Capital Crimes

Capital Crimes

George Winslow

Monthly Review Press
New York

Library of Congress Cataloging-in-Pubublication Data

Winslow, George.
    Capital crimes / George Winslow.
        p.   cm.
    Includes bibliographical references and index.
    ISBN 1-58367-002-5 (cloth). — ISBN 1-58367-001-7 (pbk.)
    1. Crime—United States. 2. Crime prevention—United States.
3. Criminal justice, Administration of—United States. 4. Social
control—United States.
    HV6789.W547 1999
    364.973—dc21   98-47887
                                                 CIP

Monthly Review Press
122 West 27th Street
New York NY 10001

Manufactured in Canada
10 9 8 7 6 5 4 3 2 1

Contents

Introduction:
Crime Pays

The American Department of Justice, ironically so called, . . . has been engaged in sharp practices since the earliest days and remains a fecund source of oppression and corruption today. It is hard to recall an administration in which it was not the center of grave scandal.

—H. L. Mencken

LIKE A PULP CRIME NOVEL, ONE TELEVISED STORY OF CRIME IN America begins on a dark and rainy night with a middle-aged woman scurrying nervously down a dimly lit street. There is fear in her eyes and apprehension in her movements. This is her neighborhood, but it is not warm and neighborly. No cafés, restaurants, or movie theaters line the streets. No families are hurrying through the rain to visit relatives. No young lovers are strolling arm and arm, oblivious to the weather. Everyone seems to be indoors, imprisoned by fear as they watch stories of urban crime and violence on the nightly news. And rightly so. As the woman runs through this no man's land, an authoritative male voiceover reminds viewers that "crimes of violence in the United States have almost doubled in recent years. . . . Today a violent crime is committed every sixty seconds, . . . a robbery every two and half minutes, . . . a mugging every six minutes, . . . a murder every forty-three minutes, . . . and it will get worse unless we take the offensive."[1]

These images could have been aired on a nightly newscast in 1996, when President Bill Clinton's tough law-and-order record helped him get reelected; or in 1994, when Republicans capitalized on widespread fear of crime to win control of Congress for the first time in decades; or even in

1988, when George Bush was elected president by convincing voters that his opponent believed in coddling black rapists. But this tale of fear and violence in America was, in fact, a paid political advertisement for Richard Nixon in 1968. Arguing in speeches and articles that "America has become among the most lawless and violent [nations] in the history of free people," Nixon made the fear of crime a centerpiece of his presidential campaign. In fact, during the months before the election all three candidates—Nixon, Vice President Hubert Humphrey, and George Wallace—promised to reduce crime and to protect the average citizen from dangerous crooks. "There are three men running for sheriff of the United States," one liberal democrat grumbled, "and no one running for President."[2]

Today virtually everyone "running for sheriff" has embraced Nixon's view that more cops, more prisons, fewer civil liberties and longer prison sentences are the true path to law and order. But whereas Nixon's law-and-order crusade was widely criticized in the late 1960s by mainstream academics and liberal politicians who believed that crime could best be eradicated by attacking the underlying social problems, few now dare challenge the conventional wisdom that more prisons and cops are the only effective cure. Law-and-order rhetoric has become a surefire path to power. Naked appeals to a law-and-order crackdown got Nixon elected in 1968, played a key role in Reagan's 1980 campaign, and revived Vice President George Bush's faltering political prospects in 1988. When Democratic nominee Michael Dukakis led Bush by seventeen points in the opinion polls, Republican strategists counterattacked by airing the famous William (Willie) Horton commercial. In only sixty seconds, by telling a simple story of an adult black man pointedly identified by a boy's nickname, that ad managed to raise nearly all the racial stereotypes and fears that have dogged debates over crime in America since the Civil War. It accused Horton of raping a young white woman after escaping jail on a work-release program while Dukakis was governor of Massachusetts. The images convinced millions of Americans that Michael Dukakis was a liberal Democrat who was laboring under the misguided notion that criminals can somehow be reformed. It didn't matter that the Horton case was one of the few failures of the generally well managed, tough work-release program that had been put in place by a rather conservative Republican governor many years earlier or that Dukakis did not have a particularly liberal record in the area of criminology. What mattered on election day was the spot's neat subliminal racism (innocent suburban whites being victimized by savage urban blacks); its implicit analysis of criminal behavior (dangerous, unrepentant, and unreformable individuals *will* commit senseless violent acts, even when offered a chance to reform themselves); its powerful political dichotomies (punitive conservatives versus permissive liberals); and its simple solution to a problem that no American politician has managed to solve (a tough law-and-order crackdown). This naked appeal to the worst fears of the American public marked a turning point in the campaign. Dukakis never recovered from the perception that the Democrats were somehow soft on crime.

A decade later, few politicians are willing to leave themselves open to that kind of attack, no matter how unfair. Shameless pandering to racist stereotypes, astonishing levels of political cowardice, and a lack of political will have produced a crime policy narrowly focused on law-and-order rhetoric. Many states have revived the death penalty, and mandatory sentences have become the rule for most crimes, from murder to smoking pot. Spending for law enforcement grew from about $6 billion in 1968 to $97.5 billion in 1993, the most recent data available in spring 1999.[3] And if present spending trends continue, the bill for the war on crime is expected to top $210 billion in 2003. Between 1982 and 1993 American officials spent an estimated $208.6 billion to build and operate prisons—enough money to provide more than four million students with $50,000 worth of tuition credits each, or to build about two million $100,000 homes. A greater percentage of the population is behind bars in America than in any other country in the world, including South Africa and Russia—governments that once had an unassailable corner on this dubious distinction.

Most of these policies are linked in the public's mind to Republicans. But Bill Clinton's administration has shown little willingness to change the way the war on crime is being fought, primarily because he learned the power of law-and-order rhetoric the hard way. In his first term as governor of Arkansas, he freed forty inmates convicted of noncapital offenses but he changed his tune when he was voted out of office for being soft on crime. Reelected governor in 1983, he became a staunch supporter of the death penalty; during his stay in the governor's mansion he signed some seventy death warrants—including one for a retarded man that most experts believe had no understanding of the crime he had committed. He also signed laws providing long sentences for selling even small amounts of narcotics, and his support of longer sentences caused the number of people behind bars to double.

Similar ideas have informed his strategies in the White House. During his first months in office Clinton unveiled a $13 billion federal anti-drug package that provided little money for education and drug rehabilitation— prompting the *New York Times* to grumble that the budget offered "little change from the widely criticized approach followed for 12 years by . . . Ronald Reagan and George Bush." That fall he unveiled a proposal to increase the number of federal crimes punishable by the death penalty to forty-seven, one more than Bush had proposed several years earlier. Even though this bill called for massive funding to hire 50,000 new police officers, the proposal proved too mild for Clinton's supposedly liberal Democratic allies in Congress. By the time it passed in 1994, the number of capital crimes had increased to sixty, and the cost of the legislation had ballooned from $6 billion to more than $30 billion. Even this budget-busting proposal proved too timid for the newly elected Republican-controlled Congress. Although the effort failed, the Republicans tried to pass legislation that would wipe out the $15.7 billion the Democrats had planned to spend on crime prevention and community policing while raising the amount that states spend on prison construction from $7.9 billion in the 1994 law to $10.5 billion. Illustrating the new mind-set was Senator Phil Gramm (R-Texas), who, when he threw his hat into the 1996 presidential race, promised to lock up all criminals "if I have to string barbed wire on every closed military base in America."[4]

Virtually everyone admits that this approach to crime control has been hugely expensive and painful. Each year, more than twelve million Americans spend at least one night in jail, and at any given moment, more than 5.5 million are in prison, or on parole, or on probation. Yet almost everyone in Washington and in statehouses around the country remains convinced that we're now winning the war on crime. Between 1991 and 1997, homicide rates in the United States fell from 9.8 per 100,000 people to 6.8, the single biggest drop since the end of the Second World War. The rates of violent crime such as assault and rape continue to drop, as do those of property crimes such as burglary. Consumption of most illegal narcotics is lower than it was in the late 1970s, and the crack plague appears to be waning. In late 1998 polls showed that public concern over crime was at its lowest level in years.[5]

There is, unfortunately, one problem with the rosy view that the war against violence is being won—it isn't true. Even though homicide rates have dropped precipitously, they are still appallingly high, four to fifteen times greater than in most developed countries. If, for example, U.S. homicide rates (9.9 per 100,000 in 1990) were as low as Japan's (0.6 per 100,000 in 1990), 22,019 of the 23,440 Americans who were murdered in 1990 would still be alive. That same year, much lower homicide rates could also be found in New Zealand (2.3 per 100,000), France (1), England and Wales (0.8), Italy (2.6), Spain (1), Germany (1), and Australia (2.2), even though all of these countries had much lower rates of incarceration and spent far less per capita on police and prisons. For example, in 1990 the United States imprisoned 292 people per 100,000, far more than Japan (32 per 100,000), France (82), Germany (78), or Italy (79).[6]

Indeed, during most of this three-decade push for law and order there has been virtually no evidence that more prisons and cops had any effect on violent crime rates, despite persistent pronouncements of progress. In 1972 Nixon claimed that the law-and-order agenda was already working its magic: Crime, he said, was "finally beginning to go back down . . . we have a remarkable record on the law-and-order issues, with crime legislation, obscenity and narcotics bills."[7]

Yet as the number of people behind bars increased from 204,211 in 1973 to 315,974 in 1980, crime victimization surveys, the most accurate measure of crime, showed that the violent crime rate grew from 47.7 per 1,000 Americans to 49.4. The violent crime victimization rates actually increased 4 percent to 51.4 between 1980 and 1994, as the number of prisoners passed one million and mandatory sentencing rules dramatically increased the average sentence inmates served. An even worse record can be found in the number of crimes reported to police, a less accurate measure that was widely used by conservatives to justify their anti-crime policies. Overall, violent crime rates jumped 89 percent between 1972 and 1991: rape rates increased by 88 percent; robbery rates, 51 percent; aggravated assaults, 130 percent; burglaries, 10 percent; larceny, 62 percent.[8] And in 1997 the murder rate, even after recent declines, was higher than in 1967, when Nixon launched his presidential campaign by promising to win the war on crime.

Unfortunately, these dismal statistics aren't the only reason to doubt the effectiveness of America's $1.5 trillion law-and-order crusade. While its leaders busily pat themselves on the back for the recent decline in street crime, some of the world's largest and most deadly criminal activities are ongoing. Back in 1970, when Nixon declared his war on heroin, the entire world produced about a thousand tons of opium a year. But by 1994, global production had topped 3,409 metric tons—a whopping 241 percent increase. And even though U.S. drug use has declined precipitously since the late 1970s, it remains widespread. In 1995 about 72 million Americans had used illegal drugs at some point in their lives, and about 12.8 million had done so within the month preceding the survey, including 5.6 million pot users and 1.2 million coke users. Even though the United States spent more than $300 billion to fight it between 1980 and 1999, the U.S. drug trade was worth more than $50 billion a year in 1993, and global narcotics trade estimates are as high as $300 billion.[9]

Similarly depressing statistics can be cited for Nixon's ill-fated war on the mob. The 1970 Organized Crime Control Bill gave law enforcement agencies wide-ranging new powers to tap phones, trample civil liberties, and invade the privacy of individuals. The House Judiciary Committee complained that the law contained the "seeds of official repression," but Nixon declared that curbs on civil liberties were necessary to win the war on organized crime.[10] But as the years passed, it became clear that new police powers were not a magic bullet against gangsters. In the Nixon years there were two major organized crime groups operating in the United States—the Mafia and the Chinese crime syndicates—and these organizations earned only a few billion dollars each year. Today, United Nations researchers estimate that powerful organized crime groups—notably the Colombian cartels, the Mexican gangs, the Chinese Triads, the Mafia, Russian crime groups, and the Japanese Yakusa—have established international operations that produce more than $1 trillion a year in revenues and that these groups control assets (property, bank accounts, securities, businesses) worth that much and more. Even the richest mobsters in Nixon's era were worth perhaps $5 or $10 million, whereas now some of the world's most powerful gangsters are regularly included in the *Forbes* list of the world's wealthiest men.

Then there is the war that Nixon *didn't* declare—on corporate crime. During his years in office the Republicans collected millions of dollars in illegal contributions, including hundreds of thousands in cash delivered directly to the White House. In some cases the Nixon administration intervened directly to protect white-collar criminals such as Robert Vesco, who stole more than $100 million from investors and was accused of smuggling drugs.[11] The spectacle of a U.S. president accepting bags of cash from large corporations seeking protection from activities that bilked consumers should have prompted a law-and-order crusade against white-collar crime. After all, the FBI believed that all the street criminals in the country managed to steal less than $1 billion in 1974, the same year that the U.S. Chamber of Commerce estimated the cost to the economy of white-collar crime at about $41 billion. Yet over the next quarter-century, many law-and-order conservatives worked to limit spending to fight corporate crime, which is generally committed by large campaign contributors, as they were beefing up spending to fight street crime, which is typically committed by poor people. In 1996, for example, FBI investigations produced convictions in only two antitrust cases, one case involving workplace safety, thirty-five environmental cases, and just 148 cases of health fraud (which cost consumers $100 billion in inflated fees each year). Given this record by the nation's premier law enforcement agency, it is no surprise that corporate crime now costs the economy $1 to $2 trillion a year, and Ralph Estes estimates that white-collar criminals cause some 150,000 American deaths each year—more than the record 24,700 murders in the 1991.[12]

Finally, it is important to stress that our crime statistics—which ignore the drug trade, organized crime, and corporate misconduct—contain no information about legalized violence. For example, the $100 billion estimate of health care fraud excludes the enormous social and economic costs created by the legal workings of the U.S. health care system. As of 1993 at least 40.9 million Americans lacked health insurance, and the Medicaid program provided services to only half of poor Americans (a proportion that will drop as massive Medicaid cuts take effect). Not surprisingly, the least affluent Americans have the worst health. One 1986 study found that the mortality rate for heart disease was 2.3 times higher for blue-collar workers than for corporate lawyers or physicians. Nationwide, blacks, who have lower incomes and higher poverty rates as a group than whites, also have shorter life spans and higher rates of mortality from heart disease and other major health problems. For lack of proper care, millions of people suffer debilitating illnesses or endure the premature loss of loved ones. Yet these victims never appear in the crime statistics. The system that permits their often preventable injuries and deaths does not violate the law.[13]

This book is about a war on crime that has proved to be one of the most shamefully wasteful and unsuccessful government programs ever conceived—a remarkable accomplishment, considering the Pentagon's propensity to buy $500 toilet seats and the Atomic Energy Commission's record of storing dangerous radioactive materials in leaky drums next to major waterways. This is not to say that violence and crime don't deserve serious attention. The levels of violence in America are an abomination. Compared with those of other developed industrial countries, they are off the radar screen, even excluding corporate malfeasance, organized crime, and the drug trade. But documenting the failure of the war on crime is only part of the story. Until the "let them eat prison" approach is challenged and we completely rethink the entire problem, there is little hope that the war against crime can be won.

Admittedly, rethinking the problem is a difficult task. Information on many crucial issues is notoriously unreliable and the data that are available have a funny way of supporting a wide range of seemingly contradictory conclusions. Worse, many conventional notions about crime and punishment turn out to be the modern equivalent of the old flat-earth theories. We are told that more prisons and more severe punishment will reduce crime, yet the massive increase in the prison population over thirty years has barely reduced street crime and has had little impact on organized crime or corporate misdeeds. We are told that overzealous judges and civil libertarians have tied the hands of police and prosecutors, thus freeing armies of criminals. Yet crime rates in the United States continued to rise throughout the 1980s as federal, state, and local courts dramatically reduced the rights of suspects. We are told that a decline in moral, religious, and family values has produced a wave of gratuitous violence. Yet little is said about the well-respected, pious, and powerful corporate executives who carry out $1 trillion worth of corporate crimes each year. We debate the merits of capital punishment but forget that executing thousands of Americans will not end crime if millions more people are willing to take their place in the criminal underworld. We are even told that we don't know what causes crime. Yet jails and prisons are packed with people who have little formal education, lousy incomes, and irregular employment.

More fundamentally, the exclusive focus on the problems created by visible crime tends to obscure the violence and pain created by the normal workings of society. The notion is widespread that criminals and law-abiding citizens inhabit two separate and unrelated universes, but it does not help to explain why certain societies manage to produce so much violence while other communities manage to live in relative peace. By concentrating on the business of apprehending, punishing, and imprisoning criminals, we forget to ask why the families, schools, workplaces, and other social institutions that are supposed to produce law-abiding citizens manage to create so many lawbreakers. Likewise, the exclusive focus on the criminal underworld ignores the role of legal economic institutions, such as banks, in laundering drug money or helping tax evaders. And even if we could completely eradicate street crime, there is little justice in a society that sentences millions of people to poverty, poor health, and dismal jobs.

To explore those issues, this book concentrates on one aspect of crime that has been virtually ignored in recent years: economics. So bloodless a science may seem to offer few insights into a topic fraught with fear, passion, anger, and hatred. Drunken husbands do not calculate the economic cost when they beat up their wives. Young men do not lose their jobs one day and start mugging old ladies the next. No one ever will draw up a supply-and-demand curve of violence that can accurately pinpoint the precise moment when a fight will break out in a bar or someone will decide to start dealing drugs. Even the most compelling economic arguments are unlikely to console those who have lost friends or family members to violence.

The impossibility of finding any single explanation for crime or a kind of single-bullet theory for its cure does not, however, diminish the value of economics to explain a problem that so often has to do with money. Three-quarters of all street crimes reported to the police involve an attempt to steal property, and the most deadly corporate crimes almost always involve greed. More fundamentally, a close look at many criminal activities indicates that both street criminals and corporate criminals are influenced by the same economic and political forces that are driving the larger legitimate economy. Criminals often try to capitalize on financial and technological change. (A revolution in the international financial system during the 1980s offered new ways to profit from securities fraud and insider trading.) They are generally constrained by the laws of supply and demand. (A glut of cocaine during the mid-1980s cut the wholesale price in half.) Even the most established criminal organizations must worry about foreign competitors. (In the 1980s the New York Mafia, which once had a virtual monopoly on the city's lucrative drug trade, lost 60 percent of the heroin market to organized Asian crime groups.)

In the 1990s it also became obvious that the business of crime was adapting to the global economic forces that were reshaping American life. As the economy became more dependent on global markets, crime became a global industry that linked street addicts in American cities with peasants in Bolivia and bankers in Switzerland. Today only a few cartels supply virtually all the cocaine that reaches America. The most successful entrepreneurs in the big business of crime are experts in government regulation and high finance. Their ability to move money secretly around the world and use poorly regulated financial centers such as Switzerland is essential to successful insider trading, tax fraud, money laundering and the movement of contraband—counterfeit goods, drugs, and illegal immigrants—across borders.

In this book, these rather impressionistic observations on the importance of economics are drawn into a detailed analysis of the political economy of crime—a pretentious way of saying that it is about the violence of power and money. The modern political economy of crime is a kind of toxic byproduct of a global economy based on profits and high finance rather than on social justice, an economy dominated by large multinational corporations and financial institutions. To explore this argument, the book explains, in detail, how the structure of the global economy has made crime such an intractable part of modern life. Even though discussion of class, abusive corporate power, political powerlessness, and inequality have virtually disappeared from mainstream discussions of the global economy, they have an enormous impact on the problem of crime in America.

During the last fifty years, dramatic changes in the global economy, in which multinational corporations enjoy new freedom to move goods and services anywhere in the world, have also created a fertile breeding ground for violence by exacerbating many social problems and reducing social services that address the causes of crime. Nixon's political advertisements in the late 1960s featured scared white women, but about half of all homicide victims in both the 1960s, as in the 1990s, were black—a group that has faced a long history of economic exploitation, political exclusion, and racism. Nor is it an accident that the highest violent crime rates can be found in America's poorest communities, or that impoverished peasants who have been devastated by changes in the global economy have turned to cultivating narcotics to survive.

Less obvious but equally important is the impact of corporate crime on poor and working Americans. In the late 1970s, for example, arson committed in decaying urban centers by wealthy real estate interests, often with the aid of organized crime groups, killed or injured more than thirty thousand people a year, destroyed desperately needed housing, and left the shells of buildings to be used for a variety of crimes. Similarly, poorer communities, disproportionally located near polluting industries and toxic waste dumps, face environmental damage that makes it difficult for them to attract investments and produces medical problems for people who lack access to adequate health care. Further, crimes such as tax fraud cause government agencies to short-change antipoverty programs, and violations of labor laws have forced millions of Americans to work in dangerous sweatshops.

These crimes impose a huge cost on poor and working-class communities that highlights the economics of community life. Almost everyone, left, right, and center, agrees that stable, prosperous communities are key to reducing violence. Unfortunately, the same global economic changes that have encouraged powerful corporations to move their operations wherever their costs are lowest, make the economics of local communities increasingly insecure. The communities that lose jobs as a result and are starving for capital not only suffer some of the worst social problems and crime rates, but find it virtually impossible to attract the investment and capital they need to rebuild.

These economic structures, which influence both street crime and corporate crime, also help explain the politics of crime. Although equality under the law is one of the most enduring and powerful traditions of American life, political power, like economic power, is not equally distributed. For most of American history Native Americans were denied the vote.

Blacks were not allowed to vote in most states until after the Civil War, and many were denied the vote and basic constitutional rights until well into the 1960s. Women were not able to vote nationally until 1920. Many poor whites were denied basic legal rights—such as constitutional protection from unreasonable search and seizure, or access to a lawyer—until after the Second World War. Even today, many people find equality under the law only a theoretical concept. Defendants who are too poor to make bail, or to afford private attorneys, find it much harder to help public defenders prepare their cases and, not surprisingly, suffer much higher conviction rates.

This enduring history of discrimination illustrates how wealthy individuals have used their economic and political power to mold the legal system. Powerful business interests, which profited from the opium trade in the eighteenth and nineteenth centuries, successfully fought to keep the trade legal, even though it produced enormous social problems, both in the colonies and the U.S. throughout the 19th century. More recently, major banks successfully battled efforts to crack down on the laundering of drug money, an expensive lobbying campaign that had the unintended effect of protecting major crime groups from effective prosecution. Likewise, the political power of major Wall Street firms prevented effective regulation of the bond market, thus costing investors billions of dollars and dramatically increasing the costs government agencies must pay to borrow funds. Today, if a young man in California gets his third felony conviction for stealing a pizza, he faces life in prison. But white-collar criminals who pollute the environment, violate labor safety rules, and defraud investors, rarely face more than a few years in prison.

This disparity between the way the criminal justice system treats corporate crimes committed by wealthy executives, and the way it punishes minor thieves, highlights another important issue—the ideology of the war on crime. Politicians who take bows for having reduced crime rates in recent years are completely unwilling to take responsibility for the simultaneous failures of the law-and-order crusade: the growth of the global drug trade, the expansion of organized crime groups, and the obscenely high U.S. murder rates. They continue to blame civil libertarians, producers of network sitcoms that feature unwed mothers, illegal immigrants, poor black mothers on welfare, rap musicians, pornographers, and promiscuous left-wing intellectuals—a cast of characters who have virtually no power over the $100 billion government agencies spend each year on crime or the 1.7 million people employed by the law enforcement system.[14]

Focusing scarce government resources on petty crimes committed by poor people while playing little attention to corporate crime does, however, have a certain economic rationality. Images of gang-banging young black men, crack-addicted welfare moms, illegal immigrants dealing drugs, and liberal politicians soft on crime not only helped conservatives get elected to political office, but also built up political support for larger pro-business agendas. Odious stereotypes of minorities made it easier to gut social programs and to cut taxes for the exceedingly rich. Attacks on liberal and progressive politicians for being soft on crime weakened political support for effective government regulation and helped conservatives pursue economic policies designed to aid exceedingly rich campaign contributors at the expense of almost everyone else.

Though conservative politicians and powerful corporations have profited from the failed war on crime, this does not mean that the problem of violence in America can be attributed to a secret conspiracy. Any attempt to blame fifty or even a thousand drug lords, inept conservative politicians, or greedy corporate executives, trivializes the powerful economic, political, and social forces that have created the modern world of crime. Throwing a few people out of office or locking up some powerful criminals is unlikely to have any long-term effect, unless much broader reforms are put in place.

Before that can be done, it is necessary to address the complex issue of what causes crime. The political and economic forces documented in this book provide a context for understanding the world of crime, but they are not much help in explaining every particular crime or the ephemeral forces that push otherwise law-abiding citizens to commit criminal acts. Criminals themselves rarely have a complete understanding of the forces that push them into violence or the impact that their violence has on the world. A wife beater, for example, may understand some of the reasons for his actions—perhaps he was angry at his wife for calling him a drunk—but may be unaware of other crucial motivations such as the abuse he was subjected to as a child. Nor can sexism be excluded from the analysis of domestic violence, just because an abusive husband rejects the criticism.

Further, it is important to stress that the social forces pushing people toward crime don't act the way gravity works on a falling object. Statistics tell us that young people living in poverty with poor job and educational prospects are at high risk of committing street crime, but the same data also show that most people in this group manage to get through life as law-abiding, gainfully employed citizens. There is little doubt that men are responsible for most domestic violence, but it is equally clear that most males do not pass their evenings beating up their loved ones. In seeking the sources of crime, it is important not to stereotype all members of a high-risk group.

More complexities appear in the attempt to define what is meant by "crime." Any student of violence knows that criminal acts have been defined in different ways in various countries and that all these definitions have changed over time. Today, any business that attempts to hold its employees in captivity faces severe legal sanctions—a major change from the colonial era, when employers had the legal power to beat, torture and in some cases kill white indentured servants as well as black slaves who attempted to escape. Rather than trying to find commonalities among usages on which to construct a definition of crime, this book uses the term much more loosely to refer to very harmful behavior. Some of the activities called crime here have in fact been defined as criminal by the legal system, but others are not even illegal.

This imprecise use of the term will certainly irritate some legal scholars and philosophers, but it reflects a major theme of this book: that all too often the social, economic, and political pressures have affected the legal definition of a crime. Some "crimes," such as murder, are statutorily defined and punished to protect the security of all citizens. But some other "crimes," have led to measures—such as the criminalization of drugs and the imposition of long prison sentences on people who have a medical problem of addiction—that serve little social purpose and frequently cause more problems than they solve. Likewise some perfectly "legal" activities, such as the existence of a health-care system that refuses to provide treatment to millions of people, impose huge costs on society and harm or even kill thousands of people each year. Hence the strict legalistic use of the term creates more conceptual confusion than it solves, whereas the seemingly imprecise colloquial meaning of "crime" as some kind of harmful activity forces one to think about the subject in a broader, more comprehensive fashion.

To tell the story of the kinds of crime and their interconnections, this book is divided into four parts, each featuring an illustrative case study. Part I, by tracing the Burmese heroin trade and particularly the activities of one drug lord, introduces the basic structures of globaization that have allowed street and corporate crime to thrive. It shows how the spread of market economies (dominated by major multinationals) into Asia and Latin America impoverished many peasant communities and created a large reserve army of labor that was recruited into the drug trade.

Part II, returning to American cities, uses an apparently senseless killing on the Brooklyn Bridge to demonstrate the vicious cycle of economic decay, social dislocation, and rising violence in urban centers. It looks at the movements of capital, jobs and factories that have bred street crime by destroying the economic and social fabric of local communities and explains how those economic changes have affected the politics of crime.

Part III takes up the trillion-dollar business of corporate crime, beginning with the example of forests in the Pacific Northwest. It shows how the growing power of major corporations over society has subjected millions of Americans to dangerous work, inadequate health care, environmental damage, and poor government services. It explores some reasons why these large and expensive causes of violence are ignored, even encouraged, while various individual misdeeds draw increasingly harsh punishment.

Finally, the conclusion of this book takes up the thorny problem of reforming the current system. The difficulties of addressing the economics of crime and the scope of the subject matter have precluded any attempt to explore specific policies that might reverse the destructive course being taken by the police, courts, and prisons. But in summarizing the book's central arguments, the last chapter highlights a number of key issues that need to be understood before the real roots of crime can be confronted.

Part I

The Rise and Fall
of the King of Heroin

Chapter 1:
Supply and Demand

The individual primarily responsible for this worldwide devastation of drug addiction is Khun Sa and his United Shan Army. . . .
He has delivered as much evil to this world as any mafia don has
done in our history. . . . For the past two years a combined group
of Thai police, narcotics units, border police, military and United
States officials . . . have targeted Khun Sa as the kingpin mafia drug
lord most important in the entire globe.

—*Thomas Constantine,*
Drug Enforcement Administration,
December 1994

The DEA already has tried to stop me, from 1972 up to this day.
What they get is four things: first, the addicts increase every year.
Second, the merchants, the traffickers, increase all over the world.
Third, the ones who go to jail increase all the time. And fourth, the
problem increases every day. That is what they get from DEA.

—*Khun Sa, June 1994*

IN 1974 A WIRY MIDDLE-AGED DRUG DEALER NAMED KHUN SA
walked out of a Burmese prison after serving five years for treason.[1] He had
a lot of experience in crime (he first began working in the opium trade at
sixteen in the early 1950s) and a flair for self-promotion (in the 1980s Khun
Sa's press secretary regularly faxed journalists his boss' thoughts on the drug
war). But like a lot of ex-cons, he faced an uncertain future. Burma, his
homeland, had for decades been wracked by a civil war, and Khun Sa, who
had been a rising star in the opium trade during the 1960s, faced an uphill

battle to rebuild his criminal empire. During his years in jail his rivals had expanded their operations at his expense, and U.S. authorities had declared a war on heroin. To survive, this forty-year-old, nearly illiterate warlord, who commanded only a few hundred soldiers, would have to battle other gangsters while fighting the world's most powerful and prosperous nation. As he walked out of jail, few people would have predicted that the U.S. ambassador to Thailand would one day call him "the worst enemy the world has."[2]

As Khun Sa was plotting ways to rekindle his career in the opium trade, events halfway around the world were creating new markets for his products. In the mid-1970s open-air drug markets had become a fact of life in many poor urban ghettos, such as the Lower East Side of Manhattan in New York City. In some ways this wasn't anything new; the vice trade had thrived on the Lower East Side since the mid-nineteenth century. By the start of the twentieth century the Bowery had become the world's most famous skid row, a center of vice and gang warfare which Hollywood used as a background for crime movies and even comedic series such as "The East Side Kids" and "The Bowery Boys." Saloons specializing in five-cent whisky and knockout drops, sensational dime museums, rat-infested beer dives, flophouses, pawnshops, opium dens, and filthy tenements radiated off the thoroughfare in all directions. Here, legendary gangsters Meyer Lansky and Lucky Luciano got their start stealing pennies from kids on the way to school.

Yet most residents found a way to make a living without beating up old ladies or robbing school kids. Famous examples of this occupational choice between terror and trade were the Jewish markets. Immigrants from the ghettos of Eastern Europe filled Hester, Orchard, Essex, Norfolk, and Ludlow Streets with pushcarts and market stalls. The art of salesmanship was so highly developed that the Yiddish word "spiel" first came into vogue in this neighborhood as the term for a sales pitch. Equally frenzied centers of commerce were the Chinese markets on Mott, Pell, and Doyers, or the Italian markets on Mulberry, Mott and Grand Streets. In fact, in the two square miles surrounding the Bowery, almost everything was for sale—even people: every morning between three and four o'clock immigrants gathered at the corner of Hester and Ludlow, then the center of the garment district, hoping to find a job for the day.

By the mid-1970s much had changed. Most of the sweatshops had moved to the American South, Latin America, or Asia, and those that remained employed Chinese or Hispanic immigrants. The flophouses, which had once housed thousands of transient laborers, had nearly disappeared, and the cheap bars were on their way out. As the city lost nearly a half million manufacturing jobs and about a million residents between 1948 and 1980, its financial condition worsened. In the late 1970s the virtually bankrupt city was forced to lay off tens of thousands of teachers, cops, and government employees, and the quality of life declined precipitously. In poorer neighborhoods such as the Lower East Side, garbage was left to rot on street corners for days or sometimes weeks at a time, and ghetto schools were so strapped for cash that many classrooms lacked such basic equipment as textbooks. Even the hookers had gone downhill: by the late 1970s, the Lower East Side was the bottom of the sex trade barrel, the last stop for women who had been used up by brutal pimps, abusive boyfriends, and addictive substances. Many were so beat up it was hard to tell their sex. On winter days they stood in the subzero weather on Houston or Delancey Street and raised their blouses whenever a truck passed, hoping to convince the drivers that they were women, not transvestites.

Nevertheless, cars from all over the tristate area flocked to the Bowery and neighboring streets. Gentrification had not yet become a household term, and the Lower East Side wasn't yet a popular residence for supermodels and bohemians with trust funds, yet there were always long lines of cars at the corner of Rivington and the Bowery. Visitors tried to park in front of the twelve-story Salvation Army flophouse (a dismal rat-infested lodging that was eventually shut down by the city) because, besides feeding hundreds of homeless men a steady diet of baloney sandwiches and religion, it employed a security guard who took a dim view of auto theft. This was, however, an unnecessary precaution. The entrepreneurs who were turning Rivington into a kind of Kmart for drug abuse, understanding that their largely white clientele were nervous about entering these mean streets, did what they could to ensure their safety. Several kids (all minorities) solicited and directed customers; older and much larger guards provided security.

On one floor of an abandoned building on Rivington you could buy heroin; on another you could score cocaine. Discarded, tattered couches and seats from stripped autos were set up in various abandoned apartments for people who wanted to get high right on the spot; if you lacked a needle or had trouble finding a vein, there was always someone to help. For a while in the early 1980s the Rivington Street shooting gallery was frequented by a large transvestite who kept half-a-dozen needles stuck in his wig. He would cook up the heroin, draw it into a needle, and tenderly insert it. He would even shoot the drug into a leg or neck if the addict's arms were too covered with scar tissue. An addict himself, he survived by collecting the drops of heroin and blood left in the syringe—a technique that says much about the devastating spread of AIDS through the city's population of 500,000 heroin addicts in the 1980s.

By 1978, no one seemed to know when this shooting gallery had first opened for business. But in succeeding years, as the traffic lines along the block grew and as the nearly bankrupt city fired thousands of cops and teachers, this shooting gallery flourished, as did scores, maybe hundreds, of similar enterprises set up in abandoned buildings in the East Village and Lower East Side of Manhattan. Heroin, pot, cocaine, speed, and occasionally even opium could be purchased in these burned-out buildings, which had frequently been torched by the landlords for the insurance money, or on dozens of street corners where open-air drug markets did business around the clock. Hundreds of people worked in these enterprises, and thousands of addicts trekked there from all over New York, New Jersey, and Connecticut to buy drugs. It was the Las Vegas of drug abuse, the center of the New York City heroin trade and, in turn, the American capital of smack. At particularly well known locations, the streets were so crowded with people that cars couldn't pass. Some of the more popular dealers even branded their goods with trade names: *E.T., Executive, Golden Nugget,* and *Toilet* (which advertised the "good shit" inside each glycine packet with a crudely drawn bathroom fixture). That way users know they are buying from a familiar and, in the duplicitous world of illegal narcotics, a relatively trustworthy source. One enterprising dealer in the 1980s even began peddling cocaine under the brand name *Trump*, a reference to the billionaire real estate developer.

Some of these retail outlets operated with the kind of intrigue that had become a cliché in Hollywood movies about Prohibition. One, located on East Sixth Street, used a candy store as its cover. Customers would arrive and wait until the appointed time. Then the doors would be locked and an employee would push aside the jukebox, revealing a small passage into another room. After everyone had climbed through, the jukebox was pushed back into place and everyone waited, quietly, until a small slot was opened, from which heroin was dispensed. Then, the entire process was repeated in reverse. Eventually the police shut down this operation by commandeering a fire truck (no easy task in a bankrupt city where a large chunk of the fire department had been fired, and landlords were torching hundreds of buildings) and ordering the firefighters to pump water into the candy store until its hidden occupants were forced to flee.

Many dealers, though, simply set up shop on a street corner or inside an abandoned building, recruiting young men and women to run their businesses. Most local residents resisted these employment opportunities, just as most of the immigrants in the late nineteenth and the early twentieth century avoided the career path of crime chosen by the Meyer Lanskys of the world. But far too many young men and women who couldn't get an education in rat-infested classrooms or jobs in crime-riddled neighborhoods did find work in the heroin trade, frequently with tragic results. Unlike the drug dealers on prime-time television series such as *Miami Vice*, few of these fledgling drug lords ended up in posh penthouses serviced by $1,000-a-night whores. Over the years, a lot of kids moved through the industry, starting as lookouts, becoming runners, and gradually developing their own habits. Most of them ended up in a nightmarish world of drug abuse, passing their time shooting up in the vestibules of apartment buildings or nodding out on street corners—homeless, old, and pathetic at the age of thirty.

This was very bad for the neighborhood and its residents—most of whom were gainfully employed and busy trying to build stable families— but great for organized crime groups. In the 1970s Mafia families not only made huge profits from the city's heroin trade but also collected large fees to burn down buildings so that sleazy slumlords could collect insurance money. In the early 1980s the mob was responsible for about 20 percent of all arson fraud nationwide, and law enforcement sources say the percentage in New York City was much higher. By the late 1970s New York City was averaging ten thousand cases of arson—and more than 150 related deaths—a year. In the South Bronx more than thirty thousand fires were set in the 1970s, and equally suspicious fires on the Lower East Side helped create the open-air drug markets and rampant crime. "In the process that leads to the kindling of buildings, landlords generally stop providing services which hastens the deterioration of the buildings and tenants move out," one 1978 report on the Lower East Side of Manhattan explained. "The blocks destroyed by fires serve the interim purpose of becoming markets for wholesale drug commerce and related crime. As addicts and drug wholesalers begin to move into the block, they replace the families who speedily move out. Other criminally related commerce such as pimping, prostitution and/or fencing and other rackets begin to blossom on the block; deterioration escalates and more fires are set. Eventually . . . these streets . . . contain less than half of the houses that were there even two years [earlier]. They look like war ravaged towns."[3] In this sequence of events thousands of apartments disappeared on the Lower East Side in the 1970s and early 1980s.

All of this was good news for Khun Sa. By 1994 he had managed to create a private kingdom in northwestern Burma (by then called Myanmar) along the border with Thailand. Here his private army of 10,000 to 20,000 troops ruled hundreds of thousands of acres where hundreds or maybe thousands of tons of opium were refined into heroin each year. With his profits Khun Sa had even built his own capital, the village of Homing, with a population of several thousand people. It wasn't listed on any official map of the region, but it was easily reached by car from Thailand on a paved two-lane highway built with the help of Thai engineers and U.S. foreign aid. Visitors, including journalists, top Thai military leaders, and many merchants, found most of the amenities of civilized life in Homing: schools, barracks, Buddhist temples, a karaoke bar, a small munitions factory capable of manufacturing crude bazookas, and a prosperous gem market where more than $80,000 worth of precious stones was traded each day. A generator supplied enough electricity in the evening so that local residents could watch satellite-delivered television channels or home videos. There were even a fax machine and pay telephone booths for journalists to file stories. Drug rehab facilities, however, were more primitive: addicts were simply tossed into a ten-foot pit to endure a painful withdrawal.

Khun Sa's success in reestablishing his power over the heroin trade and the proliferation of drug markets in U.S. cities might seem to confirm many of the common stereotypes. For thirty years Presidents Nixon, Ford, Reagan, Bush, and Clinton have argued that the best way to attack drug abuse is to crack down on the trade by hiring more police, and sentencing drug dealers to long prison sentences. In 1966, Governor Nelson Rockefeller announced New York State's first war on drugs, pushing through draconian legislation in 1973 that provided long sentences for the possession of even very small amounts, and in 1971 Nixon launched a federal war on heroin. But many cities lacked the resources to battle drug use aggressively. The severe fiscal problems that nearly forced New York City to file for bankruptcy in 1975, for example, led its political leaders to gut social services, particularly in poorer neighborhoods, and to lay off thousands of police officers. During this period the city's unofficial policy was simply to ignore the brewing social problems and hope that many of its poorest residents would simply move somewhere else. Roger Starr, who ran the city's housing programs in the mid-1970s, once ruminated that massive cutbacks in the fire, police, transit, and sanitation departments in poor neighborhoods would help the city in the long run: "We should not encourage people to stay where their job possibilities are daily becoming more remote," Starr argued, reflecting the Malthusian views of many affluent white New Yorkers. "Stop the Puerto Ricans and the rural blacks from living in the city. . . . Reverse the role of the city. . . . It can no longer be the place of opportunity."[4]

Not surprisingly, the city's most affluent neighborhoods had the best police protection and had the lowest crime rates; its poorest neighborhoods, which had the worst, suffered much higher levels of violence. As long as the drug dealers stayed in these minority communities, far away from the lily-white suburbs where many cops lived, police let them do what they liked. Such views began to change in the early 1980s, however, when some money from the city's recovering real estate market trickled into the Lower East Side. As young artists, writers, and professionals moved into the neighborhood, lured by its cheap rents, landlords seeking to attract higher-income tenants began complaining about the drug trade. In 1982 and 1983 the New York Police Department made massive sweeps, stopping, questioning, and occasionally arresting all who moved through these streets—even if they were simply walking home. As part of this crackdown the NYPD even staged a commando-style raid on the Rivington drug mall. The scale of the operation was impressive, involving paddy wagons, snipers stationed on roofs, blaring loudspeakers, fleets of cop cars, and lots of armed men wearing baseball caps and flak jackets. But no major newspaper bothered covering it, for by this time the city's drug problem was so out of control that a raid involving dozens of police didn't even merit a mention in the tabloids.

Eventually, the crackdown on drugs plus new investments improved housing stock, brought in new business, and led to improved government services. By the late 1990s crime on the Lower East Side was dropping, and it had emerged as one of the city's trendiest neighborhoods. Expensive restaurants sprang up along Tompkins Park, once so infested with heroin addicts that it was known as Needle Park, and young professionals were paying $2,000 or more a month to rent renovated one-bedroom tenement apartments that had been shooting galleries in the early 1980s. Supermodels and Hollywood stars flocked to local nightclubs, and limousines now parked on avenues once packed with drug dealers and buyers.

But the eradication of the open-air heroin markets and the urban renewal of a famously poor neighborhood did not mark the major victory in the war on drugs that many law-and-order politicians had hoped for. Rising rents pushed many poorer residents out of the area, making it impossible for them to benefit from its revival, and drug markets continued to thrive in many other rundown New York City neighborhoods. By the mid-1990s, despite a nationwide war on drugs that had cost well more than $300 billion between 1980 and 1998, heroin overdose fatalities skyrocketed in New York and other urban areas.

Such deaths usually don't get more much more attention than a line in the police blotter. In 1997 about 488,000 Americans were treated in emergency rooms for drug overdoses—70,463 for heroin. But newspapers and television run stories about those who die only if they are celebrities, not about the anonymous users who chase the dragon into oblivion, even though the number of heroin overdose cases more than doubled between 1988 and 1994. But in the late summer of 1994, the twentieth anniversary of Khun Sa's release from jail, the body count in New York seemed impossible to ignore: two deaths from heroin overdoses were reported on Thursday, August 25, followed by another on Friday, two on Saturday, and seven on Sunday. On August 31 even the *New York Times*, which normally devotes more space to endangered species than overdoses among local residents, took notice, hitting the newsstand with a lengthy article on the deaths.[5]

Initially, the police erroneously attributed the fatalities to packets of heroin sold under the brand name *China Cat* and bearing a picture of a tiger. But inside the packets of *China Cat,* users got far more octane than they had bargained for. Each packet was said to be 96 percent pure, indicating that the drug had not been cut since being refined from opium into what addicts call China White and the drug chemists call No. 4 heroin. Brownish and coarser-grained No. 3 heroin, from Mexico or Afghanistan, contains more impurities. It is produced for people who want to smoke or snort the drug; when shot into a vein, the impurities can produce huge open sores, so junkies who prefer the needle naturally embrace No. 4.

Producing this drug isn't easy. With perfect weather, the average peasant family of four workers can grow as much as ten to twelve kilos of opium a year but usually harvest only five to six kilos.[6] They first clear a hectare of land, done laboriously, with shovels, axes, and scythes and without the aid of tractors, herbicides, or other standard technologies of modern agribusiness. Then they scatter small poppy seeds over the field. Several months later each poppy plant produces a bright white flower. When the petals drop off, the peasants cut small slits on each green seed pod. A white sap oozes out of the cuts and dries into a brown gooey tar, which is carefully cut off with a flat, dull knife.

The tar is opium. Each year, 180,000 to 190,000 acres of poppy fields are cultivated in the Golden Triangle (which comprises the rich opium producing areas of Burma, Thailand and Laos), an enterprise that employs more than a million people. It takes ten kilos of opium, or the year's work of two peasant families, to produce one kilo of heroin. To supply U.S. addicts, who annually consume about twenty tons of heroin, upward of 160,000 peasants must cultivate 20,000 hectares of poppy fields to harvest at least 200,000 kilos of opium.[7]

For most of the late 1980s and early 1990s, U.S. authorities blamed much of that production on one man—Khun Sa. They alleged in 1993 that peasants living in areas of the Golden Triangle controlled by his army planted and produced opium from some 42,000 hectares of poppies each year. There is reason to doubt these numbers, which would have given him control over about one-third of the international heroin business. But there is little doubt that Khun Sa had become something of a celebrity. "He's God, man," one addict told a *Boston Globe* reporter. "He's so powerful. They would not say anything against him. They say something against him, they're dead, automatically dead. He reaches everywhere."[8]

Official U.S. statistics on the drug trade seemed to confirm that view. Over the last quarter of a century, opium warlords have created some of the largest agribusiness operations in the world. In 1970 the Golden Triangle produced about 713 tons of opium. By 1987 Khun Sa bragged to reporters that his production alone was nine hundred tons, up from six hundred tons only a year earlier. Worse, total opium production in Burma alone increased from about 600 tons in 1988 to more than 2,365 tons in 1997, producing a flood of heroin on U.S. city streets. Moreover, most heroin today is 60 to 80 percent pure, a dramatic change from the early 1970s, when the average purity was a mere 4 or 5 percent. That means an addict who used to spend $70 a day on his habit can now get the same high for $3 to $6—about the price of a six-pack of beer.[9]

New York Police Department detectives eventually admitted that the wave of overdoses recorded in the summer of 1994 could not, after all, be blamed on the unusually pure *China Cat* brand or even entirely on heroin. Six of the dead men had taken no heroin, two men hadn't taken *any* drugs, and most of the others also had traces of cocaine in their systems. And, if anyone had bothered looking beyond the publicized blip in heroin over-doses, they would have noticed that the number of people using heroin at least once a week in the United States dropped from 878,000 in 1988 to 810,000 in 1995, and the amount spent on heroin fell from $17.7 billion in 1988 to $9.6 billion in 1995.[10]

Similar numbers can be cited for most other illegal drugs. Surveys by the National Institute of Drug Abuse have shown the number of Americans using illegal drugs within the month preceding the survey dropping from 25.4 million in 1979 to 13 million in 1996. Marijuana use has been declining since 1978, heroin and hallucinogenic drugs since 1975. Despite a modest upturn in the number of users since 1992, demand and prices still remained far below earlier levels. By 1996 the number of people who had used cocaine in the previous month was only 1.7 million, far below the 4.7 million regular users in 1979.[11]

These encouraging figures reveal one of the great riddles of the global drug trade: why has the supply of illegal narcotics increased exponentially while demand in the United States, the world's largest market for narcotics, has plummeted? Part of the alleged increase in production can be traced to the notoriously unreliable estimates of the drug economy, which have been inflated by the hype surrounding the war on drugs. But even if those estimates were cut in half, user statistics contradict the notion that rising demand—created by the alleged moral decay of American society—is fueling the growth of the drug industry. In fact, even in the 1960s and 1970s, when demand was expanding in the United States, the supply exploded at a much faster rate, indicating that factors other than the desire to get high were playing a role in the development of the drug trade. Nor can the rising production be explained by rising prices, since street prices for both heroin and cocaine declined throughout the 1980s and early 1990s as the supply of drugs vastly exceeded demand. If anything, one would expect that the increase in supply would, by cutting prices, actually *create* demand and a bigger pool of potential consumers. Yet exactly the opposite has occurred.

The mystery of rising production in a period of falling demand and prices is compounded when one considers the politics of the multibillion war on drugs. The federal government devoted very few resources to the narcotics problem in the 1950s and 1960s, spending $5 million in 1968, when the number of addicts was rising from less than 60,000 in 1946 to more than 500,000 (some say 750,000) in the early 1970s. Yet between 1980 and 1998, as drug use dropped, federal, state, and local agencies spent more than $300 billion in the war on drugs. By 1999 the federal government was spending about $17 billion a year, 3,400 times more than the 1968 spending levels.[12] Why didn't the federal government launch a war on drugs in the 1950s and early 1960s, when drug use was becoming a serious problem in many American cities? Why did spending increase in the 1980s and 1990s, when drug use was dropping?

Another question is the effectiveness of law enforcement. Most of the agents who investigate the narcotics trade are hardworking, dedicated professionals. Compared with police forces in Panama, Mexico, Thailand, Colombia, Pakistan, Burma, and many other major cogs in the global drug trade, they are paradigms of virtue. They do not routinely act as armed guards for drug cartels or regularly accept huge bribes from crime syndicates. Yet their effectiveness seems to operate at an inverse ratio to their budgets. Despite an exponential increase in federal narcotics budgets over the last quarter-century, this has not produced a similar drop in drug production, or even eradicated drug use, which is lower but still widespread. Why, then, has Congress continued to pour billions of dollars into an enterprise that has obviously failed to show long-term results?

Similar points can be made about the problem of global drug cartels. Like heroin, international crime syndicates are the flavor of the month for law enforcement officials and the mainstream media. Some researchers now estimate that organized crime groups around the world produce more than $1 trillion in revenues a year from all their activities and over the last few decades they accumulated more than $1 trillion in assets. Those numbers, like all the other estimates of organized crime, are probably exaggerated, but "even if you cut these numbers in half, or a third, they are frightening," argues James Kallstrom, the former head of the FBI's New York office.[13]

Just how frightening the economic power of the crime syndicates has become can be seen in Colombia, where drug cartels own 30 percent of the farmland and earn $5 billion a year from drugs; in Venezuela, where they control nearly one-fifth of the nation's gross domestic product (GDP); in Italy, where the Mafia earns $21 to $24 billion a year; in Mexico, where drug cartels earn $30 billion a year; in Panama, where money laundering has increased since the fall of Noriega; in Asia, where the Chinese Triad gangs rake in $210 billion a year; in the former Soviet Union, where criminal gangs control 35 percent of the commercial banks and more than two thousand corporations; and in the United States, where American crime syndicates employ 280,000 people and earn about $50 billion in profits a year.[14]

No one in the top levels of federal law enforcement thinks that the drug activities of multinational criminal organizations can be obliterated by arresting or even executing thousands of low-level street dealers. They know that the real problems lie with the global organizations that produce, smuggle, and distribute hundreds of tons of illegal narcotics each year; therefore, U.S. law enforcement officials have spent billions of dollars to put top organized crime leaders behind bars. During the last fifteen years federal prosecutors have put more than three hundred mafia leaders around the country in jail, including all five heads of the traditional Italian crime families in New York. Overseas, investigators working with local police forces and occasionally the Pentagon have jailed Panamanian strongman

Manuel Noriega and many of the leaders of Medellín, Cali, Mexican, and Sicilian crime families.

Nevertheless, drug production continues to increase, and new drug lords rise to power. A crackdown on the Colombian Medellín cartel in the late 1980s allowed the rival Cali cartel to seize control of much of the U.S. market, a position they held until investigators put some of *their* leaders behind bars—leaving an opening for Mexican cartels. Since the mid-1960s, successes in curbing drug production in one area have simply shifted production to new locales, opening new markets and creating more potential consumers. In the early 1970s, for example, a U.S. crackdown on the Turkish heroin trade pressured that government to reduce the country's opium supply, but Asian crime syndicates took up the slack by boosting production in the Golden Triangle, a region that now supplies well more than 60 percent of the heroin reaching the United States. More recently, as some Asian countries—notably Thailand—reduced production, Latin American crime syndicates dramatically increased poppy farming in Colombia and Mexico. These two countries now produce 110 tons of opium each year, up from twenty-five to forty-five tons in 1985. In short, each successful prosecution of a major drug lord and every major success in cutting supply in one country has been followed by an increasing global supply of narcotics. Just as the eradication of the drug trade on the Lower East Side had little overall impact on the U.S. heroin business, the successful prosecution of various organized crime groups has not solved the problem. By 1997 more than 4,100 tons of opium was produced worldwide, quadruple the 1970 harvest.[15]

The failure of the massive federal war on crime to reduce the supply of drugs, permanently disrupt distribution networks, or radically reduce demand indicates fundamental problems with the entire effort. Although heroin abuse remains a popular subject of debate, no attempt has been made to untangle the seductive ideological and economic obsessions of earlier generations—colonialism, the war against communism, the "yellow peril" and the hunt for riches in foreign lands—that have made the drug a seemingly intractable part of the American landscape. All of these fatal attractions seem far away from the heroin induced landscapes of AIDS hospices or trendy drug users in downtown clubs. Few people think of the legacy of colonialism when they wake up in the morning and look out of their apartment through windows covered with security bars. Hardly anyone who is followed down a dark deserted street, late at night, worries about the history of the Cold War. People do not curse Nixon and the China lobby when they discover that their home has been pillaged by a junkie.

This history becomes relevant, however, for anyone who considers the development of the global heroin trade and the long career of Khun Sa, whose operations were finally shut down in late 1995 and early 1996. Khun Sa grew up in the turmoil of postwar Southeast Asia, in a world where colonial powers had already turned opium into a huge multinational business that supplied millions of addicts and financed British and French governments in India, Hong Kong, and Indochina. In the 1950s, as a young man, Khun Sa learned the opium trade from corrupt Nationalist Chinese troops who were backed by the U.S. government because of their opposition to the Communist Chinese government. Throughout his career, Khun Sa worked closely with politically powerful Chinese organized crime groups in Taiwan, Thailand, and Hong Kong, groups protected by corrupt local officials, and he established extensive ties to the Thai military, which received billions of dollars in U.S. aid. In exchange for intelligence on Communist guerrillas and a share of his opium profits, Thai military leaders sold him arms and supplies, a trade that earned them millions of dollars. Top Thai officials also allowed Chinese crime syndicates with close ties to the Nationalist Chinese government to smuggle heroin through Thailand, an agreement that enriched both parties. And as Khun Sa expanded his operations, he paid huge bribes to the Burmese military dictatorship, which made little attempt to shut down a kingdom of opium that stretched for hundreds of miles in northeastern Burma.

These tidy arrangements came crashing down with the pro-democracy rebellion in 1988 and 1989. Over the next few years Khun Sa's allies in Rangoon and Bangkok turned against him. Thai officials closed off the border to Burma, making it harder for him to buy supplies and smuggle opium, while the Burmese military deployed tens of thousands of troops against his positions. The U.S. government, which had given Khun Sa's allies in Thailand, Taiwan, and Burma billions of dollars in aid, indicted him for smuggling heroin and called on the Burmese junta to extradite him to Brooklyn to stand trial. These forces finally forced his surrender in January of 1996 to Burmese authorities.[16] Yet in the summer of 1996, six months after Khun Sa was finally put out of business, another wave of heroin overdoses was reported in the New York City press. Despite their victory against the king of heroin, Drug Enforcement Administration (DEA) agents admit that production remains at historically high levels. In 1998, when Khun Sa claimed he had retired from the heroin business and was peacefully living in Rangoon (now Yangon), Burma was still the world's largest heroin producer. The king has fallen, but the empire thrives.

This depressing fact makes the story of Khun Sa's rise and fall a useful—though exceedingly complex—outline of the global drug trade. Contrary to the usual explanations, the modern heroin trade illustrates some basic political and economic problems: abusive corporate power, unequal distribution of wealth, corrupts local elites who have close ties to organized crime groups, and right-wing American politicians who have protected the power of these various interests. The connections can be seen by simply taking a look at the flow of drugs from places like Burma to heroin addicts in the United States. At the bottom of the trade, organized crime lords, like Khun Sa, require a large pool of impoverished peasants who are willing to work for extremely low wages. Not surprisingly, the drug trade has taken root in countries such as Burma, Colombia, Peru, Bolivia, and Mexico where economic conditions have produced massive poverty. Once harvested and processed, however, the narcotics must be transported across borders, which requires the help of local elites who can protect the cartels from prosecution and launder their revenues. Then the cartels must find another group of impoverished people to sell the drugs once they reach the United States—a labor pool created by rapid changes in the global economy and the movement of low-skill manufacturing jobs out of many American cities. Finally, the cartels must launder their U.S. profits by moving the money out of the country—a process that has been aided by the rise of a deregulated global financial system—in order to expand their operations further. This entire system was set in place by economic interests that created the drug trade prior to 1945.

Chapter 2:
The Global Drug Trade

You have a row of dominoes set up. You knock over the first one
and what will happen to the last one is that it will go over very
quickly. So you have the beginning of a disintegration that would
have the most profound influences.

—President Dwight Eisenhower,
1954, announcing U.S. economic aid
to the South Vietnamese government

IN JANUARY 1950, THE SAME YEAR THAT SIXTEEN-YEAR-OLD
Khun Sa began working in the opium trade, Senator Joseph McCarthy sat
down with three friends in a posh Washington restaurant. In the late 1940s
the senator had raised a lot of campaign contributions from real estate
interests by opening fire on public housing programs. During one trip to
the Rego Park Veterans' Housing Project in New York City he denounced
the apartment blocks as a "breeding ground for communism." But this and
other projects had failed to garner the publicity and political power he
craved. Sitting with his friends, McCarthy admitted he was desperate for an
issue that would boost his reelection campaign. As they brainstormed a
series of possible winning issues, McCarthy dismissed one of his friend's
ideas that he should push harder for the St. Lawrence Seaway. "That hasn't
enough sex," he said. "No one gets excited about it." The senator's face lit
up, however, when one of his friends suggested he take up the issue of
communism. "The government is full of Communists," McCarthy said.
"The thing to do is to hammer them."

And hammer he did. One month later, he stood before a woman's
Republican club in Virginia, and waved a sheaf of papers: "I have in my

hand a list of 205 [people. It is] . . . a list of names that were made known
to the Secretary of State as being members of the Communist Party and
who nevertheless are still working and shaping policy in the State Department." The number later changed to fifty-seven and some of the alleged
Communists soon became merely "security risks." No matter. The fall of
China to Communism in 1949 and the start of the Korean War in June of
1950 prompted McCarthy and other conservatives to claim that radical
movements came to power in Asia because of "twenty years of treason" by
Communist traitors in the U.S. State Department.[1]

Although most of McCarthy's charges about treason in the highest levels
of government were simply manufactured, there is little doubt that the
United States faced an economic and political crisis of enormous dimen-
sions in the late 1940s. Socialist parties had taken power in India and Burma
after successfully demanding independence. Communist forces had taken
over North Korea, and left-wing labor movements were active in South
Korea. By 1948, Communist guerilla movements had been launched in
Malaysia, Indonesia, Burma, and the Philippines. In 1949, Mao Zedong's
Communist forces toppled the U.S.-backed government of Chiang Kai-
shek. And in 1954, after a lengthy war, Vietnamese Communists defeated
France, a victory that led to the creation of a Communist state in the north.

These movements also threatened longstanding American and European interests in the region. European interests, which date back to the
fifteenth century, played a key role in shaping Asia's modern history and
some understanding of their impact is crucial for understanding U.S.
policies after the Second World War. Marco Polo and others spoke of the
region's riches in glowing terms, and in the late medieval and early Renaissance periods a booming trade developed between Europe and Asia, producing a flow of gold out of Europe into India, China, and the Arab world.
Portuguese sailors reached India by sea in the late fifteenth century and took
over direct control of the spice trade from Arab merchants in the early
sixteenth century by establishing bases in Africa and India. By 1506, gold
from Africa and spices from Asia made up half the revenues of the Portuguese state, and "profits were extraordinarily high. Pepper bought in the
east fetched forty times its price in Europe."[2]

In the late sixteenth and early seventeenth centuries, Portuguese domi-
nance of the trade came under attack from Dutch and British merchants,

who gradually established their control of the region. In 1641 the Dutch capture of Malacca from the Portuguese gave Holland control over the Indonesian trade, while the British gradually expanded their domination of India. Spain took over the Philippines in 1571, and in the seventeenth century France began expanding to Indochina. By the start of the First World War the British had established colonial rule over India (conquered between 1757 and 1858), Brunei and Malaysia (1874 to 1914), Hong Kong (1842), Singapore (1819), and Burma (1826-1885). Meanwhile, the French had taken control of Vietnam, Cambodia, and Laos (1862-1904); the Dutch ruled Indonesia and Java; and the once-powerful Portuguese global empire shrank to only Macao and East Timor. Thailand (called Siam until 1939) and Japan remained nominally independent, but military threats had forced both countries to open their borders to Western trade and investments, and China was forced to cede some of its territory to foreign powers.[3]

The United States entered this game of conquest and trade relatively late. American forces invaded the Philippines in 1899, after Filipino nationalists revolted against Spanish colonial rule. Rather than turn the country over to local rebels—who planned to set up a U.S.-style democracy—the United States embarked on a brutal campaign of repression that featured concentration camps and mass murder. "Kill and burn, kill and burn," General Jacob F. Smith told his troops. "The more you burn, the more you please me. This is no time to take prisoners." Historian D. R. SarDesai estimates that a million people, about one-seventh of the population, died before the country was "pacified."[4]

European forces had already conquered most of Asia by the early twentieth century, however, and U.S. efforts there focused on trade and finance. American merchants began trading with China in the 1790s and during the 1830s and 1840s played a key role in the China trade of tea, silk, and opium. In the 1850s U.S. traders exported and imported more goods with Thailand than did any other country except Britain, and the appearance of U.S. warships off the coast of Japan in 1855 forced the Japanese to open their country to foreign trade and investment. Total U.S. imports from and exports to Asia grew steadily, from a mere $7 million in 1821 to $14 million in 1850, $41 million in 1870, and $2.3 billion in 1920. Between 1880 and 1940, U.S. businessmen managed to export more than $14.8 billion worth of goods to Asia, and by 1940 U.S.-Asian imports and exports to the region accounted for 24 percent of all U.S. trade.[5]

These imperial maneuvers were part of a global battle for raw materials and cheap labor in the developing world. The lure of profits in foreign lands, increased competition from foreign competitors, a wealth of raw materials in many third world countries, and cheap labor pushed many companies to expand overseas during the nineteenth and early twentieth centuries. Foreign investment by British companies, for example, increased from 144 million pounds sterling ($72 million) in 1862 to nearly 1.7 billion ($850 million) by 1893. As global trade grew twentyfold between 1840 and 1913, many countries established direct colonial control over third world territories to ensure ready access to markets and raw materials. Between 1876 and 1915 about one-quarter of the globe's land surface was distributed or redistributed as colonies, and by the start of the First World War, most of the world area outside Europe and the Americas was formally partitioned into territories under the formal or informal political domination of a handful of Western industrialized nations.[6]

During this same period, direct U.S. investments in Europe, Latin America, Asia, Africa, Canada, and the Middle East, grew from only $700 million in 1897 to $17.2 billion in 1930, and exports of goods and services from $1.2 billion in 1897 to $10.2 billion in 1920. By 1914 overseas loans from U.S. banks topped $1 billion. Overall, the United States increased its share of the world's exports from 11.7 percent in 1899 to 20.4 percent in 1929, and U.S. companies exported more than $152.9 billion worth of merchandise between 1880 and 1940.[7]

Unfortunately, the expansion of Western corporations into Asia and the growth of colonialism also created the basic structures of the modern drug trade that would be so crucial in Khun Sa's rise to power. In the sixteenth century Arab and Indian traders sold opium throughout the region, and the Portuguese and the Dutch began selling the drug throughout Asia in the sixteenth and seventeenth centuries. Spectacular profits as high as 400 percent convinced European traders and governments to expand their opium operations in Asia.[8]

This trade was extremely important for the development of the European economy. Its profits increased the power of the merchant classes and the banks that financed the colonial commerce. The growing power of these groups helped break down traditional relations and accelerated the growing importance of market economies. The most active trading empires of the Netherlands and Britain were also the areas that made the most rapid industrialization in the seventeenth and eighteenth centuries; meanwhile, the declining trading empires of Spain and Portugal made little industrial progress.

But the global trade that laid the groundwork for modern European industrial economies crippled the economic development of Asia, Africa, and Latin America. Initially some Asian rulers and merchants profited from the European trade by acting as middlemen between Western merchants and the producers of valuable local commodities such as silk or tea. But as European countries increasingly sought to control the supply of valuable commodities, the direct colonial rule they established over certain territories accelerated the development of market economies and European economic power. Colonial governments typically enacted legal systems that gave local residents few political or legal rights, thus making it difficult for Asians to own and exploit lucrative natural resources. Likewise, corrupt colonial governors and administrators showed a marked bias toward foreign investors. Many Asian peasants were forcibly removed from the land, and rich natural resources were virtually given away to foreign investors, who established direct control over the production and distribution of such valuable commodities as rubber, tea, spices, and precious metals. As a result, large amounts of capital flowed out of Asia into the pockets of Western companies, while many local residents became landless laborers forced to work for less than subsistence wages on colonial plantations.

This economic revolution affected the opium trade in some obvious and not so obvious ways. After their 1764 conquest of Bengal, the British faced the difficult task of financing the colonial administration and expanding their commercial interests. Traders made huge profits selling tea from China to Europe, but because the Chinese were not interested in buying many British products, and alarming amounts of silver began flowing out of Britain into China. British administrators sought to find a product that China would buy. One such commodity was opium, so British agents fanned out in the rich opium-producing regions of India, advancing peasants money and supplies to grow poppies. Chinese imports of opium skyrocketed from 75 tons in 1775, when the British started the Bengal opium monopoly, to 270 tons in 1820 and 2,555 tons in 1840.[9]

New England merchants also created commercial fortunes by smuggling opium into China. By 1815 about 30 percent of all American cargos to China involved opium. In 1856 the American government even sent gunboats to China to force it to open its ports to trade, which by then was primarily opium, and one American merchant described the U.S. opium trade by saying, "We're all equally implicated."[10]

Still, the U.S. role in the nineteenth-century opium trade never rivaled that of the Europeans, who set up colonial empires built on it. Although opium was illegal in China, massive corruption among local officials allowed it to enter Chinese ports, where merchants bribed other officials inside China to distribute it. When Chinese officials attempted to end the corruption and crack down on the trade, the British responded by sending in warships and 7,000 troops, who captured Canton in 1839. In 1842, at the end of the first so-called Opium War, the Chinese were forced to sign a humiliating treaty that gave the British colonial rule over Hong Kong and rights to trade at five Chinese ports. China, however, refused to legalize opium until after the Second Opium War (1856-1958) which also forced the country to open more ports and cede some land to the British. Thanks to the forced legalization of the drug, about 27 percent of all adult Chinese males smoked opium in 1907, and the country had some 13.5 million addicts consuming 39,000 tons of opium each year.[11]

Other colonial empires also moved heavily into the trade and, like Britain, used the revenues to finance their colonial systems. The British ruled Burma as part of its Indian colony and established an official opium monopoly in the country, which in 1930 had 55,000 legally registered addicts (another 45,000 purchased their drugs illegally). The Dutch expanded their opium monopoly in Java to the point of importing 208 tons of opium in 1904, and after the French conquered Vietnam, Laos, and Cambodia they too expanded state-controlled distribution of the drug. By 1930 French Indochina had 3,500 state-run opium dens that served some 125,000 opium smokers. The United States initially set up state-run opium dens in the Philippines, but political protests resulted in their abolition in 1906. Even countries that maintained nominal political independence began to use opium as a lucrative source of income. Thailand ended its ban on opium, and by 1930 the kingdom was selling 84 tons of opium a year in 972 dens to 164,300 opium smokers. "While addiction weakened the local populations, it strengthened the finances of colonial governments," Alfred McCoy has argued. "In 1905-1906, for example opium sales provided 16 percent of taxes for French Indochina, 16 percent our Netherlands Indies, 20 percent for Siam, and 53 percent for British Malaya. These revenues, sometimes reaching as high as 50 percent of total taxes, financed construction of cities, canals, roads and rails that remain as the hallmarks of the colonial era."[12]

Meanwhile, the political and economic turmoil created by the expansion of colonial rule and Western corporations exacerbated social problems that encouraged drug production and abuse. European power in China accelerated the decline of the central government and touched off political rebellions in the mid-nineteenth century. During the nineteenth century, a number of the opium-growing hill tribes moved south into Southeast Asia to escape the unrest and increased opium production in what is now called the Golden Triangle. At the same time, colonial expansion drove many Asian peasants into major cities, where they could be recruited to work on plantations or in a variety of criminal activities such as prostitution. Some poor migrant laborers were actually paid in opium, and others sought refuge in the drug to relieve their misery. Overall, it is believed that something like twenty million Chinese emigrated to other parts of Asia in the nineteenth and early twentieth centuries.

During the same period the turmoil of the colonial era created the new elites who, one day, would play an important role in Asia's postwar development. The expansion of the pan-Asian trade also helped some major Chinese merchants to build their operations, and in the early twentieth century wealthy Chinese entrepreneurs set up business empires that came to dominate the economies of several Southeast Asian countries, including Indonesia, Malaysia, and Thailand. Most colonial systems relied on local residents to staff the military forces that enforced colonial rule, thus creating a class of military officers who were well placed to set up military dictatorships after colonial rule ended. Similarly, colonial administration relied on Western-educated local elites, thus creating a class of professionals who had the skills to run civilian governments.

While some of these elites fought against European rule, the thoroughly corrupt colonial systems also created close ties between criminal elements and powerful Asian businessmen and politicians. The Chinese Triads developed in the seventeenth century as a resistance force to the invading Manchu Dynasty and members of these secret societies played an important role in several rebellions against the British in the late nineteenth century. But as the century wore on, they increasingly reached an accommodation with British authorities in Hong Kong, who allowed them to run the vice trade that supplied prostitutes and opium to Chinese addicts. Their power took another leap forward in 1912 when Dr. Sun Yat-sen overthrew the imperial dynasty and established a Republican government. Sun, who was a member of the Triads, did attempt to improve the life of the average Chinese, but his successor, General Chiang Kai-shek, another Triad member, showed no interest in attacking China's rampant corruption and crime.

By this time the Triads had evolved from a political organization into a group that was involved in a wide variety of both legal operations—such as providing coolie labor to colonial enterprises—and illegal activities ranging from gambling and prostitution to opium trading. Increasingly, Chiang Kai-shek relied on them as a paramilitary wing of his army, using the Triad gangs to quash strikes and assassinate political opponents. During the political and economic turmoil of the 1920s and 1930s, warlords allied with the Triads and the Kuomintang carved out and ruled whole sections of the country with little outside interference. Many became active in the opium trade, supplying opium to China and Southeast Asia.[13]

This nasty mix of corrupt political leaders, organized crime groups, and an exploitive economic system eventually laid the foundation for the modern drug trade. But before it assumed its modern form the Great Depression and the Second World War brought a state of crisis that dramatically weakened the colonial system and led to the creation of an economy dominated by multinational corporations. Initially, the crisis caused a profound contraction in the global economy. U.S. exports fell from $7 billion in 1929 to only $2.4 billion in 1932 (the same level as 1911). By 1946 foreign investments by U.S. companies totaled only $13.5 billion, lower than in 1929. In the 1930s President Franklin D. Roosevelt attempted to solve the crisis by increasing spending for social welfare programs. But the economy stagnated, and unemployment remained high (19.1 percent in 1938) until massive military expenditures returned the country to nearly full employment (1.9 percent unemployment in 1945). Then, as victory over Japan and Germany became more likely, political and business leaders worried about the future. In 1944 Dean Acheson, who as Harry Truman's secretary of state was influential in shaping America's Cold War economic and political strategies, expressed many of these fears in testimony before Congress: "The important thing is markets. We have got to see that what the country produces is used and sold....You must look to foreign markets." Should the United States be denied access to those markets, Acheson warned, "we are in for a very bad time so far as the economic and social position of the country is concerned. We cannot go through another ten years like the ten years at the end of the twenties and the beginning of the thirties without having the most far-reaching consequence upon our economic and social system."[14]

U.S. dreams of finding prosperity in global markets faced a number of political and economic obstacles, however. Large parts of the world—Russia, China, and Eastern Europe—had embraced Communist policies that restricted U.S. investments; third world leaders demanded economic and political independence from the West; guerilla wars broke out around the world. Many U.S. policymakers worried that the rise of a generation of radical third world leaders would limit U.S. economic expansion and trade.[15]

The solution was found by creating, in the words of Richard Barnet and Ronald Muller, a new world order "based on the dollar and backed by the atomic bomb." As the sole Western power that emerged from the war with its industrial base and military power intact, the United States was able to use its immense political and economic resources to create a global economy dominated by American corporations. The carrot of massive foreign aid, which totaled $133.7 billion between 1945 and 1970, gave many governments a strong economic incentive to pursue pro-U.S. policies. And when the carrot didn't work, the big stick of military intervention in dozens of countries over the next half-century enabled American corporations to maintain access to rich natural resources and lucrative markets throughout Europe, Asia, Africa, and Latin America. U.S. exports of goods and services grew by an astonishing 15,335 percent, from $5.5 billion in 1944 to more than $848.7 billion in 1996. Between 1946 and the end of the Cold War, U.S.

corporations capitalized on the military power that gave them access to global markets by exporting more than $7.15 trillion dollars in goods and services, ranging from wheat and cars to television programs and computer software. In 1996 American foreign investments topped $1.5 trillion, up from $29.1 billion in 1955.[16]

In Asia, however, the new world order based on the dollar and backed by the atomic bomb faced enormous opposition. Rivers of blood and millions of lives were lost in the battle for the region's rich economic resources. Soon after the end of the Second World War anticolonial movements in Asia began clamoring for independence, and various Communist-backed guerilla groups took up the fight. Faced with mounting unrest throughout the region, the United States and Europe battled left-wing movements by installing a number of repressive pro-Western regimes in power. In Vietnam the United States backed away from its wartime promise of supporting independence and helped France try to hold on to its colony with billions of dollars in military aid. The French were defeated in 1954, after a bitter eight-year war, but the United States refused to allow the Communists to take power and installed a series of corrupt governments that imprisoned, tortured, or executed thousands and thousands of people. By the time South Vietnam fell to Communist forces in 1975, more than 2.2 million Vietnamese and 50,000 American troops had died in the conflict.[17]

Meanwhile, in South Korea, which had rich deposits of rare metals such as tungsten, needed for U.S. military hardware, the United States backed the regime of Syngman Rhee. In exchange for the use of miliary bases and lucrative deals to American investors for gold, tungsten, and other natural resources, the United States turned a blind eye to the regime's corruption and massive human rights abuses. To maintain his power, Rhee turned to high-ranking police and military officers who had served the Japanese during the war, protecting them from prosecution for war crimes and using them in a massive crackdown on the political opposition. As protests by peasants and unions broke out in 1946 and 1947, Rhee's paramilitary organization under the control of his police apparatus jailed, tortured, and killed tens of thousands of people. A 1948 uprising in the areas around the port city of Yosu produced at least 500 dead civilians and left more than 3,000 people in jail, of whom at least 866 were executed. A crackdown on a 1949 rebellion in Cheju left more than twenty-seven thousand dead. Guerrilla warfare continued in South Korea until the North Korean Communists invaded in 1950. When United Nations troops led by General Douglas MacArthur counterattacked and, later, the Chinese entered the fray, Rhee's Axis-trained police and military forces embarked on a massive campaign against anyone they viewed as a Communist sympathizer. In November the South Korean government announced that nearly 56,000 people had been arrested in one day alone and one Japanese source estimated that the Rhee regime executed or kidnaped about 150,000 people during the Korean War. By the time it was over, 111,000 South Koreans had been killed and another 57,000 were missing. No one knows how many North Korean civilians died, but the Communists lost as many as 70,000 troops, and the United States suffered 2,954 dead, 13,659 wounded, and 3,877 missing in action.[18]

Although Korea and Vietnam provide the most graphic reminders that the Cold War was waged with white-hot terror, other examples of the region's turmoil abound. In Thailand the United States backed a military dictatorship that overthrew a democratically elected government, even though the leaders of the coup had run a pro-Axis dictatorship that declared war on the United States. In the Philippines the United States installed a government headed by Manuel Roxas, who had run the government during the Japanese occupation. In Taiwan, the United States supported Chiang Kai-shek's Kuomintang (KMT) government, despite that party's long history of corruption and brutality, and Washington remained silent when the Nationalist dictatorship for decades refused to allow democratic elections, a policy that effectively reduced the local residents to colonists in their own country. In 1947, for example, when local nationalists protested the invasion of their country, KMT machine gun squads toured the country randomly firing into homes, and anyone suspected of dissent was imprisoned, tortured, or executed. By the time it was over, the KMT had massacred as many as 28,000 civilians.[19]

This detour into the political turmoil of the Cold War may seem at first glance far removed from the career of Khun Sa and the global heroin trade. But over time, as U.S. military and economic aid strengthened the power of authoritarian regimes in many Asian countries—most of which enthusiastically protected the power of major American multinational corporations—

their corrupt leadership laid the foundation for an explosion of drug production in the Golden Triangle. Military dictatorships in countries such as Thailand, receiving massive aid from the United States to crack down on left-wing guerilla groups, also received massive bribes from the drug cartels and used their political power to protect drug traffickers. Thanks to this protection, organized crime groups were able to build up global distribution networks and rapidly expand the production of drugs. Meanwhile, peasant economies were disrupted by the economic policies of these elites and the bloody guerilla wars of the period, which created a large pool of desperately poor people who would work in both low-wage factories and the drug trade.

This was wonderful news for Khun Sa, but for countries such as Burma it spelled disaster. At the end of the Second World War, Burma was one of the most promising of emerging Asian democracies. The leaders of the difficult revolt against British rule hoped to find a middle way between the Russian and American models. Unfortunately, their inability to find a "third way" quickly plunged the country into political turmoil and eventually led to the creation of one of the world's most brutal military dictatorships—which had a significant impact on the political economy of crime.

Chapter 3:
The Narco-Dictators

We have to continue to fight the evil of communism and to fight you must have an army and an army must have guns and to buy guns you must have money. In these mountains the only money is opium.

—*General Xiwen Duan of the Kuomintang, 1967*

IN THE 1970S AND EARLY 1980S, MAI HONG SON, A SMALL BORDER town in the north of Thailand, established a well-deserved reputation as a Wild West outpost for opium smugglers and speculators of all stripes, and as late as 1990 Khun Sa maintained an office in town, right next to the Thai police station. Today, however, the drug trade has taken a back seat to a more lucrative industry: the village receives more than 200,000 visitors a year. It is filled with burger stands, English pubs, tourist agencies, and trinket shops that sell fake opium pipes. Each year guides take thousands of young people on long hikes up to the hill tribes, where they can smoke opium in a culturally correct setting; others escort busloads of sightseers up to visit the long-necked women, Burmese women whose necks have been artificially elongated with brass rings fitted over their neck during their childhood.

Mai Hong Son has even become a popular destination for movie-makers seeking to capture the mystique of the East on film. About fifteen kilometers outside of town is a resort where Mel Gibson stayed while filming *Air America,* a fictionalized account of the CIA's involvement in the Southeast Asian opium-smuggling business. The owners charge visitors ridiculous sums of money to stay in air conditioned grass huts surrounded by over-logged and badly eroded hills.

A very different view of the region, however, can be found by driving northwest from the village over a dirt road that is little more than a series of potholes through the jungle. Only a few miles out of Thailand into Burma, everything changes. The tacky shops selling opium pipes and running gear emblazoned with poppy plants give way to rice paddies and isolated farming villages. The peasants who live here are no longer major opium growers, as they were twenty years ago. Instead, at harvest season every November, after six months of torrential rains, the lush green rice paddies have ripened into golden seas, shimmering and rippling in the warm autumn winds, and the hills are dotted with peasants working in the hot sun.

Behind this bucolic picture, however, lies great misery. Many peasants are so heavily indebted that they must sell their younger sons or daughters to outside labor recruiters for brothels and sweatshops inside Thailand. Intravenous heroin abuse has become a serious problem, and the picturesque native costumes of some hill tribes hide HIV infection rates as high as 30 percent. Even those who can supplement their income by smuggling opium, or by growing it in small plots, rarely make more than a few hundred dollars a year. Worse, many of these peasants have had their lives turned upside down by the political turmoil in Burma that has produced more than one million refugees and so many casualties no one even bothers to keep an exact body count.[1]

The Burmese border near Mai Hong Son is dotted with guerilla camps. One such camp, which had to be reached by a three-hour truck drive from Mai Hong Son and a one-hour hike into the jungle, seemed at first glance an unusual launching pad for a political revolution. Here the guerrillas, members of a pro-democracy student group, asked new arrivals to sign a guest book. Their commander, Sonny, had been studying for a Ph.D. in physics before his political activities landed him in jail. Moscow, the Burmese student who shepherded visiting journalists, was three months away from an advanced degree in zoology when a military coup forced him to flee to the jungle. Richard, a tiny, gentle-looking man who used his two-year exile to become an expert on the jungle and its plants, had studied accounting; at thirty-three, he was the oldest person in residence. He seemed happiest when talking about the ecology of the jungle, showing visitors plants that he claimed could treat everything from diarrhea and the flu to gunshot wounds and sprained ankles.

The camp's purpose became more apparent when a young man who looked barely old enough to be in high school explained that he had been fighting the military junta for six years and displayed his gun. It was not one of the featherweight, high-tech semiautomatic weapons favored by drug gangs in Hollywood films, but an old, beat-up Uzi that he claimed was captured in a raid on a Burmese military outpost. Cradled in his young arms, the gun looked like an old toy used by generations of kids.

The seriousness of their struggle also became apparent inside their hospital, a grass hut with a dirt floor, three bare bamboo cots, and a small medicine cabinet. Moscow explained that forty students from this camp had been treated for gunshot wounds; they regularly carried out military operations far inside Burma. In six years of armed struggle this tiny camp of a hundred guerrillas had suffered twenty-five casualties. Within a year, however, this area was also overrun by Burmese troops, forcing the students to move to a new location.

Moscow spent most of his time in guiding tourists into the jungle from Mai Hong Son and explaining the intricacies of this forgotten war to visiting journalists. Nevertheless, like the others in the camp, he had experienced the ravages of war firsthand. Raised in a wealthy Shan family, he got involved in politics in 1987 and 1988, when millions of students and citizens hit the streets of Rangoon and other major cities to demand democratic rights. After hundreds, maybe thousands of people were killed in an attempt to quash the uprising, Burma's longtime dictator Ne Win agreed to step down. In August and September 1988, hundreds more unarmed demonstrators died in clashes between authorities and dissidents, but the military's power was clearly ebbing. For a few weeks it seemed as if the pro-democracy forces might win.

Then, on September 19, the military formed the ominous sounding State Law and Order Restoration Council (SLORC) and brutally cracked down on the dissenters. No one will probably ever know how many people were killed in that fighting, in part because the military disposed of many bodies before they could be counted. "Witnesses at the cemetery said they heard cries of shooting victims who had been brought to [a crematorium] . . . while they are still alive—and were cremated with the corpses," *Newsweek* reported. By year's end, human rights groups estimated that three to ten thousand people had been killed by SLORC and that another ten thousand students and dissidents had fled into the jungle to launch a guerrilla war against the military.[2]

Hoping to defuse the tensions, the military agreed to democratic elections in 1990. When it lost, however, SLORC arrested the leader of the main opposition party, Daw Aung San Suu Kyi. The daughter of the Aung Sang, leader of the nationalist opposition to British colonial rule in the 1940s, she had given up a secure life in Oxford, England, to join the popular resistance. That heroic decision and her work fighting the military junta won her the Nobel Peace Prize in 1991. But she remained under house arrest until 1995, and as late as the fall of 1998 her political activities were still severely restricted. As the fighting, the torture, and the executions drag on, more articles are written in the U.S. press about Burma's heroin problem than its human rights abuses.

The crackdown ended Moscow's dreams of becoming a zoology professor. He was thrown in jail, an experience that gave him the nickname he still uses. "Thousands of people were arrested," he says. "My best friend was gunned down in a demonstration. I was arrested and spent two weeks in prison. The jail [where I was held] was called Moscow because our society is like a locked prison, without freedom. The inmates suffered like [the citizens of] Moscow. There were forty people in a small room with only two mats to sleep on. We had to cut up the mats [to wipe ourselves] when we wanted to go to the bathroom. We were given only two cups of water a day to drink and to wash. The smell was unbearable. At night we couldn't sleep because of the screams of people being tortured. Every day, the police came in and beat people with their batons. That is how I got my name."[3]

After two weeks of incarceration Moscow confessed—on camera—the error of his ways and renounced his opposition to the government. When the tape was aired on state-controlled television, he and other student leaders were released from the jail. But his confession—like those of many others threatened with torture or worse—was only a matter of convenience. The day after his release he fled into the jungle, joined the armed resistance, and hasn't been home or seen his family since. "When we first got here, we thought it would be over soon," he says. "Now we know it will be a long struggle. Many of us have died. Many more will die. The military is stronger now than it ever has been."

Understanding how that military dictatorship took power and why it has remained in power, Moscow and other dissidents admit, isn't easy, but there is little doubt that this history, going back, once again, to problems created by colonial rule, has played an important role in the region's heroin trade. Prior to independence, The British, who had actively encouraged ethnic conflicts as a way of destroying political opposition, made no attempt to prepare the country for independence. Despite hopes that those ethnic conflicts might be smoothed over, Aung San, Burma's revered nationalist leader, and six cabinet members were assassinated by right-wing forces six months before independence. Their replacements were quickly overwhelmed by the enormous political and economic problems left over from colonialism. Within months after independence the loose political alliance of communists, socialists and ethnic nationalities that Aung San had held together degenerated into political infighting. In late March 1948, after a crackdown on Communist labor and peasant strikes, the Communist Party of Burma (CPB) resorted to armed struggle. In August, part of the army mutinied, and unrest spread to some of the country's ethnic groups. That same month, members of the police and army in Karen State also revolted and joined militants in that region, who had been demanding their own independent state since the end of the Second World War. Some groups in the southern district of Karenni also took up arms after the murder of a prominent Karenni nationalist. By the end of the rainy season in 1949 more than a thousand people were dead, Communist forces controlled 71,000 square miles where about six million people lived, and a number of ethnic groups were in open revolt. Communist leader Thakin Than Tun confidently predicted that "we will surely defeat the enemy within two years."[4]

This political turmoil, which would eventually allow drug lords such as Khun Sa to establish control over large territories, was compounded by America's Cold War policy of backing corrupt anticommunist dictatorships such as that of Nationalist China. For example, during the Second World War, the United States decided to bring KMT forces from the south of China into Burma to mount a counteroffensive against Japanese forces and a right-wing Axis dictatorship headed by Ne Win—despite objections from British officials, who pointed out that KMT warlords were making huge profits by supplying the Japanese army with opium. The United States also escalated the old British practice of recruiting the hill tribes as soldiers and paying them in opium. One British soldier wrote that "U.S. air force aircraft flew in large qualities of opium from India . . . and distributed it with typical efficiency, in ample, generous doses." Two U.S. advisers later rationalized this policy: "If opium could be useful in achieving victory, the [answer] . . . was clear. We would use opium."[5]

The colonial powers had a long history of using narcotics to preserve their power in the region, but the U.S. decision to back the KMT laid the foundation for a new empire of opium dominated by American-backed dictatorships and local warlords such as Khun Sa. After China fell to the Communists in 1949, several KMT armies that had been involved in the opium trade invaded Burma, hoping to use the north of the country as a staging ground for a guerrilla war against Communist China. Once inside Burma these armies received military aid from the Nationalist Chinese government in Taiwan and the United States, which viewed the KMT presence in Burma as a second front against China during the Korean War. Companies financed by U.S. intelligence agencies made regular flights into KMT headquarters in Burma, bringing arms, food, and ammunition and flying opium back out. Using these resources, the KMT commanders (who had been heavily involved in the Chinese opium trade during the 1930s and the 1940s) quickly expanded opium production in the Golden Triangle as a way of financing their armies and their secret war against China. They forced the hill tribes to expand their opium production by imposing heavy taxes and by threatening them with violence. KMT troops, armed with U.S. weapons, then collected the drug and, with the help of the U.S. backed Thai military and companies financed by U.S. intelligence agencies, shipped it into Thailand and Hong Kong. The opium was refined into heroin by Chinese organized crime groups with close ties to the KMT in Hong Kong and shipped overseas by other crime groups. As it poured into America, the number of heroin addicts, which had dropped to about 20,000 in 1944, began to rise dramatically.[6]

Burma quickly protested the invasion and, after mounting several un-successful attacks on the KMT forces, took its case to the UN. In 1953 international pressure forced Taiwan to agree to evacuate the troops, but the withdrawal was never really carried out. KMT troops in Burma, Thailand,

and Laos continued to dominate the opium traffic in Southeast Asia until well into the 1970s, and many of their descendants and former allies are still active. Khun Sa, for example, got his start working for the KMT in the 1950s, and Lo Hsing-han, who is still a major player in Burma's drug business, worked for a KMT-backed warlord. A number of Khun Sa's top advisers were KMT soldiers, and most of his drugs were distributed by Chinese crime gangs that flourished because of their ties to local governments.[7]

The KMT invasion, which occurred in the middle of a civil war between central authorities and the Communist Party of Burma and a variety of ethnic minorities, played a key role in the country's political turmoil and the collapse of its fledgling democracy. As KMT forces provided some of the rebels with arms, Rangoon responded giving greater power and increased freedom to crack down on the minorities to army forces under former Axis dictator General Ne Win. During the 1950s Ne Win's attempts to reconquer territories held by the KMT produced massive human rights abuses. Villages that were already heavily taxed and frequently terrorized by marauding KMT troops were burned to the ground by the Burmese army. Although the Shans, who lived in the KMT opium areas, had supported the founding of a democratic republic, these abuses pushed them into open rebellion by the late 1950s. To support their war for national independence, the Shans and some other ethnic minorities increasingly turned to the opium business to finance their political agendas, selling opium to the KMT in exchange for arms and supplies.

Britain and other Commonwealth countries provided generous military aid to help Rangoon fight the rebels. Although Ne Win made little headway against the rebels, the massive military spending, which ate up about 30 percent of the country's budget, allowed him and the military to increase their power base at the expense of democratic institutions. In 1962, when it appeared that civilian leaders were trying to make peace with the minorities, Ne Win overthrew the government and engineered a brutal crackdown on the opposition. The military dynamited the Student Union in Rangoon, killing hundreds of students, and most well-known civilian politicians were jailed.[8] Ne Win described his policies as the Burmese way to socialism, but the repression of unions and ethnic minorities and the absolute power of the military more closely resembled the pro-fascist policies of the wartime government he had headed. Under the junta's rule a cycle of domestic repression, torture, civil war, and corruption pushed Burma into a long period of political turmoil and economic decline that eventually killed hundreds of thousands of people.

This carnage was immensely profitable for Khun Sa and other drug lords, however. Soon after overthrowing the democratically elected government in 1962, General Ne Win established closer ties to opium warlords. Hoping to use them to fight the Burmese Communist Party and ethnic insurgents, the military junta allowed several to turn their private armies into government-sponsored local militias known as KKY militias. Khun Sa was put in charge of one of these in 1964, and like the other militia leaders he was allowed to grow and smuggle opium as long as he used his army to fight rebels. In the 1960s Burmese officers, who regularly received bribes from these warlords, used official army trucks to help them transport drugs.[9]

This alliance was not without its problems. On several occasions in the 1960s and 1970s, Khun Sa broke with the government, and he was jailed by the junta for treason in 1969. His troops kidnapped two Russian doctors and held them hostage until he was released from jail in 1974. By 1976, however, he was back in business and once again a close ally of the Thai and Burmese military dictatorships. In 1992 André and Louis Boucard, who have journeyed deep into the opium-producing regions of the Golden Triangle many times over the years, noted that in 1984 "the Burmese military offered Khun Sa free trade in narcotics if he used his troops . . . against the minorities and CPB's guerrillas. . . . [Since then] Khun Sa has continued to expand his power over the Thai border area. . . . [He] has evolved into a figure of significant political influence and has increased his forces to an extent previously not thought possible. . . . Because he was not considered a threat by Burmese leaders, . . . he roamed, unchecked, dealing with whomever he wished."[10]

Yet Khun Sa's ties to the military don't explain his rise or his actual role in the global drug trade. Thanks to huge profits from the heroin trade, Khun Sa became a powerful, almost mythic presence in this part of the world. In the mid-1990s guides regaled visiting tourists with stories about his career. For a small fee it was possible to visit tiny Chinese villages two hours north of Mai Hong Son which housed the descendants of the Nationalist Chinese troops that used American aid and profits from the opium trade to finance a secret guerilla war against Communist China. As late as 1995 some of these officers, who trained Khun Sa and gave him his start as a mercenary, were still playing a key role in his operations, helping him to smuggle drugs into Thailand and to launder his profits.

Likewise, tourists still regularly visit his former headquarters in Ban Hin Taek, a small northern Thai town a few miles from the Burmese border, where Khun Sa entertained top Thai generals in the late 1970s and early 1980s, paying them large bribes to allow him to smuggle heroin. Visitors to the north of Thailand can even visit the spot where Khun Sa fought a vicious battle with the U.S.-funded Nationalist Chinese troops and U.S.-backed Laotian generals for control of the opium trade in the late 1960s. Near that spot there is an opium museum, and at dozens of tacky huts are sold souvenirs and opium paraphernalia: poppy-decorated sweat pants and tote bags, Golden Triangle T-shirts, opium pipes.

But Khun's Sa's real role in the heroin trade is harder to define than his legend. He is half Chinese by birth, but near the end of his career he was trying to pass himself off as a Shan nationalist who was simply protecting that minority from massive human rights violations of the Burmese military. The United States has described him as the mastermind of a sophisticated multinational empire that produced $100 to $200 million in annual revenues, yet Khun Sa was, by all accounts, virtually illiterate until very late in life. He was supposedly responsible for much of the heroin that reached the United States, yet he had little control over the crime syndicates that imported the drug, and he lacked the education and financial expertise to launder his huge profits. For most of his career he was heavily backed by both the Burmese and the Thai military, both of whom received large bribes from his operations. Yet in 1993 the Burmese launched a massive military campaign against him and his longtime supporters in Thailand suddenly cut off the supplies of food and weapons that he had once easily purchased there.

Answers to many of these riddles can be found in the workings of global economy. After the Second World War, American corporations were able to expand their operations by working closely with local dictatorships, many of whom used U.S. aid and military support to stay in power. Unfortunately, some of these dictatorships were also heavily involved in a variety of criminal activities, which U.S. officials, more interested in fighting Communism than corruption and crime, ignored.

The subsequent alliance of political leaders, legitimate capital, and criminal money is a crucial feature of the political economy of crime. One obvious example of this dynamic can be found in Thailand. A 1994 U.S. State Department review of Thailand's war on the heroin trade noted that "widespread police and military corruption, expanding narcotics trade with Burma, and the involvement of influential Thai and Sino-Thai private citizens and government officials undermine the effectiveness of law enforcement counternarcotics units." Frustrated U.S. officials even went so far as to leak news that the head of the military-backed caretaker government was once denied a visa to visit the United States because he was alleged to be involved in narcotics trafficking. In the uproar that followed it was revealed that seventeen other members of the Thai parliament had also been denied visas because of drug trafficking. One outraged Thai journalist even suggested that all Thai M.P.s should apply for a U.S. visa and that those who couldn't get one because of narcotics trafficking should resign. "If they [took the visa test to prove their honesty] it's doubtful that enough would be approved for that august body to get a quorum," quipped *BurmaNet*. "Thailand has been the largest single smuggling route for heroin for decades. . . . [Yet] the number of major traffickers extradited from, or prosecuted in Thailand is exactly, none."[11]

The American frustration with Thai anti-narcotics efforts is particularly ironic because the Thai government has been one of the staunchest U.S. allies in the region and a major recipient of American aid: more than $1.1 billion worth of military aid between 1951 and 1972—about 54 percent of all Thai military spending—and another $91.4 million in aid to Thai police forces between 1957 and 1972. As part of these programs, the United States provided training for 34,983 Thai military officers.[12]

Much of this aid obviously reflected Thailand's economic and political importance as an anticommunist ally during the Cold War. "The U.S. was . . . concerned with expanding export markets in Thailand after the war," historian and political scientist Surachart Bamrungsuk notes. "Thailand was also seen as the only important independent Eastern source of rubber and tin. Furthermore, the U.S. expected to stimulate and expand production in industry and agriculture in Thailand and free Thai international commerce from [the] Thai government's restrictions. . . . Hence the U.S. insisted [over the objections of Britain] that there would be no military occupation of the country [even though the Thai pro-Axis government had declared war on the U.S. and the Allies].... This policy also affected the war criminal trials in Thailand. For instance, the Allies did not demand very strongly that Thai war criminals should be punished. All of them were released by the Thai Supreme Court ... [and Marshal Phibun Songkhram], the wartime Premier, spent only five months in jail."[13]

Thanks to strategic objectives that gave a higher priority to the war against Communism than the war against dictators and narcotics, American officials refused to criticize Phibun and other war criminals who overthrew Thailand's fledgling democratic government in November 1947. The United States provided Thailand with little aid during its experiment with democracy but responded more generously to the old pro-fascist military dictator. After Phibun and the junta offered to send troops to South Korea to fight the Communists, the United States increased military aid from $12 million in 1952 to $55.3 million in 1953. In 1954 it began constructing airstrips and bases in Thailand, and American intelligence services built up Thai counterinsurgency and paramilitary units. Meanwhile, the Office of Policy Coordination (a predecessor to the CIA) had also provided millions of dollars in aid to set up the Border Patrol Police (BPP) of Thailand (which operated both as a security and an intelligence agency) and a border police force on the north, and U.S. intelligence agencies spent $35 million to establish Sea Supply, which ferried guns and supplies to KMT rebels in Burma. Sea Supply trained three hundred members of Thailand's Police Aerial Unit and worked closely with the BPP, which had grown to 4,230 members by late 1953. By the mid-1950s there were seventy-six covert U.S. intelligence advisers and perhaps as many as three hundred American spies working at Sea Supply. "With CIA support the number of Thai police grew," explains Surachart Bamrungsuk. By 1955 to 1956 there were "some 48,000 men stationed throughout Thailand, with 10,000 stationed in the capital alone. [The] ... regular army had only 45,000 men."[14]

In the 1950s and 1960s these U.S.-financed police and military officials repaid their American allies by enacting policies to protect and encourage foreign investors. In 1954 only nine U.S. firms had investments—a total of only $1.6 million—in Thailand, but U.S. investments grew to $15.2 million by 1971 and U.S. companies exported more than $1.5 billion to Thailand between 1964 and 1970. By that time the war in Vietnam was also helping fuel Thai economic development. As the number of U.S. military personnel stationed in Thailand rose from 6,300 in 1964 to 43,994 in 1968, the United States spent $561.8 million constructing bases and American troops on leave from Vietnam spent $111.4 million in Thailand between 1965 and 1972. By 1969 U.S. military installations were employing 34,436 Thai workers. Although the end of the war reduced the direct economic impact of U.S. military operations, foreign investment continued to expand. Foreign companies invested $2.2 billion in Thailand between 1965 and 1985, of which $842 million came from the United States, and another $9.4 billion between 1986 and 1992. U.S. companies also exported $31.3 billion worth of goods to Thailand between 1976 and 1992.[15]

Initially, little of this wealth trickled down to the average Thai peasant and worker. Average per capita income grew only 1.5 percent a year between 1950 and 1960, in part because the military junta siphoned off much of the wealth. Following the 1947 coup Phibun and top military officials set up a number of state-owned enterprises that were run by military officials. Most of these companies were not profitable, but they provided military and police officers with lucrative sources of fees and bribes. In addition, Thai military leaders established policies that discriminated against the ethnic Chinese who dominated the economy. To avoid persecution major Thai companies bribed military and police officials, started joint ventures with military leaders, or put top government officials on their boards of directors. Multinationals, who also saw the beauty of working with local partners, established joint ventures with prominent Thai businessmen allied with the military. Between 1952 and 1957, sixty-one Thai cabinet ministers sat on the board of directors of 107 major firms, and the seven major leaders of the 1947 coup sat on ninety-one boards. Investments "by military leaders and bureaucrat capitalists . . . extended to almost all industries and sectors including banking, trading, mining, manufacturing, construction and services," as Suehiro Akira explains.[16]

Not surprisingly, military leaders used this power to accumulate vast wealth. By the late 1950s the former head of the Thai police department was described as one of the richest men in the world. In the 1960s it was also revealed that Field Marshal Sarit Thanarat, who ruled the country after Phibun was overthrown, had accumulated a personal fortune of well more than $600 million and that he had used American aid to maintain more than one hundred mistresses. By this time, Thai military leaders had also accumulated huge profits from the heroin trade, despite the fact that the U.S. government had spent millions to modernize Thai police forces and create the Thai Border Patrol, which was theoretically in charge of preventing narcotics smuggling. The TBB, trained by the same company that carried KMT opium out of Burma, worked closely with the KMT inside Burma and helped transport drugs, supplies, and arms. General Phao Sriyanon, whose police forces had been virtually created by American intelligence officials and U.S. aid, also used his ties to the KMT and its American allies to set up one of Asia's largest opium syndicates. "The connection between Phao and the KMT through the CIA eventually provided Phao with the ability to build a virtual opium monopoly," writes Surachart Bamrungsuk. When Phao and Phibun were ousted from power in 1957, the new military leader, Sarit Thanarat, publicly attacked their corrupt ties to the opium trade. But behind the scenes he continued the same old alliances with the merchants and businessmen who ran the trade. Bertil Lintner notes that "a fair portion of his wealth [which totaled as much as $600 million] . . . came from the drug trade."[17]

Despite a level of official corruption that allowed Thai military leaders to use U.S. tax dollars to smuggle drugs and hire mistresses, American officials continued to back the Thai government and provide aid to its police forces well into the 1970s. Between 1957 and 1961 the U.S. pumped $2.4 million into the Thai police under the Civilian Police Administration program and in the 1960s, the U.S. funded Thai police through the Office of Public Safety at Aid for International Development. Both programs were sold to the American public as a way of improving police forces around the world, but in Thailand most of the money went to corrupt officials in the border patrol, which continued to work with a variety of opium smugglers. Worse, Thai and U.S. officials (about one-third of the Americans involved in the Thai police training program were actually CIA agents) continued to use KMT troops and ethnic minorities involved in the opium trade to gather intelligence and as paramilitary forces to wage a secret war against Communist guerrillas in Thailand, Laos, and Vietnam. In short, the Cold War policy of supporting corrupt military dictatorships consistently took precedence over anti-narcotics efforts, which were virtually ignored.[18]

The same policy warped Thailand's internal economic development in a way that made it much harder for U.S. officials to attack the heroin trade in the 1980s and 1990s. Obvious examples were the alliances of Thai officials with opium warlords and rebels inside Burma. Between 1950 and the early 1990s, Thai military leaders sold guns and supplies to the rebels and the opium warlords, a trade that allowed Khun Sa to expand his operations. The increased political turmoil that helped fuel the opium business proved enormously profitable for Thai elites, who made huge profits exporting guns and supplies and importing raw materials such as gems, logs, and opium from Burma. "For many years, Thailand wanted Burma to be in a state of war," one Burmese student guerilla complained. "The Thais took bribes from opium smugglers. They sold rebels arms, food and supplies. They got contracts to log off the forests. They traded in gems."[19]

The importance of this traffic for wealthy Thais and the country's economic prosperity can be seen by taking a look at the heroin business. Chao Tzang Yawnghwe estimates that in the early 1980s the Thai output of 80,000 kilograms of heroin sold at $5,000 a kilo pumped about $400 million into the Thai economy. That would make heroin Thailand's seventh largest export earner, behind maize, rubber, sugar, textiles, tapioca and rice. In the early 1990s, however, corrupt Thai officials allowed some 190,000 kilos of heroin to move through the country (by this time most of the drugs were refined in Burma). Selling it at the going rate in northwest Thailand of $5,000, for a total value of $950 million, would make heroin Thailand's fifth largest export, behind textiles, precious stones, shrimp, rice and rubber. But if traffickers obtained the Bangkok price of $10,000 to produce $1.9 billion in revenues, heroin would have been Thailand's number two export, topped only by textiles ($4.6 billion).[20]

Equally important, close ties between the military, the business community, and the opium trade created a mix of legal and illegal capital that continues to bedevil law enforcement officials. Bertil Lintner notes that Phao, the head of the Thai police force who controlled the opium trade in the 1950s, "had accumulated not only political power through his powerful police force, but also economic influence through banking and corporate ownership, which owed much to money derived from the opium trade with KMT." Phao's banker, for example, was Chin Sophonpanit, who founded the Asia Trust, which became the center of most foreign exchange dealing in Thailand, and the Bangkok Bank, which is today one of the country's largest banks. Likewise, explains economist Suehiro Akira, in the 1960s "Field Marshal Sarit Thanarat, Field Marshal Praphat Charusathian, Field Marshal Thanon Kittikachon, and Police Director General Prasoet Ruchi-rawong . . . built new alliances with local commercial bankers and several multinational manufacturers. . . . In 1969, 143 government officials or their family members participated as board members in a total of 347 firms." Field Marshal Praphat, who Lintner says took over Phao's role in the opium trade, was on the boards of forty-four firms; he held stock in the Bank of Ayudhya and was a director of, for example, the Bangkok Bank, Capital Insurance, and the Provincial Bank. By the end of the 1960s, three of the four major business groups had placed top military and police officials on their boards.[21]

The extensive ties between opium-dealing military leaders and the banking sector help explain both the rapid expansion of Thailand's finan-cial industry and a number of its current problems. The Bangkok Bank, which had police and military officials involved in the heroin trade on its board of directors in the 1950s, saw its deposits burgeon from $64 million in 1962 to $4.1 billion in 1981 while the Bank of Ayudhya, established by the Phibun group, saw its deposits grow from $19 million to $580 million. Overall, Thai bank holdings rose from $292 million in 1961 to $11.7 billion in 1981. Thai officials who maintained close ties to the banks, through stock ownership and directorships, also set up a lax system of financial regulation that made it easy to launder drug money. "Money laundering increased as Thailand became a more significant financial center, but the government has not enacted money laundering legislation," a 1994 U.S. State Depart-ment report complained.[22]

Without the complicity of Thai officials, opium warlords in the Golden Triangle would not be able to buy arms or supplies, or men like Khun Sa to sell their opium. The U.S. officials who pumped millions of dollars into corrupt Thai police agencies gave officials the resources they needed to expand the trade. Khun Sa's reliance on corrupt military leaders in both Burma and Thailand was a persistent feature of his career. He used his ties to former KMT army officers to launder money, distribute drugs around the world, and establish connections with the Thai military. It was the head of the Thai Third Army, based in the north of Thailand, who negotiated

Khun Sa's release from jail in 1974, and when Khun Sa reestablished his operation in the 1976, he provided thugs and troops from his army for a Thai military crackdown on leftist students during the military coup that ended a three-year experiment in democracy. And in the early 1980s, when the leaders of the military coup launched their own National Democratic Party, Khun Sa contributed $50,000.[23]

As the U.S. war on drugs heated up in the 1980s, however, Thai military leaders faced pressure to crack down on the trade. Realizing there was money to be made both from U.S. anti-narcotics aid and from from warlords, they adopted a dual strategy of publicly attacking Khun Sa while privately aiding his enterprises. After years of allowing him to maintain a large military operation at Ban Hin Taek in the north of Thailand, the Thai military drove him over the border in 1982. Khun Sa, however, had been warned of the attack and fled with few losses, nor did the much-publicized 1987 Thai offensive against him have much impact. That same year the Thai military used U.S. aid to complete the two-lane highway from Thailand to Khun Sa's headquarters in Burma. This road allowed the warlord to ship opium to Thailand conveniently and Thai merchants to export arms, food, and supplies for Khun Sa's army. Powerful Thai military and police officers were frequently seen driving up the road to attend lavish parties given by Khun Sa.[24] Environmentalists in Thailand also contend that he sold lucrative logging concessions in the areas he controlled to top men in the Thai military and that he was actively involved in the sale of gems and endangered species to Thai merchants. "The Thai government is not willing to cooperate with us," the Burmese border minister Lieutenant General Maung Thint told the *Bangkok Post* in 1994. "They get food, supplies, arms, and ammunition from Thailand. That is why he still survives. His survival depends on Thailand."[25]

By the late 1980s, however, Khun Sa's cozy ties with military leaders in both Thailand and Burma had begun to unravel. Economic and political changes were forcing elites in both counties to reexamine their alliance with the warlord. Although his operations had long been a lucrative source of profits for both countries, Burmese and Thai leaders were developing new economic agendas that increasingly made Khun Sa a political liability. Thailand, which had long backed Burmese rebels because the illegal cross-border trade was so lucrative, now realized that there was more money to be made by doing business with the Burmese military.

At the same time, Burmese military leaders faced new challenges to their authority that forced them to rethink their support for the warlord. Their vicious treatment of peaceful democratic protesters had made them pariahs in the Western world. Even the United States, with its long history of supporting anticommunist dictatorships, refused to go along with those policies; it cut off all aid and vowed to block all international loans from the International Monetary Fund (IMF) and the World Bank until the junta stepped aside. Desperate for cash, SLORC wondered what it could do to appease the United States without giving up power. One easy answer to that question was to attack Khun Sa, for by this time, the U.S. Justice Department and the DEA had labeled him the world's worst gangster. If Burma's dictators could capture their former ally and deliver him to an American courtroom, the junta reasoned, Washington might reconsider its opposition to the regime. After all, U.S. officials had sent billions in foreign aid to leaders in Taiwan and Thailand who were up to their eyeballs in the opium trade. Why should Burma be denied American support simply because it was a corrupt military dictatorship?

Chapter 4:
Corporate Connections

Heroin and AIDS have become an horrible problem [throughout the Golden Triangle]. Some of the Hill Tribes have very high HIV infection rates . . . 20 percent or more. . . . [I]n Rangoon there is an enormous amount of intravenous drug use. Everyone is very poor but you can get high for pennies [about 50 cents a shot]. I visited one place where a dealer was shooting up eight or nine addicts with the same needle. I asked him if he'd ever heard of AIDS. He said sure, but he said his customers didn't have any good reasons to worry about the future. I asked him if he knew that AIDS was transmitted by sharing needles. He just shrugged and said it was the only needle they had. I told him that he should use bleach to clean the needle to prevent AIDS. But, he said . . . it was very expensive and almost impossible to find. So, I asked him what he would do when this needle wore out. He said he'd already had it for two years. Whenever it got dull, he just sharpened it on a sandstone.

—An anonymous human rights worker

IN JULY 1994 SEVERAL HELICOPTERS SETTLED DOWN ON A heavily fortified hill, known as Point 4410, in the Shan states of northeastern Burma. Protected by a squadron of heavily armed Burmese soldiers, a group of journalists, DEA agents, and foreign diplomats warily climbed out of the helicopters. Point 4410 was one of seven heavily fortified mountaintop strongholds that the Burmese miliary had recaptured in an offensive against Khun Sa's army. The Burmese military had made dozens of air strikes before bringing in more than ten thousand troops to invade Khun Sa's position.[1]

The fighting had ended only two days earlier and the delegation stepping off the helicopters was treated to a gruesome scene of mass graves, bomb craters, and fortified trenches. Khun Sa's forces still controlled many nearby hills, and he had vowed to retake the territory, but the Burmese military was eager to show off its victory to the international community. During the military briefing that followed, SLORC officers showed journalists heavily fortified trenches that had been breached only by hand-to-hand combat and heavy shelling. When Khun Sa's stronghold had finally fallen, soldiers discovered over "163 firearms, as well as mortars, rocket launchers, hand grenades, mines and over 10,000 rounds of ammunition."[2]

But the most significant find, from SLORC's perspective, was a cache of 3.3 kilos of heroin. Within days after bringing foreign journalists to Point 4410, SLORC leaders told the *New York Times* that they were serious about capturing Khun Sa and delivering him to the United States, where he faced a massive indictment for drug trafficking. "We've begun to hurt him," said Lieutenant Colonel Kyaw Thein, but he was quick to add that the Burmese military needed U.S. help to destroy Khun Sa's army. "What we need from America are helicopters and smaller arms, which we can use in the mountains."[3]

The push to show the world that Burma was serious about ending Khun Sa's career undoubtedly surprised the drug lord and a few journalists who had tracked his longstanding ties to Burma's military establishment. But SLORC had played the anti-narcotics card almost as soon as it took power. In 1988, before the crackdown on pro-democracy protests, Burma received $12.2 million in U.S. assistance, including $5 million in anti-narcotics aid. And it had garnered more than $80 million in U.S. anti-narcotics aid since 1974—including eleven airplanes and twenty-eight helicopters—most of which had been used to fight the rebels, not the drug lords. Eager for more U.S. aid, officials from SLORC military intelligence units began secret meetings with DEA agents stationed in Rangoon in 1988, even though the U.S. Embassy had prohibited such contacts. One DEA agent was ordered to leave Rangoon after these meetings were discovered that fall, and in 1989 the United States cut off all anti-narcotics aid, because, the U.S. State Department reported, the junta "has facilitated the drug trade and limited any potential enforcement efforts. . . . The GOB [Government of Burma] clearly condones drug production and trafficking by ethnic groups [with] which it has reached an accommodation."[4]

Yet even though Burma's drug production soared from 1,285 in 1988 to 2,575 in 1993, DEA agents continued contacts with the government, arguing that any anti-drug activities in the region would require help from the military junta. In a move much like the letters the DEA sent Panamanian strongman General Manuel Noriega, congratulating him on his "vigorous anti-drug trafficking policy," DEA agents began helping SLORC burnish its international reputation. In March 1991, DEA attaché Angelo Saladino wrote to a Burmese military leader, Major General Khin Nyunt: "I believe that many critics of Myanmar's [Burma's] government for reasons based on their own narrow political considerations have purposefully ignored SLORC's current efforts to build up a viable narcotics program. I would also respectfully point out that the government of Myanmar can count DEA among its staunchest supporters.... I and my staff [will go] to great lengths to make sure that the SLORC anti-narcotics successes are given the widest possible dissemination. Be assured that I, and my staff... will support your efforts with all the means available to us."[5]

In February 1990—only two months before SLORC refused to honor the results of a democratic election—the DEA had organized a public bonfire of opium that SLORC had supposedly captured. It was timed to coincide with the visit of top SLORC officials to Washington. But State Department officials refused to see them, and the bonfire captured little international press attention. Nevertheless, the DEA and Burmese military leaders organized several more opium bonfires, going so far as to arrange visas for foreign journalists who were normally banned from visiting the country. At a July 1994 ceremony, journalists, "senior diplomats, military attach[e]s and anti-narcotics officers witnessed the burning of 162 kilos (356 pounds) of heroin and nearly 1,300 kilos (2,860 pounds) of opium." Burmese authorities announced the destruction of 18,080 pounds of opium, 2,880 pounds of heroin, and 7,860 pounds of marijuana in a dozen other bonfires around the country and held forth at length on their commitment to the war against drugs. "I would like to proudly declare that the Union of Myanmar [Burma] is always ready to act and always welcomes sincere cooperation in solving mankind's most serious problem," said Police Colonel Ngwe Soe Tun, the joint secretary of the committee for drug abuse control. He added that many lives had been lost in the fight against narcotics, citing the soldiers killed during forty-five days of continuous fighting with Khun Sa in May and June.[6]

These events put the U.S. Drug Enforcement Administration, at odds with the U.S. State Department, which continued to back the arms embargo and the suspension of all international aid. DEA agent Saladino was removed from his post when his congratulatory letter to Khin Nyunt was discovered, and his successor, Richard Horn, also got in trouble for maintaining contacts with SLORC. The DEA "is trying to run its own foreign policy," an anonymous State Department source complained in 1994 to the *Far Eastern Economic Review*.[7]

While the DEA pushed to end sanctions against Burma, corporate lobbyists also descended on Washington, arguing that it was best to "engage" Burma with closer political ties and foreign investments. With more than $200 million worth of U.S. investments in the country and the DEA insisting that SLORC could help win the war on drugs, the Clinton administration waffled. During a May 1994 tour through Asia, Lee Brown, director of the Office of National Drug Control Policy, told the Associated Press that "if we're going to deal with the problem of opium in Southeast Asia, Burma has to be dealt with as well." Timothy Wirth, a State Department counselor, agreed: "We have a national interest to become more engaged in Burma, engaged in terms of dealing with that government and dealing with the narcotics issue," he said. "We're on the edge of an epidemic of cheap and very pure heroin and that's going to demand more aggressive action by us because that directly impinges on our national interest. I'm thinking of young people on the streets of the United States of America.... That should be our first priority. First of all [we have to] start to deal with them [the junta]. It seems to me you have to do that." At the end of the year the *Wall Street Journal* reported that U.S. officials had opened talks with the miliary dictatorship about normalizing relations.[8]

Ultimately, however, SLORC refused to give in to the Clinton administration's very modest demand that pro-democracy parties be allowed to operate, and in 1997 Washington imposed tighter economic sanctions on Burma, outlawing all new foreign investment by American companies. Unfortunately, this decision was about nine years too late. In 1988, when more than a million Burmese citizens joined pro-democracy protests, the military dictatorship had been nearly bankrupt, but the junta had used this grace period to bolster its economic and political power. Just as lucrative trade and investment opportunities caused Western governments to turn a blind eye to massive corruption and state-sanctioned crime in Taiwan and Thailand during the 1950s, a new battle for Asia's rich natural resources had allowed one of the world's most noxious dictatorships to thrive and prosper. As late as the summer of 1998, Aung San Suu Kyi, the winner of the Nobel Peace Prize for her courageous stand against dictatorship, still lived as a virtual political prisoner; when she attempted to journey to a provincial town to meet with other pro-democracy activists, she was surrounded by the military, creating a standoff that left her stranded on a bridge for days.

Worse, as major corporations made large investments in Burma and corporate lobbyists argued against economic sanctions, the Burmese government carried out a reign of terror against the opposition. Soon after outlawing the pro-democracy movement, the junta turned to slave labor and other human rights violations to carry out its economic policies. The *Working People's Daily,* a state-owned publication, admitted that 800,000 people were conscripted to work on a railroad built to take tourists to posh resorts and thus produce badly needed foreign exchange. In August 1994 the *Daily Telegraph* reported that "tens of thousands of villagers from the Karen and Mon ethnic minorities are being treated as little more than slave labor as they build a 100-mile extension to the railway from Ye to Tavoy in appalling conditions."[9]

Similarly, the *Los Angeles Times* reported in 1993 that villagers were regularly kidnapped and forced to work as porters for troops who were fighting Karen and Karenni rebels: "During the last four years, as SLORC has stepped up its campaign to subdue the country's 12 million ethnic minority members, tens of thousands of villagers have been abducted. . . . Because the Myanmar [Burma] army has no pack animals, and since few roads penetrate the rugged terrain of northeast Myanmar, the porters are used to carry army supplies and ammunition over endless waves of jungled mountains. According to the stories the porters tell, the pattern seems invariably the same. The government soldiers move into a village and confiscate rice as tax. They arrest and spirit away those they believe to be rebel sympathizers. They take items from shops and refuse to pay. They rape the women. And finally they conscript villagers as porters and assign them to units moving to the front lines. Men, women and some children have been taken. The treatment of the porters varies. Several said they had seen soldiers bury the extremely sick, those who had lost consciousness, in leaves, then set fire to the leaves. The soldiers waited until the victims awoke screaming, then left the victims behind to suffer an agonizingly painful death. Some units released their porters after a few days or weeks, when they became too weak to work. Other porters were never heard from again. Women porters undergo the worst treatment. They report being raped by one or more soldiers nearly every night and still being forced to carry supplies or ammunition every day. The [surviving] porters . . . may find only burned-out homes when they return to their villages."[10]

A traumatized labor force also helped the junta raise badly needed cash for guns to repress Burmese rebels. In 1989 SLORC reduced government regulation, relaxed foreign exchange controls and offered foreign investors lucrative tax breaks and access to cheap labor by outlawing unions and strikes as well. The clamp-down on protests kept wage rates artificially low—about a dollar a day.[11] Further, the dictatorship offered to sell off natural resources and distributed a secret report to foreign investors which outlined potentially profitable investments in agriculture, timber, fishing, manufacturing, textiles, telecommunications, energy, and mining. "Myanmar could be classified as a country rich in natural and human resources because of her vast cultivable land and a long coastline, navigable river system, lush forests, abundant minerals, gems and literate population," the report claimed. "What she really need[s] to reap the benefits of such endowment is capital for exploiting the same. . . . In this regard it is evident that foreign direct investment can play a significant role."[12]

Major multinational corporations agreed. By March 1994, Burmese government officials claimed, investors from sixteen countries had set up ninety-one enterprises and invested more than $1 billion in oil and natural gas ($381 million), hotels and tourism ($332 million), mining ($155 million), manufacturing ($96 million) and fisheries ($88 million). Thai companies led the list with investments of more than $211 million, but U.S. corporations were a close second with $203 million, followed by Singapore ($108 million), Japan ($101 million), the Netherlands ($80 million), Austria ($72 million), Korea ($60 million), Hong Kong ($58 million), Malaysia ($54 million), the United Kingdom ($43 million), Australia ($27 million), and France ($10 million).[13]

U.S. officials publicly attacked SLORC's human rights record while privately encouraging American corporations to move into the area. In 1993 the U.S. Embassy in Rangoon reported investment opportunities in telecommunications, mining, wood-based industries, agribusiness, and natural gas, and the American press soon spread the good news that Burma was open for business. "Burma, one of the world's poorest, most autocratic states, is riding a wave of foreign business interest to greater international prominence," the *Wall Street Journal* gushed in November 1994. "The country's military regime is relaxing some political controls and accelerating economic change. . . . [The United States], until recently opposed to contact with the regime, has opened talks with it. . . . [this] 'constructive engagement' as opposed to international isolation . . . has produced a flurry of business activity. . . . Foreigners, mainly Asian, are building hotels, factories and mines and infrastructure. Unocal Corp. of the U.S. is a partner in a historical $500 million project signed in September to pipe natural gas from Burma into Thailand. [The number of cars has swelled to 300,000 from 72,000 five years ago, prompting interest from automakers]. . . . Banks are opening offices in the Burmese capital, even though the government still can't obtain international loans."[14]

The military regime attempted to remain in power by auctioning off the country's rich natural resources to the highest bidder, helping change Thailand's view of Khun Sa as a result. Although the country achieved an annual growth rate of 7.9 percent between 1970 and 1990, its rapid development was increasingly threatened by mounting shortages of energy and water. Despite massive dam projects, the heavy use of water in industry and in government-promoted agribusiness projects with major multinational corporations had reduced the amount of drinking water available for Thailand's rapidly growing population, and electricity needs were increasing at about 1,000 megawatts per year. Thailand was desperate for ways to build new dams for energy and water, reported *The Nation*, a Thai newspaper, in 1994.[15]

To solve those problems, Thai leaders increasingly saw Burma's natural resources as the key to their country's future growth and began to forge closer ties to the Burmese military junta. In September 1993 Thailand and Burma signed a memo of understanding on joint development of dams along Salween, a major river system that runs through both countries, and

Thailand began working with Burma to develop its rich natural gas reserves. In 1989, as the junta was jailing and torturing thousands of dissidents, eight major oil companies signed agreements with SLORC to explore for natural gas and oil, deals that gave the cash-strapped junta $40 million to buy arms to repress the democratic opposition. Several companies pulled out after their concessions failed to produce marketable quantities. But when large natural gas reserves were found in the Andaman Sea, Premier, Texaco, and Nippon signed a contract to develop the Yetagun gas field (fifty thousand square kilometers), and Total signed a deal with Myanmar Oil and Gas Enterprise (MOG), to develop the Martaban field. Unocal later became a partner in Martaban, acquiring 47.5 percent of the shares; Burma's state-owned MOG and Thailand's state-owned oil companies both got options to buy shares, and Thailand agreed to build a $1 billion conversion plant to handle the flow of gas from Burma to Thailand.[16] Eventually protests forced Texaco and ARCO to pull out of Burma.

These deals, producing huge profits for Thai and Burmese elites, have had disastrous consequences for both the region's ecology and peasants in the Golden Triangle. Rampant logging by Thai firms in Burma has already caused massive problems of soil erosion, and developing the offshore gas fields requires the oil companies to build pipelines. Burma has no environmental laws and the junta's corrupt record raises serious concerns about the government's ability to protect the environment. Moreover, the military's practice of conscripting slave labor to build roads into logging areas, or to construct army barracks to secure the areas to be used for pipelines to carry out new projects, convinced more than one million people to flee the country between 1988 and 1994. Kevin Heppner, who works with the Karen Human Rights Group, says that "95 percent of the refugees say they have not fled military battles, but systematic oppression by the SLORC military. Several new railway and road projects are being built entirely with the slave labor. . . . If they fail to provide slave labor, their village leaders are tortured or killed and their village and crops are burned."[17] He documents these allegations with horrifying slides of people injured by torture, overwork, and sexual abuse.

This flight of workers has been good news for the Thai business community. With about 350,000 illegal Burmese immigrants working in Thailand, many Thai businesses have been able to remain competitive with other low-wage Asian countries. The Burmese illegals are typically paid about sixty dollars a month, well below the minimum wage for unskilled Thai labor and some maids make as little as twenty to thirty-two dollars a month. "Cheap labor from Burma will remain cheap for Thai entrepreneurs who exploit them to maximize their profits with no concern for their basic human rights," writes Thailand's *The Nation*.[18]

The worst abuses of this system are to be found in Thailand's sex industry, which employed some eight hundred thousand to two million prostitutes in the early 1990s. Since 1988, up to 1,200 women a month have fled to Thailand, where they must work illegally in low-wage sweatshops or in the sex trade. In 1994 *The Nation* in Thailand estimated that twenty to thirty thousand Burmese women were working in the sex trade, with about ten thousand new recruits arriving each year. "Peasants with heavy debts and in desperate economic straights often sell young boys and girls to agents," said one activist, who didn't want her name used for fear of reprisals from Thai authorities. "The agents work with Thai and Burmese officials to keep a steady stream of women coming across the border. Thai police are bribed by the brothel owners, and . . . prostitutes who attempted to escape have been raped or badly beaten by the Thai police. The brothel owners do not let them complain if a customer does not want to wear a condom and many become IV [intravenous] drug users."[19]

The Women's Rights Project and Asia Watch confirmed that "the trafficking of Burmese women and girls into Thailand is appalling in its efficiency and ruthlessness. Once the women and girls are confined in the Thai brothels, escape is virtually impossible. Any Burmese women or girl who steps outside the brothel risks physical punishment . . . and/or arrest as an illegal immigrant—by the same police who are often the brothel owner's best clients. The worst brothels . . . are surrounded by electrified barbed wire and armed guards. The women and girls face a wide range of abuse, including debt bondage; illegal confinement; forced labor; rape; physical abuse; exposure to HIV/AIDS; and in some cases murder." As a result of increased intravenous heroin use and unsafe sex, more than 70 percent of all prostitutes in Thailand are HIV positive.[20]

Not only is this nasty mix of environmental degradation, slavery, prostitution, AIDS, greedy multinational companies, human rights abuses, and arms peddlers one of the great political tragedies of the twentieth century;

it also goes a long way toward explaining why Khun Sa lost his crown as the king of heroin. Business deals gave the Burmese military the income it needed to buy arms and remain in power. At the same time, closer economic ties between Burma and Thailand showed the Thai leaders that more money was to be made in Burma, which could provide the energy Thailand needed for the twenty-first century, than from Khun Sa. Even better, by joining Burma's war on Khun Sa they might curry some favor in Washington, which was getting increasingly irritated by Thailand's lack of interest in cracking down on major heroin traffickers. In the fall of 1994, then, after Burma launched its first attacks on Khun Sa, Thai leaders began closing the border with Burma. That made it harder, though by no means impossible, for smugglers to supply the drug lord and various rebel groups with arms and supplies. There were news reports that Khun Sa's demise was imminent.

By this time it was also clear that the junta's war on drugs was nothing more than a cynical political maneuver. Even the military's offensive against Khun Sa did not seem to signal any real change, since the government continued to have close relationships with such warlords as Lo Hsing-han, a longtime rival of Khun Sa. Like Khun Sa, Lo Hsing-han got his start in the opium business in the 1960s as a KKY militia leader. After Khun Sa's 1969 arrest, Lo Hsing-han took over many of his operations. By 1973 a U.S. official told Congress that the "kingpin of the heroin traffic in Southeast Asia. . . . Lo Hsing-han is an international bandit and responsible for a growing proportion of Asia's and America's drug-caused miseries." That wasn't quite accurate—several other producers were larger—but the bad publicity (and an offer to give up the trade if the United States would buy all his opium) led to his arrest in 1973. In 1980, however, the military released him and allowed him to smuggle opium as long as he ran a militia that pursued local rebels.[21]

Lo Hsing-han's career really took off after the junta's brutal repression of the pro-democracy movement. As part of its divide-and-conquer policy, SLORC sent him to negotiate with rebel Wa ethnic groups and the remnants of the Communist Party of Burma, and he worked out an agreement that essentially revived the old KKY militia system: rebels who signed a cease-fire with the central government were allowed to smuggle opium as long as they fought other rebels and supported the government. By 1994 eleven groups of ethnic rebels and CPB units had signed on, and these new government allies were increasingly dominating the heroin trade. Heroin refineries appeared in former CPB territory and SLORC-controlled areas, and the drugs continued to move over roads controlled by the military.[22]

Major traffickers with close ties to the military dictatorship—Lo Hsing-han, the Pheung brothers, Lin Minxian, and Zhang Zhiming—remained enormously powerful, generally operating with the implicit blessing of the Burmese military. They produced opium in the north, refined it into heroin, and worked with Chinese organized crime syndicates to smuggle it through China to North America and Europe. As a result, total opium production remained at historically high levels even after the junta launched its attack on Khun Sa. Two years after his surrender, Burma was still supplying 60 percent of the world's heroin.[23]

The junta's official policy of encouraging opium production by allies while repressing opposition groups also helps explain the government's decision to attack its former ally, Khun Sa. Burma not only hoped to gain political good will in Washington but recognized that Khun Sa controlled the last well-armed force capable of resisting the junta's power: a ten-thousand-man army that ruled the Shan area of northeast Burma. Initially, Khun Sa seemed genuinely surprised by the Burmese offensive. But when it became clear that the junta was actually serious about wiping out his operations, he attempted to bolster his political position by declaring an independent Shan state in the territories he controlled. Many Shan political leaders remained privately skeptical—in the 1980s the warlord's men had assassinated prominent Shan politicians who were living in exile in Thailand—and U.S. authorities have long maintained that his attachment to the Shan cause was only a front for protecting his drug business.[24]

Still, Khun Sa's troops were the only sure protection the Shans had against a government that regularly burned down villages, tortured dissidents and forced tens of thousands of people into slave labor on government projects. "No one from the outside world has ever helped us," grumbled one Shan activist in 1994, who had been fighting the military for decades. "The whole world attacks us because of Khun Sa. They say he is a drug lord. If the Shan States were independent and we had free democratic elections, he would lose. But right now he is all we have. People support him because he is fighting for our independence. No one else can protect us."[25]

In 1994 and 1995 the junta's assaults on Khun Sa produced massive human rights abuses in the Shan areas. The military forced local villagers to carry supplies ahead of advancing troops so that they would be the first killed by land mines or attacks. Others were driven out of the area by the incessant fighting and hunger; more than five thousand starving peasants fled over the border into Thailand during the fighting in the spring of 1995. "[Their] food is running out and Thai authorities are not allowing supplies to pass border checkpoints," reported a refugee worker. "They are now surviving on the small amounts that can be smuggled through."[26]

Yet because of Khun Sa's odious reputation, few human rights groups took up the cause of the Shans. No Hollywood movies were made about their plight. No government wrung its hands about the mistreatment of Shans living in the war zone between Khun Sa and SLORC, even though their villages were regularly torched, their legal crops burned, and their families torn apart. No one pointed out that Shan peasant families rarely made more than a few hundred dollars a year growing opium, or that few Shans liked working in a trade that invariably produced more mayhem than money. For most it was simply the only way of making a living; all other avenues of survival had been closed off by decades of civil war and political turmoil. In the eyes of the outside world, they were pariahs—drug producers, dealers, and smugglers. "Every week, I get new reports of women being raped, of villages being destroyed, and of young men being kidnapped to serve in the Burmese army," explained another refugee worker. "We regularly send out reports to the press about these human rights abuses. What has happened to the Shan is one of the worst tragedies of the twentieth century. Yet no one . . . [wants] to be seen as helping drug dealers. They won't acknowledge that these refugees are simply fleeing oppression."[27]

In 1994 and 1995 Thailand even drove some Burmese refugees back over the border, a move that was designed to hurt Khun Sa and to burnish Thailand's reputation with Burma and the United States but that in fact simply left thousands of impoverished peasants at the mercy of the Burmese military. Burma's military junta continued a thoroughly cynical policy of profiting from the drug trade while simultaneously scoring points with foreign investors and governments by attacking Khun Sa. The United States, which claimed to be interested in human rights in Burma, did nothing for the Shans living in Khun Sa's territory, nor did it impose tough sanctions on foreign investment.

Meanwhile, Khun Sa's position was becoming more untenable. Lucrative deals with Burma's military dictatorship had convinced Thai leaders to abandon their traditional ally. In 1994 they closed the border, and in the spring of 1995 Burma stepped up its offensive, hoping to score political points with the United States by capturing the warlord. In early 1996 Khun Sa's headquarters fell to Burmese troops, and the warlord surrendered.[28] Yet by 1999 there was little evidence that the fall of the king of heroin had produced any long-term impact. The Burmese junta, which feared that the warlord would tell some very nasty tales about their operations, refused to extradite him to the United States to stand trial. As part of the surrender agreement, Khun Sa moved to Rangoon, where he is busy spending his drug profits. The agreement may also have allowed some of his associates to remain in the drug trade, for it seems clear that Khun Sa's fall simply allowed others to step into his shoes. As a number of opium producers continued to operate with the implicit blessing of the military dictatorship, the largest dealers were establishing a stranglehold over the legitimate economy, creating an alliance of legal and illegal capital that would make it much harder for law enforcement officials to eradicate the opium trade.

Consider, once again, Lo Hsing-han, who negotiated the cease-fires with other major Burmese opium groups that allowed them to remain in business. Little has changed since the *Washington Post* noted in 1990 that "when Lo Hsing-han visits the Burmese capital these days from his home in the country's far north, he is fond of indulging a passion for golf. This might not seem unusual for a wealthy, 56-year-old ethnic Chinese, except that he has been publicly identified as one of Southeast Asia's leading heroin traffickers, and some of his partners on the links are top Burmese military officers."[29]

Other partners seem to include major multinational corporations and foreign businesses. Sources in Thailand say Lo Hsing-han owns hotels, auto dealerships, trading companies involved in the arms business and logging companies. Despite his involvement in the drug trade, his compound is guarded by Burmese troops and he has become a much sought after political fixer, working with foreign investors to negotiate deals with

SLORC. Further, he is the chairman of Asia World Company Ltd. (AWC), one of Burma's fastest growing conglomerates, with interests in trade, manufacturing, real estate, construction, transportation, and distribution. The company has also set up joint ventures with firms owned by the Singapore government and other foreign investors, even though law enforcement officials believe that Lo Hsing-han and his son use AWC's investments (which include a container-shipping business in Rangoon, a toll highway through the poppy-growing regions of northern Burma, hotels, and an industrial park outside the capital) to smuggle drugs and launder money. The U.S. Secretary of State was forced to admit in the summer of 1997 that "drug traffickers who once spent their days leading mule trains down jungle tracks are now leading lights in Burma's new market economy. We are increasingly concerned that Burma's drug traffickers, with official encouragement, are laundering their profits through Burmese banks and companies—some of them joint ventures with foreign business."[30]

Nor is Lo Hsing-han the only drug lord to establish close ties to foreign capital. His younger brother, who is the government liaison officer in the largest opium-producing regions, also operates a lucrative distillery and transport company as well as teak logging in the Kachin state. Likewise, Zhang Zhiming, a former Red Guard member who joined the Burmese Communist Party in 1968, has become one of the region's largest opium and heroin refiners, enjoying "excellent relations with local Chinese police, army and military intelligence officers" in southeastern Yunnan, Lintner says. He and Lin Minxian, another former Red Guard fanatic turned opium warlord, also have business deals with Chinese officials to export gems and logs to China.[31]

This sort of alliance of corrupt government officials, heroin smugglers, and foreign investors has not only been a major factor in the political survival of a regime that has one of the world's worst human rights records; it also goes a long way toward explaining the ill-fated U.S. war on drugs. Just as commercial interests financed the colonial system by establishing the opium trade in the eighteenth and nineteenth centuries, the marriage of dictatorships and major corporations has allowed the drug trade to thrive today. It is no accident, for example, that U.S.-backed militaries and governments in Peru, Mexico, Colombia, Guatemala, Haiti, Bermuda, Costa

Rica, Paraguay, and Panama played a key role in shipping much of the cocaine that reached U.S. shores.

Nor is it an accident that the largest crime groups have flourished in countries that were major U.S. allies during the Cold War period. Many of these crime groups, though badly weakened by the Second World War, rebuilt their operations by establishing close political ties to U.S.-backed elites. Besides the Triads, who capitalized on Cold War politics and their ties with corrupt dictatorships to control the Asian heroin trade, the Yakusa in Japan revitalized their power by helping the right crush left-wing labor unrest in the 1950s and by establishing close ties to the conservative Liberal Democratic Party (LDP). That alliance continued until the 1990s, when a corruption scandal that involved organized crime figures and massive economic woes forced the LDP to move against the gangs. In France the Corsicans reestablished their control of the heroin trade after they helped repress left wing labor unrest. In Italy an alliance was formed between the Mafia and U.S.-backed Christian Democrats, who were saved by $10 million in covert U.S. aid from possible defeat by the Communists in 1948; eventually, Christian Democrats' political protection allowed the Mafia to rebuild and to establish a global organization that produced an estimated $21 to $24 billion in revenues in 1994.[32]

These examples illustrate how intricately the history of the narcotics traffic is entwined with the history of U.S. and European corporate interests. They do not mean, however, that the drug trade can be explained as some kind of massive conspiracy. Any attempt to reduce its rise to an evil plot by a few middle-aged white men in Langley, Virginia, tends to obscure much more important economic issues. Postwar economic restructuring produced millions of impoverished peasants, who began growing drugs, and large numbers of unemployed poor Americans, who could be recruited as users or as low-level dealers by global drug cartels run by organized crime groups. Corrupt local elites, who received U.S. aid and military support because they offered multinational corporations lucrative investment opportunities, protected these crime groups from effective prosecution. Finally, changes in the international financial system created new offshore banking havens that allowed organized crime groups to launder their profits. As long as the multitrillion global economy creates and encourages social and political problems that sustain the drug trade, U.S. law enforcement officials have no hope of success.

Still, the existence of these larger economic forces does not mean that the law-and-order politicians who have guided the war on crime are blameless. There is little evidence to suggest that Richard Nixon, J. Edgar Hoover, Ronald Reagan, and other law-and-order politicians consciously encouraged the drug trade, but their uncritical support of anticommunist elites did allow the drug trade to thrive in many countries around the world. Moreover, a number of prominent conservatives during the McCarthy period received money, valuable intelligence information, and public support from foreign governments that were heavily involved in a variety of illegal activities.

Nixon, for example, built his political career around the idea that Communists had infiltrated the State Department; his charges convinced many Americans that China had fallen to the reds because of traitors in the Roosevelt and Truman administrations rather than because the Nationalist government was corrupt. During the Cold War and the McCarthy period, few government officials, journalists, and politicians dared criticize these ideas, and the so-called China Lobby—an informal group of powerful U.S. Cold War figures—became an important political force in Washington. Over the years the China Lobby was heavily funded by the Nationalist government in Taiwan, which was up to its eyeballs in the Southeast Asia heroin trade, and wealthy Chinese businessmen had close ties to the Triad societies that ran much of the trade. By means of a well-financed propaganda campaign and hefty political contributions, the lobby developed close ties to such Cold War conservatives as Barry Goldwater, Richard Nixon, Ronald Reagan, and J. Edgar Hoover. Nixon, for example, received more than a quarter of a million dollars from the China Lobby for his 1968 presidential campaign—which ironically featured endless speeches blaming drug use on the political left.[33]

In the 1950s and early 1960s the China Lobby worked tirelessly to promulgate the idea that the heroin trade was controlled by the Communist Chinese. Senator Frederick G. Payne, a member of the China Lobby's Committee of One Million, argued on the floor of the Senate in 1954 that "Communist China is the leading source of supply of the illicit drugs being used to corrupt our young people." Likewise, Commissioner of Narcotics

Control Harry J. Anslinger, also a member of the Committee of One Million and prominent in the China Lobby, declared that "millions of dollars obtained through the sale of opium and other narcotics are used by the Communist regime of mainland China for political purposes and to finance [agents] who have been found actively engaged in subversive activities." This statement, from an advertisement placed by the Committee of One Million in the *Washington Post* and other major newspapers, and similar assertions in the *New York Times, Time,* and elsewhere, persuaded U.S. anti-narcotics officials to pay little attention to Southeast Asian opium. Anslinger refused to assign enough agents to the region, and the United States made no attempt to investigate charges that Thailand and Taiwan were heavily involved.[34]

Yet there was no evidence then or now that the Chinese Communist regime was extensively involved in the trade. In fact, soon after taking power this vicious dictatorship embarked on a brutal law-and-order campaign that managed to reduce drug addiction significantly by means of systematic human rights abuses. In the 1960s, after Anslinger retired, the U.S. government finally realized its error, fired many anti-narcotics agents for corruption, and issued a report stating, "There is no evidence that the People's Republic of China sanctions the illicit export of opium . . . or is involved in the illicit trafficking of narcotic drugs."[35] Today, DEA agents acknowledge that the strategy of blaming heroin on Communist China crippled U.S. anti-narcotics efforts until the late 1960s.

Similar points can be made about Nixon and Reagan's longstanding support for the corrupt South Vietnamese government in the 1950s and 1960s. Researchers such as Alfred McCoy and Gerald Posner have noted that after the United States installed Ngo Dinh Diem in power in 1955, American officials allowed the anticommunist government to become heavily involved in the opium trade. Nguyen Cao Ky, for example, became a major smuggler while he headed the air force, a career he continued as the country's vice-president and premier. Likewise, South Vietnamese officials used the air force and government trucks to transport opiates from the Golden Triangle to Saigon. Ky's brother-in-law, who ran the Saigon port, oversaw their shipment out of the country. Worse, Triad groups and dealers with government ties marketed the drugs to U.S. soldiers. Thanks to those seedy alliances—indirectly financed by the dollars Washington spent to prop up this criminal regime—American troops were easily able to buy heroin, and by 1971 about 15 percent were addicted. Meanwhile, the CIA's secretly funded airline, Air America, was still flying opium out of the Golden Triangle as late as 1973—two years after Nixon declared his war on heroin and attacked the opiate as "public enemy number one."[36]

The failures of law-and-order policies illustrate why the Burmese heroin trade is such a useful case study of the basic features of the political economy of crime. Although Burma's recent history is far too tragic to sum up in a single chapter, even its outlines highlight issues that are rarely mentioned in the current debate over crime in America. The Burmese heroin trade shows how changes in the legitimate economy mold the workings of the illegitimate economy and demonstrates how powerful legitimate interests frequently profit from the violence and social decay created by the world of crime. It explains why crime thrives in a world dominated by economic inequality and exploitation, and why law-and-order politicians with close ties to corporate interests choose to pursue such disastrous policies.

The forces that propelled Khun Sa to the top of the heroin trade in the 1980s also led to his downfall in the 1990s. He was much more powerful than the small-time drug dealers of the Lower East Side that helped fuel his rise, but like theirs, his prosperity relied on powerful outside interests. As long as the Burmese military was willing to tolerate his operations and the Thai military profited from the trade in logs, teak, and gems, as well as heroin, with Khun Sa and other rebels, he thrived. When the Burmese launched their phantom war on drugs to burnish their odious reputation, however, and the Thais decided that their future growth depended on Burma's rich energy resources, Khun Sa's days were numbered. He had outlived his economic usefulness.

Unfortunately, as leaders in Washington, Rangoon, and Bangkok plotted his downfall, they ignored the impoverished peasants who were raped, tortured, abused, and kidnapped simply because they lived in opium producing regions controlled by Khun Sa. Because they were "drug producers," few people defended their rights. And in contrast to Khun Sa, who was allowed to surrender peacefully and move into a life of luxury in Rangoon, these peasants continue to face severe human rights abuses as they continue to produce the drug for new opium kingpins. The king has fallen, but the kingdom of heroin thrives, thanks to poverty, human rights violations, corruption, and powerful business interests.

A similar dynamic can be found much closer to home. Just as Khun Sa profited from a global economy that created millions of impoverished peasants, U.S. crime groups such as the Mafia relied on millions of impoverished farmers who migrated from rural communities in the South and Midwest to urban centers between 1900 and 1970. These poor blacks, whites, and Hispanics provided the labor force for criminal activities—drugs, prostitution, gambling. In the most recent period, the global economy encouraged businesses and wealthy individuals to move money out of American cities. The results were disastrous, affecting availability of jobs, government services, housing, and capital for infrastructure.

Part II

The American Way of Crime

Chapter 5:
The Road to Violence

The bald truth is that we do know something of the sources of crime and we obstinately refuse to remedy them. . . . If we look at the system as "wanting" to reduce crime, it is an abysmal failure—and we cannot understand it. If we look at it as not wanting to reduce crime, it's a howling success. . . . All we need to understand is why the goal of the criminal justice system is to fail to reduce crime.

—*Jeffrey Reiman*

ON MARCH 1, 1994, HEROIN WAS THE FURTHEST THING FROM THE minds of fifteen orthodox Jewish students who were returning from a visit to their spiritual leader, Rebbe Menachem Schneerson, in a Manhattan hospital. Some of the students were praying for the Rebbe; others were sleeping or talking as their van headed toward their homes in the closely knit orthodox Jewish communities of Brooklyn just over the river.

But as the driver turned onto the entry ramp of the Brooklyn Bridge, there was an explosion of flying glass inside the van, and the prayers stopped. Thinking there was something wrong with the van, the driver pulled over to the side of the road, where he noticed that one of the students sat slumped over in his seat as if the exploding glass hadn't waked him from his slumber. But before he could assess the damage, a blue Chevy Capri roared up beside the van, and two machine pistols opened fire. Realizing that they were actually under attack, the driver sped away, while the gunman, weaving in and out of the traffic on the Brooklyn Bridge, fired shots at one side of the van and then the other. After what seemed like an eternity of gunfire and violence but was probably only a few moments, the attacker sped off into the traffic and disappeared into Brooklyn.

By the time it was over, one student was dead, and three others were wounded—one so seriously that he spent more than seven months in a hospital with head injuries that will leave him crippled for life. The dead student, sixteen-year-old Aaron Halberstam, had not even planned to take the van back to Brooklyn. At the last moment he made the fatal mistake of asking the driver if there was an empty seat. Aaron's mother was so shocked by the gratuitous act of violence that killed her son, she complained about the fact that New York State did not have the death penalty in 1994. "Death would send a message to the world that America knows how to deal with terror," she said. "And death, too, might have brought a measure of finality to the horror me and my family have to live with."[1]

To many commentators this attack on defenseless students seemed to encapsulate everything that was wrong with American cities. The Brooklyn Bridge, which had been a powerful symbol of urban progress for millions of immigrants, had become nothing more than a dismal backdrop for an act that seemed to defy explanation. Like the serial killers that have been headline news for decades in America, the Brooklyn Bridge killer entered his victims' lives at a moment when they least expected to be harmed. The incident involved complete strangers and no visible economic motive. It would be hard to imagine a case further removed from the world of economics.

Yet on closer inspection even the most random acts of violence seem to be guided by larger forces. Civil wars in Beirut, corruption in Burma, illegal arms deals in Central America, and fanaticism in the Middle East have become more than distant events. Violent criminals have learned how to "think globally and act locally."

This new world of global crime came into sharp focus when police investigating the case arrested a Muslim immigrant, Rashid Baz, who as a youth had fought in a brutal Lebanese civil war. Baz was working as a Brooklyn cab driver when he was arrested, but ABC and the *Daily News* quickly alleged that the gunman had ties to Hizbollah, a militant Muslim fundamentalist organization that has been involved in a number of bombings. Soon commentators and journalists began speculating that Muslim terrorists had ordered Baz to attack the Jewish students.[2]

No such connection was ever found. In Baz's case, FBI officials and the mayor of New York City took the unusual step of holding a press conference to deny that Hizbollah or any other terrorist organization had backed the violence. At his trial, prosecutors painted a portrait of the gunman as a violent anti-Semitic loner who had brought his hatred of Jews from the Middle East to the Big Apple, a view that was accepted even by Baz's attorneys. In their client's defense, they argued that Baz suffered post-traumatic stress syndrome. Only a few days before the Brooklyn Bridge shootings, far-right racist Jewish settlers had opened fire on unarmed Muslim worshipers in Jerusalem, killing and wounding scores of people. Upset by the Jerusalem massacre, Baz claimed the sight of the orthodox students made him believe that he was still fighting in Lebanon. "He did kill and he did witness people being killed," argued a defense psychiatrist, who explained that Baz began fighting in one of the militias when he was only nine years old. "He always had his back to the wall and was waiting for a catastrophe or something to go wrong. . . . These were clearly Jewish passengers, and he really perceived them as the enemy. . . . His idea was to protect himself by killing before he was killed himself." The jury and judge didn't buy this controversial defense. Baz was convicted and sentenced to 141 years in jail.[3]

The lack of terrorist conspiracy in the killings, which had been blindly accepted by so many local journalists, wasn't the only peculiar twist in this case. The killing fields of Lebanon had certainly provided Baz with a racist motivation and the military skill to carry out the shootings, but problems in the Middle East did not explain why Baz owned two machine pistols or how he had purchased them. Then NYPD detectives and agents from Bureau of Alcohol, Tobacco and Firearms (ATF) discovered Baz had been investigated in several heroin smuggling cases in the early 1990s in Los Angeles and New York City and that two of his brothers had eventually been arrested for smuggling drugs. Baz also worked in a small gang that dealt heroin and robbed drug dealers on the Lower East Side of Manhattan. "You could say drugs killed those students," grumbled one investigator. "It's a trade that requires guns. Far too often, those weapons get used for things that have nothing to do with narcotics."[4]

More complexities emerge when law enforcement officials try to explain how heroin flows from warlords like Khun Sa to people like Baz at the bottom end of business. Commentators have attempted to compare the global drug cartels to large multinational corporations, but there is little evidence that the problem of global crime can be reduced to a few foreign conspiracies or a handful of powerful godfathers like Khun Sa. About 60 percent of the heroin reaching New York is now from Asia, but Chinese organized crime groups do not monopolize the trade from top to bottom. Sometimes overseas Chinese groups will sell the drug to a variety of Chinese gangs. These gangs then sell it to other middlemen, who in turn sell it to street gangs. Quite often, however, the heroin may pass through the hands of a variety of organized crime groups on its way from Asia to the streets of New York. Mafia families, Sicilians, Russians, Israelis, Turks, Albanians, Mexicans, and Colombians may smuggle the drugs into the United States or buy heroin from other smugglers. "There is so much money to be made that rival gangs who normally hate each other will work together on any deal that comes their way," says one DEA agent.[5]

Such confusing alliances are rarely examined by the mainstream media or Hollywood scriptwriters, who prefer simple, dramatic stories of crime organizations groups that operate like multinational corporations, with clear lines of authority and power. But dozens of law enforcement officials argue that this bewildering web of criminal activity is frequently the rule in the international drug trade and that few narcotics deals are orchestrated by an omnipotent godfather. Even the American Mafia, which operates under a feudal system of godfathers, capos, and soldiers, generally sells its drugs to street-level drug gangs that behave more like anarchists than devoted underlings.[6]

However, as the global drug business tends to view its employees as disposable cogs in a multinational enterprise, this tends to produce a steady output of mayhem, which is exacerbated by the chaos and rivalries of the trade. At the low end the competition for market share is fierce. "Guns are an essential part of doing business," says Henry J. Ballas, special agent in charge of the New York office of the ATF. "There is a tremendous amount of money exchanging hands in the drug trade. If you've got a corner that is bringing in $50,000, people are going to notice. Someone will try to take it away from you. So you need guns to protect your business. You can't stay in business without them. Guns are a means of making a lot of quick money and the only way you're going to keep your share of the pie."[7]

The New York Police Department has estimated that local residents own as many as a million guns, and no one knows how many other guns are in the hands of low level dealers like Baz. Because of the easy availability of guns, the NYPD believed that about half of all homicides in the city were drug-related in an eight-month period in 1988. In Miami one study found that of all homicides between 1978 and 1982, 24 percent of them were drug related; in Washington, D.C., the figure was 53 percent in 1988. Overall, a 1990 Justice Department survey of twenty-three cities found that 68 percent of those arrested for burglary tested positive for illegal drugs, as did 66 percent of those arrested for robbery and 52 percent of those accused of murder. Prison inmates often admit that they turned to crime to finance their drug habits. About 27 percent of all inmates in state prisons in 1991 for robbery and 30 percent of those jailed for burglary had used drugs in the month prior to their arrest.[8]

Such studies are often cited as proof that drug use leads to violent crime. Yet a close look at the data reveals a different conclusion. To begin with, there is little evidence that most criminals start using drugs before they began a life of crime. Criminologist and sociologist Elliot Currie points out the "recurrent finding that most people who both abuse drugs and commit crimes began to commit crimes *before* they began using drugs—meaning that their need for drugs cannot have caused their initial criminal involvement (though it may have accelerated it later)." One twenty-five-year study of heroin addicts found that more than half were "known to have been delinquent before drug abuse," a finding confirmed by a 1986 Justice Department survey of inmates in state prisons: more than 60 percent of those who had been daily users said they had not used illegal narcotics until *after* their first arrest.[9]

Another point is that many addicts are not criminals. A 1992 federal study of people entering outpatient methadone or other drug programs found that about one-third had committed a crime to make money in the preceding year—another high rate often cited to show that drugs cause crime. But note that *two of three* addicts who sought outpatient treatment *did not* rob old ladies, break into apartments, deal drugs, or prostitute themselves to support their habits. Except for the purchase of drugs, these addicts had managed to remain law-abiding citizens. Similarly, a 1991 study of juvenile delinquents found that contrary to "folk wisdom, . . . even among the heaviest drug users and delinquents, the majority did not report engaging in any illegal behavior to obtain drugs or alcohol"; only 20 percent engaged in non-drug crimes to get high.[10]

Moreover, there is a great deal of confusion over the exact relationship between violence, drug use, and addiction. Heroin, for example, depresses the central nervous system, and a long history of research indicates that it decreases the user's likelihood of responding violently to a provocative situation. As a result, the 1973 National Commission on Marijuana and Drug Abuse, which was appointed by the Nixon administration, concluded that "assaultive offenses are significantly less likely to be committed by . . . opiate [heroin, morphine and opium] users." Medical evidence also suggests that some drugs, including heroin, are not as addictive as commonly thought. A massive study of U.S. servicemen in Vietnam found that 250,000 soldiers had used heroin, yet only 80,000 had become addicts—meaning that they used heroin every day or suffered withdrawal symptoms if they did not. More significantly, follow-up studies found that only 6 percent of the addicts and only 1 percent of the users continued to take heroin in a two-year period after they left the army. In short, heroin has been widely used by people who did not become addicts, and the vast majority of those who did become addicted were able to quit.[11]

Research denying a direct link between drugs and violence has caused some experts to reexamine police studies that purport to establish such a connection. One researcher who reexamined 414 murders that the New York City Police Department blamed on drugs—primarily crack—found that only 31 were related to the physiological effects of drugs, and 67 percent of those involved alcohol. He found only five cases where the murderers were high on crack, and only one case where the killer had used only crack. In sharp contrast, about three-quarters of the murders had been committed by drug dealers battling for territory—a problem related to the illegality of drugs but not to the way narcotics use influences behavior. The psychological effects of alcohol caused many more murders than crack, but no one was killed trying to buy booze—a legal mind-altering substance. Drugs that are illegal must be purchased from dealers who may also be involved in gangs or organized crime. As a result, casual users are more likely to meet addicts or street criminals, and this may increase their chances of getting involved in illegal activities or developing more serious abuse problems.[12]

A final twist to the Baz story leads even further from foreign conspiracies or simplistic explanations that illegal drugs inevitably produce crime. Some of the worst violence created by the drug trade would not be possible without the complicity of legitimate businesses and their political allies. Just as corrupt elites and businessmen supplied Khun Sa with the arms he needed to control large areas of the Golden Triangle, U.S. businesses provide essential services for the drug trade—laundering drug money and selling guns to people like Baz—and frequently use their political power to protect their profits. The National Rifle Association (NRA), which is heavily funded by the gun producers, dealers, and owners, bills itself as an anti-crime organization, but pursues policies that in effect protect shady gun dealers and other crooks from serious legal sanctions. The NRA overall political contributions of $3,359,413 between 1985 and 1995 paid off in political support for lax government regulation. Many southern states, which are strongholds of NRA lobbyists, have extremely lax gun control laws that allow dealers to ship thousands of guns illegally each year to major urban centers. On the federal level, NRA lobbyists successfully cut ATF budgets, making it impossible for the agency to investigate and prosecute illegal gun trades adequately. Until the late 1980s the NRA managed to defeat virtually every single serious gun control measure, and the existing regulations face continual NRA attacks. In 1996, for example, House members who voted to repeal the ban on assault rifles each received an average of $14,056 in NRA political action committee contributions.[13]

Thanks to this massive political support, the production of guns that Americans all too often use to shoot one another has become a very big business. Between 1983 and 1995, U.S. manufacturers, who supply about 80 percent of the American market, sold more than $16 billion worth of guns and ammunition at wholesale prices—goods that probably fetched some $32 billion at retail outlets. Today there are some quarter-billion guns in the United States, more than double the number owned by Americans at the end of the Second World War. In 1993 there were more than 1,000 U.S. gun producers, about 900 companies that imported guns, and some 284,000 federally licensed dealers—or thirty-one times more gun dealers in the United States than McDonald's restaurants. And even though a 1994 law cut the number of gun dealers by about one-third, there are still only about 240 ATF agents in charge of regulating them.[14]

Wittingly or unwittingly, gun dealers play a key role in the violence. One U.S. Justice Department study estimated that 27 percent of all felons, who in theory are prohibited from buying weapons, purchased their firearms from licensed dealers. ATF agents tracked one of Baz's guns, a semiautomatic pistol, back to a Homestead, Florida, gun shop, where it had been purchased by Albert Jeanniton using his Florida driver's license. Jeanniton was arrested in 1993 for selling a DEA agent three kilos of cocaine, but like some other small-time drug dealers, he had supplemented his income in the black arms trade. Between October 1991 and December 1992 Jeanniton purchased 132 guns and delivered them to Anthony Hernandez in the Bronx, who in turn sold them to various people, including Baz.[15]

State and federal rules designed to restrict illegal firearms sales are filled with loopholes. As the Baz case indicates, criminals can take advantage of the lax regulations in the South to purchase weapons that are easily transported to states such as New York, that have tighter gun control laws. Gun owners are also legally allowed to sell their own weapons at flea markets, and black arms manufacturers use that right to their advantage. Then there is the mail-order trade, which has produced millions of dollars in advertising revenues for the gun magazines that are among the most vocal and effective opponents of gun control. "Just pick up a gun magazine," says one AFT agent. "There are dozens of them and they're all filled with ads for gun parts. One manufacturer will sell you a kit for the barrel; another guy will sell you a kit for the rest of the gun. Anyone can buy these kits. The manufacturer will say they're following the law. They're not selling complete guns. But, they have to know why people are buying these kits." Baz's second gun, the machine pistol, believed to have killed Aaron Halberstam, had been assembled from a kit advertised in a magazine.[16]

Over time, large corporations have made hundreds of millions of dollars from gun sales. In 1992 the National Sporting Goods Association (NSGA) estimated that discount retailers, primarily Kmart and Wal-Mart, accounted for $81 million of the $488 million in annual sales of rifles sold in all retail outlets and $77 million of the $433 million annual sales of shotguns. During the 1980s and early 1990s, as gun-related homicides skyrocketed, these large discount retailers increased their share of the shotgun and rifle market. The NSGA estimates that major retailers, such as Wal-Mart, sold from $225 million to $300 million worth of guns in 1992.

Although these sales figures account for a small percentage of the goods that large chains sell, marketing experts say the gun trade is important to the discount retail chains' strategy: they "use the weapons to draw male customers into their stores," as *Business Week* explains. "Once there, these shoppers often buy other highly profitable items, such as hunting clothing and accessories. In certain stores firearms can lead to a 50 percent increase in hunting gear sales," a Kmart spokesman told the magazine.[17]

With so much money on the line, retailers have sometimes been less then diligent in following regulations designed to prevent criminals from buying firearms. In 1987, one Kmart store violated gun laws by selling a gun to a man who was so drunk he was unable to sign the requisite forms, forcing the clerk to fill them in for him. The customer later used the weapon to shoot his estranged girlfriend, leaving her a paraplegic for life. *Business Week* found that the undermanned ATF had not inspected the store since 1980, and when the agency did get around to inspecting six Kmart stores, it cited three for "numerous" violations.[18]

Adverse publicity and several large lawsuits from crime victims persuaded some companies to get out of the gun business in 1993 (a move that Sears and J. C. Penney had made in the early 1980s). By that time, however, the damage had been done. In 1993 alone, guns were used in about 1.3 million murders, robberies, rapes, and assaults, and in 1990 the health care costs of treating firearm injuries totaled $20.4 billion.[19]

Baz received a 141-year sentence for murdering one student and injuring three others, but no executive of a major retailer has ever gone to jail for the violence caused by the guns it sold. This discrepancy points to another paradox in the seemingly obvious connection between illegal drugs and violence in America: not all violence is created equal. Some organized activities that directly contribute to violence in America are allowed, even encouraged, while other types of violence are attacked and punished in the harshest possible way. By any objective standard, Baz's crime, however heinous, was far less damaging to society than the poorly regulated gun trade. Yet no news networks speculated that highly organized corporate chains orchestrated the Brooklyn Bridge killing, or attacked the manufacturer of the gun that killed one of the students, or called for tougher restrictions on the mail-order gun trade that made it easy for Baz to carry out his private jihad. Instead they speculated that a cabal of anti-Semitic

Muslims had concocted a global conspiracy to assassinate harmless Jewish students.

The differences in approach to various kinds of violence goes to the heart of the problem of crime in America. Just as the Asian heroin trade is ruled by forces that are rarely mentioned in the long-running war on drugs, the problem of street crime is, if anything, even more misunderstood. Like the Baz case, the complexities of street crime go far beyond the usual headlines and proposed panaceas. On close inspection, seemingly obvious truths turn out to be misconceptions. The numbers endlessly cited to prove conventional views of violence turn out to be misleading if not erroneous. Cases of heinous violence that seem to justify an even more draconian law-and-order crusade have a funny way of showing the futility of that crusade. Facts about crime are regularly distorted to support policies that are contradicted by available evidence. Certain crimes are widely publicized, while much graver examples of mass violence are virtually ignored. "Commonsense" solutions—building more prisons, imposing tougher sentences, giving police more power to curb civil liberties—are rarely questioned.

It's worth taking a look at some prominent assumptions about crime in America. Like the Baz case, they provide a quick overview of the confusion that has obscured the subject. They offer a basic, albeit superficial introduction to the landscape of crime in America and go a long way toward explaining why violence in America has proved to be such an intractable problem.

> Commonsense solution #1: *Since the 1960s, liberals have spent hundreds of billions of dollars on social programs designed to end poverty and other social problems that were said to cause crime. These programs haven't solved poverty, and they certainly didn't lower crime rates. Today, a number of criminologists even admit we don't know what causes crime. So the best policy is to forget about the causes of crime and adopt tough laws. That will take criminals off the streets, make our neighborhoods safer, and deter people from committing new crimes.*

This "let them eat prison" view of the sociology of crime was the central assumption of federal law enforcement during the Reagan-Bush years and has helped shape the policies of the Clinton administration. Speaking at a summit on violence and crime in 1991, then U.S. Attorney General Richard Thornburgh argued that "We are not here to search for the roots of crime" but rather to stop the "carnage in our own mean streets." Likewise in 1994, House Speaker Newt Gingrich and twenty-seven other Republican members of Congress wrote to President Clinton, "The American people are tired of being hostages to violent crime and looking for action to put a stop to the crime epidemic now. They are fed up with discredited theories that 'it is society's fault' or that we have to wait to solve the 'root causes' of crime before we can take action."[20]

Preventing crime is not a task that current social welfare programs have shown much ability to perform. Nor are the causes of crime as obvious as some liberal commentators have liked to argue. Conservative criminologists are right in pointing out that it is impossible to demonstrate a one-to-one correspondence between violence and such problems as unemployment, poverty, poor housing, and limited educational opportunities. If poverty were the only cause of crime, it would be hard to explain how the vast majority of poor people manage to stay out of jail. And poverty and unemployment do not explain corporate crime, which is typically committed by top executives who live in affluent neighborhoods. So what do we know about the structure of street crime? Where does it occur? Who commits it? Who is victimized by it?

Anyone who considers these questions soon realizes that some answers simply aren't available. U.S. researchers rely on two major surveys, the National Crime Victimization Survey (NCVS) and the FBI's Uniform Crime Reports (UCR). Both are severely flawed in that they exclude data on corporate crime, the narcotics trade, and organized crime—the three largest and most deadly criminal enterprises in the world. Their cost to the economy of $1.2 to $2.7 trillion a year dwarfs the $17.2 billion a year that the FBI believes people lost to burglars and robbers in the 1992 and even the $105 billion in stolen property, medical expenses, and lost productivity that the National Institute of Justice estimates is caused annually by violent crimes.[21]

Even if we ignore corporate crime, tax fraud, narcotics, and organized crime, the FBI's index of serious crimes—which includes murder, forcible rape, aggravated assault, robbery, burglary, larger larcenies, and auto theft—remains a hopelessly inaccurate measure of street crime. For one thing, the index is based on the number of crimes reported to local police departments. Unfortunately, many crimes are not reported to the police; moreover, for many years local police departments were simply too lazy, incompetent, or corrupt to record accurately those that were. Consequently, official FBI statistics prior to 1970 are highly suspect. The statistical incompetence of local police forces in the 1940s and 1950s tended to exaggerate the rise in crime during the 1960s, when departments began to keep better records and social changes—from higher levels of home insurance to the civil rights movement—encouraged people to report crimes that weren't brought to police attention in earlier years.

To deal with these problems, in 1973 the Justice Department established the National Crime Victimization Survey, which measures the number of crimes by interviewing a representative sample of households. It is considered by most criminologists to be far more accurate than the UCR, but the NCVS also has its problems. Because it goes back only to 1973, comparison with earlier years is impossible; it offers only national data; and it is issued only annually. Reporters therefore still turn to local police departments for local data or for quarterly reports.

Over time, the limitations of both surveys have allowed American politicians to manipulate the problem of violence in America for narrow political or economic gain, and the confusion created by political posturing has been compounded by the way the media covers crime. In the 1980s and 1990s the increasingly competitive economics of the modern news business pushed journalists toward an increasingly sensational approach to crime. By the early 1990s, "true crime" television programs such as "America's Most Wanted" were featuring gruesome crimes almost every night. And between 1993 and 1996 American television networks increased their coverage of murders by 700 percent, even though the actual murder rate in those years fell by 20 percent. As a result, one survey found that only 14 percent of Americans knew that the national crime rate was lower in 1995 than in 1975. According to another poll, 91 percent erroneously believed that crime rates had risen in 1995, whereas in fact they had dropped faster than any year since 1973.[22]

All this might be forgiven if the media actually provided some insight into the causes and nature of crime in America. But coverage of crime, like government statistics, is markedly skewed toward street crime and presents a misleading view even of this problem. For example, newspapers and television stations typically give wide play to cases of affluent white women murdered by strangers, when in fact most murder victims are men (78 percent) and nonwhite (52 percent). Contrary to regular news stories about women being raped, mutilated and murdered by psychotic strangers, government statistics for 1992 show that female victims knew their attackers in 47 percent of cases, and that past or present husbands and boyfriends committed 29 percent of the single-offender violent crimes against women. Strangers commit only 20 percent of the 500,000 rapes and sexual assaults against women reported each year.[23]

In short, the problem of understanding crime in America is made unnecessarily complex by the fact that some crimes (such as corporate crimes committed by rich people) are excluded from crime data and rarely covered at length by the media, while other crimes (generally street crimes committed by poor people) are given the widest possible coverage and punished in the harshest possible manner. But even if one focuses on street crime and ignores problems of corporate crime, it is still apparent that the current law-and-order policy of dismissing the economic and social sources of crime is disastrous. For starters, violent street crime is a problem that disproportionally afflicts poorer neighborhoods. For example, NYPD figures for 1993 show that twelve of the city's seventy-four precincts—all located in impoverished neighborhoods of Harlem, the Bronx, and Brooklyn—reported a total of 854 homicides or 43.6 percent of the city's 1,960 murders; twelve other precincts, all located in more affluent terrain, reported only thirty-seven homicides.[24]

This distinction can be seen without multiple regressions or other complex statistical methods. Simply take a map of New York City, and put a tiny drop of red ink wherever there was a homicide. Soon small red lakes form in the city's poorest neighborhoods. Similar results could be produced for 1895, when the most violent neighborhoods in New York City were white and poor, or 1995, when the Big Apple's high-crime areas were black, brown, and poor. Today, this exercise in criminal cartography could be repeated in virtually every major city in the United States. Wherever there are neighborhoods that have been plagued by extreme poverty and unemployment for many years, there are extraordinarily high levels of violent crime—and many poor people who are victimized by violent crime. In the nineteenth century, studies have shown, the poorest immigrants had the highest crime rates. In the 1850s and 1860s about 80 percent of both homicide victims and their killers were foreign-born, mainly Irish and German. Subsequently, crime rates for those groups declined, while the rates rose for the more recent immigrants who replaced them at the bottom of the social totem pole. Between 1900 and 1920 in Philadelphia, Italians were twenty times more likely than other whites to be sent to prison for murder. More recently the ethnic composition of poorer neighborhoods continues to change, but the poorest residents of American cities are still much more likely to be murdered. In Boston, for example, low-income whites were 2.7 times more likely to be murdered than high-income whites in the 1970s, and low-income blacks 1.8 times more likely than high-income blacks. Likewise, in three major Ohio cities low-income black kids under the age of fifteen were 7.9 times more likely to be murdered than upper-income black kids between 1974 and 1984, and their white counterparts 5.2 times more likely.[25]

Detailed statistics on poor ghetto neighborhoods throughout the United States are not readily available—in part because such figures are so politically embarrassing—but a clue can be found in the annual Justice Department survey of crime victims. In 1992 this survey found that 7 percent of all Americans who had incomes less than $7,500 were victims of a violent crime, and 3.9 percent were victims of a serious violent crime—rape, robbery, or aggravated assault—whereas the figure for those who had incomes more than $50,000 were only 4.3 percent and 1.9 percent. More affluent groups are generally more often victimized by property crime—reflecting the fact that they have more assets worth pilfering—yet 6.1 percent of those in the lower income bracket were victims of a burglary compared with 3.8 percent of those in the upper bracket. In sum, the poorest Americans, owning the least property worth stealing, were 63 percent more likely to be victims of a violent crime, 105 percent more likely to suffer from serious violent crime, and 61 percent more likely to have their homes burglarized—simply because they lived near other people who engaged in acts of violence. For such victims, the problem of crime in America can be reduced to one simple root cause—decent-paying jobs; after all, with higher incomes they could afford to move to a neighborhood with lower crime rates.

The links between poverty, unemployment, poor education, and violence become more obvious in studies of prison populations. One 1994 Justice Department survey of inmates who had entered state prisons in 1991 found that 64 percent had never graduated from high school (compared to 19.8 percent of the general population), and only 8 percent had attended college (compared with 71 percent of all Americans). Also in 1991, about 45 percent did not have a full-time job when they were arrested; 33 percent were unemployed. About 70 percent earned less than $15,000 a year, and only 15 percent earned more than $25,000 (compared with 23.5 and 59.2 percent respectively of all American households).[26]

Inmate populations are also dramatically skewed toward the minority groups that face the worst problems with poverty and unemployment. As a group, Blacks have unemployment rates about twice and poverty rates more than three times those of whites, and make up 30 percent of federal inmates and 46 percent of those in state prisons, even though they constitute only 12 percent of the U.S. population. Similarly, Hispanics, whose unemployment rates are nearly twice and poverty rates nearly three times those of whites, make up 28 percent of the federal and 17 percent of the state penal population, even though they constitute only 10.2 percent of the population. In short, the higher incarceration rates of blacks and Hispanics are almost directly correlated with their higher unemployment and poverty rates.[27]

Other social problems—instability of families, child abuse, alcohol and drug abuse, poor housing—can also be seen in the personal histories of inmates. Only 43 percent of all state inmates and 58 percent of all federal inmates were raised by both parents and nearly four of ten state prisoners said they had a relative in prison. A 1992 study funded by the National Institute of Justice found that "being abused or neglected as a child increased the likelihood of arrest as a juvenile by 53 percent, as an adult by 38 percent and for a violent crime by 38 percent." A survey of 2,621 juvenile offenders conducted by the U.S. Bureau of Justice Statistics found that 52 percent had one or more close relatives who had been incarcerated and that 34 percent had a mother or father who had been in jail. In addition, about 53 percent of all mothers in prison had a history of physical abuse, and 42 percent had been sexually abused, according to a study done by the National Council on Crime and Delinquency.[28]

Such statistics, which seem to add up to a profile of potential criminals, can be misleading, however. To begin with, it is important to stress that the presence of adverse social factors, ranging from poverty to illiteracy, does not support the notion that certain groups of people are more criminal than others or that a member of a high-risk group will automatically commit crimes. Anyone who takes a close look at all types of crime soon realizes that it is difficult to compare crime rates for one group with those of another group because some groups are more likely to commit certain crimes than others. For example, men are arrested at much higher rates for violent street crimes than women, whereas females have higher arrest rates for prostitution. Corporate crimes are disproportionally committed by people from affluent backgrounds. In the absence of good statistics about corporate and white-collar crime, it is virtually impossible to say whether rich white men who pull off multimillion-dollar scams are more or less criminal than poor blacks who work overtime to steal a few purses. And again, though much has been made of the fact that one-third of all younger black males are in prison, on parole, or on probation, very few commentators have given similar attention to the two-thirds of this population who are by all accounts law-abiding citizens.

This last point cannot be overemphasized. For many year outsiders have harped on the higher crime rates to be found in poorer neighborhoods and twisted them into stereotypes that make the problem of living in a poor neighborhood even more difficult. Thanks to the erroneous stereotype that young blacks are more criminal than middle-aged white men, all young black men are frequently treated as if they were criminals. But this stereotype ignores the fact that most black men do not commit violent acts and the fact that poor blacks rarely run drug cartels, launder drug money, or mastermind lucrative corporate crimes.

Even less defensible is the odious view that crime and violence are either racially determined or somehow an intrinsic part of certain ethnic cultures. In fact, dramatic changes in the ethnic face of crime over the last half-century indicate that the behavior of various ethnic groups is far too malleable to be blamed on either biology or deep-seated cultural traditions. As noted earlier, in the nineteenth and early twentieth centuries poor immigrants had high rates of street crime, and the intellectual godfathers of the law-and-order crusade used those statistics to argue that Irish, Italian, and

Jewish Americans were the human equivalent of pond scum. Yet, leaping to the end of the twentieth century, only a heartbeat in the history of human evolution, these supposedly criminal ethnic groups now have relatively low crime rates, and descendants of these "dangerous classes" have become successful FBI agents, judges, prosecutors, and even law-and-order criminologists.

> Commonsense solution #2: *Of course, we should do something about the causes of crime, but solving those problems could take years, maybe decades. In the meantime, criminals will commit fewer crimes if we spend more money to make certain they are caught and severely punished.*

This view has been the guiding principle of the Clinton administration, which pushed through a $30 billion crime bill in 1994 that offered a politically appealing package of new funding for prisons, federal money for 100,000 new cops, making about sixty crimes punishable by the death penalty, and some money—about $10 billion—for social programs designed to prevent juvenile delinquency and drug addiction. Clinton's dual-pronged approach, which emphasizes programs designed to strengthen law enforcement while dealing with some social problems, is part of the Democrats' strategy of showing the electorate they are not a party of free-spending liberals whose crime policy is limited to giving speeches about the root causes of crime.

Such views have also found support among conservative economists. In a seminal 1968 article, Gary Becker attempted to apply his laissez-faire economic ideas to the problem of crime. Arguing that criminals decide to commit crimes based on the risks they face, Becker contended that street criminals—the supply side of murder and mayhem—are influenced by the profits their illegal activities produce. Like other entrepreneurs, they will increase their crimes if they believe their efforts will pay off and reduce them if they become convinced that crime doesn't pay. In short, Becker, who is a staunch opponent of social welfare programs designed to help the poor, believes that billions of dollars of government spending to hire more police, build more prisons, and sentence criminals to long periods behind bars will increase a criminal's perceived risk and therefore reduce crime.[29]

Unfortunately, Becker's theories ignore many basic economic issues and bear little resemblance to the real world. Is it reasonable to assume that most criminals actually behave like a tenured university professor, carefully adjusting the optimal allocation of violence to changes in the supply and demand for mayhem? Do drunks calculate the odds of going to jail before they beat up their wives? Will serial killers such as Son of Sam, who believed a barking dog ordered him to kill people, become peaceful and law-abiding citizens if they are threatened by the death penalty? Does a prostitute ponder the odds of getting AIDS or going to jail when she needs a fix? Alternatively, is it reasonable to suppose that economic calculation will always lead to less violence? Imagine a young man robbing a liquor store with a shotgun in a state that has just passed a mandatory life sentence for any violent crime committed with a gun. Will this bandit drop his gun and surrender if a cop accidentally walks into the store? Or will his economic instincts push him into an even worse crime? After all, if he shoots the cop and walks out of the store, he might escape arrest and avoid spending the rest of his life in jail.

These examples are not meant to argue that most criminals are irrational, savage beasts who operate outside the forces of reason or economic pressure. Obviously, there are powerful incentives at work in the business of crime. The problem is constructing an economic theory that might actually help explain the way crime works. This effort is sabotaged from the start if one assumes that all people operate like miniature corporations, studiously calculating the costs and benefits of every decision. By imagining that crime is a well-thought-out career move, Becker and other conservative economists ignore the large number of crimes committed by juveniles, who are hardly old enough to memorize complex mandatory sentencing charts, or by drunk and drug-addicted people, whose medical problems affect their judgment. Their theories do not account for the 40 percent of all violent crimes that are committed by relatives or acquaintances of their victims.[30] Here, longstanding feuds, momentary fits of anger, and drunken passion are more important than supply and demand. This economic model of crime also fails to ask a fundamental question: Why do millions of people embark on poorly paid, dangerous occupations as muggers, drug dealers, or burglars? Why wouldn't these supposedly rational economic actors become, say, economists who rake in large consulting fees from major corporations?

More problems can be found in the application of Becker's ideas. Under Becker's supply-and-demand view of the world, the solution to the problem of crime should be a simple matter of determining the risks faced by criminals and making the odds of going to jail so high that they would be forced to find new occupations. To do this, the government would first have to calculate the risks of going to jail for any particular crime. This isn't easy to do, but in the early 1990s about thirty-five million crimes were committed each year, of which about twenty-five million involved violence or sizable amounts of property. In the end, however, judges send only about 500,000 people to jail. That means the average criminal faces only a 1.4 percent chance of being imprisoned for committing one of the nation's 35 million crimes, and only a 2 percent chance for one of the 25 million serious crimes.[31]

That very low probability of doing jail time for any given crime would seem to support the quick fix for violence: increased government spending for police, prisons, and courts so that law enforcement could put more people behind bars for longer periods of time. This would take more bad guys off the streets and send a message to the rest that they were involved in a very risky business. Unfortunately, this seemingly irrefutable logic ignores a simple economic problem that any good free-market economist would highlight: the cost of law enforcement and prisons. In 1993, the entire law enforcement system—prisons, police, prosecutors, courts—that managed to put someone in jail for only 2 percent of all serious street crimes cost about $97.5 billion. So to increase to 20 percent the chances of a criminal's being convicted will require increasing the money tenfold to $975 billion a year.

No one has actually advocated spending nearly a trillion dollars a year to battle crime, since this would probably bankrupt the poor taxpayers left outside prison to foot the bills. But the absurd magnitude of such an expenditure and its unimpressive ability to increase the chance of jail time for any individual crime to a mere 20 percent illustrates a fundamental flaw in recent law-and-order policies. As government spent hundreds of billions of dollars to build and operate federal and state prisons between 1970 and 1997, the number of inmates jumped from 196,441 in 1970 to 1,725,842 in the middle of 1997—yet U.S. crime rates remained higher than in any other Western developed country.[32]

Moreover, there was little direct correlation between crime rates and prison populations. Street crime rose in the 1960s, as the number of prison inmates stagnated, and continued rising in the 1970s, when the number of prisoners increased. Crime rates dropped in the early 1980s as the prison population skyrocketed but went back up between 1984 and 1992, when the prison population increased even faster, and even more draconian laws were passed. Crime rates dropped in the mid-1990s as still more people were put behind bars, and law-and-order fanatics have taken credit for this decrease, but the overall figures do not demonstrate a connection between stiffer punishments and lower crime rates. Even with doubling or tripling the number of people behind bars and keeping them there for long periods of time, crime will not disappear as long as poverty, unemployment, drug addiction, child abuse, and illiteracy create millions of new criminals.

> Commonsense solution #3: *Since the 1960s, court decisions have tied the hands of the police and given criminals more rights than their victims. We need to free law enforcement officials from silly legal technicalities and get tough on crime so that the victims can see justice. Whatever professors of criminology may say about ineffectiveness of punishing bad guys, any fool can see that tough law enforcement and severe punishment, such as the death penalty, make our streets safer. After all, crime rates were much lower in the 1950s, when police were not handicapped by liberal court rulings. And increasing the power of police will not cost a cent.*

The notion that law enforcement must be given more freedom to do its job is one of the most persistent law-and-order arguments. Barry Goldwater raised the point in 1964, and Presidents Nixon, Ford, Reagan, and Bush made it the centerpiece of their wars on crime. During the 1980s and 1990s federal, state and local officials also pushed to expand the power of law enforcement officials. By the end of 1993 a survey of state laws by the Sentencing Project found that thirty-five states had mandatory penalties for offenders who had two or three prior felony convictions. In May 1994 the National Conference on State Legislatures noted that ten states had passed so-called three-strikes legislation—requiring life imprisonment after the third felony convictions—and similar bills were pending in twelve other states. By the start of 1994 thirteen states had restored the death penalty, and about three thousand people were on death row—triple the number in 1982. Today, only three countries in the world execute more prisoners than America: China, Iran, and the former Soviet Union, countries not known for tying the hands of police with legal technicalities.[33]

Unfortunately, there is little evidence that the crusade to beef up the powers of law enforcement has actually helped police and prosecutors do a better job. It is rarely mentioned that in fact civil liberties have actually improved the efficiency and professional skills of U.S. law enforcement over the last century. One of its great strengths, compared with many police forces around the globe, is its attention to civil liberties, however begrudging, and the fact that it operates under a system of public oversight, however flawed. Because of civil liberties, police must actually investigate crimes—as opposed to simply torturing a suspect until a confession is obtained. Because evidence has to stand up in court, police have been forced to become more effective investigators and to acquire techniques such as forensic evidence that can bolster their cases. The results, however limited, have made American investigators some of the best in the world. Their expertise in forensic science, their experience in tracking convoluted cases of organized crime, and the necessity of diligence to prove their cases "beyond a reasonable doubt" have produced some of the greatest successes in American law enforcement.

In sharp contrast, police forces not bound by "silly technical rules" designed to protect individual rights have a shocking record of corruption, crime, and incompetence. Police in Thailand, Burma, Colombia, and Mexico do not have to worry about Miranda warnings, probable cause, protection against self-incrimination, or any of the other rights we take for granted. They routinely beat confessions out of suspects, ransack homes without search warrants, and toss people in jail for little apparent reason. Yet there is no evidence to suggest that their "freedom" from civil liberties has eliminated crime. In all these countries the drug trade continues to flourish, and major crime groups operate with impunity, in part because the lack of public oversight and real democratic institutions makes it much easier for crime lords to bribe police, prosecutors, and judges.

Similar tales can be found in American history. Before the Second World War suspects were frequently beaten to obtain information, arrestees were regularly denied access to a lawyer, and few people were informed of their rights—yet organized crime groups thrived. Working with corrupt political machines that controlled the hiring and firing of police, crime families built up large criminal empires in bootleg liquor, prostitution, and gambling. The lack of real public oversight and of concern for civil liberties in these years allowed such organizations to flourish in many American cities, a development that increased crime, extortion, corruption, and violence. By any comparative measure, cops who are bound by civil liberties do a better job of putting serious criminals behind bars.

Proponents of expanded police freedom would, of course, argue that this detour into police incompetence and brutality in Thailand, Mexico, and prewar America misses the point. Even the staunchest law-and-order conservatives don't advocate the imposition of a police state or the abolition of civil liberties; they argue simply that the balance of power has swung dangerously to the left, creating a legal system that coddles criminals, and cripples the police. But there is little evidence to support these very popular views. In the late 1970s the General Accounting Office found that only 0.8 percent of all federal cases were lost because of the exclusionary rule, which requires that courts disregard evidence obtained illegally by police, and in 1978 the Institute of Law and Social Research found that less than 1 percent of all felony arrests were tossed out of urban courts because of that rule.[34]

Those studies date from the late 1970s, when court rulings on evidence and civil liberties were far more liberal than today. Since then, there is even less evidence that hordes of dangerous crooks are going free, for the Supreme Court has dramatically limited the power of defendants to argue that evidence was obtained by illegal searches and expanded the investigative powers of both federal agents and local police. "Under the Burger and Rehnquist courts, the kinds of situations in which government agents must obtain judicial warrants before they act have slowly been reduced," writes David Burnham in his detailed history of the U.S. Justice Department. For example, anyone riding a bus, car, or train can now be detained and searched without a warrant, an action that would have been declared unconstitutional in 1970. Similarly, Burnham points out, the courts have issued a number of rulings that have abandoned the traditional legal standard, that police must show "probable cause" in order to get a warrant; now only "reasonable suspicion" is needed. Yet as the Supreme Court was freeing the hands of law enforcement to ignore the constitution, the crime rate rose steadily between 1984 and 1993.[35]

Like civil liberties, capital punishment is a subject often heatedly argued in emotional, moral, philosophical, and legal terms. Lost in these debates is the fact that the death penalty has never proved to be an effective law enforcement tool. Between 1928 and 1949 homicide rates in states that had the death penalty were two or three times higher than in those that had abolished capital punishment. In the 1930s the United States had record-breaking homicide rates even though it executed about 150 people a year. In the early 1960s, with executions at about twenty-four people a year, homicide rates were 30 percent lower; some states saw murder rates drop after abolishing the death penalty. Similar numbers can be found from the 1980s and 1990s, after a number of states reinstated the death penalty. Texas has executed the most people, ninety-two, since it reinstated the death penalty in 1976, yet in 1992 it was tied with California for the third highest murder rate in the country. In contrast, the murder rate in Massachusetts, which has no death penalty, was 3.6 that year—less than a third of the 12.7 rate in Texas. On the whole, the Capital Punishment Research Project estimates that states with the death penalty generally have higher murder rates than those without.[36]

Nor is there any evidence that the threat of execution actually deters crime, given the fact that the chance of it being carried out is extremely small. Writing in *Liberty* magazine in 1932, when the United States was executing record numbers of people, conservative commentator H. L. Mencken grumbled that "there were 11,000 homicides in the U.S. . . . [and] we executed only 130 murderers, a proceeding as silly as trying to hold Niagara with a tennis racket." Similarly, between 1976 and 1993 only 253 prisoners were actually put to death, a tiny fraction of those who committed 381,790 murders and nonnegligent homicides in those years. It seems unlikely that a 0.07 percent chance of being executed would prevent a "rational" criminal from killing.[37]

In addition to decades of research showing that the death penalty does not reduce murder rates, there is mounting evidence that, actually, the current obsession with executing convicted criminals makes protection of the average citizen less likely. Currently, it costs taxpayers about $100,000 to build a prison cell and about $30,000 to put someone in jail for a year.

That means that it costs about $12 million to keep ten convicted murderers behind bars for forty years, and another $1 million to build jail cells to hold them. This sounds expensive, but consider that prosecuting a death penalty case costs prosecutors about $2.3 million in Texas and $3 million in Florida, or $23 to $30 million for ten cases.[38] The $10 to $17 million the state could save by not executing ten people would pay for 142 to 242 new police officers at $70,000 a year in wages and benefits. Equally important, the prosecutors who work overtime fighting appeals of death penalty convictions would have much more time to devote to other cases. By any measure, this sensible allocation of resources would put more police on the streets, give prosecutors and judges more time for other cases, and keep murderers behind bars for a very long time.

A similar point can be made about the economic efficiency of the entire law-and-order crusade. Spending trillions on new prisons and cops would bankrupt the entire country, whereas if prisons were reserved for violent criminals, police, prosecutors, and judges would have more money to deal with the serious crimes of murder, rape, and really vicious assaults. Yet while increased public spending for police and prisons and tougher sentencing laws are dramatically increasing the number of people behind bars, smaller proportions of inmates are actually being sentenced for violent offenses. In 1980 about half (48 percent) of the 131,215 people sent to state prisons had been convicted of violent crime. In 1992, however, only 29 percent of the 334,301 new state prison inmates were violent criminals. Overall, violent crimes accounted for only 16 percent of the increase in state inmates; 46 percent of the increase could be traced to drug offenses.[39]

In other words, the law-and-order dragnet leaves less prison space for violent felons, primarily because the number of drug convictions has increased so rapidly. And in 1994, a Justice Department survey found that more than one third of all federal prisoners incarcerated under mandatory laws for drug offenses, constituting 21 percent of all federal inmates, were considered "low-level" offenders. In 1991 the federal government spent about $6.1 billion to house low-level drug offenders but only $4.4 billion for treatment and prevention programs. Worse, the General Accounting Office estimated that there were drug treatment slots for less than one-fifth of the 500,000 state prisoners who were drug addicts at the time of their arrest, and in many cities the waiting period for treatment programs is six

months or longer. Removing at least some of these inmates to drug treatment facilities would give them an opportunity to deal with medical
problems that might otherwise lead them back into criminal activity and,
in the process, save a lot of money. In New York State, for example, it costs
about $26,000 a year to put someone behind bars, compared with $16,000
for a residential drug treatment center and less than $7,000 a year for
outpatient treatment. If, for example, about one-sixth of the drug offenders
were taken out of prison and put in treatment programs, prisons would be
less crowded, and hundreds of millions of dollars could be freed up for
more police or for social programs that could more effectively target the
causes of crime.[40]

Even bigger costs can be found by looking at families and neighborhoods
devastated by the alarming rise in the number of women imprisoned. In
1991 researchers for the National Council on Crime and Delinquency
estimated that more than 87,000 women were behind bars (triple the
number in 1980), meaning that on any given day in 1991 there were 125,000
kids in America whose mothers were in prison (compared with 36,000 in
1986). Justice Department studies show that 55 percent of the increase in
female inmates between 1986 and 1991 was caused by a huge jump in drug
convictions. In New York state alone the number of women committed to
prison for drug offenses jumped an astonishing 1,863 percent between 1982
and 1993. Over time, the growing number of women behind bars and
children with mothers in jail, creates serious worries about the future of
crime. Kids who grow up in broken homes have high rates of delinquency,
and adolescents whose parents have spent time in jail are at much greater
risk of ending up in prison as adults. Justice Department surveys indicate
that only 43 percent of all state inmates were raised by both parents. Nearly
four in ten state prisoners said they had a relative in prison, and a survey
of 2,621 juvenile offenders conducted by the U.S. Bureau of Justice Statistics
found that over half had one or more close relatives who had been incarcerated; for 34 percent it was a mother or father. In short, putting women
behind bars for minor drug offenses not only costs more than drug rehabilitation, but it makes it much more likely that their children will become
juvenile delinquents.[41]

> Commonsense solution #4: *So the war on crime hasn't been very*
> *efficient, but that doesn't excuse violent crime. Violence is wrong, and*

the state has an obligation to protect its citizens by quickly and speedily punishing violent criminals. This is not only moral. It is just.

Justice is one of the most enduring and powerful symbols of government, but its actual working has far more to do with politics and economics than with high-minded morality and philosophy. One obvious bias can be found in the way the criminal justice system deals with minorities. As already noted, the proportion of blacks and Hispanics in prison far exceeds their proportions of the U.S. population, and by 1994 nearly one in three of all black men between the ages of twenty and twenty-nine was either in jail, on probation, or on parole. In 1997, one Justice Department study found a black man had a 28.5 percent chance of going to jail at some point in his life and a Hispanic man, a 16 percent chance—about six and four times more likely to be incarcerated than a white man (4.4 percent).[42]

Although most of the debate over racism has focused on the sea of black and brown faces to be found behind bars, the most telling symptom of racism in the criminal justice system is the attitude of officials toward the victims of crime. Over the years studies have shown that people who commit crimes against whites consistently get higher sentences than those who commit crimes against minorities. In examining Florida homicides between 1973 and 1977, researchers found that no white who killed a black was sentenced to death, and only 0.5 percent of blacks found guilty of killing blacks were sent to death row. But of the 286 blacks convicted of killing whites, forty-eight (16.8 percent) were given the death penalty, whereas in the 2,146 cases of a white murdering a white, only seventy-two (3.4 percent) were sentenced to death. In a study of a thousand homicide trials in Georgia between 1973 and 1980, law professor David Baldus found that a white defendant convicted of killing a white victim stood a chance of being sentenced to death eight times greater than the chance of a white who killed a black, and a black defendant was thirty-three times more likely to face execution if he killed a white than if he assassinated a member of his own race.[43]

More recently, a smaller study of homicides and rapes in Dallas County, Texas, in 1988 found that higher sentences were passed out for interracial homicides and rapes. A white convicted for killing a white got a median sentence of thirty years; a black convicted for killing a white, thirty-five years; a black convicted of killing a black, twenty years; a Hispanic convicted of killing a Hispanic, seven and a half years. Likewise, white/white rape cases typically brought a five-year jail stint, while blacks found guilty of raping whites got nineteen years. In contrast, a white convicted of raping a black got ten years; black/black rape cases got only one year, and Hispanic/Hispanic cases received two and a half years.[44]

These studies provide grim examples of how selectively punishment is used to control crime and resources allocated to fight it. If one accepts the law-and-order assumption that punishment should be designed to deter crime, then one would expect law enforcement to pay particular attention to the problem of black-on-black violence and pour large amounts of money into protecting minority neighborhoods, which are victimized at much higher rates than others. After all, about half of all murders and nonnegligent homicides in 1992 involved black victims, and 92.7 percent of all these black victims were killed by other blacks—about the same rates as in the 1960s. Yet under the current law-and-order crusade, black-on-black murders get lighter sentences than white-on-white or white-on-black.[45] Obviously, the goal is not so much to deter crime with more severe sentences as to send a message that violence against whites is more important than violence against blacks.

One explanation for this discrimination is the lack of minority influence in the criminal justice system. Despite the increased number of elected black officials (from virtually none) in the last few decades, in 1993 there were only thirty-nine black members of Congress and 525 black state legislators around the country. That is, although blacks made up 14.7 percent of the voting-age population, they held only 9.5 percent of the legislative seats. Similarly, blacks are strikingly underrepresented in all levels of the legal system. In 1992 only 3 percent of the nation's lawyers, less than 6 percent of all federal judges, only 4.5 percent of judges in the highest state courts and none of the country's ninety-three U.S. attorneys were black. Finally, blacks are still underrepresented among the nation's police, despite enormous progress since the 1960s, when American police forces tended to be all-white institutions. In New York City, for example, blacks were 28.7 percent of the population but comprised only 11.4 percent of the police force in 1992, a story replicated in Chicago (39.1 percent of the population versus 24.9 percent of the police force), Houston (28.1 percent versus 14.7 percent), Philadelphia (38.9 percent versus 25.7 percent), San Diego (9.4

percent versus 7.5 percent), Detroit (75.7 percent versus 58.3 percent), and Dallas (29.5 percent versus 19 percent). Of the major cities only Los Angeles had achieved racial parity, with blacks constituting 14 percent of the population and 14.1 percent of the police force.[46]

Underrepresentation helps explain why blacks fare worse than whites at every step of the legal system. For example, a *San Jose Mercury News* study of 683,513 criminal cases between 1981 and 1990 in California found that nearly half of all white, but only one-third of all black and Hispanic defendants were able to plea-bargain for a reduction of charges. Likewise, about one-third of all whites but only a quarter of all blacks and Hispanics were able to get the charge against them reduced from a felony to a misdemeanor. Blacks and Hispanics were also less successful in getting all charges dropped and, if convicted, more likely to be sent to jail. Similar results can be cited for Dallas, Sacramento, Dayton, New York State, Kansas, and elsewhere.[47]

Does this mean that racism—by itself—accounts for the high proportion of people of color locked up in America's prisons? Probably not. Factors such as the length of a defendant's rap sheet and his or her age and socioeconomic status also enter into the decisions of police, prosecutors, judges, and juries. Judges are more likely (and under current sentencing rules are often required) to impose longer sentences on repeat criminals than on a first-time offender. Similarly, a man who holds a decent job and supports a family may be given a lighter sentence than a person defined as more "socially marginal." A 1980 Rand study of more than 11,000 criminal cases in California that compared white and black inmates who had similar criminal backgrounds found very little evidence that whites received lower sentences.[48]

But the Rand and similar studies do not attempt to analyze the racial, economic, and class biases that may cause police to arrest more blacks. The issue of why blacks are arrested at higher levels than whites becomes particularly important when one looks at police and law enforcement strategies. In 1990, for example, only 10 percent of all blacks had ever used cocaine, compared to 11.7 percent of whites and 11.5 percent of Hispanics. Blacks showed slightly higher rates of having tried heroin but lower rates for pot, hallucinogens, and alcohol. Yet between 1976 and 1992 arrests of blacks on drug charges more than tripled (103,615 to 364,546). By 1992 blacks accounted for 40 percent of all drug arrests (up from 22 percent) and whites for about 59 percent (down from 77 percent in 1976).[49]

One obvious reason for these dismal numbers is the way the war on drugs has been fought. For example, police who sought to raise their arrest records by targeting open-air drug markets tended to ensnare black urban drug dealers; white suburban dealers did business in the privacy of their own homes. In 1960 about three in ten people sent to federal and state prisons were black, but by 1990 more than half were black. This increase, many criminologists point out, is not because blacks are committing more violent crimes or using more drugs than whites: "Crime by blacks is not getting worse," writes Michael Tonry. "Since the mid-1970s, approximately 45 percent of those arrested for murder, rape, robbery and aggravated assault have been black. . . . [Yet] since 1980, the number of blacks in prison has tripled. . . . Incarceration rates for blacks in 1991 . . . were nearly seven times higher than those for whites. . . . Disturbing though the numbers are on the surface, what lies below is even more disturbing. . . . Particularly since 1980, the effects of crime control polices have been a major contributor to declining levels of lawful employment by young black males. . . . Many disadvantaged black males start out with bleak life chances and disadvantaged young men ensnared in the criminal justice system have even bleaker prospects."[50]

Tonry's point raises a widely ignored issue in the debate over racial bias. Although it is difficult to quantify the role of racism in the criminal justice system, policies that spend billions every year to lock up poor people impose a huge economic burden on blacks and other minorities. Whether these policies result from racism or economic bias, the important point is that the failure to address the social conditions that breed crime destroys the chance of achieving social justice for many Americans, particularly minorities. This state of affairs wastes scarce resources, separates parents from children, and tears apart the social fabric of poorer neighborhoods, where increasingly large numbers of young minorities end up with police records that dramatically reduce their economic potential.

To see how this occurred requires a careful look at the impact of capital investment, class, race, and political power on the economics of crime. Conservative economists have generally ignored those problems. If put into practice, their bromides touting the efficacy of punishment would bankrupt American capitalism. Even the limited application of their theories has systematically sabotaged the workings of law enforcement, shifting tens of billions of dollars each year away from measures that might actually make neighborhoods and communities safer. But simply marshaling statistics showing the failure of the current approach or pointing out its ineptness in dealing with what we do know about the causes of crime would not have much of an impact. The real problem is understanding why such self-destructive policies have been so popular.

Some answers can be found by taking a look at the history of the American legal system. Just as the history of the drug trade in Asia reveals the economic forces that launched Khun Sa's career, the history of American law enforcement highlights economic forces that have helped guide its evolution.

Chapter 6:
Policing America

Lenin and Trotsky are on their way.

—Wall Street Journal, *describing a 1919 strike by Boston*
police officers for better pay and working conditions

Each and every adherent of this movement [the American left in 1920] is a potential murderer or a potential thief. . . . Out of the sly and crafty eyes of many of them leap cupidity, cruelty, insanity and crime; from their lopsided faces, sloping brows and misshapen features may be recognized the unmistakable criminal type.

—*U.S. Attorney General Mitchell Palmer,*
justifying the arrest of thousands of immigrants

IN JUNE 1857, SEVERAL HUNDRED POLICE OFFICERS LINED UP in and around New York's City Hall. They were not there to provide security for a visiting dignitary or to protect the citizens of the city from attack, but to prevent the arrest of Mayor Fernando Wood. They had already tossed Police Captain George Walling out of the building when he'd tried to apprehend the leader of America's largest city. But Walling, who was operating under orders from the state legislature to disband the pro-Wood police force and set up a new one, quickly returned with reinforcements. They stormed the building, and for nearly half an hour these two rival police forces battled each other on the steps and in the corridors of City Hall with clubs and fists until Walling was once again forced to retreat, leaving behind more than fifty-two injured officers. One was hurt so badly that he remained an invalid for life.

A short time later the National Guard arrived and helped Walling capture Wood. But the mayor, quickly released on bail, refused to disband the police forces who had protected him at City Hall. So, in the weeks that followed, rival police forces battled for control over the streets of New York—one representing the mayor and the other representing the state legislature—leaving the city's residents at the mercy of thugs. "Respectable citizens were held up and robbed in broad daylight on Broadway and other principal streets," notes Herbert Asbury. "Policemen belabored each other with clubs, trying to decide which had the right to interfere, [and] . . . the gangs . . . took advantage of the opportunities to . . . engage in almost constant rioting." The disorder was not quelled until three army regiments were called in, and that violent military operation left eight dead and more than two hundred injured.[1]

Welcome to the politics of crime in America. The battle for control of New York City's police department provides one extreme example of the economic and political forces that shaped American law enforcement. In the early nineteenth century most eastern cities relied on watchmen to patrol the streets. Although they were paid by the cities, they did little to police poorer neighborhoods and primarily worked to guard the warehouses, businesses, and property of wealthy elites. This was an inexpensive form of security, but the watchmen were ill equipped to deal with the problems of rapidly industrializing cities. By midcentury, industrial life had already taken its toll on urban America. Long hours, poor wages, and frequent crushing depressions produced increasingly serious riots and social disturbances. In 1845, after witnessing huge riots in the 1830s, businessmen and wealthy residents persuaded New York City to create a twenty-four-hour police force, an innovation that was quickly imitated in by other cities.

While the cities badly needed a means of dealing with violent crimes, the rise of corrupt urban political machines quickly derailed early attempts to produce a truly professional police force. In New York and elsewhere, police officers had to bribe city officials to obtain their jobs and were expected to kick back a portion of their salaries to political leaders. Frequently, police officers were used to collect graft and as go-betweens in arranging questionable deals for politicians. Not surprisingly, Asbury points out, "the entire force was bewildered and demoralized and the few honest officials could do little towards enforcing the laws, . . . for the arrest of a notorious thug was quickly followed by the appearance of an indignant ward-heeler who demanded and procured his release."[2] Worse, corruption allowed ethnic gangs with close political ties to machine politicians to thrive. These gangs, which would evolve in the twentieth century into major organized crime groups, were allowed to control the vice trade in gambling, prostitution and clip joints as long as they paid off local politicians and provided political muscle to maintain the machine's power—beating up political opponents, bribing voters, and stuffing ballot boxes.

But as urban gangs prospered, poor workers and labor unions did not. Throughout the later nineteenth century police forces and military troops were used to quash labor strikes. More than eighteen hundred soldiers with thirty cannon quelled an 1873 railroad strike in Pennsylvania, and in 1877 three thousand federal troops crushed a nationwide rail strike that left more than a hundred strikers dead. Likewise, police forces and troops put down the 1886 strikes for an eight-hour day and the 1892 Homestead strike in Pennsylvania that broke the steel union and left dozens dead. At least a thousand troops brutally crushed a 1903-1904 mining strike in Colorado by deporting scores of activists, thus destroying the union.[3]

Even worse problems faced blacks in the south. The first modern police forces in the South trace their origins to patrols that were hired to capture escaped slaves. The law gave slaveowners wide power to punish and in certain instances even kill their walking, breathing "property." Although slaves had some legal rights and a few owners were punished for extreme brutality, such cases were investigated by whites working for plantation owners, tried by a judge who was frequently part of the planter class and adjudicated before an all-white jury more likely to acquit than to convict.

After the Civil War, attempts to give former slaves the right to vote, to own property, and so on, faltered. Wealthy southern businesses and landlords encouraged the Democratic party to launch a crackdown on poor blacks and whites that was designed to create a secure supply of cheap labor. In the 1880s, after the federal government agreed not to interfere in "states' rights," southern politicians began setting up a system of legalized segregation in which blacks were denied basic rights and government services. Heavy taxes and regulations imposed on small farmers and agricultural workers—both white and black—put many of them heavily in debt to wealthy landlords.

The reduction of blacks and poor whites to a state of virtual economic slavery known as sharecropping created a pool of captive labor that was legally required to work long hours for less than subsistence wages. In addition, the onerous regulations and taxes produced a huge increase in the penal population, disproportionally black. Convicts were then leased to local industries, who ran prisons as brutal but quite legal gulags. "In some states where convict labor is sold to the highest bidder the cruel treatment of the helpless human chattel in the hands of guards is such as no tongue can tell," wrote one white southerner. "Prison inspectors find convicts herded together, irrespective of age; confined at night in shackles; housed sometimes ... in old box cars; packed almost as closely as sardines in a box. During the day all worked under armed guards, who stand ready to shoot down any who may attempt to escape from this hell on earth—the modern American bastille." Of 285 convicts sent to build the Greenwood and Augusta Railroad between 1877 and 1880, 45 percent were dead by the time the rail line was completed. During this period convict labor, widely used in coke mills, sawmills, and cotton plantations, as well as railroad construction, depressed wages for other workers and was also used to break strikes. Later, chain gangs played a key role in building the infrastructure that aided the eventual transition of the South from an agricultural to an industrial region. "Hundreds of southern fortunes have been amassed by this enslavement of criminals," W. E. B. Du Bois complained in his history of the period.[4]

Farther west, the legal system and corrupt law enforcement officials also played a key role in the control of labor and the acquisition of lucrative natural resources by wealthy landowners and businessmen. As social and economic conditions in China deteriorated following the Opium Wars, between 1860 and 1880 hundreds of thousands of Chinese were brought into the United States, where they were contracted to employers who gained the legal right to force them to work for years at practically nonexistent wages. By 1875 there were more than 105,000 Chinese workers in the American West, where they constituted about one-quarter of the male labor force. Although many hoped to earn enough money either to return home or to send for their families, their economic conditions were so marginal that most ended up stranded in the New World, facing a nativist backlash that was frequently supported by white-led unions and that severely restricted their civil liberties and economic future. Nativist sentiment led to the end of Chinese immigration in 1882, a move that made it impossible for these men to bring their wives and families to America. Some states, notably California, passed strict legislation that severely restricted their legal and economic rights.[5]

Throughout this period, the weakness of state power to control unrest and unruly lower classes frequently prompted local elites to take the law into their own hands, often with the implicit support of local law enforcement. When police forces proved no match for striking or rioting workers, companies frequently hired private security forces or recruited vigilantes. Between 1866 and 1892, the Pinkerton detective agency was hired by employers in at least seventy strikes, many of which produced serious violence. In the 1892 Homestead strike, for example, a riot between laborers and Pinkertons left forty workers and seven detectives dead.[6]

Likewise, wealthy southern elites heavily supported the creation of the Ku Klux Klan, which embarked on a wave of terror against blacks after the Civil War. One South Carolina investigation found that the Klan had "lynched and murdered 35 men, whipped 262 men and women and otherwise outrages, shot, mutilated, burned out, etc. 101 persons." Another reported that more than two thousand people were killed, wounded, or injured in Louisiana a few weeks before the presidential election of 1868, much of the violence being carried out by organized bands of white supremacists who were financed by rich white southerners. This kind of violence played a key role in quelling black militancy, and it continued after the passage of Jim Crow legislation in the 1880s and 1890s, which enforced a rigid system of racial segregation and economic exploitation. Nearly four thousand people—almost all of them black—were lynched between 1889 and 1941, and blacks who moved north in the early twentieth century were met by more violence. As the black population of northern and western states swelled by 330,000 people, white mobs frequently attacked black urban neighborhoods in the 1910s. In East St. Louis, for example, after a few blacks were given factory jobs by a government contractor, white mobs went on a rampage, clubbing, stabbing, and hanging, that resulted in forty deaths. In 1919, race riots broke out in more than twenty U.S. cities; white mobs who invaded black neighborhoods in Chicago left thirty-eight dead, more than five hundred injured, and more than a thousand homeless.[7]

The legal system also gave wealthy elites free rein to exploit children and operate dangerous factories that killed and maimed thousands of workers each year. Just how many children worked in U.S. factories in the nineteenth century will never be accurately known—the government made little attempt to regulate the practice, or keep statistics on the problem. In 1900, one study found that 284,000 youths between the ages of ten and fifteen spent their days in mills, factories, mines, and ships, often working sixty hours a week or more. Although many states banned youths under the age of fourteen from work, the laws were rarely enforced and typically opposed by business. Asa Candler, the founder of the Coca-Cola company (which pushed a then cocaine-spiced product to millions of Americans in this period), once argued that "the most beautiful sight that we see is the child at labor; as early as he may get at labor, the most beautiful, the most useful does his life get to be."[8]

Less beautiful were the dangerous workplaces that massacred large numbers of people each year. Between 1890 and 1930 a total of 81,274 miners perished—a death toll the size of a small city. A 1904 study of 19.6 million workers found that in just one year 15,136 manufacturing employees and 12,005 transportation and agricultural laborers were killed by workplace accidents or diseases acquired on the job. Even these death rates probably only hint at the extent of the problem. According to a report covering a million workers in 1916 and 1917, doctors treated about 197,000 cases a month, indicating that one worker in five suffered some injury or disease every month because of their working conditions.[9]

Union organizers attempting to fight these brutal conditions were not lauded as farsighted social reformers but attacked as common criminals. Drawing on English common law, most American courts from the colonial period viewed labor unions as a "criminal conspiracy." As early as 1677, strikes in New York City were held to be in contempt of court and participants were prosecuted, as were union organizers of strikes in 1684, 1741, and 1836. In the first three decades of the nineteenth century, unions in Philadelphia, New York, and Pittsburgh were prosecuted as "conspiracies in restraint of trade" under English common law doctrine that a combination of workers to raise wages was a conspiracy against the general public. Not until 1842 did a Massachusetts court ruled that unions were legal organizations. Well into the 1930s, however, courts continued to issue legal opinions that made organizing unions extremely difficult. Businesses regularly got the courts to issue injunctions that made strikes illegal; judges used criminal syndication laws to put radical union leaders behind bars, and union leaders were convicted of violent acts that occurred during labor disputes even though those leaders had no role in the violence.[10]

Wealthy businessmen ran dangerous factories, lynched blacks, forced workers to live in slums, and used police and military forces to smash labor unions. Here lies a fundamental feature of the American legal system: not everyone has equal access to economic and political power. Those with at least modest wealth—which allowed them to acquire some education, at least some initial capital, and, equally important, the possibility of gaining access to political elites—dominated the industrial and political landscape of the late nineteenth century and early twentieth centuries. Despite the popularity of Horatio Alger stories in those years, one study found that only 3 percent of the executives heading major textile, railroads, and steel firms in the 1870s had foreign-born fathers; the rest dated their ancestry back to the revolutionary war. About 90 percent grew up in upper- or middle-class families, and in a period when advanced degrees were rare, one-third had a college education.[11]

Thanks to a legal system that encouraged the creation of a large, heavily exploited, low-wage labor force, wealthy businessmen were also able to create major corporations that increasingly dominated the country's economic wealth. Between 1895 and 1904 a merger boom created some of the country's largest firms, such as U.S. Steel (with 62 percent of the market at the time of its creation in 1901), International Harvester (85 percent market share in 1902), Anaconda Copper (39 percent in 1895), and American Can Company (90 percent in 1901). By the end of this period, one or two companies in each of seventy-eight key sectors of the American economy controlled over half of that industry's output, and only three hundred companies controlled 40 percent of the country's industrial wealth.[12]

This concentration of economic power in a few hands was mirrored in the political system. Early in the country's history only white males who owned property—and in some cases belonged to a specific religious denomination—could vote, a policy that disenfranchised 80 percent of the population. Although voting rights were expanded in the nineteenth century, women, Indians, and blacks were still denied the vote in the early twentieth century, and local regulations such as poll taxes disenfranchised many poor whites. As late as 1912 U.S. senators were elected by state legislatures, a practice that kept Congress under the tight control of party machines and wealthy elites, and throughout much of the twentieth century, candidates for most public offices were nominated at political conventions rather than by primaries.[13]

As a result, the democratic process was consistently controlled by powerful political machines, most of which were dependent on wealthy campaign contributors for their continued prosperity. The most notorious examples of the consequent corruption were to be found in city governments dominated by Boss Tweed of Tammany Hall in New York City, Boies Penrose in Pennsylvania, "Bathhouse John" Coughlin in Chicago, "Doc" Ames in Minneapolis, Colonel Butler in St. Louis, and the "Old Regulars" in New Orleans, who worked with local organized crime groups to loot city coffers. But most other political institutions were also compromised by the power of big money. One historian has noted that corruption in state legislatures, which handed out lucrative subsidies and public lands to major corporations, "was so pervasive that [business money] was sometimes able to control entire legislatures. It was often said, for example, that Standard Oil did everything to the Pennsylvania legislature except refine it." As a result, major railroads and timber and mining companies accumulated publicly owned lands worth hundreds of billions of dollars, while influence-peddling by major corporations forced millions of Americans to work in dangerous low-paying jobs with few legal protections or social services. As one U.S. senator explained, when asked why he refused to support legislation to regulate child labor, "I can't stand for a bill like that. Why those fellows this bill is aimed at—those mill owners—are good for $200,000 a year to the party. You can't afford to monkey with businesses that friendly."[14]

The system that allowed wealthy businesses to crush labor unions and run dangerous factories paying bare subsistence wages played a key role in the country's early economic development. By the early twentieth century, however, it was clear that this system was increasingly dysfunctional. Wrenching financial crises, severe depressions, poverty, income inequality, and burgeoning urban slums produced massive social unrest and made it difficult to build up a middle class that would be a reliable base for economic and political stability. Radical political movements that attacked the very premises of industrial capitalism became increasingly popular and the status quo of lax government regulation and laissez-faire economics was increasingly unable to provide a stable business climate. Large industrial enterprises needed an educated professional class of managers and engineers, a better infrastructure of roads, and a more stable economic system—all of which required more government intervention in the economy. To address those needs, reformers pushed for better government regulation, improved social programs for immigrants and the poor, and a more effective criminal justice system. They wanted to create more professional police forces, eliminate corruption in the judicial system, reform brutal prison systems, prevent crime by reforming juvenile delinquents, and end the political corruption that allowed organized crime to flourish.

These very sensible proposals to reform law enforcement and attack the social origins of crime shaped the direction of the criminal justice system for some decades. Unfortunately, the movement to reform law enforcement and turn it into a useful tool for social change achieved only limited success. Although the 1890 to 1920 period of American history saw many long overdue judicial and some political reforms, such as the decision to give women the vote, it was also a period of enormous social upheaval and political repression. Faced with widespread dissent, business elites supported modest reforms in government regulation and social conditions; however, conservative politicians also mobilized support for a massive crackdown on radical social movements, unions, and immigrants. In 1917 Congress passed an immigration act that allowed foreign-born radicals to be deported. "We are going to love every foreigner who really becomes an American and all others we are going to ship back home," said the chairman of the conservative Iowa Defense Council.[15]

Following the First World War, as labor strife intensified and many cities were shut down by general strikes, fourteen states passed criminal syndicalism laws. These allowed local authorities to prosecute and jail members of organizations that were deemed socialist or radical. In early 1919 the Immigration Bureau attempted to deport thirty-nine members of the Industrial Workers of the World, a radical union that advocated revolutionary change. On November 7, 1919, the U.S. Justice Department staged raids in eleven cities, arresting hundreds of Russians and deporting 249. An even larger raid on January 2, 1920, rounded up thousands of foreign-born suspected radicals. Very few of those arrested had ever been involved in any act of violence, and the vast majority had not even participated in a recent labor strike. Their only crime was belonging to organizations that advocated radical or revolutionary change. Nonetheless, most of them were denied access to families or lawyers after their arrests, which were frequently made without search warrants, and many were subjected to extreme brutality.[16]

Vigilante attacks on minorities and radicals also increased, sometimes sanctioned by the authorities. During a 1919 steel strike, mill owners had the local police deputize hundreds of people, who were thus given the legal power to beat, maim, and kill strikers. Mounted state police galloped "through the streets, beating up men and women, shooting them, dragging them to jail, tramping them under their horses' hoofs. . . . At Braddock, Pennsylvania, the Constabulary attacked a funeral procession from ambush, clubbed the participants and scattered them. In the same town a Slovak Catholic congregation leaving the church was suddenly attacked by the Constables, clubbed and trampled by the horses, for no reason whatever except that the priest was known to be a passionate strike sympathizer. . . . In Farrell, Pennsylvania, three people were killed by the [mounted police] in one day and eleven wounded, one of them a woman. She was shot in the back while on her way to the butcher shop." During this affair, strikers were frequently jailed for even nonviolent picketing, but no criminal charges were ever brought against vigilantes or the police who beat and murdered local citizens. By the time it was over, union membership had been dramatically reduced—between 1921 and 1923 it fell by more than a million members, to only 3.8 million. The most radical unions, such as the IWW, had been virtually obliterated.[17]

Much of this repression was justified by racist stereotypes of immigrants and minorities. Like conservatives in the 1960s who turned black males into a popular symbol of urban violence, propagandists of the late nineteenth and early twentieth centuries insisted that Jews, Eastern Europeans, Irish Catholics, and Italians—groups that today have low rates for common street crimes—were culturally and genetically predisposed to violence. In what might be called a dress rehearsal for the law-and-order crusades of the 1960s, which blamed social disorder on the poor blacks and radical students, thousands of books and articles blamed poor immigrants for the country's social problems.

By citing Charles Darwin, the recently discovered genetic theories of Gregor Mendel, and the racist views of nineteenth-century anthropology, a group of conservative intellectuals known as eugenicists attempted to prove that there were specific cultural traits associated with various biological groups and that the betterment of mankind could be accomplished only by improving the "inborn qualities" of "the human breed," in the words of the movement's English founder, Sir Francis Galton. The eugenicists, who wanted the U.S. government to create a kind of master race by outlawing immigration, developed elaborate theories attempting to show that northern, Teutonic races (the ethnic groups that had created the opium trade) were in fact responsible for almost everything wonderful about American life—science, capitalism, democracy, technological advances. In contrast, they argued, Eastern Europeans, Irish, and Mediterraneans (who sprang from the Greek, Roman, Hebrew, Celtic, and Byzantine civilizations) produced despotic, corrupt societies that were riddled with crime and violence. "Nothing will save the life of this free Republic if these foreign leeches are not cut and cast out," exclaimed the president-general of the Daughters of the American Revolution.[18]

As these ideas spread, Harry Laughlin, who was hired by Congress as its "expert eugenics agent," argued that the new immigrants had, because they were overrepresented in jails, mental hospitals, and poorhouses, "inborn socially inadequate qualities." By 1914 popular magazines were carrying more articles on eugenics than on slums, tenements, and living standards combined. Writing in the *Saturday Evening Post*, Kenneth Roberts warned that the deluge of Alpine, Mediterranean, and Semitic immigrants would invariably produce "a hybrid race of people as worthless and futile as the good-for-nothing mongrels of Central American and Southeastern Europe." Such arguments provided a pseudointellectual justification for the crackdown on radical political groups in the 1910s and a backlash against all immigrants that produced tough laws restricting immigration in the 1920s. The 1924 Johnson-Reed Act, for example, explicitly stated that it was designed to maintain the "racial preponderance [of] the basic strain on our people." Moreover, "influenced by ... European racist theoreticians, major political figures such as Henry Cabot Lodge unblushingly defended Anglo-Saxonism, the superiority of the 'original' American stock," notes historian David Bennett. "[As the] eugenics movement flourished . . . Theodore Roosevelt and Woodrow Wilson embraced racist theories, Henry Adams, Henry James, the president of Harvard and other cultural heavyweights did the same. Many key members of a new generation of social scientists . . . doubted the intellectual capacity of racial and ethnic minorities."[19]

Such theories may now seem laughable, but their effects are still with us. The anti-immigrant backlash ended the reform movements of the early twentieth century and brought conservatives back to power, a position they used to pursue pro-business policies in the 1920s. In the process they ignored the role of major corporations in creating problems like crime, drug abuse, and alcoholism. After all, the sturdy Protestant merchants of New England, who provided much of the capital for America's Industrial Revolution, grew wealthy in the eighteenth century by importing rum and molasses (90 percent of which was refined into rum) from the West Indies; between 1768 and 1772 the colonies imported about 477,000 pounds sterling worth a year. Some of the rum was sent to Africa, where it was used to buy slaves, but much of it was sold to poorer colonists and Indians. Eventually, these profits helped create a culture of heavy drinking, particularly on the frontier. By 1830 the average American was consuming the equivalent of seven gallons of pure alcohol a year (nearly triple the 2.7 gallons consumed in the 1970s), and the expansion of grain production made whiskey and beer incredibly cheap for consumers. Beer production jumped from 6.6 trillion barrels in 1870 to 60.8 trillion in 1917, and distilled alcohol skyrocketed from 72.6 million gallons in 1870 to 286.1 million in 1917, creating large production, distribution, and marketing networks. To protect their markets, brewers and distillers came to control many retail outlets, and they pressured saloonkeepers to sell as much booze as possible. "We must create the appetite for liquor in the growing boys," one dealer explained in 1912. "Nickels expended in treats to boys now will return in dollars to your tills after the appetite has been formed." Illustrating the success of that formula, American liquor manufacturers netted about $1.5 billion in 1911, an amount that was then higher than the national debt.[20]

As already noted, New England merchants were also very active in the nineteenth-century China trade, smuggling opium out of China, and the growth of the opium trade in Asia and Turkey brought quantities of addictive drugs into the United States. Laying the foundations for many of our current problems, British and New England merchants imported about twenty-five thousand pounds of opium in 1840—a figure that jumped to half a million pounds in 1870. As drug companies began to discover ways to peddle narcotics to the public, opium was not only smoked but turned into patent medicines or refined into morphine, which was originally marketed as a cure for almost everything—including opium addiction. Merck of Germany, now one of the world's largest pharmaceutical companies, became a commercial producer of morphine in 1827, and Rosengarten and Co., which is now part of Merck, began production in 1832 in the United States. Merck also became the first to market cocaine, which in the late nineteenth century was praised by writers such as Freud for its power to cure morphine and alcohol addiction. The Parke Davis pharmaceutical company of Detroit became one of the world's largest manufacturers of cocaine, selling coca cordials, capsules for hypodermics, sprays, and cocaine cigarettes. The Coca-Cola formula included the drug until 1903, and cocaine and opiates were the basis of many patent medicines, such as Mrs. Winslow's Soothing Syrup, an opiate-laced cocktail that was liberally dispensed by parents seeking to sedate their kids. In 1898 Bayer began marketing heroin as a nonaddictive alternative to morphine and as a panacea for infant respiratory diseases. Given the flood of opium out of the European colonies and heavy promotion by pharmacists and patent-medicine makers, American consumption of opium quadrupled from twelve grains per person in the 1840s to fifty-two grains in the 1890s.[21]

The number of addicts in nineteenth-century America will never be accurately known, but some historians believe that the numbers rose steadily to about 250,000 by 1900. Initially, the huge advertising revenues received from patent medicines prevented most newspapers from attacking drugs, but exposés began to appear as the public came to perceive the problems. Early exposés focused on middle-class users, who acquired their drugs from doctors, and the major corporations that supplied them. But as labor and social unrest escalated, elite reformers focused on lower-class drug use as a symbol of how dangerous lower classes threatened the prosperity and values of American capitalism. "Addicts were identified with foreign groups and internal minorities who were already actively feared and the objects of elaborate and massive social and legal restraints," explains historian David Musto.[22]

By the first decade of the twentieth century the same elaborate racial stereotypes that built political support for a crackdown on immigrants and radicals were also used to justify a massive crusade against drug addiction. In the South, politicians blamed much of the black crime on cocaine. "The colored people seem to have a weakness for it," a pharmacist told Congress in 1910. "Persons under the influence of it, believe they are millionaires. They have an exaggerated ego. They imagine they can lift buildings.... They have no regard for right or wrong. It produces a kind of temporary insanity. They would just as leave rape a woman as anything else and a great many of the southern rape cases have been traced to cocaine." Some newspaper accounts even claimed that blacks under its influence were almost impossible to kill. As mythic tales of black superhumans on cocaine circulated, southern police departments even justified their switch to using .38 caliber bullets by saying that blacks when high were almost unaffected by .32 caliber bullets.[23]

Similarly, the Chinese were said to be congenitally drawn to opium, and in the 1930s Hispanics were believed to become raging criminals and rapists of white women under the influence of marijuana. In the early twentieth century, police departments—which had said little about narcotics abuse when nineteenth-century big business was making huge profits from the trade—began to blame street crime on narcotics use, and commentators increasingly identified drug abuse with urban gangs, unemployed young men, and immigrants. "Heroin addiction is a public menace, as it increases the rebellious attitude of anti-social youth, and obliterates all controlling influences of the herd instinct," one doctor wrote in the 1920s, reflecting widely disseminated views. "Heroin ... is naturally the drug of choice of the criminal class. It gives them the desired inflation of personality, the reckless daring, the indifference to crime and the lack of all remorse, no matter what crime is committed."[24]

Of course, no drug has ever been developed that allows men, black or white, to run unharmed through hails of bullets, and decades of studies show that those who indulge in heroin—which depresses the nervous system—have lower crime rates than other drug users. No matter. In the early twentieth century—a period of massive social unrest, labor violence, racist attacks on immigrants, and red scares—the older stereotype of the middle-class addict "trying to seem normal" was transformed into "a new image of the user who denied social conventions and threatened progress and stability," explains drug historian H. Wayne Morgan. Such stereotypes helped develop political support for anti-drug laws. Dr. Hamilton Wright, who drafted the first anti-narcotics legislation, frequently complained that the Chinese were the primary causes of the problem: "One of the most unfortunate phases of the habit of smoking [opium is] ... the large number of women who have become involved and are living as common-law-wives . . . with Chinese in the Chinatowns of our various cities." From these women, Wright argued, the problem spread to other whites and to blacks (a rather bizarre opinion, considering that most addicts got their drugs from white doctors, white drugstore owners, or patented medicines that were produced and sold by white-owned corporations). Likewise, he also argued that the problem of black cocaine abuse, despite hysterical newspaper reports all over the South, had not been adequately publicized: "Cocaine is often the direct incentive to the crime of rape by the Negroes of the South and other sections of the country."[25]

Pharmaceutical companies and patent-medicine producers fought the legislation, but in 1914 Congress passed the Harrison Act. By that time, there was broad political support for it, largely because of increased fears of social disorder. "Prominent newspapers, physicians, pharmacists and Congressmen believed opiates and cocaine predisposed habitués towards insanity and crime," explains Musto. "Cocaine raised the specter of the wild Negro, opium the devious Chinese, morphine the tramps in the slums; it was feared that use of all these drugs was spreading into the 'higher classes.'"[26]

A similar dynamic pushed the federal government to move against alcohol. By 1917 twenty-seven of the forty-eight states had outlawed liquor sales, and the Eighteenth Amendment was quickly ratified. As with narcotics, much of the debate over alcohol was closely tied to the anti-immigrant and anti-radical fears of the age. "The Eighteenth Amendment attempted an unprecedented regimentation of morality by law," explains immigration expert John Higham. "Riding the wave of 100 percent Americanism, the Drys identified their crusade to regulate behavior with the preservation of the American way of life. . . . Americanizers set about . . . to transform the immigrants . . . [and] prohibitionists carried the point that outlawing alcohol would accomplish a general moral improvement."[27]

These attacks on drug and alcohol use by immigrants and minorities helped build political support for the larger anti-union and anti-radical crackdown, a policy that would protect big business from increased government interference. But the conservative backlash against immigrants and poorer Americans that led to the prohibition of drugs and alcohol would prove to be one of the most disastrous movements in the history of American law enforcement. Saloons and alcohol had played a major role in the profitability of criminal gangs, but the strategy of criminalizing liquor allowed organized crime to establish huge empires. Organized crime expert Alan Block notes that "the more illicit an activity became, the greater the profit margin for its vendors. . . . Prohibition has stood as a historical gateway . . . when mobs first made really big money on a national scale."[28]

Less obviously, the scapegoating of immigrants and minorities by conservative elites systematically sabotaged efforts to reform corrupt political machines, to create more efficient police forces, and reduce the power of organized crime. Throughout the nineteenth and early twentieth centuries the business community railed against these machines, but its vocal hostility toward immigrants and social programs that might deal with causes of urban violence generally left many poor Americans with only one political choice: vote early and often as instructed by their ward bosses.

In the 1930s and 1940s, when government officials did attack those problems, the ethnic character of the urban gangs that were the farm system for major organized crime began to change. Less than a century after journalists, academics, and politicians built lucrative careers by claiming that Italian, Jewish, and Irish Americans were genetically predisposed toward violence and gang warfare, the sons and daughters of those immigrants began to play prominent roles in the government war against organized crime. They risked their lives as undercover cops to infiltrate the mob. They ran federal anti-crime task forces and sat as judges in federal courts where mobsters were put on trial.

Yet the purveyors of organized mayhem still thrive. Just as massive economic and political changes in Asia allowed warlords to recruit millions of impoverished peasants to grow opium, the global economy would create fertile conditions in America—poverty, urban decay, rampant unemployment, and social unrest—for a new generation of gangs to build even bigger enterprises. The postwar economy and the Cold War, enormously profitable for large multinationals and conservative U.S. politicians, would wreck the manufacturing base of American cities, leaving millions of poor urban residents with dismal economic prospects. Some, like the Asian peasants working for Khun Sa, would turn to crime to survive.

Chapter 7:
The Short Arm of the Law

No matter how much we seize, it doesn't seem to change the amount [of drugs] coming into the country. . . . The price doesn't go up, the purity doesn't go down.

—*Thomas A. Constantine, DEA administrator*

IN THE EARLY 1940s, THE WAR AGAINST FASCISM BROUGHT WITH it one of law enforcement's few victories in the battle against crime. After reaching record levels in the depressed 1930s, homicide rates dropped from 9.7 per 100,000 people in 1933 (about what they were in 1991) to 5.1 in 1943. And thanks to the Second World War, which disrupted drug production and distribution networks, the number of U.S. addicts fell to forty-eight thousand in 1949, a dramatic drop from the 150,000 to 200,000 addicts in 1915. But as the war ended, law enforcement officials began to worry about the future. "A new upsurge in crime is gaining headway rapidly in this country," *U.S. News and World Report* warned in May 1946. "Crime rates [rose] . . . relatively little in wartime. The big reason was that millions of men under 30 years of age were overseas. . . . Now that demobilization is filling out this age group again . . . the result is a new crime wave. If the trend is not checked quickly, this year will see a crime rate at least 25 percent worse than any previous year."[1]

The so-called postwar crime wave, which saw violent crime rates rise every year between 1945 and 1954, may seem like a modest, almost genteel event to readers inured to nightly news reports of drive-by shootings and cannibalistic serial killers. Yet policymakers had real reason to be worried. The war had ended the Great Depression but peace brought many pressing social and economic problems. As millions of veterans returned home, the economy struggled to provide them with jobs. Unemployment rose from 1.2 percent in 1944 to 5.9 percent in 1949, and the number of people on welfare increased 135 percent between 1945 and 1950. Organized labor, which had moderated its wage demands and avoided strikes in order to help the war effort, flexed its muscle in a record number of strikes. Veterans and city residents demanded better housing and social services. In 1940 the U.S. census found that 38.5 percent of non-farm housing was "unsatisfactory," and after the war housing expert Charles Abrams claimed that one-third of the nation's housing stock was substandard. Hubert Humphrey prophetically noted that "slums, rotten broken-down areas, are the ulcer which may develop into the cancer that will consume the physical and economic structure of the industry[sic] city. . . . Either we lick the slums or the slums will destroy the city."[2]

Most economists realized that the economy needed larger markets, both abroad and at home, to avoid another collapse, but there were serious political disagreements on how this could be accomplished. In 1945 and 1946 Democrats proposed massive new social programs, including national health insurance and a widely backed proposal to make full employment a national policy. In 1947 they battled conservatives over legislation to limit the power of organized labor. In 1948 President Truman attacked Republicans for having changed their 1928 campaign slogan of "two cars in every garage" to "two families in every garage."[3]

The outcome was that instead of embarking on a crusade against poverty, racism, poor housing, rotting cities, dangerous working conditions, and dismal schools, the United States launched a very heated Cold War that would consume trillions of tax dollars over the next half-century. Washington's success in containing communism and keeping many markets open to U.S. corporations made it possible for American companies to export an astonishing $7.15 trillion worth of goods and services between 1944 and 1990, creating a political climate in which global multinational corporations could thrive. By 1995 the 2,600 largest American multinationals accumulated more than $7.2 trillion worth of assets.[4] But the restructured American economy also created economic and social structures that allowed crime to flourish in many major cities and fueled the expansion of criminal organizations such as the Mafia that profited from booming underground economies. Understanding how that occurred requires a close look at the way the Cold War affected the movement of capital in and out of American communities, particularly the poor urban neighborhoods with high crime rates.

The government-sponsored shift of capital out of the cities actually began in the 1930s and accelerated with the start of the Second World War, when non-defense public works projects and many social programs were abolished. During the war, a group of wealthy industrialists, put in charge of the wartime economy by the Roosevelt administration, embarked on policies that hurt the older industrialized northern cities. "Considering that the existing manufacturing investment was valued at only $39.5 billion in 1939, wartime investment [$35.5 billion between 1942 and 1944] amounted to an unparalleled expansion of the nation's productive capacity," urban affairs expert John Mollenkopf notes. Unfortunately, these investments were designed to improve the profitability of major corporations, not the long-term economic future of the cities: generally, they channeled manufacturing capital away from unionized urban areas to suburbs and to regions with weak traditions of unionism—primarily the South and the West. In Detroit, for example, the government invested $713 million in new plants in the surrounding suburbs, while putting only $311 million into the central city. Mollenkopf's research indicates similar discrepancies in New York ($380 million investment in the central city and $492 million in the suburbs), Los Angeles ($149 million versus $664.9 million), Boston ($81 million versus $181 million), Pittsburgh ($58.7 million versus $428.2 million). In addition, wartime investment created an industrial base in Sunbelt cities such as Houston, San Diego, Denver, San Jose, and Phoenix—cities that had few industries before the war. As a result, Sunbelt cities and suburbs, which had weak traditions of unions, came out of the war with the most modern manufacturing plants, making it tough for many central cities to compete economically or provide jobs for their residents.[5]

Equally egregious problems were created by defense spending, which helped some regions of the country at the expense of others. During the postwar period the Defense Department's outlays worked as a federally mandated system of transferring capital—in the form of taxes and government contracts—from central cities to suburbs and cities in South and the West. "Few northeastern cities have benefited from defense spending," notes Mollenkopf. "Between 1947 and 1967, the suburban rings captured 111 percent of the manufacturing employment gain [meaning that central cities actually lost jobs] and 100 percent of the population gains in the sixty-nine largest [metropolitan areas] with populations over five hundred thousand. During these two decades the sixteen largest and oldest central cities, located primarily in the belt stretching from New York and Boston to St. Louis and Chicago, lost an average of 34,751 jobs, while their suburbs gain an average of 86,358. . . . Federal defense spending during and after World War II fostered 'new industries' [closely tied to the military-industrial complex] which chose an even more pronounced pattern of suburban location. . . . As a recent Congressional research service literature review noted, 'a definite shift from the Northeast and North central regions to the South and West' has occurred in the awarding of prime [military contracts] between 1950 and 1976, especially in the years after 1968."[6]

Meanwhile, the rise of agribusiness and capital-intensive farming methods drove millions of poor whites, blacks, and Hispanics off the land. Between 1940 and 1970 nearly 4.5 million blacks left the South, and the number of Puerto Ricans in the mainland United States jumped from about 50,000 in 1940 to 1,379,100 in 1970, of which about 811,800 made their home in New York City. White southern migration is less easy to track, but Appalachian whites are believed to have accounted for about 10 percent of all the migrants to Chicago, Detroit, and Cleveland between 1955 and 1970, when about 200,000 former residents of Appalachia lived in just those three cities.[7]

The arrival of these black, white, and Hispanic workers who had little education and few skills came at a time when many skilled blue-collar workers were leaving the cities, many to work in the new suburban factories. New York City is believed to have lost one million whites prior to 1965, and more than 2.5 million moved out of Chicago, Baltimore, Cleveland, Detroit, and Philadelphia between 1950 and 1970, while the percentage of blacks more than doubled in most large northern cities over the same two decades.[8]

There is little doubt that the mass migration of people into and out of the cities had a devastating impact on many neighborhoods, contributing to the decay of social and economic institutions that had helped preserve public safety. But the problem was not so much the changed racial and ethnic composition of urban areas as the differences in opportunities that cities could offer. Massive federal programs had not only created factory jobs in the suburbs but subsidized the construction of inexpensive suburban housing with cheap home-financing schemes and offered returning veterans a free college education. These programs allowed many earlier immigrants to improve their lot and played a key role in the rising standard of living. Median family income tripled from $3,031 in 1947 to $9,867 in 1979 (in constant 1967 dollars). In principle, there was little reason to believe that the millions of people who migrated to the cities in the postwar era would not also benefit from new government programs and investment to stimulate jobs, housing, and education.[9]

Unfortunately, the response of federal, state, and local agencies to the challenge was at best ineffective and at worst hostile to the future of the cities. During the Great Depression only 160,800 residential units were built, and the Second World War forced a temporary end to public housing programs in 1943, before much progress had been made. By 1947, 2.7 to 4.4 million families had to live with other families, with another half-million living in transient shelters or in buildings not designed for residential use; more than six million poor urban families were looking for better housing or planned to do so. But as the need increased, various business groups and real estate interests—notably the National Association of Real Estate Boards, the National Association of Home Builders, and the U.S. Chamber of Commerce—labeled the limited public housing programs of the New Deal a Bolshevik plot, and the Cold War escalated their attack on public housing as "socialistic." Overall, real estate, construction and business interests are believed to have spent $5 million (about $30 million in 1995 dollars) to shape federal housing legislation, and their tactics were so aggressive that a full-scale congressional investigation was launched. The final legislation drastically limited the amount of public housing and included provisions designed to ensure that "private enterprise shall be encouraged to serve as large a part of the total need as it can." Thanks to those efforts, urban historian Sam Bass Warner notes, "after a generation of construction, from 1934 to 1970, only 893,500 [public housing] units were completed and in operation around the country. Of this total 143,400 were for the benefit of the elderly. Less than 2 percent of our metropolitan population occupies such structures. . . . For most spaces there are long waiting lists."[10]

Meanwhile, real estate developers, financial institutions, and construction companies reaped billions from corporate welfare programs designed to subsidize the private housing industry. To stimulate the construction industry and help revive the economy, the Roosevelt administration had created the Federal Housing Administration and a variety of public works programs. Under the FHA the federal government agreed to insure home mortgages made by private financial institutions, and after the war the Veterans Administration provided low-interest, insured loans to returning servicemen. Thanks to these subsidies, which included tax deductions for home buyers, contractors and developers would make a mint building houses for consumers flush with mortgage money from FHA or VA loans. Banks and thrifts also collected hefty fees making federally guaranteed loans. In short, the same industry lobbyists who railed against socialist programs like public housing, which they said would destroy the nation's entrepreneurial spirit, pushed through massive government programs that protected them from competition and the vagaries of the market.

Everyone made out marvelously except poorer Americans and major cities, in part because wealthy elites warped a variety of urban programs to suit their interests. The 1949 and 1954 housing acts contained provisions for urban renewal, slum clearance, and public housing intended to revitalize inner cities. In practice, however, the new laws were a disaster. The 1954 law shifted control over urban renewal programs away from the federal government to local authorities who cared more about political contributions from real estate interests than about housing for poor blacks and whites. In many major cities, business interests also financed urban planning groups that focused on renewal programs for revitalizing downtown areas—where the business interests who financed the planning associations owned land—and paid little attention to the cities' worst slums, which were desperate for housing and economic development.

Overall, local redevelopment agencies funded by the federal government acquired and cleared more than 57,300 acres of central-city land between 1954 and 1969 and set up some 1,600 redevelopment projects—about 60 percent of which were designed for nonresidential uses. To make way for office buildings, research hospitals, symphony halls, and educational institutions that would enhance the property values of powerful real estate interests, more than a quarter-million central-city housing units were demolished prior to 1966 and more than a million people displaced. Yet only 114,829 new units were built, and only 45,861 of those were subsidized. In effect, many poor whites, blacks, and Hispanics who had been forced off the land by declining demand for agricultural labor arrived in urban slums at a time when schemes for newly beautified central cities left no place for them. Hundreds of thousands of blacks and Hispanics were pushed out of downtown districts into segregated urban ghettos, prompting one critic to describe the urban renewal programs of the 1950s and early 1960s as "negro removal."[13]

Government officials also made little attempt to protect blacks and Hispanics from racism in the housing market. Blacks who moved into the cities in large numbers in the 1910s were met with violence and legal restrictions. After scores were killed by white mobs during race riots, a number of cities attempted to pass laws mandating segregated housing. The Supreme Court overturned those laws in 1917, but neighborhood associations widely used racial covenants—which prohibited whites from selling homes to blacks and quite often to Jews, Italians, and certain immigrant groups—to prevent racial and ethnic integration, and in 1924 the National Association of Real Estate Brokers adopted policies that actively encouraged segregated neighborhoods. Racial covenants were overturned by a 1948 Supreme Court decision, but many real estate agents simply adopted the unwritten policy of not showing homes in white neighborhoods to black buyers.[12]

Meanwhile, most federal housing programs of that period, which provided insured mortgages, were designed to be profitable or break-even enterprises, and officials adopted an extremely conservative approach to housing finance. In the 1930s the federally financed Home Owners' Loan Corporation "initiated and institutionalized the practice of redlining," according to historians Douglas Massey and Nancy Denton. Its maps highlighted poorer neighborhoods in red and established lending rules that made it virtually impossible for homeowners to get loans in those areas. "The HOLC rating procedures thus systematically undervalued old central city neighborhoods that were racially or ethically mixed. . . . Black areas were invariably rated as fourth grade and 'redlined.' . . . The HOLC did not invent these standards of racial worth in real estate . . . [but] it lent the power, prestige and support of the federal government to the systematic racial discrimination of housing," Massey and Denton explain.[13] A 1939 HOLC manual even specified that "if a neighborhood is to retain stability, it is necessary that properties shall continue to be occupied by the same social and racial classes."

These policies were expanded by the Federal Housing Administration, established in 1937, and the Veterans Administration. Between the 1930s and the 1970s federal authorities distributed their redlined maps of urban neighborhoods to private lenders, and banks used these maps to make lending decisions, making it extremely difficult for homeowners in poorer neighborhoods to get either private or public money. In addition, by making few loans for remodeling existing structures, the FHA favored new suburban development over inner-city renovation. The vast majority of FHA and VA mortgages went to white suburbs, and it was extremely difficult to obtain loans in central cities. For example, one suburb of St. Louis received five times as many FHA mortgages as the city did. In New York, likewise, FHA lending to suburban Nassau County was eleven times that in Brooklyn and sixty times that in the Bronx.[14]

In effect, this system of financial and social segregation concentrated some of the country's poorest and least educated citizens in some of America's worst neighborhoods at the same time that other government policies were systematically encouraging the transfer of capital out of the cities. That reduced opportunities for education (essential because the segregated South had provided almost no effective education), decent-paying unskilled jobs (crucial because many of the recent migrants to the cities came from agricultural economies), and housing (important because bad housing encourages young people to hang out on the streets).

Although conservatives have argued the only way out of this dilemma is for local residents to rebuild their lives, it should be stressed that the typical ghetto economy offered them virtually no opportunity to accumulate capital legally or to build up a successful economic infrastructure. In this sense, the ghetto economy is reminiscent of the Asian peasant communities involved in the Asia heroin trade, which have little capital and minimal control over the economic decisions that affect their lives. Impoverished peasants in Asia are paid only a few hundred dollars for a year's opium production, and most of the profits move out of the producing countries into the pockets of global crime groups. Likewise, most of the money made by ghetto residents leaves the community, and most of the assets in the community are owned by outsiders: its apartments, its stores, its banks, and its factories.

Most ghetto dwellers with jobs not only work elsewhere but spend a large chunk of their wages outside their neighborhoods, which frequently lack supermarkets, banks, and other basic services. As a result, the money pouring out of urban ghettos totals much more than the money put back in. For example, one researcher found that residents of Bedford-Stuyvesant, New York City's largest ghetto, sent $641.2 million out of the community in 1969 (much of it to landlords or banks for housing and to retailers), whereas the private sector of the ghetto brought in only $564.5 million (mostly in wages and sales to nonresidents). That produced a shortfall of $76.7 million, which was only covered by $288.2 million in government aid. Similar studies of Harlem and ghettos in Newark, Cleveland, and Washington, D.C., came to similar conclusions. In Cleveland, for example, ghetto dwellers spent only thirteen cents in the neighborhood for every dollar earned.[15]

Over time, this disinvestment had an enormous impact on crime. In areas lacking jobs, decent housing, government services, and functional public schools, crime rates have remained very high throughout the twentieth century. Don Wallace and Drew Humphries investigated crime rates in twenty cities between 1950 and 1971, analyzing the effects of key economic indicators—a region's economic prospects, labor-force changes, levels of poverty and unemployment—on different types of crime. Overall, they found, the older industrial cities that had lost jobs, suffered from high unemployment, and faced large numbers of new migrants had increased levels of murder, robbery, auto theft, and burglary. "Two crimes against persons—homicide and robbery—tend to be associated with the most extreme hardship levels . . . indicating that formerly active sites of industrial accumulation (that is, the older industrial cities that lost jobs in the postwar period) are now the sites of high rates of interpersonal violence," the authors concluded. "Theft as well as violence . . . is associated with the metropolitan pattern of accumulation that relocated industry to the suburbs . . . [and] turned parts of central cities into repositories for low-paid workers, the unemployed and welfare dependents. . . . An examination . . . shows that manufacturing job losses lead to high rates of auto theft . . . and burglary. . . . The old industrial centers bear the cost of the abandonment of obsolete production sites in favor of more profitable investment sites. These deteriorating cities not only lose employment, but suffer high property crime rates along with community decline and neighborhood disruption. Conversely, the increase in the size of the manufacturing labor force connected with the shift in investment patterns decreases the rate of crime. This result supports . . . earlier studies linking industrial employment, community stability and low crime rates."[16]

No similar study has been done for more recent periods, but a quick look at FBI crime data supports similar conclusions. In 1991 the cities with populations more than 250,000 accounted for about 20 percent of the nation's population but 51 percent of all homicides, 47 percent of all violent crimes, and 61 percent of all robberies. The eight U.S. cities with more than a million residents accounted for a mere 9 percent of the country's population but were responsible for 27 percent of all homicides, 26 percent of all violent crimes, and 36 percent of all robberies. In sharp contrast, suburban counties, which have been the chief beneficiaries of government subsidies, held 21 percent of the nation's population but suffered only 12 percent of all homicides, 14 percent of all violent crimes, and 9 percent of all robberies.[17]

Unlike the Wallace and Humphries study, these data do not separate the northern, more heavily unionized cities from Sunbelt urban centers that received heavy government subsidies in the form of defense spending. Nor do they separate the poorer urban neighborhoods, which have been most plagued by disinvestment, from more affluent communities. Even so, the gross FBI crime data for urban and suburban regions indicate that cities plagued by disinvestment and government disdain have crime rates two or three times those of suburbs that have benefited from corporate investment and government welfare programs for the affluent.

This difference can't be traced to the usual bugaboos of the law-and-order right. Suburban teens watch the same movies and television programs as urban youths yet commit far fewer serious crimes. Suburban police are no less bound by Supreme Court decisions protecting civil liberties than are their urban brethren, yet these generally better behaved officers manage to produce much lower crime rates. And although there are many firearms in the suburbs, more people die by the gun in urban centers. Finally, drug use by whites, who tend to live in suburbs, is very similar to that of blacks, who are disproportionately congregated in depressed urban centers, yet there is far less drug-related violence in white suburbs. In short, areas that have benefited from large investments and government subsidies have low crime rates; areas whose economies have been destroyed by disinvestment and government policies have epidemic levels of violence.

Law-and-order politicians not only ignored this problem but systematically pursued policies that made American cities less habitable, more violent places. At the start of the Cold War, Richard Nixon, Joseph McCarthy, and other public figures pushed for a conservative social agenda that gutted public housing and discouraged urban investments. By the mid-1960s their misguided policies had produced rising crime rates and growing social disorder. Yet instead of being voted out of office for pursuing a course that created these problems, conservatives used urban riots and rising crime to rebuild their careers. In the 1960s they capitalized on the political disorder of the era to build support for a law-and-order crusade. Then, after taking power in the 1970s and 1980s, they used law-and-order rhetoric to launch a rearguard attack on the minimal social programs of the 1960s. The net result: conservative politicians, who received massive political contributions from major corporations, embarked on programs designed to protect their wealthy benefactors at the expense of almost everyone else. Crime, which law-and-order politicians promised to end soon after taking power in 1968, continued to be a severe problem.

Chapter 8:
The Politics of Retribution

God knows how little we've really moved on this issue [racism and poverty], despite all the fanfare. As I see it, I've moved the Negro from D+ to C-. He's still nowhere. He knows it. And that's why he's out in the streets. Hell, I'd be there too.

—*Lyndon Johnson*

The whole secret of politics [is] knowing who hates who.

—*Kevin Phillips, Nixon adviser*

WHEN SENATOR BARRY GOLDWATER STRODE TO THE PODIUM to accept his party's presidential nomination in 1964, the Republicans had already thrown down the gauntlet on the issue of crime and social disorder. Former President Dwight D. Eisenhower had attacked rising crime rates, and Republican strategists hoped to link corruption scandals in the Johnson administration with increased crime and growing social disorder. "Tonight there is violence in our streets," thundered Goldwater, "corruption in our highest offices, aimlessness among our youth, anxiety among our elderly and . . . despair among the many. . . . Security from domestic violence, no less than from foreign aggression, is the most elementary and fundamental purpose of any government and a government that cannot fulfill this purpose is one that cannot long command the loyalty of its citizens. . . . Nothing prepares the way for tyranny more than the failure of public officials to keep the streets safe from bullies and marauders."[1]

In the months leading up to the election, Goldwater hammered away at those themes, laying out the basic outlines of what would become the politics of law and order. He denounced judges and particularly the Supreme Court justices, arguing that all too often "a criminal defendant must be given a sporting chance to go free, even though nobody doubts in the slightest he is guilty." He blamed crime on the disorder and rioting that accompanied the civil rights movement, and he attacked the Johnson administration's efforts to deal with violence by attacking the problems of poverty and racism. Crime, he declared at one point, is "the final terrible proof of a sickness which not all the social theories of a thousand social experiments have even begun to touch." But he wasn't opposed to all government intervention, for in another speech, he argued, "We have . . . seen many wars in the time of the present administration. But have we yet heard of the only needed war—the war against crime? No."[2]

In Goldwater's message, as in earlier debates, radicals and political leaders who attempted to do something about the poverty and racism that allowed crime to flourish were labeled instigators of violence. Their proposals to deal with the causes of crime were attacked as social "engineering" that would destroy individual responsibility and accelerate moral, social, and religious decay, the real cause of crime. Goldwater's solutions were also remarkably similar to the policies deployed in the late 1910s, when a crackdown on immigrants and labor led to the prohibition on alcohol and a federal war on drugs that allowed organized crime to grow into a multi-billion-dollar enterprise. In Republican campaign rhetoric, police forces who deployed attack dogs and whips against peaceful protesters were cast as heroes in the fight for law and order, while civil rights activists were recast as "bullies and marauders." The problem was not racism or poverty but the failure of government to hire more police and pass tougher laws.

In 1964, the American public turned away from this solution. They were appalled by Goldwater's initial unwillingness to disavow the Ku Klux Klan, which was busily blowing up black kids sitting peacefully in churches, or the John Birch Society, which had branded the Second World War hero and former president Dwight D. Eisenhower a Communist "traitor." Johnson swamped Goldwater at the polls, sweeping in the most liberal Congress since the New Deal. But with widespread public support for liberal social programs came another shift. As the Vietnam War escalated, radical student organizations emerged, draft cards went up in smoke, administration buildings were occupied, and the civil rights movement took a radical turn. The Cold War political consensus faced its first serious political test since the rise of McCarthyism. The social turmoil produced 329 significant urban riots in 257 cities, killing scores of people between 1964 and 1968.[3]

Federal, state, and local governments responded with an alphabet stew of government agencies and commissions. Federal spending on income security (which includes welfare) jumped from $9.7 billion in 1964 to $86.5 billion in 1980, and the public welfare expenditures of state and local governments from $6.3 billion to $54.1 billion. In the early years of these programs some progress was made, but the federal government's commitment to fighting poverty never matched the policies that encouraged capital to move out of the cities, primarily because military spending continued to outpace social spending. Even at the height of the war on poverty, while total spending on Social Security, medical care, health, and income security, increased from $28.8 billion to $58 billion between 1965 and 1970, the military budget remained about $22 billion higher, rising from $50.6 billion to $80.1 billion. As late as 1968, programs designed to benefit urban areas accounted for only 2 percent of all federal outlays.[4]

Meanwhile, conservative politicians deftly manipulated the disorder and urban decay to build political support for a range of right-wing agendas, finding strength in problems they had created in the first place. The postwar economic order, disastrous for the cities and many poor Americans, was a political windfall for the right. Government subsidies for the suburbs encouraged many whites to move out of the cities. Likewise, more conservative regions—notably the South, the Southwest, and southern California—benefited heavily from the military-industrial complex, producing a staunch base of support for military adventurism and anti-radical politicians.

The first inklings of this government-financed political shift to the right came in the Eisenhower era. In 1952 Eisenhower drew strong support from white ethnics fleeing the cities, and he became the first Republican presidential candidate to capture more than half of the southern white vote. That trend continued in every subsequent election except Johnson's 1964 landslide, and even then, Goldwater—who had voted against the 1964 Civil Rights Act—did remarkably well in the South. He openly courted the white vote and became the first Republican candidate to win the southern states—Mississippi, Alabama, South Carolina, Louisiana, and Georgia—most opposed to ending segregation. He also drew strong support from working-

and lower-middle-class white voters, indicating that race could be used to divide the Democrats' working-class base.[5]

Also noting that George Wallace, running on a third-party platform, did very well in several southern and northern states by capitalizing on white ethnic discontent, Republican strategists began turning away from the party's longstanding commitment to civil rights. Until 1964 the party of Lincoln had been far more liberal on racial issues than the Democrats, who had a long history of supporting segregation, organized lynchings, and other attacks on blacks. But the success of Wallace and Goldwater in breaking the Democratic monopoly in the South prompted a shift in the Republican party's thinking. Kevin Phillips, one of Nixon's key campaign advisers in the 1968, argued for "a Southern strategy" that would target disgruntled white voters. "Who needs Manhattan when we can get the electoral votes of eleven Southern States?" Phillips wrote. "Put those to-gether with the Farm Belt and the Rocky Mountains and we don't need the big cities. We don't even want them. Sure Hubert [Humphrey] will carry Riverside Drive [in Manhattan] in November. La-de-dah. What will he do in Oklahoma?"[6]

Following Phillips's advice that "the whole secret of politics [is] knowing who hates who," Nixon pursued a carefully crafted policy of divide and conquer. He worked hard to rebuild his alliances with the Republican Goldwater right and established close ties to old segregationists such as Senator Strom Thurmond, whom one columnist called "Nixon's great Southern vassal." Then, to bolster his appeal in the South and among disenchanted whites, he chose as his running mate Spiro Agnew, the Republican governor of Maryland who had built a career on blaming black civil rights leaders for the urban riots. And he wasn't alone. Between 1964 and 1968, conservative Republicans had kept up a steady drumbeat of attacks on social disorder, antiwar protests, and crime, using crime the way McCarthy had used Communism to bash liberals. "For such a deterioration of respect for law to occur in so brief a time in so great a nation, we must look for more important collaborators and auxiliaries," Nixon said in the summer of 1966, drawing on the old code words of the McCarthy period to accuse liberals of secretly collaborating with criminals to subvert law and order. "It is my belief that the seeds of civil anarchy would never have taken root in this nation had they not been nurtured by scores of respected

Americans, public officials, educators, clergymen [and] civil rights leaders as well."[7]

These themes were enormously appealing to many voters who got their information about urban problems from short news clips of rioting which failed to deal with underlying economic problems. Isolated from the realities of black urban ghettos, many whites who lived in the suburbs and Sunbelt cities accepted the same racial stereotypes that had persuaded middle-class elites to join the anti-immigrant and anti-radical crusades of the early twentieth century. In 1968 a Gallup poll found that 81 percent of Americans agreed with the statement that "law and order has broken down in this country"; another 63 percent believed that the courts were "too soft" on criminals; and a Harris poll taken shortly before the Democratic convention found that the public rated "organized crime," "negroes who start riots," and Communists as the key causes of the current violence. About 38 percent of all voters believed that Nixon would do the best job of ending the disorder—a higher rating than received by Humphrey and Wallace at 26 and 21 percent. Thanks to those perceptions, Nixon squeaked out a razor-thin victory in November.[8]

Ironically, many of the men who led the law-and-order charge—Richard Nixon, Ronald Reagan, Spiro Agnew, George Wallace, Barry Goldwater, and J. Edgar Hoover—had played a pivotal, though unintended role in allowing crime to become a major problem in the first place. Their slavish support of anticommunist dictators in countries such as Thailand and Taiwan protected corrupt pro-U.S. elites around the world and it made it much easier for the crime syndicates allied with those dictators to engage such enterprises as narcotics smuggling. Nixon, Goldwater, and Reagan were staunch supporters of the Taiwanese government that was responsible for revitalizing the heroin trade in Burma and all three politicians also supported a corrupt South Vietnamese regime that was involved in the drug trade.

Closer to home, McCarthyism helped Cold War politicians carry out conservative anti-labor policies and it prevented the left from pushing for the kind of serious social reforms that might have ameliorated the poverty and urban decay that fed the crime wave of the 1960s and 1970s. In 1945 and 1946 U.S. Chamber of Commerce publications had blamed Communists for the surge of labor unrest, arguing that "whoever stirs up needless strife in American trade unions advances the cause of Communism," asserting that the Communist Party had "gained control of at least 20 of the most important unions," and alleging that "about 400" Communists held positions of power in Washington. Similarly, the National Association of Manufacturers, representing about 17,000 companies, spent several million dollars a year attacking any legislation that protected unions' rights, and powerful conservative organizations such as the American Veterans of Foreign Wars (VFW) spent huge sums attacking Communist infiltration of all aspects of American life.[9]

These campaigns strengthened the power of conservative trade unionists and assisted in the passage of labor laws, such as the Taft-Hartley Act, that would cripple the power of unions to press for more social programs. At the same time, allegations that the Truman administration and the unions were harboring Communist traitors weakened political support for a variety of social programs championed by New Deal liberals and strengthened the power of major business groups to promote conservative agendas and finance the political careers and policies of men such as Joseph McCarthy and Richard Nixon. "What these businessmen sought was a firm anti-Soviet foreign policy combined with a domestic anti-communism program aimed primarily at labor unions and animated by hostility toward the social programs of Roosevelt's New Deal," writes historian Peter Irons. By attacking the New Deal as a Communist plot, conservatives were able to defeat liberal programs to guarantee everyone a job, health insurance, and housing. Federal programs to replace urban slums with new public housing were gutted; jobs left the cities as their housing stock decayed, and trillions of dollars were channeled out of urban areas into suburbs or non-union southern states.[10]

All these problems were compounded by the fact that Goldwater, Wallace, J. Edgar Hoover, and other law-and-order conservatives were staunch opponents of the civil rights movement in the 1960s. Their opposition to laws that would have ended segregation denied many southern blacks basic educational and economic opportunities, and it forced minorities who migrated north to live in segregated high-crime ghettos. In addition, antilabor legislation passed at the height of the red scare made it easier for major corporations to move jobs out of the heavily unionized northern cities to areas that offered lower wages and fewer unions. In the late 1940s the CIO embarked on a major campaign to organize southern workers, but the

South's strong anti-union laws, organized lynchings of rebellious blacks, and red-baiting by conservative politicians crippled the campaign. Employers continued to move south to avoid unions, and the job losses in major cities accelerated. After peaking at 35 percent of the labor force in 1945, union membership dropped to 31 percent in 1960 and 27 percent in 1970. Today it is less than 14 percent.[11]

The red scare not only sabotaged efforts to deal with the underlying causes of crime, but also bolstered the political power of government officials such as J. Edgar Hoover and allowed them to embark on disastrous law enforcement strategies. Hoover had made a name for himself in the anticommunist witch hunts of the 1910s and played a key role in the Palmer raids that rounded up thousands of workers and immigrants after the First World War. In 1924, as a reward for those efforts, he was put in charge of what is now the FBI and managed to revitalize what had been a corrupt, inept agency. But the FBI's obsessive interest in garnering publicity for its director and attacking alleged radicals prevented any effective attacks on problems like organized crime and political corruption. Fearing that the narcotics trade would corrupt his agents and produce unfavorable publicity, Hoover refused to work with anti-narcotics and prohibition officers at the Treasury Department. The FBI also antagonized local law enforcement officials by taking charge of high-profile investigations and taking credit for arrests that were primarily due to hardworking local cops. Thousands of agents were assigned to investigate auto theft, which is best left to local law enforcement, while the agency ignored white-collar crimes, political corruption, and organized crime. Since Hoover claimed there was no such thing as organized crime, the FBI's ten-most-wanted list invariably included garden-variety bank robbers and murderers rather than major crime bosses. As late as the 1950s, Hoover's FBI refused to assist a congressional investigation that documented the growth of organized crime into a huge enterprise.[12]

Meanwhile, Hoover channeled most of the agency's resources into a massive witch hunt for radicals and subversives of all stripes. By the early 1960s the FBI had more than 1,500 informants inside the Communist Party—indicating that about one in six members was actually working for Hoover. Yet in New York City, where hundreds of agents were investigating Communism, less than ten FBI employees were tracking the mob, which controlled many key sectors of the city's economy. When antiwar protests and urban riots prompted Presidents Johnson and Nixon to spend huge sums investigating their political opponents, Johnson's Justice Department set up an Interdivisional Intelligence Unit, and Hoover launched his infamous COINTELPRO operation, "designed to expose, disrupt, misdirect, discredit or otherwise neutralize the activities of black nationalist[s]." Under that program, the FBI infiltrated radical groups, employed agents provocateurs to create divisions within them, fabricated cases against political activists (and may even have assassinated some of them). By the mid-1970s, FBI headquarters in Washington had more than five hundred thousand domestic intelligence files. Similarly, the CIA's Operation Chaos, created in 1967 to investigate antiwar activists, had produced information on more than three hundred thousand Americans by the time it was shut down in 1974. Meanwhile, the army accumulated more than one hundred thousand files on suspected radicals, and the IRS collected some eleven thousand files on political opponents.[13]

Many cities too had set up "red squads" during the anti-radical hysteria of the 1910s, and throughout the next fifty years these units devoted substantial resources and manpower to the task of monitoring labor strikes, protests, political meetings, rallies and parades. By 1940, police forces in Chicago, where organized crime groups prospered, had accumulated dossiers on five thousand local and seventy-five thousand suspected Communists around the country. In the 1960s, more than a decade after a Senate investigation (the Kefauver Committee) had documented the pervasive power of organized crime, Frank Donner notes that "in cities such as Chicago, Philadelphia and San Francisco, more police personnel were on political intelligence assignments than were engaged in fighting organized crime. Similarly, the police in small and medium-sized cities plagued by organized crime, proudly boasted that they were hot on the heels of radicals." By then, special anti-radical units in local police forces may have employed more than three hundred thousand men. Yet the American Communist Party of the era is believed to have had no more than five to ten thousand members, suggesting that there were thirty to sixty cops investigating every card-carrying red.[14]

Over time, law enforcement's lack of interest in political corruption, money laundering, and organized crime would also allow crime groups to sink their roots deep into the legitimate economy. In the early 1900s gangsters extorted money from garment-industry sweatshops and were hired as thugs to break up strikes on the Lower East Side of Manhattan. By the 1930s, Lepke Buchalter, one of Meyer Lansky's fellow gang members, employed about two hundred and fifty gunmen and thugs, giving Lansky power over New York City's garment district and other industries. Although local prosecutors had begun to crack down on the mob in the 1930s and 1940s, in the 1950s the Kefauver Committee (despite the fact that the FBI refused to cooperate, still arguing that the mob didn't exist) produced 11,500 pages of testimony from 600 witnesses showing that organized crime had infiltrated some 50 industries. It listed the names of 514 mob-related individuals and companies involved in legitimate businesses; some had lucrative contracts with Fortune 500 companies such as Ford. The Kefauver investigation also found that official corruption played a key role "in facilitating and permitting organized crime." The committee's final report complained that top mobsters remained "immune from prosecution and punishment. . . . At the local level this committee received evidence of corruption of law-enforcement officers and connivance with criminal gangs in practically every city in which it held hearings."[15]

New York City provides a particularly odious example of how Hoover's policies allowed gangsters to exert enormous power over the economy. In the late 1970s more than twenty garment companies were under the direct control of syndicate figures. Similarly, mobsters moved into the liquor, shipping, trucking, warehouse, food, and construction industries. Their control of the International Longshoremen's Association gave them power over many businesses on the New York City docks, and corrupt unions also allowed Mafia figures to dominate local meat markets, which processed about one-fifth of the meat sold in the United States. In the construction trade, Mafia family cartels got a 2 percent kickback on every bit of concrete poured during the early 1980s, controlled hiring and firing at many construction sites, worked to rig bids for city projects, and in one case got lucrative contracts to install new windows in public housing projects—deals that allowed them to inflate construction costs by 5 to 20 percent a year. Likewise, mobsters set up a cartel of commercial carting companies that forced local businesses to pay an extra $200 to $500 million a year to have their trash removed. Mobsters even managed to infiltrate the school bus industry; as late as 1995, mob-owned school bus companies had contracts with the city school system to drive kids to their classes.[16]

No one will ever know how much violence was produced by Hoover's policy of ignoring organized crime and its corrupt political allies between 1920 and 1960, but there is little doubt that the lack of federal attention allowed crime groups to become hugely profitable enterprises. In a 1986 study of the costs of organized crime Wharton Econometrics, a consulting group, estimated that extortion, fraud, price fixing, labor racketeering, and other activities increased prices by 2 percent in such industries as construction, trucking, warehousing, and waste hauling; by 1 percent in the garment industry; and by 0.5 percent in the wholesale and retail trade, personal and business services, banking, and real estate. "Wharton's estimate of $47 billion in 1986 for organized crime equals 1.13 percent of U.S. gross national production," the study concluded. "At $47 billion, organized crime is about the same size as all the U.S. metal producers (iron, steel, aluminum, copper, etc.), is larger than the U.S. paper industry, is larger than the U.S. rubber and tire industry and is about the same size as the textile and apparel industry."[17]

The 1986 Wharton study further estimated that organized crime groups were responsible for 100 percent of the narcotics trade, the loan-sharking business, cargo (trucking, air, and railroad) theft, and cigarette smuggling. Because of their ability to fence stolen goods and organize groups of thieves, organized crime groups accounted for half of all shoplifting and employee theft, about one-fifth of all household and personal theft, 30 percent of the counterfeiting trade, 20 percent of the prostitution trade, and about half of all arson fraud.[18]

As usual, the impact of these incredibly costly crimes fell most heavily on poor and working Americans. Some of the biggest job losses in New York City have occurred in the blue-collar industries systematically looted by the mob and their corrupt political allies in the Democratic Party. Mob-run trucking companies made it prohibitively expensive to operate a garment factory in New York City. Meat packers had to endure mob-controlled unions and unfair competition from mob companies that sold rotten meat. Shipping companies were forced to pay kickbacks and inflated bills or endure organized pilfering. Not surprisingly, many companies simply packed up shop and moved. By the early 1990s large sections of the New

York City port, once the nation's largest, was filled with ancient, empty, rotting piers. The Fulton Street Fish Market had lost hundreds of millions of dollars worth of annual business to competing markets outside the city. And tens of thousands of jobs had been lost in the garment industry.

The decline of these industries can't be blamed on the mob alone—technological and economic changes played an even larger role—but the higher costs that mob-run business imposed on the economy certainly exacerbated the flight of jobs and capital. And decline of the meatpacking, shipping, and garment industries cost the city many other jobs. Companies that had produced goods and services for these industries also departed, leaving in their wake a decaying industrial infrastructure in Brooklyn, Manhattan, and the South Bronx. Young men and women, who could once find unskilled work in these enterprises, now found few opportunities to make a living in the legitimate economy, a factor that has fueled the rise of a huge underground economy.

By the late 1960s it was clear that the basic premises of the law-and-order crusade added up to a recipe for creating street crime. Its leaders' Cold War obsessions revitalized the global drug trade and crippled law enforcement. Their antipathy to social programs made it impossible to deal with the economic changes that were creating a fertile breeding ground for crime. Racism and segregation ensured that millions of blacks and Hispanics were forced to live in decaying urban centers with epidemic levels of violence. One would expect such a failed approach to produce a political backlash and renew debate over violence in America.

In fact, precisely the opposite occurred. As it became increasingly clear that the war on crime was a dismal failure, the debate over the issue narrowed. Democrats worked overtime to show that they were even tougher on crime than Republicans, proposing legislation that made Nixon look suspiciously left-wing. Debates over crime bills came to revolve around whether chain gangs should be tethered together or individually shackled. Issues such as rehabilitation, civil liberties, urban renewal, and poverty were ignored.

Washington's decision once again to ignore the sources of crime could be traced to changes in the global economy. In the 1940s American business elites had supported government programs designed to create a consumer economy that would allow a large class of decently paid blue-collar and white-collar workers to buy homes and consumer goods. Unfortunately, Washington's policy of subsidizing business interests, the military-industrial complex, and the suburbs, created massive social problems that boosted urban crime rates while ignoring the cities and poor farmers. Liberals in the 1960s attempted to address these problems by increasing spending for social programs. But before these programs could have much impact, global economic changes made it harder for government agencies to finance their war on poverty.

Between 1967 and the early 1980s the country was hit with one economic catastrophe after another. As inflation soared in the late 1960s, a stock market crash pushed several brokerages into bankruptcy and prompted an industry-wide consolidation. During the humiliating U.S. withdrawal from Vietnam, American politicians found new evidence of their weakening global power in the Mideast. Oil-producing nations began an embargo to protest U.S. support of Israel, and oil prices skyrocketed, fueling even worse inflation. As employment and productivity slumped, the economy fell into the worst recession since the 1930s. Then new financial problems loomed. In the mid-1970s many savings and loans began to show rising losses and in the early 1980s many commercial banks began reporting huge losses on their loans to third world countries.

This economic crisis grew out of the internal contradictions of the postwar economic system. Initially the opening of foreign markets gave U.S. corporations an enormous competitive advantage over those of other countries, and in the 1950s the whole notion of multinational corporations was inextricably tied to major U.S. industrial firms. But the revival of the European and Japanese economies created powerful global competitors, and investments in the third world by U.S. and other multinational corporations established low-wage, low-cost factories that could undercut the wages paid and prices charged by American factories. Meanwhile, the expansion of U.S. corporations abroad and the military costs of protecting those investments weighed heavily on the economy. The $4.9 trillion spent on the U.S. military in the Cold War era, between 1946 and 1991, channeled investment and research away from civilian uses and manufacturing.[19] Military research produced a number of technological breakthroughs such as the transistor, but the massive Defense Department expenditures gave U.S. companies few incentives to find ways to market new technology to consumers. Overseas corporations, such as Sony, grew to dominate the consumer electronics market in the 1970s. Even in the late 1950s and early 1960s, an era that has been mythologized as a heyday of American economic and military power, signs of economic decay were evident. As U.S. corporations dramatically increased their foreign investments, their aging U.S. factories became less able to compete with Germany, Japan, and the newly industrializing nations of the third world.

Given these problems, it is not surprising that manufacturing productivity grew only 2.7 percent a year in the United States between 1960 and 1985, far lower than that of Japan (8 percent), France (5.5 percent), Germany (5.4 percent), or any other major foreign competitor. The U.S. trade deficit that began in 1971 widened to more than $152 billion by 1987. At home, this translated into massive layoffs and declining living standards. One Labor Department study found that more than 9.7 million Americans lost their jobs to plant closings, layoffs, and bankruptcies between 1979 and 1987—a crucial period in the restructuring of the U.S. economy. Of the 1.8 million workers in the manufacturing sector who lost their jobs, only two-thirds had found full-time employment by 1990, and 28 percent of those were forced to accept pay cuts of more than 20 percent. As a result, median family income, adjusted for inflation, fell from $36,893 in 1973 to $35,419 in 1982, and hourly earnings in the private sector declined from $8.55 in 1973 to $7.40 in 1994 (in 1982 dollars).[20]

To deal with these problems, major corporations and the government embarked on several policies that would have an enormous impact on the war on crime. To improve corporate profits, government officials encouraged a boom in global trade and finance by reducing regulations and laws that limited the free flow of capital and by creating free-trade zones, such as the European Union and the North American Free Trade Agreement (NAFTA). These policies, which made it easier for corporations and investors to move their operations to regions that offered the highest-profit markets, were further encouraged by government to deregulation of financial markets in many countries. Nixon's decision to take the United States off the gold standard and the exponential expansion of the amount of money flowing through the global financial system gave speculative capital still more economic power. Internationally, speculators and major investors were increasingly able to veto basic government policies, such as budget deficits or plans to tax major corporations, by driving down the price of a currency or by moving their money to more business-friendly regions. Closer to home, the boom in global finance allowed speculative capital to touch off a wave of foreign investments, mergers, hostile takeovers, leveraged buy-outs, and financial speculation in the 1980s and 1990s that dramatically restructured the way American corporations did business. To avoid take-overs or to make their companies more attractive to fickle investors, they trimmed costs by laying off millions of workers and shutting down many factories. Finally, as large amounts of capital were moved out of older industrial enterprises and regions in search of higher rates of return on investments, governments found it increasingly difficult to levy new taxes and regulate business activity. To keep major corporations happy, they cut regulations, taxes, and social spending. But as they deregulated the economy, they increased the power of the state to intervene militarily in foreign countries and to crack down on crime with more police and prisons.

Over time, this bitter medicine did improve the bottom line. Corporate profits soared from $188.3 billion in 1980 to $827.3 billion in 1997 and increased from 6.8 to 10.2 percent of GDP, indicating that a much larger share of the nation's economic activity was being grabbed by wealthy investors who were increasingly demanding much higher rates of return. Unfortunately, changes in the global economy that have allowed major corporations to burnish their balance sheets also produced problems for U.S. policymakers seeking to deal with the problem of crime. For starters, the growth in global trade and the movement of manufacturing plants to low-wage centers outside the United States reduced the number of unskilled blue-collar jobs that had been the bedrock of many urban neighborhoods. In 1992 *Business Week* pointed out that almost three million manufacturing jobs had been lost nationwide between 1979 and 1990 and that the work force in some light manufacturing—industries such as apparel that employed many city residents—was down by more than a quarter: "For urban workers who counted on steady factory jobs that require little education, the losses have been devastating." Moreover, from 1973 to 1989, increased competition from low-wage offshore factories had reduced pay for many low-skilled jobs in the United States: for white men in their twenties, pay was reduced by 14 percent; for white school dropouts, by 33 percent; for black men in their twenties, by 24 percent, and for black dropouts, by 50 percent.[21]

The impact was particularly hard on inner cities. Between 1970 and 1992 middle-class taxpayers flocking out of the cities produced massive population losses in New York City (583,000 residents), Chicago (601,000), Detroit (502,000), Philadelphia (396,000), Baltimore (180,000), Cleveland (248,000), Milwaukee (100,000), Boston (89,000), Pittsburgh (237,000), and Buffalo (140,000)—urban centers that had already suffered large declines in the 1960s. Worse, these population shifts were accompanied by large job losses. Researchers at the Urban Institute found that urban city centers "lost 288,000 manufacturing jobs while the outer areas gained 353,000." Losses like these are particularly worrisome because manufacturing is "the industry best-suited to providing higher-wage employment to lower-skilled workers."[22]

Even with the growth of jobs in the service sector, which mainstream economists claimed would rescue urban economies, the job picture remained dismal. The Urban Institute found that between 1976 and 1986, two-thirds of all new jobs were in the suburbs. In 1976 more jobs were available in center cities (17.4 million) than the suburbs (16.0 million), but by 1986 the situation had reversed itself: 24 million jobs in the suburbs, 21.2 million in central cities. Between 1980 and 1986 the suburbs produced all the new jobs in the metropolitan regions of Chicago, Cleveland, Dayton, and Detroit and 75 to 97 percent in Los Angeles, Newark, Washington, D.C., Philadelphia, Milwaukee, and St. Louis. The result, was a dramatic increase in poverty and a noticeable drop in wages for unskilled inner-city residents: "In 23 of the 30 largest cities, the poverty rate increased during the 1980s." Even in metropolitan areas where poverty declined, it dropped at a faster rate in the suburbs than in the inner cities.[23]

In short, the restructuring of the 1970s and 1980s greatly reduced the availability of manufacturing jobs, which had anchored the economy of many urban neighborhoods, and made it much harder for unskilled workers to find jobs—an economic catastrophe that played a crucial role in the rise in crime rates between 1983 and 1991. One sign of this can be found in a precipitous drop in the number of poorly educated men in the labor force. Between 1967 and 1982 the number of men who were not either in school or in the labor force more than doubled for both whites and nonwhites, and by 1992 about one-quarter of all male high school dropouts had no official employment. Similarly, the wages of the lowest-paid workers dropped about 30 percent between 1970 and 1989. Such trends cut across racial lines but were particularly evident for black men. The number of black high school graduates who had not worked in the preceding year jumped from 9 percent in 1974 to 22.9 percent in 1982.[24]

Although conservatives have attempted to blame these dismal numbers on the debilitating effects of welfare, more obvious culprits were the changing job market and the poor educational opportunities offered by cash-strapped cities. More than one million jobs that did not require a high school diploma were lost in inner-city areas of Boston, Chicago, Cleveland, Detroit, and New York in the 1970s. By 1980, Thomas Edsall notes, "in Baltimore only 29.6 percent of the jobs . . . did not require a high school education but 54.4 percent of the black men in the city did not have high school degrees and 67.5 percent of those black men who were not working did not have high school degrees." Similar numbers could be found in New York City and Philadelphia. As a result, the unemployment rate for black high school dropouts in the three cities jumped from between 23 and 28 percent in 1970 to between 43 and 50 percent in 1980. Nationwide, the number of black high school dropouts who had never held a job climbed from 15.1 percent in 1974 to 40.1 percent in 1982, and the percentage of black men between the ages of twenty and twenty-four who had a job or who were looking for work dropped by 25 percent between 1973 and 1986.[25]

Likewise, the economic diaspora played an important role in the creation of gangs in the urban ghetto, a booming underground economy, and some of the worst violence associated with the drug trade. Research on gangs, going back to the days of the murderous white ethnic gangs of the Lower East Side of Manhattan, have shown that young people once tended to get involved in gangs in their teens and then to drift out of crime as they acquired families and jobs. In a study of young men between 1976 and 1989, researcher Delbert Elliot confirmed these earlier findings: "Participation in serious violent offending behavior (aggravated assault, forcible rape and robbery) increases from ages 11 and 12 to ages 15 and 16 and then declines dramatically with advancing age." But as jobs disappeared, so did opportunities for a way out of petty crime and gang membership. Elliot found that crime rates for blacks youths did not decline as fast as for whites as they aged, a difference paralleling higher unemployment rates among blacks.[26] In short, the disappearance of low-skilled jobs and the decline in wages for such work made it much harder for inner-city youths to abandon gang violence and crime. Lacking legitimate work, many turned to the underground drug trade, which was increasingly controlled by violent gangs.

In 1995, according to a city comptroller's report, New York City's underground economy topped $58 billion—almost equal to one-fifth of the $300 billion worth of goods and service the city produces each year. Most of that cash ($42.4 billion) comprises untaxed income from legitimate activities carried out by people and businesses looking for ways to make ends meet: street vendors who don't report their income to the IRS, hairdressers who work off the books, small businesses that don't pay sales taxes, waiters who underreport their tips, sweatshops that pay their workers under the table. About $16.2 billion, however, can be traced to illegal enterprises such as drug deals, extortion, prostitution, gambling, and auto theft.[27]

Nor is New York a unique case. The expansion of the global economy in the postwar world that forced impoverished Asian peasants into the opium trade had similar effects in Latin America, where mechanized agribusiness, imported manufacturing goods, and the debt crisis of the late 1970s and early 1980s destroyed peasant economies. In Peru alone, some 70,000 people moved into coca-producing regions in the 1980s as the economy shrank by 20 percent, inflation hit 2,775 percent, and real wages dropped by 60 percent. Similar stories could be found in Colombia, where the cocaine trade boomed as coffee prices fell more than 33 percent between 1980 and 1986, and Bolivia, where production of coca leaves skyrocketed as prices for tin and natural gas plummeted. By the late 1980s Peru earned about $1 billion a year by exporting drugs, primarily cocaine, and Colombia earned $7 to $15 billion in net profits. By 1995 the U.S. State Department estimated that more than 194,100 tons of coca leaves were being produced annually in Latin America, a significant jump from the 105,000 to 147,000 metric tons produced in 1984. Peasants who once planted coffee or produced handicrafts now till fields of coca shrub or work in the mobile cocaine-refining labs run by global drug cartels. U.S. Department of Justice researchers estimate that about a million people grow, process, and smuggle cocaine in Peru, Bolivia, and Columbia. Just how many people are employed in illegal activities in the United States isn't known, but a Justice Department study estimates that there were about 249,324 gang members and 4,881 gangs in 1992.[28]

Surveying drug economies in 1989, researcher Jo Ann Kawell found that "about 600,000 people in [Colombia, Peru, and Bolivia] are directly employed in the production and distribution of cocaine. They include nearly 450,000 coca farmers and about 150,000 people employed in making paste. . . . Then there are the almost 15,000 people who transport the paste, the over 2,500 people who refine it into cocaine, and some 1,000 people who work in the import-export end of the business, including the big traffickers." Those at the bottom of the drug trade rarely see much profit from their activities. Researchers note that Andean peasants who grow the coca leaves rarely earn more than a few thousand dollars a year, and in Southeast Asia the average peasant family of four earns no more than $375 to $450 a year cultivating opium. Higher incomes can be found in the U.S. street-level drug trade, but a 1989 Rand Corporation study of drug dealers at the height of the crack plague found that the typical dealer made only $10,000 a year—less than the official poverty-level income for a family of four.[29]

The booming underground economy has been very good for global crime groups, however, who have capitalized on economic desperation to recruit new members, smuggle goods, and launder money. Xavier Tang, superintendent of the Organized Crime and Triad Bureau in Hong Kong, points out that the lion's share of profits from the global drug trade goes to middlemen who bring the drug from peasant growers to the streets of New York. "You can buy a unit of heroin [about 700 grams] from a factory in the Golden Triangle for about $2,500," Tang explained during a 1995 interview. "The price for the same amount will double or triple in price by the time it reaches Bangkok and increase by ten to fifteen times by the time it reaches Hong Kong. By the time it reaches New York City, it will sell for $125,000 to $250,000." Tang and other law enforcement officials say it is impossible to know how much illegal money these groups move through the global financial system, though some have estimated more than $300 billion a year in drug money is laundered each year. It is clear that dramatic changes in the global financial system—electronic money transfers, twenty-four-hour trading of stocks and bonds, the establishment of loosely regulated offshore financial centers, computerized currency trading—have made it much easier for crooks to move money around the world. "It is very difficult to trace money once it's been moved into offshore havens that have strict bank secrecy laws," explains Raymond Kerr of the FBI's New York office. "In a few hours, you can send the money through five countries, but it can easily take us four months or a year to track that money. By that time, it's often long gone."[30]

This ability to move assets around has allowed organized crime groups to accumulate large financial resources, making them economic power-houses in many parts of the world. Similarly, the liberalization of global trade rules and the creation of free-trade zones have allowed organized crime groups to expand their criminal empires. Brookings Institution researcher Peter Andreas points out that about 80 percent of the cocaine, 20 percent of the heroin, and 60 percent of the marijuana that flows over the Mexican border into the United States can easily be hidden among the 232 million people, 82.3 million cars, and 2.8 million trucks that annually cross the Rio Grande. "Hiding drug shipments within the growing volume of U.S.-Mexican trade has become the favorite method of smuggling co-caine into the U.S.," Andreas explains. "A 1993 report written by an intelligence officer of the U.S. embassy in Mexico City claims that cocaine traffickers are establishing factories, warehouses and trucking companies as fronts in Mexico to take advantage of the boom in cross-border com-merce now occurring under NAFTA."[31]

The growing power of organized crime groups makes programs to improve education, attack poverty, and revitalize urban centers more cru-cial than ever before. In the 1940s and 1950s, massive government subsidies raised the living and housing standards of the white ethnics who had once produced the nation's most vicious mobsters. But the collapse of the postwar economic order has made it much harder for governments around the world to attack the root causes of crime. Footloose capital, which has decimated the economic base of many cities, has also encouraged govern-ments to back away from the kind of social welfare spending that charac-terized the Johnson administration's war on poverty.

Former Citibank chairman Walter Wriston argued in 1993 that the rise of hugely profitable international markets has made it easier for major companies to move their capital and operations to countries that provide the best investment climate. "As recently as 1980, the daily volume of trading in the foreign exchange market in the U.S. was estimated at only $10.3 billion," Wriston has noted. "By 1989, this total had grown to an average of $183.2 billion per day. Now including Eurodollars, estimates are that two to three trillion dollars a day are exchanged in Manhattan alone. ... This huge floating pool of capital goes where it is wanted and stays where it is well-treated. If people who own that capital perceive that a nation's economic policies are bad or that the return on their investment ... is higher in another country, it goes. ... Thanks to the growing power of technology, the ability of a sovereign power to dictate investment is overwhelmed by the new world order of traders sitting in front of flashing computer screens. ... Borders are not boundaries anymore. Foreign exchange control is no longer possible. In effect, technology gives governments a choice: create hospitable climates for capital or suffer the consequences."[32]

Many governments complied. On a regional level, Europeans radically opened their borders by expanding their free-trade zone in 1992; the United States concluded a free-trade agreement with Canada and Mexico; Latin American governments in the Southern Cone have established their own free-trade zone, and Asian governments are slowly moving toward the creation of a free-trade union. Throughout Europe, both right-wing and left-wing parties cut social programs and deregulated their economies in the 1980s and 1990s. Meanwhile, the massive third world debt crisis of the 1980s forced many Latin American countries to cut back on social services and liberalize trading rules—a trend that helped large organized crime groups expand their power over the legitimate economy in Colombia, Peru, Venezuela, Panama and Mexico. More recently, Asia's economic woes have forced governments in many countries to liberalize their economies and open them up to foreign investment in order to attract badly needed new capital and loans from international agencies such as the IMF.

A similar story can be found in Washington. According to the Center on Budget and Policy Priorities, between 1981 and 1992—a crucial period in the restructuring of the global economy and rising crime rates—federal spending for subsidized housing fell by 82 percent, job training and employment programs were cut by 63 percent, and the budget for community development and social-service block grants was trimmed by 40 percent. The federal government and the states allowed inflation to eat away at welfare benefits, which once permitted a family of four to live at the poverty level; no state currently provides grants and subsidies equal to 100 percent of the poverty level. In 1991 alone, thirty-one states froze Aid to Families with Dependent Children (AFDC) benefits, and nine states reduced them.[33]

Meanwhile, economic and political policies put in place decades ago continue to siphon huge sums out of major urban centers. For example, in 1994 the average New Yorker got back only $3,948 in services per $5,000 in tax dollars sent to Washington: the city as a whole ran a deficit of about $9 billion; and New York State sent Washington $18.9 billion more in taxes than it got back. In sharp contrast, Virginia got back $13.7 billion more than it paid. Four northern states—New York, Illinois, New Jersey, and Michigan—all with large numbers of poor urban residents who desperately needed federal aid—were in effect cheated out of $61.8 billion in social services. Not surprisingly, given this enormous transfer of wealth, between 1991 and 1993—when the rest of the nation created 2.3 million jobs—New York State lost 300,000.[34]

Government policies have encouraged capital to move out of the cities for quite some time, but the Reagan, Bush, and Clinton administrations have made it even harder for them to finance social programs that might do something about the sources of crime. Federal cutbacks in the 1980s cost New York City a whopping $33.7 billion in federal aid, and the federal government's contribution to the city's budget fell from 17.9 percent in 1980 to only 9.3 percent in 1990. Clinton too continued the trend by signing bills reducing social spending for the urban poor. Cutbacks to Medicaid alone will probably reduce the already inequitable share received by New York State by another $24 to $27 billion between 1996 and 2002, and welfare reform proposals could cost New York City another $1.5 billion in federal aid.[35]

Further, federal tax breaks continue to encourage wealthy Americans and corporations to move capital out of the cities and poorer communities. For example, multinational corporations are allowed to deduct foreign taxes from their U.S. bill, a system that promotes them to move factories from older industrial cities to low-wage zones, which also tend to offer low tax rates. This tax loophole will cost the federal government at least $95 billion in lost revenues between 1996 and 2003, enough to fund the $6.5 billion spent on worker-retraining programs for fourteen and a half years. Accelerated depreciation, which encourages companies to build new factories rather than remodel old ones located in cities, will cost $259 billion over the same period; capital gains tax loopholes, which primarily benefit the wealthy and do little for property owners in depressed urban centers, will cost $258 billion. Other breaks include $204 billion for the insurance industry and its products; $21 billion in oil, gas, and energy tax breaks; $10 billion for timber, agriculture, and minerals; $7 billion for banks and other financial institutions. In 1996 alone, the federal government handed out nearly $450 billion worth of tax breaks that specifically benefited wealthy Americans and large corporations.[36]

Over time, these trends have produced a nation-state that is miserly to its citizens, generous to major corporations. It has abdicated many of the traditional functions of government, leaving basic decisions about monetary policy, interest rates, employment, regulations, and movements of capital to the invisible hand of the international market. And as the new global economy exacerbates social problems and government agencies reduce funding for programs designed to address those problems, the state has responded by becoming a more direct instrument of social control. Even after the collapse of Communism in Russia and Eastern Europe, the United States continued to spend heavily on the military to protect foreign investment, while at home it launched an unprecedented crackdown on the forces of social disorder—again, with disastrous results.

Chapter 9:
Addicted to Crime

There is no people so prone as the American to take the law into their own hands when the sanctity of human life is threatened and the rights of property invaded. . . . Judge Lynch is an American by birth and character. . . . Every lamppost in Chicago will be decorated with a Communist carcass if necessary.

—Chicago Tribune *editorial, 1875*

Casual drug users should be taken out and shot.

—*Chief Daryl Gates, Los Angeles Police Department*

EVEN AS HE LEFT OFFICE, PRESIDENT REAGAN WAS demonstrating his genius for creating powerful political myths. "I wasn't a great communicator, but I communicated great things," Reagan noted in his farewell address in January 1989. "They didn't spring full bloom from my brow, they came from the heart of a great nation—from our experience, or wisdom, and our belief in the principles that have guided us for two centuries. They called it the Reagan revolution. Well, I'll accept that, but for me it always seemed more like a great rediscovery, a rediscovery of our values and our common sense." The result, he added, was that "we meant to change a nation and instead we changed the world."[1]

There is little doubt that life in America changed, but there are good reasons for doubting the inevitability of that transformation or its beneficial consequences. Economic restructuring was hardly a return to the natural order of things or an effort to create a world based on common sense. To carry out its agendas, the right had to build political support for distinctly unpopular government policies—cutting taxes for the rich,

slashing government social programs, and deregulating corporate crime—
that improved corporate profits and transferred wealth from the average
citizen to the rich. Between 1977 and 1989, taxes were cut by an average of
$49,262 for the wealthiest 1 percent of the population, while they were
raised another $81 for 80 percent of the population. Domestic spending
declined from about 5 percent of the gross domestic product (GDP) in 1980
to about 3.5 percent in 1990: in 1996 major corporations and the rich
received $455 billion worth of tax breaks, about 2.5 times the federal
spending on means-tested entitlement programs, such as welfare and Medi-
caid, designed to help less affluent Americans. In 1976 the top 1 percent
owned 19 percent of all private wealth, but by 1995 they owned 40 percent.
Between 1979 and 1993 the income of the wealthiest fifth of the population
grew by 18 percent and that of the upper-middle fifth by 5 percent, while
the bottom fifth saw their real income drop by 17 percent, the lower-middle
fifth recorded an 8 percent loss and the middle fifth lost 3 percent.[2]

Meanwhile, Reagan, Bush, and Clinton pushed for programs that hurt
blacks, women, immigrants, and labor. Conservative appointees to the
courts gutted affirmative action programs, reduced welfare benefits, and
boosted poverty rates for minorities and women. The federal government
did not effectively enforce existing labor laws and continued to encourage
U.S. corporations to move their jobs overseas, thus crippling organized
labor and reducing the number of decently paid manufacturing jobs. Tough
anti-immigrant laws encouraged the growth of sweatshops and increased
discrimination against native-born Hispanics, Asians, and legal immigrants. By 1993 there was a shortage of 4.7 million low-rent homes forcing
60 percent of all low-income families to pay more than half their incomes
in rent. By 1990 average wages for black Americans had fallen about 15
percent since the early 1970s, and even when overall unemployment rates
dropped to 6 percent in the mid-1990s, black unemployment rates remained at 11 percent for all black men and around 25 percent for those
under the age of twenty-five. Between 1970 and 1995 the minimum wage
lost 30 percent of its purchasing power; welfare benefits, 20 percent of their
value. Average weekly wages dropped 18.8 percent between 1973 and 1994.
Among teenagers, in 1993 some two-fifths of low-income Hispanics, a
quarter of all low-income blacks, and a fifth of poor whites dropped out of
school. Of all U.S. children under the age of eighteen, about 20 percent live

in poverty—far more than in Canada (9.3 percent), Australia (9 percent), Britain (7.4 percent), France (4.6 percent), Germany (2.6 percent), or Sweden (1.6 percent). Finally, the United States has the most inequitable distribution of wealth of any developed nation. Given the longstanding relationship of poor education, unemployment, poverty, and crime, it is not surprising that American homicide rates remained far higher during this period than those in any other developed country.[3]

Although few politicians seem particularly concerned about such issues today, it is important to remember that after the passage of significant civil rights legislation, Watergate, and the defeat of U.S.-backed forces in Vietnam, liberals, blacks, women, and Hispanics pushed successfully for further reforms, thus building up an institutional base for long-term progressive agendas. Feminists came within a few states of passing an equal rights amendment that would have constitutionally guaranteed women's rights, and consumer and environmental groups succeeded in getting Nixon to set up the Consumer Products Safety Commission, the Environmental Protection Agency, and the Occupational Safety and Health Administration. Drug policy reformers even convinced several states, notably Oregon and Alaska, to reduce penalties for marijuana or legalize possession of small amounts of pot.

Even after Reagan took power, many polls indicated strong support for liberal agendas. Between 1981 and 1983 the number of Americans who believed Reagan was going too far in cutting back government social programs jumped from 37 percent to 52 percent and in 1982 large majorities favored retaining government regulations that protected the environment, industrial safety, and government lands. About three-quarters of all Americans said they supported traditional Democratic positions on typical New Deal issues—government management of the economy, protection of Social Security and worker welfare—and large majorities also supported abortion rights, affirmative action when not linked to specific quotas, and social spending designed to benefit the poor.

In short, the Reagan revolution had to be created from the top down. The rise of the right was not a return to the natural order of things or "a rediscovery of our values and common sense." Elites had to mold popular opinion to suit their economic and political interests. To do that, the right mobilized billions of dollars in campaign contributions from major corporations and wealthy individuals who were struggling to overcome the economic crisis of the 1970s. The number of corporate political action committees (PACs) grew from 89 in 1972 to 1,251 in 1980, when they poured $39 million into House and Senate races. PACs from oil, chemical, lumber, paper and other industries that had been hurt by increased government regulation provided the financial backing for a surge of GOP House and Senate victories in 1978 and 1980. In the 1977 to 1984 period Republicans raised better than half a billion dollars more than the Democrats ($766.9 million compared with $201.4 million). Corporate advocacy advertising, much of which was designed to burnish the image of business and to attack regulations, grew from $400 million a year in the mid-1970s to nearly $1 billion in 1980. Major foundations and wealthy entrepreneurs also spent huge sums, pouring money into the Law and Economics Center at Emory University, the New Coalition for Economic and Social Change, the Heritage Foundation, the American Enterprise Institute, the Committee on the Present Danger, and other think tanks that became leading proponents of free-market policies, deregulation, decreased social spending, and increased military spending.[4]

Money, however, was not enough to carry the day. The right also needed a large cadre of dedicated followers and found it in the growing Christian right, which was heavily subsidized by wealthy conservatives such as the Hunt brothers. By the early 1980s such right-wing evangelical ministers as Jerry Falwell and Pat Robertson were said to have be pulling in $500 million to $1 billion a year in contributions. They used this wealth, their tax-free status, and government giveaways of public air time to preach conservative agendas over 1,400 radio stations, 3,500 local television and cable channels, and 4 satellite systems. In 1981 the top ten religious programs reached about 14.9 million viewers, and a research team at the Annenberg School of Communications found that about 13.2 million people (6.2 percent of the television audience) viewed religious programming each week. By 1985 Pat Robertson, who had received a $10 million donation in 1970 from the oil-rich Hunt brothers, had a budget of about $230 million and broadcast on some 200 television stations. In 1981, Jerry Falwell's various enterprises—which included the Moral Majority (said to have about 400,000 members), the Old Time Gospel Hour, and Liberty Baptist College—brought in more than $70 million. Oral Roberts pulled in some $60 million, and Jim Bakker,

$51 million. Bill Bright's Campus Crusade, which received millions in contributions from the Hunts, spent nearly $1 billion between 1976 and 1980.[5]

The shift of big business and many wealthy elites to Reagan and the right obviously provided conservatives with the money to get their message to a larger public through think tanks, paid advertising, political campaigns, and televangelists. But they still had to craft a message that would convince many people to embrace policies that would primarily benefit the rich. In the 1910s, radicals, immigrants, and the IWW were portrayed as terrifying symbols of social decay and subversion that conservatives used to mobilize political support. In the 1950s, reds under the bed and behind the iron curtain performed that function; in the 1960s, conservatives invoked urban violence, khaki-clad black-power revolutionaries and pot-smoking radical students to attack the civil rights movement, the war on poverty, and anti-war protesters. Not surprisingly, then, in the 1980s and 1990s the right once again launched a campaign against the dangerous classes, using stereotypes of Hispanic drug dealers, black teen gangs, unwed welfare moms, drugged-out kids, and secular liberals to boost support for conservative agendas.

The impact of that campaign of fear was particularly evident in the mobilization of the so-called New Right and conservative white evangelicals, who had a history of supporting white supremacist and segregationist policies. Three prominent new right leaders—Richard Viguerie, Howard Phillips, and Paul Weyrich—first attracted national attention in an unsuccessful 1976 attempt to take over George Wallace's American Independent Party, which was a bastion of the old racist southern right. Southern New Right ministers had established all-white private schools in the 1960s after court decisions forced public schools to desegregate, and other ministers and their congregations joined the New Right when the Carter administration attacked the tax-exempt status of such schools. Ultimately, white evangelical voters accounted for two-thirds of Reagan's ten-point-margin over Jimmy Carter.[6]

The right also used fear tactics to mobilize disgruntled middle-class and working voters in the South and the North who had traditionally voted for Democrats. Like Nixon before him, Reagan used coded attacks on affirmative action and welfare that played well in the South, where he garnered at least 141 electoral votes—about half the number he needed for victory—in the 1980 and 1984 presidential campaigns. In the North he deftly used attacks on minorities to court white voters who faced rising crime and slumping economies. A mid-1980s poll of Democrats who had just become Republicans found that "these white Democratic defectors express a profound distaste for blacks."[7]

Nor were blacks the only groups targeted by the right. Conservatives courted votes from blue-collar workers by blaming immigrants for high unemployment rates and by passing draconian laws that made it harder for immigrants to find work legally or receive social services. New Right evangelicals were mobilized for conservative causes by attacks on abortion rights and feminist causes. The wealthy flocked to politicians who blamed high taxes on spendthrift liberals.

Significantly, the groups that were the focus of larger conservative attacks on the welfare state were the same as those blamed for the problem of crime: minorities, women, labor, young people, civil libertarians, and liberals. Of course, women, blacks, and young people, who were heavily victimized by street crime, had little control over the judicial system, and were at most minor players in the more costly corporate and organized crime. But such details scarcely mattered to the spendthrift generals of the war on crime; political expediency was more important, and symbolic images of the alleged enemies in the war on crime and narcotics helped them shift the political spectrum to the right. When criminal suspects were released because the evidence against them was improperly obtained, civil libertarians were blamed—not incompetent or corrupt police officers. Racially oppressed blacks were transformed into Uzi-toting gangsters. Desperately poor women became crack-crazed, sexually promiscuous welfare moms. Liberals who had fought for social justice in the 1960s evolved into elitist propagandists of drugs and moral decay. Young people who had hit the streets to oppose U.S.-backed drug-dealing dictatorships in the 1960s mutated into potent living symbols of drug abuse, senseless violence, and sexual promiscuity. "Fighting drugs in the eighties and nineties [was a way to fight] a rearguard action against full equality for racial minorities and whipping young people (and often cultural liberals) back into line after they threatened to [achieve power] . . . in the 1960s and 1970s," argues criminologist Diana Gordon in *The Return of the Dangerous Classes.* "Resistance to race and gender equality, greater emancipation of youth and civil liberties would be limited to the authoritarian fringe if it could not assume the cloak of righteous containment of identifiably dangerous people. Targeting druggies and kingpins ensures both legitimacy for political actors' embrace of 'traditional values' and a mass following for cultural conservatism."[8]

Still, the focus on narcotics to mobilize political support for larger conservative agendas did not occur overnight. In its early years the Reagan administration actually cut funds for anti-narcotics efforts. In 1982, when the United States was in the middle of a severe recession, a Gallup poll found that crime ranked as the tenth most pressing problem facing the country—down from sixth in 1976 and first in 1968.[9] The drop in public concern reflected widespread economic problems such as joblessness and inflation, and Reagan deftly used the economic malaise to mobilize political support for tax cuts, deregulation, and reduced social spending. But as the economy improved, conservative politicians increasingly turned to the symbolism of the war on drugs to promote larger conservative agendas.

This increased emphasis, it should be stressed, was not related to either increased drug use—which had been declining since the late 1970s—or rising public concern. Only 2 percent of the American public identified drugs as the most important problem facing the nation in 1985, when politicians began jumping on the anti-drug bandwagon, and only 11 percent in 1988, when Congress passed increased sentences for drug possession and made certain drug offenses punishable by death. As the *Washington Post* admitted in 1994, the "hyper-concern about drugs was largely the result of the media's sudden interest in the subject, rather than an increase in the prevalence or use of illicit narcotics. . . . When the media lost interest in the drug story, [after 1992] it fell like a rock from the top of the polls," even though teen drug use was once again increasing.[10]

While there was little relationship between the media hype surrounding the drug war and the severity of the problem, the portrayal of the war on cocaine closely mirrored the larger political debates of the period, indicating its symbolic role in the rise of the right. In the 1970s the Carter administration considered proposals to decriminalize pot and to enact more humane policies toward drug users; drug policy reformers convinced several states, notably Oregon and Alaska, to reduce penalties for pot or legalize possession of small amounts. But this willingness of the liberal establishment to consider and occasionally embrace alternative drug policies—

as well as civil liberties, racial and gender equality, gay rights, and alterative lifestyles that challenged traditional values—left it open to attacks. Carter's move to liberalize drug policies was abandoned after several White House employees were accused of snorting cocaine, and the administration's drug czar was forced to resign after prescribing Quaaludes for a White House aide. By 1979 the Carter administration had abandoned efforts to include tobacco in its drug policies, and to ward off conservative attacks it declared a "war on marijuana" and began pushing the line that permissive social values were the major cause of drug abuse.[11]

Meanwhile, conservatives seized on the drug scandals of the Carter administration to blame narcotics use on liberal social attitudes and the rejection of mainstream values. These stereotypes were reinforced when John Belushi and David Kennedy died of drug overdoses, and a number of celebrities—musician John Phillips, actors Richard Dreyfuss and Stacy Keach, and auto tycoon John DeLorean—were put on trial for narcotics. Under attack from the right, liberals quickly abandoned their lukewarm support for changes in drug laws, and a mainstream consensus emerged that made moral values and legal retribution at the centerpiece of the drug war. By the late 1980s Bush's drug czar William Bennett would declare that "the drug crisis is a crisis of authority—in every sense of the term 'authority.' What [we] . . . can do is exert the political authority necessary to make a sustained commitment to the drug war. We must build more prisons. There must be more jails." Even critics of these policies took care not to challenge their basic terms. In 1992, Senator Joseph Biden's Judiciary Committee issued a 192-page critique of the Bush administration's drug policy that never once mentioned the words "racism," "AIDS," "poverty," "tobacco," or "civil liberties." When Surgeon General Joycelyn Elders indicated that the Clinton administration might study the issue of legalizing some drugs, a White House spokesman immediately told reporters that "the President is against legalizing drugs . . . and he is not interested in studying the issue."[12]

The shift in public debate was mirrored by a stampede to pass one piece of repressive legislation after another. In the late 1970s Senator Ted Kennedy joined Senator Strom Thurmond to sponsor legislation that would completely overhaul federal law enforcement, touching off a process that eventually created mandatory sentences for all federal crimes. Following Reagan's declaration of a war on drugs in 1982, Congress passed the

Comprehensive Crime Control Act of 1984 (which established tough minimum sentences and increased by 40 percent the average sentences served
by federal drug offenders between 1985 and 1990) and the Bail Reform Act
of 1984 (which made it harder for suspects to be released on bail before
trial). The death of basketball star Len Bias, erroneously attributed to crack,
prompted the Democrats to bolster their credentials five weeks before the
fall election by passing the Anti-Drug Abuse Act of 1986, which increased
sentences for most drugs and established draconian punishments for crack
possession: 1.7 ounces would bring a mandatory ten-year sentence (compared with 11 pounds of powdered cocaine or 2.2 pounds of heroin). Then
in 1988 the so-called Kingpin Act established the death penalty for major
traffickers and made a five-year sentence mandatory for possession of only
five grams of crack. In fiscal 1989 federal spending to fight illegal narcotics
jumped to $6.6 billion, a huge increase from the $1.5 billion spent in 1981.[13]

These efforts reached a fever pitch with the election of George Bush, who
had directed an ineffective Miami task force against the cocaine trade in the
early 1980s. After using the infamous Willie Horton ads to overcome an
eighteen-point deficit in the polls during the 1988 campaign, Bush consistently attacked as "un-American" liberals who wanted to deal with the
causes of crime. Speaking to a group of Ohio policemen a month before
the election, he blasted critics who, he said, were "lost in the thickets of
liberal sociology. Just as when it comes to foreign policy, they always 'Blame
America First,' when it comes to crime and criminals, they always seem to
'Blame Society First.'" Federal spending to fight illegal narcotics almost
doubled, to $12.7 billion, in 1992, and Bush expanded the Reagan admini-
stration's policy of using the Pentagon in the drug war, going so far as to
invade Panama to oust the drug-dealing dictator Manuel Noriega. By the
end of his four-year term, Bush had spent more than $45 billion to fight
the war on drugs, more than double the amount Reagan spent in two
terms.[14]

Bush eventually vetoed his own crime bill—which featured forty-four
new crimes punishable by death—because Congress added tough anti-gun
restrictions. But crime legislation took on new life after the election of Bill
Clinton, who had spent much of his career proving his law-and-order
credentials. As governor of Arkansas he signed some seventy death warrants
and laws providing long sentences for selling only small amounts of nar-

cotics, thus doubling the number of people behind bars in Arkansas. Meanwhile, as head of the Democratic Leadership Conference, a conservative policy group massively funded by major corporations, Clinton worked to shift the crime debate from causes and long-term solutions to short-term responses such as more prisons and tougher sentences.[15]

Not surprisingly, Clinton's much awaited anti-crime proposals were difficult to distinguish from those of his Republican predecessors. Besides signing a $30 billion anti-crime bill that designated sixty new capital crimes, the Clinton administration spent $54.4 billion between 1993 and 1997 to fight the war on drugs, more than any previous administration. While slashing programs that helped young people and signing a welfare reform bill that will push more than a million people, most of them children, into poverty, Clinton championed such measures as school uniforms, mandatory curfews, and drug tests for any youths seeking a driver's license. Any opinion challenging the far-right orthodoxy that putting large numbers of young black men behind bars was the best way to fight the war on drugs was quickly suppressed by the Clinton White House. Surgeon General Joycelyn Elders was pushed out of office for remarks that legalizing drugs should be considered. A Justice Department study showed the amount wasted in prosecuting and incarcerating low-level, nonviolent drug offenders; it was censored, delayed, and then ignored. Likewise, research on needle exchange programs was quashed, and the Sentencing Commission's report that crack sentences were racially biased was rejected. In 1997 the administration pledged to crack down on stores that sold pot to patients who used it to treat AIDS and glaucoma. Frustrated by Clinton's adoption of so many conservative policies, Republican presidential candidate Bob Dole was driven to complain in 1996, "There's no reason for him being president if he listens to me all the time. I might as well be president."[17]

Law-and-order policies were making similar gains on state and local levels. By the start of 1994 thirteen states had restored the death penalty; thirty-five had mandated additional penalties for offenders who had two or three prior felony convictions; and ten had passed three-strikes legislation—requiring life imprisonment following three felony convictions. At least fifteen states increased penalties for drug crimes between 1987 and 1990, and all but one lengthened the sentence for peddling drugs to minors. The average sentence for drug offenders in federal courts jumped from 47.1

months in 1980 to 85.4 months in 1995 (doubling the federal prison population) and in state courts from 27 months in 1986 to 40 in 1995; the number of people in state prisons for drug offenses jumped 665 percent between 1981 and 1989. By 1995, 23 percent of all inmates in state prisons and 60 percent in federal prisons were drug offenders (up from 6 and 25 percent respectively, in 1980) and 21.4 percent of people on probation had violated drug laws. With less room for really violent criminals the percentage of people sent to state prison for violent crimes dropped from 48 percent in 1980 to 18.9 percent in 1995.[18]

The seemingly irrational policy, focusing scarce law enforcement resources on nonviolent drug offenders while violent crime was rising, did follow a certain logic, however. Virtually every aspect of the war on drugs was deftly utilized by law-and-order politicians to support larger conservative agendas. Even in foreign policy and military spending it played an important role in the right's campaign to revive the Cold War, which had been under attack since the ill-conceived Vietnam War and Nixon's move toward detente with Russia and China. "President Reagan came to office with a mission: to roll back the frontiers of world communism, especially in the third World," note Peter Dale Scott and Jonathan Marshall. "With the American public's anticommunist sentiments dulled by a decade of detente and memories of Vietnam, his administration [faced an uphill battle to] revive support for [this crusade]. . . . One answer was to invent a new threat, closely associated with communism and even more frightening to the public: narcoterrorism. . . . As two private colleagues of Oliver North noted in a prospectus for a propaganda campaign to link the Sandinistas and drugs, 'the chance to have a single issue which no one can publicly disagree with is irresistible.'"[19]

Just as conservatives had used booze and drugs to bolster support for an anti-radical crackdown after the First World War, Reagan and then Bush blamed the drug problem on Communist governments and foreign conspiracies. "The link between the government of such Soviet allies as Cuba and Nicaragua and international narcotics trafficking and terrorism is becoming increasingly clear," Reagan argued in 1986. "These twin evils— narcotics trafficking and terrorism—represent the most insidious and dangerous threats to the hemisphere today." Likewise, Secretary of State George Shultz attacked the "complicity of communist governments in the drug trade that . . . also includes support for international terrorism and other forms of organized violence." By the end of the 1980s the U.S. government had issued reports arguing that guerrillas, terrorists, or Communist Party officials in Peru, Syria, Cuba, Bulgaria, Nicaragua, Colombia, Bolivia, and Afghanistan were deeply involved in the global narcotics trade.[20]

At the same time, Reagan and Bush pushed to get the military more involved in the drug war as a way of justifying the Pentagon's bloated budgets. Particularly in Latin America, their administrations attempted to link major cocaine cartels to Communist guerrillas and international terrorists—an idea coined by Lewis Tambs, whom Reagan appointed as ambassador to Colombia in 1983. An ardent supporter of the far-right Guatemalan and Honduran militaries, which were involved in the cocaine trade, Tambs chose to ignore trafficking by U.S. allies and focus on left-wing governments or movements. He had, he said, only "two songs on my harp: marijuana and Marxists; cocaine and communists."[21]

U.S. policies against narcotics thus took on the character of a Cold War military operation. Although the U.S. military had traditionally refused to become involved in fighting drug trafficking, Congress passed and Reagan signed a 1985 bill requiring the armed services to do so. Reagan became the first president to declare drug production, smuggling, and processing a threat to national security: in 1986 he issued a secret directive that authorized greater use of military equipment, troops, and intelligence resources to assist domestic and foreign drug police. Very quickly, the militarization of the drug war became a new rationale for military intervention. Reagan used allegations of drug trafficking by the Sandinistas to justify massive U.S. support for the contras who were seeking to topple the left-wing government. In 1986 he sent 160 troops into the Bolivian jungle to attack cocaine-processing labs in a move the Pentagon called Operation Blast Furnace. President Bush, who continued to send troops to Bolivia for annual military exercises in the cocaine-producing regions, signed another secret national security directive that allowed U.S. military officials and personnel to work with foreign police in drug-producing regions, and in September 1989 he announced that "for the first time [he would] make available the appropriate resources of America's armed forces" to foreign governments seeking help in the war against drugs.[22]

Following up on these policies, in 1989 Bush dispatched Special Forces units to Peru to help the local military attack drug-processing plants and guerrillas who were allegedly protecting the cocaine farmers, processors, and smugglers, and it was soon thereafter that he sent twenty thousand troops to overthrow President Manuel Noriega of Panama. Virtually all Latin American governments condemned that invasion, but a decade of militarizing the war on drugs made the invasion easy to sell to the American public. Public opinion polls generally supporting Bush's policy also seemed to convince the Pentagon that the war on drugs would be useful in winning approval for the military budget and future invasions. U.S. troops became increasingly active in training local military commanders to fight narcotics traffickers, and the U.S. government began providing aid directly to Latin American militaries so they could fight guerrilla groups with alleged ties to drug traffickers. The Pentagon asked U.S. commanders to develop plans for military campaigns against drug producers and smugglers and in 1989 the secretary of defense said that "detecting and countering the production and trafficking of illegal drugs is a high priority national security mission." By 1998 the Pentagon was spending $1 billion a year to fight drugs.[23]

The symbolism of the drug war also helped conservatives mobilize public support for cutbacks in domestic social programs. News coverage of cocaine abuse in the early 1980s emphasized horror stories of respectable businessmen trading wives for cocaine or professionals degenerating into drug addiction and prostitution. In a massive study of network news coverage of the cocaine crisis, Jimmie Reeves and Richard Campbell note that in the period from 1983 to 1985 most of the victims portrayed in these stories were "white, relatively affluent at one time, [and] now in some kind of formal therapy program" that cost $1,000 a week or more. Increasingly, however, news coverage emphasized that permissive drug use among the liberal upper classes was having a cancerous effect on the rest of society. "Cocaine is widely perceived as the drug of choice for celebrities, including professional athletes and show business luminaries," CBS news anchor Dan Rather noted in a February 1983 newscast. More and more stories showed the spread of cocaine into middle- and working-class homes.[24]

By the end of 1985 the problem of class contagion—a media-created disease whereby permissive ruling-class attitudes corrupted regular folks—had taken a racial turn as news organizations discovered the crack plague. Reporters increasingly featured stories of violent inner-city drug-dealing gangs, law enforcement teams knocking down the doors of crack houses, moms abusing their kids while high on drugs, teens who killed for drugs, and grim urban landscapes of violence and addiction. Nonwhite males had been featured in only 13 percent of such newscasts between 1983 and 1985; they starred in 40 percent of them from 1986 to 1988. Meanwhile, as the proportion of nonwhites appearing in newscasts jumped to 57 percent by 1988, the proportion of whites dropped to only 30 percent, even though whites accounted for about two-thirds of all crack users. "These numbers support our view that during the Reagan era, the cocaine problem as defined by the network news became increasingly associated with people of color," argue Reeves and Campbell, who conducted a wide survey of how the networks covered crack in the 1980s and early 1990s.[25]

Clearly, the war on drugs was being waged against poor Americans, who not coincidentally were also the targets of attacks on social spending and political reform. By the mid-1980s police were instituting huge, almost military-style operations against drug dealers in poor urban neighborhoods, producing an enormous disparity between the way various racial groups were treated by the police. One study estimates that 92 percent of those caught in drug busts in New York City were black or Hispanic. Nationwide, only 3 percent of those sentenced under federal guidelines for crack were white, even though 64 percent of all crack users were white. In 1992, blacks and Hispanics made up 89.7 percent of all those sent to state prison for narcotics.[26]

Women faced a conservative assault on social programs, abortion rights, and feminism. While cutbacks in social programs boosted the number of women living in poverty, the number of women sent to prison also skyrocketed. Between 1980 and 1992 the female prison population jumped 276 percent, in part because of drug arrests, which rose 89 percent between 1982 and 1991. This crackdown largely fell on poor women of color who had already seen their welfare benefits plummet. Nationwide, the number of black women in jail for drugs increased by 828 percent and the number of Hispanic women by 324 percent between 1986 and 1991.[27]

The war on drugs also aided a large attack on organized labor. As the Reagan and Bush administrations were cutting the budgets of federal agencies in charge of enforcing labor laws, conservatives attempted to blame reduced productivity and the declining competitive position of the

United States on drug use in the workplace. "Joint by joint, line by line, pill by pill, the use of illegal drugs on the job has become a crisis for American business," *Newsweek* asserted in January 1983. "Some experts even suggest that one reason the United States is losing its industrial leadership to Japan is that America's work force is so stoned." Buoyed by the public reaction to this and similar articles, many major corporations instituted mandatory drug tests, and by 1990, the business of making workers pee in a bottle had grown to $300 million a year.[28]

Over time, the daily barrage of political speeches and newspaper articles blaming the entire drug problem on moral decay, dangerous social groups, and the permissive purveyors of secular humanism helped mobilize support for a variety of conservative programs. Liberal defenders of civil liberties and more humane approaches to substance abuse could be blamed for spreading the cocaine contagion from affluent whites to lower-class blacks, where the problem assumed deadly proportions. Women, kids, and teens—who were the chief victims of the cutbacks in social programs and who had no control over the war on crime—were symbolically transformed from the "deserving poor" into crack-crazed unwed teens, gangbangers and "children with guns," a favorite Clinton phrase. Hispanics and immigrants—targeted by a campaign to blame economic problems on foreign labor—were cast as minions of foreign organized crime groups. Organized labor, hurt by reduced federal regulation and the anti-union campaigns of many major corporations, saw its membership continue to plummet.

Moreover, blaming the problem on minorities, poor Americans, immigrants, and progressives proved a disastrously ineffective method of fighting the war on drugs both at home and abroad. Just as law-and-order conservatives sabotaged the war on drugs in the 1950s by supporting corrupt anticommunist dictators, the Reagan administration in the 1980s cozied up to a long list of anticommunist groups who were heavily involved in the drug trade. In the 1980s and early 1990s the United States supplied more than $2 billion in secret aid to fundamentalist Afghan Muslim rebels and provided Pakistan with another $3.2 billion to fight the Soviet-backed Afghanistan government, even though both the rebels and the Pakistani military were implicated in the heroin trade. The DEA had an office in Pakistan, but no major arrests were made in the area during the 1980s. As the *Washington Post* pointed out in a front-page article in 1990, U.S. officials had refused to investigate charges of heroin deals by the guerrillas and the Pakistani officials who worked with them "because U.S. narcotics policy in Afghanistan had been subordinated to the war against Soviet influence there."[29]

Even as Ronald and Nancy Reagan were touring the country telling teens to "just say no" to drugs, the United States continued to support pro-American allies that had dominated the Latin American cocaine trade for decades. In the 1960s much of the trade was controlled by anti-Castro guerrillas, who were heavily funded by the CIA, and in 1973 *Newsday* reported that "at least eight percent of the 1,500-man [Bay of Pigs] invasion forces has subsequently been investigated or arrested for drug-dealing." Later, Noriega is believed to have received as much as $10 million in bribes from Colombian cartels to allow them to smuggle drugs and launder money in Panama while he was making millions from U.S. government agencies for his help in supporting the contras in Nicaragua.[30]

Less well known ties were maintained between the cartels and U.S.-backed leaders elsewhere throughout the hemisphere. In Haiti, several top military leaders were indicted for drug smuggling, and several commanders involved in the coup that overthrew the democratically elected government of Aristide were linked to the drug trade. Paraguay's longtime dictator Alfredo Stroessner and the leaders of a military coup that overthrew him in the late 1980s had extensive ties to smugglers. A military coup in Bolivia in 1980 was led by military leaders "involved in the extraordinarily lucrative drug trade," the *New York Times* reported, and elite Bolivian police forces have maintained close ties to the traffickers even after U.S. troops were sent to the region in 1986.[31] According to *Vanity Fair*, top Honduran military leaders—who were supported by the Reagan administration—established such close ties to the cartel that "during a 15 month period lasting until 1988, perhaps as much as 50 tons of cocaine moved through Honduras . . . amounting to half the estimated consumption in the U.S."[32]

In 1988, when U.S. troops arrived in Peru to work with a military leadership, an internal Pentagon memo acknowledged that the Peruvian military was a "quagmire of deceit and corruption," besides having a record for "widespread and egregious human rights violations." Institute for Policy Studies researchers add that numerous reports accused Peruvian "military personnel of firing on anti-drug police, reselling cocaine seized in drug raids and allowing traffickers to use military controlled landing strips."[33] Likewise,

Argentinean military leaders, who tortured and massacred thousands of their own citizens in the 1970s, became heavily involved in the trade during the late 1970s and 1980s. General Carlos Guillermo Suarez Mason, who played a key role in setting up death squads and killing dissidents, was described in the Italian press as "one of Latin America's chief drug traffickers" in the mid-1980s, after a democratically elected government forced him into exile in Miami. In 1984 he was charged by Argentina for drugs and arms trafficking and deported from the United States.[34] Finally, U.S. officials now admit they tried to bolster political support for NAFTA by downplaying the corruption and drug trafficking of top Mexican government officials.[35]

One of the most controversial cases, however, concerned the Nicaraguan contras, who engaged in a brutal and successful civil war against the left-wing Sandinista government. A 1988 congressional investigation led by Senator John Kerry found "there was substantial evidence of drug smuggling through the war zones on the part of individual Contras, Contra suppliers, Contra pilots, mercenaries who worked with the Contras and Contra supporters throughout the region" and that U.S. officials "failed to address the drug issue for fear of jeopardizing the war efforts against Nicaragua." Subsequent investigations, notably Peter Dale Scott and Jonathan Marshall's book *Cocaine Politics,* added more details, and in the summer of 1996 the *San Jose Mercury News* published an explosive series detailing contra leaders' sale of large amounts of crack cocaine to dealers in poor black neighborhoods of San Francisco and Los Angeles.[36]

This government-aided foreign drug flow had economic consequences. As noted, problems caused by the drug flow were exacerbated by the right's targeting of minorities, women, and kids. A prison record, of course, dramatically reduces a person's future job prospects, making it hard to break the cycle of crime and drug abuse. One study found that soaring imprisonment rates accounted for nearly three-quarters of the sharp drop in the employment of young black high school dropouts between 1979 and 1989. Noting that about 25 percent of all black men between the ages of twenty and twenty-nine were in prison or on parole or probation in 1990, the Sentencing Project observed that "given these escalating rates of control, we risk the possibility of writing off an entire generation of black men from having the opportunity to lead productive lives in society."[37]

Further, while the nation's drug warriors were blaming drug abuse on the decline of traditional family values, their longstanding lack of interest in gender issues—particularly domestic violence, equal pay, and child care—was making it more and more difficult for poor women to raise healthy, law-abiding children. The median income of women increased in constant dollars from $7,599 in 1970 to $10,791 in 1991, a period when median male income declined from $22,659 to $21,055, but the gender disparity still meant that many women were unable to ascend into higher-paying jobs. Cuts in welfare spending hit women and children hardest, since they constitute the vast majority of those receiving aid. By 1991, 68.1 percent of all black women and 73.1 percent of all Hispanic women who had any income earned less than $15,000 a year—barely above the federal poverty level of $14,000 for a family of four. About two-thirds of all households headed by women had less than $15,000 a year in income, and 58.9 percent of all children under the age of six who were growing up in these households were living in poverty.[38]

These discouraging economic statistics become particularly important when one considers the sources of female and juvenile crime. Throughout the 1970s and 1980s, while conservatives were attacking measures that would provide women with better legal protection, domestic violence remained a major problem and one of the chief causes of juvenile delinquency. Because many women do not report domestic violence, estimates of its occurrence range widely, from 3 percent to 50 percent of all families. One study, for example, has claimed that about half of all married women (27 million) are beaten by their husbands at some point and about one third (18 million) are repeatedly battered. Whatever the exact numbers, there is little doubt that domestic violence is the leading cause of injuries to women aged fifteen to forty-four, and women are nine times more likely to be victims of a crime in their own homes than in the street.[39]

Although gender violence cuts across class lines, its impact is strongly affected by economic background and opportunities. A 1990 study of women in prison found that most had never earned more than $6.50 an hour and two-thirds were minorities, who tend to have much higher poverty rates than others. Women from poorer communities are victimized by violence at much higher rates than more affluent women: half of these women in prison reported that they had been physically abused, more than a third had been sexually abused, and half had run away from home when they were children. Very few of these women were serving time for serious crimes, but most of the women who were had attacked men who repeatedly battered them. For example, 59 percent of all women who were in jail for homicide in New York, and 40 percent in Chicago, had been abused by either a family member or a lover whom they eventually killed.[40]

The problem of domestic violence is also related to narcotics use, the single most important factor in the huge rise in the number of women behind bars. Studies have shown that a higher percentage of women who are arrested used drugs than male arrestees, and that sexual abuse and domestic violence are the major causes of drug abuse. "Recent studies of black women crack users . . . describe a complex pattern whereby users initiate crack use to relieve the symptoms of depression or trauma associated with victimization, become traumatized by their efforts to secure it (often involving dangerous or degrading sex in exchange for drugs) and then receive the new trauma by seeking additional occasions to obtain the drugs," argue Marc Mauer and Tracy Huling at the Sentencing Project. "Since these efforts all too frequently provide added opportunities for trauma, the cycle is re-initiated."[41]

The right's decision to ignore this cycle of violence, poverty, substance abuse, and crime is also likely to have an enormous impact on American children who are now growing up in poverty. About 68 percent of all those arrested for serious crimes in 1992 were under the age of twenty-five, and the number of young people has always had an important impact on the nation's crime rates. Street crime dropped in the early 1980s as the proportion of young people in the overall population declined, and a dramatic rise in youth crime between 1984 and 1992 played a major role in the rising crime rates of that period. At least part of the recent reduction in crime can be attributed to the renewed decline in the proportion of young people, but that proportion is expected to rise at the turn of the century, as the sons and daughters of the baby boomers come of age—prompting fears that crime rates will again turn upward. An exhaustive August 1995 report commissioned by the U.S. Justice Department noted that arrest rates among juveniles doubled between 1983 and 1992 and that the number of homicides involving handguns and kids under the age of seventeen increased fivefold. Looking forward, the Office of Juvenile Justice and Delinquency Prevention noted in 1995 that 14.6 million young Americans were living below the poverty level—a 42 percent jump since 1976—and that "the juvenile population is projected to reach 75 million by year 2010, . . . [leading] to an increased number of juvenile victims of abuse and neglect [and] more juvenile offenders." Another study has estimated that if juvenile crime increases at the 1982 to 1992 rates, the number of violent crimes committed by young people will double to more than 210,000 by the year 2010. Even a glowing 1996 *Time* cover story on slumping crime rates called the rising numbers of young people with poor job prospects "a teenage time bomb."[42]

Most of these worries can be traced to the growing social problems faced by America's youth, especially those who live in worsening economic conditions. For example, California researcher Mike Males reports that "thirty-one suburban and rural California counties with a population of 2.5 million, in which a quarter-million teenagers reside, experienced zero teenage murders in 1993. Zero. No small trick in a year in which 4,000 people died at the hands of their fellow Californians. [These teens grew up with the] same rock 'n' roll furies, same rap concerts, same TV barbarisms (worse since suburban and rural families are more likely to subscribe to graphic cable channels), same guns on every block (more in rural towns), [and] no shortage of drugs and alcohol. . . . Yet, central Los Angeles census tracts [with very high poverty rates and] the same youth population . . . in these 31 counties experienced more than 200 youth murders."[43]

It is important to stress once again that the cycle of domestic violence, which is compounded by economic problems, affects children as well as women. Violence in the home makes children almost twice as likely to commit crimes when they get older and much more likely to commit sexual assaults. Moreover, violence against children too often occurs in homes where women are abused, and the cycle of violence continues into the next generation: men who have witnessed their fathers beating their mothers are nearly three times more likely than others to assault their wives. And juveniles who have been abused are 53 percent more likely to be arrested. An Oregon study found that 68 percent of juvenile delinquents had been abused or had seen their mothers beaten, and a National Institute of Justice study found that teen girls who had been abused were 77 percent more likely to commit crime. Moreover, abused children tend to commit twice as many crimes when they grow up as non-abused kids. Not surprisingly, virtually all the two thousand inmates on death row in the United States have histories of abuse as a child.[44]

In short, the law-and-order crackdown of the 1980s and 1990s can be described as a system that created violence and crime. Street-level drug arrests disrupted the economic viability of many families, making it hard for their members to find jobs in the legitimate economy. Family violence, compounded by poverty, created substance abuse, which in turn produced profits for organized crime groups and engendered a cycle of crime and incarceration. Attempts by authorities to crack down on this ever growing problem temporarily disrupted the distribution networks of organized crime groups, producing violent gun battles for turf. Children forced to grow up with violence at home and in their communities increasingly turned to violence themselves, creating a new cycle of domestic abuse and street crime. Over time, the social service cuts justified by images of violent, degenerate inner-city youth resulted in manifestations of desperation that echoed the stereotypes. The officially subsidized destruction of poor communities created a new generation of delinquents, who in turn could be used to justify even more suicidal policies.

Many voters who are the bedrock of law-and-order politics, isolated from the real problems of urban communities, accepted the politically expedient explanation that the poor are to blame for their own problems. They supported cutbacks in social welfare; they sanctioned attacks on affirmative action programs that have provided educational opportunities for at least some minorities. As job opportunities for unskilled workers dried up, declining federal aid for education, and the dismantling of affirmative action programs reversed the surge in black college enrollment. By 1995 black men in prison or on parole or probation dramatically outnumbered those in college.[45]

Contrary to all the projections of conservative economists who believed that a massive prison-building boom would change the economic calculus of crime, violence has remained a basic fact of American life. Worse, there is mounting evidence that the law-and-order crusade has actually made it harder for police and prison officers to do their jobs. The next chapter explores the problem of corruption and brutality in the law enforcement field and investigates the powerful special interests that continue to back this dysfunctional system.

Chapter 10:
The Prison-Industrial Complex

Any animal with teeth enough will chew off its leg to escape a trap. Human beings behaved similarly when chain gang imprisonment—a successor to slavery—swept through the labor-starved South during reconstruction. Beaten and driven like maltreated beasts, shackled to one another around the clock, prisoners turned to self-mutilation to make themselves useless for work. They slashed their bodies, broke their own legs, crippled themselves by cutting their tendons.

—Brent Staples

I love seeing 'em in chains. They ought to make them pick cotton.

Elderly white woman describing the 1995 return
of the chain gang to Alabama

We throw our children away in bad homes, bad schools, bad environments and this is what we get 10 years later.

—An Alabama chain gang guard who calls himself
"the highest paid babysitter in the state"

IN THE SUMMER AND FALL OF 1995, JOURNALISTS FROM ALL OVER the world flocked to Alabama Limestone Correctional Facility to see the latest trend in the American war on crime—the chain gang. To get some insight on this phenomena, some journalists had guards fit them with steel shackles and attempted to walk around with the chains. But most members of the media sat under a white tent, drinking lemonade, as shackled prisoners stumbled up the road to a large pile of rocks.

Earlier in the year the gangs had been clearing weeds and picking up trash along local highways, but eventually they ran out of work. So the warden hit on the idea of having them break rocks into gravel for the road leading to the prison. Thanks to that brainstorm, forty inmates, chained together in slow-moving groups, used fifteen-pound sledgehammers to attack rocks that a machine could have crushed into gravel in minutes for a fraction of the money it costs to hire a squad of prison guards. The prisoners work on the pile for twenty minutes, making almost no progress, and then rest for forty minutes. Days turn into weeks and weeks turn into months before a significant amount of gravel is produced. "[It's] like building the pyramids [in that it's incredibly expensive and labor intensive], but less useful," quipped a journalist from the *Washington Post*.[1]

In Alabama, Florida, Arizona and Missouri where chain gangs have been reintroduced, these slow-motion road crews stumble along the highways at the speed of their least energetic worker, accomplishing only a fraction of what they might do if they were individually shackled: "You can get more work done if people are not chained together," explained Eugene Morris, a Corrections Department spokesman. However, the law-and-order fanatics who control this massively dysfunctional war on crime were not pleased by this modest attempt to improve productivity and save money. "We said chain gangs and that means chained together," insisted Charlie Crist, a Republican legislator who had sponsored the bill that led to the reintroduction of chain gangs.[2]

Such symbolism and cynical political posturing have completely overwhelmed any pretense of creating a functioning criminal justice system. In statehouses around the country legislators routinely waste tax dollars debating some of the silliest anti-crime measures ever promulgated. Arizona not only brought back the chain gang but required inmates to wear pink underwear. Florida decided to make its notoriously barbarous prisons even more inhumane; besides bringing back the chain gang, the legislature outlawed cable TV and decided that new prisons would not be air-conditioned, despite the state's sweltering heat. In virtually every state, bills have been introduced that would abolish weight-training facilities—even though research suggests that inmates who exercise are less violent. At least eight states now have laws on the books denying prisoners access to air conditioning, cable TV, or weight rooms. These policies, which simply make inmates angrier and more violent, also illustrate that the modern criminal justice system is giving up on rehabilitating criminals in favor of inflicting meaningless—but exceedingly expensive—punishment as the only cure for crime. Although law-and-order politicians make political hay by attacking the prison system as a kind of country club for the morally challenged, many American jails are nothing but holding pens. In 1995 only 60 percent of all prisons offered employment counseling, and just one-third offered college course work. At that time there were fewer than eleven thousand educators employed in our nation's prisons—ninety-three inmates for every teacher. Not surprisingly, only 23 percent of all inmates were enrolled in education programs.[3]

Overcrowded conditions, poor educational programs, and lax supervision of guards add up to a recipe for violence. Nationwide, there were more than 40,000 assaults on prisoners and staff members in American prisons in 1995 and 3,311 deaths, nearly double the number in 1990. The prisoners' rights organization Stop Rape estimates that some 80,000 unwanted sexual acts take place behind bars in the United States every day and that 364,000 prisoners are raped every year. Human Rights Watch concluded that "being a woman prisoner in the U.S. state prisons can be a terrifying experience," in part because of evidence that "male correctional officers have vaginally, anally, and orally raped female prisoners and sexually assaulted and abused them [and] have not only actually used and threatened physical force, but have used their near total authority . . . to compel them to have sex or . . . to reward them for having done so." By the start of 1993 conditions were so bad that judges in forty states had issued court orders requiring that something be done to ease overcrowded and brutal living conditions, and in 1995 about 27 percent of all U.S. prisons were under court orders. As one doctor at Chicago's notorious Cook County Jail explains, "All we do is produce someone meaner and angrier and more disillusioned with himself and society."[4]

Throughout the nineteenth and twentieth centuries, reformers have worked for more professional police forces and a better penal system. They noted correctly that police corruption and brutality allowed organized crime groups to flourish in the early twentieth century and that brutal prisons turned first offenders into hardened thugs. "Anarchy for the coming year is being bred today by the lawless practices that have entered the enforcement of the law," one prominent reformer complained in *Our Lawless Police*, a book that popularized the findings of President Herbert Hoover's National Commission on Law Observance and Enforcement.[5]

Unfortunately, past and present law-and-order crusades have generally been concocted to create political support for larger conservative agendas. In the 1910s, conservatives and major business interests were faced with rising political protests and radical unions that threatened their economic power. They counterattacked by blaming social disorder on union leaders and on immigrants, who were said to be genetically predisposed to crime, and they embarked on a massive anti-radical campaign that culminated in the red scare of 1919, anti-immigrant laws, and the prohibition of drugs and alcohol. Their efforts put conservative Republicans in the White House, allowed the Ku Klux Klan to flourish in the 1920s, and destroyed political support for reformers, unions, and radicals who wanted to address the social problems that encouraged street crime. The prohibition of alcohol and narcotics encouraged the growth of nationwide organized crime gangs and made police corruption virtually impossible to deal with. Crime sky-rocketed during the Great Depression, and homicide rates hit record levels. The conservative policy of ignoring social problems and using fear tactics to build support for their pro-business agenda crippled attempts to reform U.S. police forces and prisons. When crime rates began to rise once again in the 1950s and 1960s, thanks to the economic policies that destroyed American cities, American law enforcement was ill-equipped to deal with the problem.

Police brutality and corruption actually helped law-and-order politicians in the 1960s. Not only did Nixon win votes in 1968 by defending inept local law enforcement agencies (most of which had been staffed and created by corrupt Democratic party machines); he also built support for his law-and-order crusade by blaming urban riots on radicals. In fact, many of the worst disturbances (New York City and Philadelphia in 1964, Watts in 1965, San Francisco and Atlanta in 1966 and Newark and Detroit in 1967) erupted after allegations of police brutality or widespread complaints about the way police treated minorities. Ultimately, the Kerner Commission (which was chartered by the Johnson administration to study the roots of urban unrest) found "deep hostility between police and ghetto communities . . . a primary cause of the disorder."[6]

This was nothing new. A 1935 commission had blamed Harlem riots on widespread police brutality; the 1947 President's Commission on Civil Rights had uncovered extensive evidence of illegal police violence; the 1961 U.S. Civil Rights Commission found that "police brutality is still a serious problem"; and a 1967 crime commission called it a "significant problem." According to a 1968 study of police brutality in fifteen cities, done for the Kerner Commission, 20 percent of all black men believed that the police used insulting language to local residents; 7 percent believed that police roughed people up unnecessarily, and 22 percent believed police frisked or searched people without good cause. Likewise, a 1967 study of the Los Angeles police found that 36.9 percent of all Watts residents had witnessed police brutality, and 7.8 percent said they had been victims of it. Researcher Rodney Stark's estimate that some three million Americans were brutalized by the police in the early 1970s indicated the average police officer used excessive force 7.5 times during his or her career.[7]

Today, massive spending on law enforcement has professionalized police forces in many ways. Local cops are better educated and trained than ever before. They are better equipped and in many cases can draw on the new technology—from massive computer databases to better forensic tools—to solve crimes. Unfortunately, the law-and-order policy of ignoring police brutality persists. It is hard to measure, in part because the federal government did not bother collecting statistics on the problem until relatively recently. Nonetheless, one 1991 survey of police departments in areas where the population totaled twenty-seven million Americans found 11.1 complaints of excessive force per 100,000 people.[8]

In Los Angeles, more than a dozen local residents died in choke holds between 1978 and 1982, and the city paid out more than $20 million in damages to victims of police brutality between 1986 and 1990. Yet one study found that in the 1986-1990 period the city rarely punished any of the sixty-three "problem officers" even though *each* been accused of twenty or more cases of either brutality or corruption. As relationships between law enforcement and poor communities continued to deteriorate, the Los Angeles Police Department made mass sweeps of poor neighborhoods and arrested anyone who happened to be near an open-air drug market. In April of 1988 more than fourteen hundred minority youths were arrested in one such sweep. Mounting resentment and the LAPD's failure to police itself exploded into violence in 1991, after the acquittal of several white police officers who had been videotaped beating a black man. As a number of commentators noted, the subsequent riot, which resulted in more than $1 billion in damages and scores of injuries, was eerily similar to the 1965 Watts riot. Illustrating how little progress had been made, Amnesty International issued a report that accused the city's police department of often having "resorted to excessive force, sometimes amounting to torture or other cruel, inhuman or degrading treatment. . . . The evidence suggests that racial minorities, especially blacks and Latinos, have been subjected to discriminatory treatment and are disproportionally the victims of abuse." Yet because of political pressure to crack down on crime and the lack of media attention to the problem of police brutality, Amnesty International also found that the officers involved "appear to have acted with impunity" or received only minor disciplinary actions.[9]

Another graphic example of how law-and-order policies have derailed efforts to create a more professional police department can be found in New York City. Like many other cities that had serious crime problems when Nixon launched his war on crime, New York had a long history of police brutality and corruption. Serious government investigations included hearings by New York State Senator Clarence Lesow in the 1880s and the 1930 Seabury investigation (both of which found ties between cops, local politicians, and major gangsters). In 1966, given clear evidence that the police department's failure to manage itself allowed crime to thrive, Republican Mayor John Lindsey attempted to improve matters by establishing a Civilian Complaint Review Board. But even this modest attempt to force cops to follow the law ran afoul of law-and-order fanatics. The police union and conservatives used a campaign of racial innuendos and lies to get the review board abolished. This delayed long overdue reforms until the early 1970s, when yet another corruption scandal broke. The Knapp Commission, appointed as a result of this scandal, documented rampant corruption inside the NYPD, poor management, and other problems that protected criminals from effective prosecution. Although the commission's work brought about some important reforms, the city's fiscal crisis in the late 1970s led to the laying-off of hundreds of officers, and the department's longstanding lack of interest in providing decent security for poor communities allowed open-air drug markets to take hold in many neighborhoods, such as the Lower East Side. In the early-1980s, when the NYPD finally got serious about enforcing the law in these neighborhoods, the lack of an effective mechanism for controlling police behavior produced mounting complaints of excessive use of force. Between 1987 and 1991 complaints of police brutality increased by 25 percent and the city was forced to pay out more than $44 million to victims.[10]

In 1992 these problems—bearing an uncanny resemblance to the complaints reformers had made about the department since the nineteenth century—exploded into yet another scandal: six cops were indicated for dealing drugs and protecting a large drug gang. In 1993 the city's political leaders authorized yet another investigation. The Mollen Commission found extensive evidence that police officers were beating up suspects, stealing drug money, routinely fabricating evidence, taking bribes, and even selling drugs, a system that allowed some major drug gangs to earn huge profits in East New York, Harlem, and the Bronx, where thirty-eight officers were indicated in 1995 for charges ranging from brutality to drug dealing. But Republican Mayor Rudolph Giuliani was so politically dependent on the police union that he made the Mollen Commission's report virtually impossible to obtain, and there was little effort made to improve the department. Between 1994 and 1996 the city paid out another $70 million to settle damage suits.[11] In 1997 several police officers were accused of brutally torturing a Haitian Immigrant with a toilet plunger, inflicting anal injuries that left him hospitalized for weeks. Then in 1999 widespread protests broke out after police mistakenly killed an unarmed African immigrant in a fuselage of forty-one bullets.

Examples of how the law-and-order crusade has failed to reform and professionalize police departments can be found all around the country. In Chicago, even though local residents file more than two thousand complaints of excessive force each year, the U.S. Civil Rights Commission found that "officers are rarely found guilty of misconduct and disciplined." In Washington, D.C. more than two hundred police officers were arrested for criminal offenses between 1989 and 1995. In Philadelphia a 1995 investigation into police corruption found that police officers routinely took bribes and fabricated evidence. Forty convictions were overturned and prosecutors were forced to review another thousand cases. In 1994 and 1995, four police officers in New Orleans were charged with murder.

Another 179 officers of the 1,400-person police force were either suspended, disciplined, or fired in that period. Also in the 1990s, narcotics units at the Los Angeles sheriff's department were accused of stealing drug money and taking bribes; a group of officers at the Denver Police Department set up a burglary ring; a Detroit police officer absconded with money from a narcotics investigation fund; in Newark, New Jersey, twenty-six officers were accused of raping, beating, and robbing prostitutes, and four others were arrested for stealing cars; Jersey City cops highjacked 113 cars from the city pound, and Boston police officers were accused of stealing drugs, beating suspects, and protecting drug gangs.[12]

Similar complaints can be leveled against prison officials. Despite the fact that reformers have been complaining about prison conditions almost as long as there have been prisons, between 1951 and 1953, these conditions produced forty separate prison riots. In one case, thirty-one inmates imprisoned at Angola, Louisiana, were so despondent over mistreatment that they slashed their Achilles tendons. Protests led to some long overdue reforms: professionals increasingly replaced the corrupt political appointees that ran many prisons, and better programs for education and rehabilitation were established. But conditions remained so poor in most institutions that in the 1960s inmates began pushing for more rights. As Supreme Court rulings gave them a legal basis for attacking widespread abuses, increasingly radicalized inmates—inspired by the civil rights movement—embarked on more direct protests. On September 9, 1971, inmates at Attica, New York, seized forty hostages and took control of the institution. Angry about overcrowding, brutal prison guards, inedible food, poor educational programs, and other problems at the dilapidated facility, they issued a manifesto declaring, "We are men! We are not beasts and do not intend to be beaten or driven as such." But Governor Nelson Rockefeller, whose draconian anti-drug laws and disdain for prison reform had exacerbated the conditions at Attica, refused to negotiate with the prisoners or consider their generally modest demands. On September 13 he ordered an armed invasion of the prison which led to the deaths of forty-three people, including ten hostages.[13]

The Attica uprising marked a watershed in efforts to reform American prisons. Few protests were dealt with this brutally, and though inmates did win some victories, the reform efforts of the 1960s and 1970s were quickly sabotaged by conservative politicians. In 1974, as administration officials were being sent to jail for the Watergate scandal, there were 218,466 people behind bars in federal and state prisons, about the same number as in 1960. But as Nixon's law-and-order crusade took on a life of its own, federal, state, and local officials began to back away from the idea of rehabilitating prisoners. The Committee for the Study of Incarceration, formed in the wake of the Attica rebellion, issued a 1976 report that attacked the philosophy of rehabilitation, and conservative criminologists such as James Q. Wilson built academic careers by claiming to show that the only solution to crime was longer sentences and more prisons. The number of inmates more than doubled, to 437,248 in 1983, and prison conditions so deteriorated that the courts ordered forty-four states and territories to improve the way prisoners were treated. Law-and-order politicians, however, sabotaged court orders by gutting programs designed to provide inmates with health care, counselling, education, exercise, and entertainment. Forty states were still under court order for illegal prison conditions in 1993 and more than a quarter of all prisons faced court requirements to improve conditions in 1995. By the middle of 1996, despite a massive prison-building program, federal prisons had 25 percent, and state prisons 16 percent more inmates than they were designed for.[14]

Worse, the sabotage of penal reform allowed corruption to thrive. A 1995 *New York Times* investigation, for example, found that "evidence of the prison drug trade abounds" all over the country. In the first half of the 1990s twenty-six prison guards in New York City's jails were charged with drug smuggling. In Washington, D.C., one inmate was convicted of running a major heroin distribution ring inside the capital's jails. In Mississippi, investigators found so many drugs in one local jail that dealers were forced to smuggle their unsalable stock back out of the institution. Today, drug use and overdoses in prison are common. One 1992 survey found that 6 percent of all inmates tested positive for marijuana and about 3 percent for cocaine. In short, the hugely expensive law-and-order crusade not only scorned efforts to rehabilitate inmates but allowed drug abuse as well as violence to thrive inside prisons.[15]

Over time, the effect on the war on crime has been disastrous. American police departments and prisons, which should have been reformed a hundred years ago, are still riddled with problems that prevent the adequate protection of Americans from violence. Thanks to a long tradition of police racism, corruption, and brutality, many poor urban residents view local officers with fear, skepticism, or outright contempt. Poor relations with residents of high-crime areas make it harder for honest cops—the vast majority of law enforcement officials who *don't* beat up people or steal drug money—to investigate crimes, let alone prevent violence before it happens. Likewise, brutal prison conditions make it much more likely that inmates will continue to commit crimes after leaving jail. Denied educational programs, inmates increasingly leave prison angry, drug-addicted, and schooled in gang violence. The prison reformers who called jails school-houses for criminals in the early twentieth century might today call them boot camps for mayhem.

What's more, the enormous cost of this crusade has made it increasingly difficult for local governments to fund other programs. Even if one takes the decidedly uncharitable view that prisons exist purely to punish people, incarcerating 1.7 million people is a mean-spirited luxury that few cash-strapped government agencies can afford. Only 11 percent of all U.S. classrooms have been built since 1980, and decayed and obsolete older buildings need $100 billion worth of work to bring them back up to standard. Yet instead of investing in schools, the United States spent $208.6 billion between 1982 and 1993 to build and operate prisons. And whereas it costs $20,000 to $30,000 a year each to lock up criminals—many of whom are functionally illiterate—it costs only about $5,600 to send a student to a public high school and perhaps $10,000 a year at the average state university.[16]

Nevertheless, as early as 1991 Washington, D.C., was spending more of its budget on police and prisons than on any other part—education came in a distant third—and in 1995 Mayor Giuliani tried to cut more than $1 billion from New York City's social welfare, health, and school programs so he could avoid cutting funds for police. Between 1984 and 1994 more than eight thousand jobs were cut in California's colleges and universities while the state's Department of Correction hired 26,000 employees to guard 112,000 new inmates. By 1996 California was spending more on prisons than it did on its once-vaunted system of higher education. Nationwide, the National Conference of State Legislators found, the fastest-growing segment of state budgets in fiscal 1994 was for correction: "For the third year in a row, corrections received more new state dollars than higher education."

The more funds you put into police and security, one mayor explained in 1994, "the less funds you have for kids, parks, and recreation and job training. . . . These [high crime areas] become the areas that need jobs. The cab drivers don't want to go there, the business people don't want to locate there, the tax base erodes. And these are the very areas that require the most services."[17]

The failure of our law-and-order crusade to reform American law enforcement and to address other social problems, however, has been enormously profitable—both politically and economically—for major corporations and conservative politicians. In 1969, when Nixon was ratcheting up the federal war on crime, a Wall Street research firm, Equity Research Associates, estimated that public and private expenditures on security services and law enforcement equipment would top $1 billion a year and grow by more than 20 percent a year for the next five to ten years—a development that writer Lee Webb called an emerging "police industrial complex." In fact, public expenditures on law enforcement and security skyrocketed from $12 billion in 1972 to $39.7 billion in 1983 and $97.5 billion in 1993 (the most recent data available in 1998). And even this mind-numbing figure doesn't include the $14.3 billion spent in 1993 by government regulatory agencies or private security expenditures, which topped $170 billion in 1993. (Today there are more than 1.5 million private security guards—double the number of police officers and up 80 percent since 1980.) In other words, total public and private spending to fight crime topped $280 billion in 1993—not to mention legal services, which topped $111 billion that year.[18]

Whatever you may want to call this industry—the business of law enforcement, the crime- or prison- or police-industrial complex, or simply Big Brother—it is clear many major corporations now profit from violence at home. A cynic might say that prisoners—who are primarily poor people of color—are now more valuable to the economy than black slaves of the nineteenth century. The incarceration of poor minorities produces huge profits for the major defense contractors who supply police departments with high-tech weapons and equipment. Wall Street firms collect lucrative fees for issuing bonds to build new prisons, and wealthy investors collect tax-free interest on the bonds, which can double the cost of building a $100,000 cell. Contractors have grown rich on the prison construction boom. Phone companies and managed health organizations aggressively bid on contracts to provide prison services. The private companies that now run prisons that house about 70,000 inmates expect to see their revenues top $1 billion in 2000, and businesses have set up factories inside prisons that earned $1.8 billion in revenues in 1995. And in a period of corporate downsizing, prisons and law enforcement have offered secure employment for millions of people. Servicemen and servicewomen work on the Pentagon's $1 billion-a-year war against drugs. In the private sector, besides the 1.5 million private security guards, 960,000 people find employment in the $124 billion legal services industry. Finally, more than 1.8 million people are employed by government agencies in law enforcement.[19]

Not surprisingly, economic sectors that profit from violence are among the staunchest political supporters, in both money and votes, of law-and-order politicians. Police officers, prison guards, military personnel, and others in the military-industry complex have long records of supporting conservative politicians and in 1997 constituted a powerful block of several million voters. At the same time, the policy of arresting poor people for minor drug offenses while ignoring corporate criminals has decimated the political power of many communities and reduced the number of minorities who are eligible to vote. By the mid-1990s, when some twelve million Americans were arrested each year, it was estimated that about 80 percent of all black males under the age of thirty-five had police records and that some five million Americans had lost the right to vote because of felony convictions—a block of potential voters that could have provided a crucial swing vote in future presidential elections.[20]

This dynamic—huge political contributions, secure voting blocks, and policies that reduce the political power of the groups that would oppose law-and-order politicians—has made conservative policies on crime almost irresistible to mainstream politicians. Every homicide victim meant more votes. Every celebrity drug overdose added more momentum to the anti-drug crusade. Every mugging victim made it easier to pass more repressive legislation. Every unrehabilitated convict who went on to commit more crimes produced more political pressure to build even more prisons that made no attempt to educate or train their inmates. Pursuing policies that objectively encourage poor Americans to murder other poor people was the best vote-getting mechanism that conservatives ever discovered.

The popularity of this conservative war on street crime did not only create new business opportunities for companies seeking to profit from the growing prison-industrial complex. The stereotypes that were used to justify self-defeating cutbacks in social programs and suicidal law enforcement policies also allowed the right to build political support for larger economic agendas: deregulation and trillion-dollar corporate welfare schemes that have allowed white-collar crime to grow into a $1 trillion problem.

Very few people think of corporate crime when considering the problem of violence in America, and those who do rarely attempt to see how crimes in the streets are related to crimes in the suites. But both are influenced by changes in the legitimate economy, and many legitimate businessmen have direct or indirect ties to the criminal underworld. Besides making huge sums of money from heroin, Khun Sa also profited from the workings of the legitimate economy. He sold off rich timber resources to his allies in the Thai military, whose logging practices created severe environmental damage, and he laundered drug money through shady banks that cheated depositors out of billions of dollars. At the same time, impoverished peasants working for the druglords sold off their sons and daughters to work in factories or brothels for businessmen in Thailand. Thus many, seemingly varied types of crime—environmental degradation, human rights abuses, bank fraud, dangerous sweatshops, and the heroin trade—are in fact closely related.

Closer to home, the small logging towns of the Pacific Northwest may seem far removed from urban ghettoes plagued by drugs and violence, but closer inspection shows that these communities have been devastated by the same economic forces: changes in the global economy and government policies designed to protect the interests of U.S. and multinational corporations. Powerful business interests in America have used their economic power to dominate the legal and political systems—to the detriment of poorer communities and, often, the benefit of criminal organizations.

Part III

The Trillion Dollar Gang: Corporate Crime in America

Chapter 11:
Clearcut Crimes

It always annoys me to leave anything on the ground when we log our own land. We don't log a 10-inch top, we don't log to an 8-inch top or a 6-inch top. We log to infinity. It's out there, it's ours, and we want it all. Now.

—*Harry Merlo, president of Louisiana Pacific*

In essence we [the communities of the Pacific Northwest] have been relegated to the role of a colony—exporting relatively low value raw materials and importing high value manufactured products—even though we have the best timber and the most efficient mills in the world.

—*U.S. Representative Joleen Unoeld
(D-Washington), 1989*

THE PICTURESQUE NORTHERN COAST OF OREGON IS RARELY associated with crime. On a clear day the mountains of the Coast Ranges, some rising hundreds of feet straight out of the ocean, offer spectacular views of clean white sands and rocky cliffs stretching miles up and down the Pacific. But behind this beauty lies an uglier vista. Many hills that were covered with magnificent old-growth conifers early in the twentieth century have now been heavily logged. In some places the loggers left swatches of woods along the highway, known as beauty strips, so that outraged tourists would not call their congressmen to complain about clear-cutting—the profitable and widespread practice of chopping down every tree in sight. But far too often the land was left naked, stripped to bare red clay that is easily washed down the slopes into the rivers. In less than a century of logging, hundreds of thousands of acres of forests that took a millennium to develop have disappeared. Although many acres of land have been replanted in the last thirty years, these second-growth trees are but a pale reminder of the old-growth forests that once covered the land and local residents once took for granted. No one will see such forests again until well into the twenty-fifth century; indeed, many environmentalists wonder if anything like those ancient conifers will ever reappear.

The destruction of old-growth forests isn't just socially and environmentally troubling; it is also a grim reminder that corporate crime can be an economic disaster. Measured in terms of biomass, biologists claim that the temperate rainforests of northern California, Oregon, Washington, British Columbia, and Alaska were the largest in the world, bigger than the tropical rainforests of the Amazon or Southeast Asia.[1] They were not only the lungs of North America—a vital ecological resource playing a crucial role in the long-term survival of the planet—but also the economic backbone of the region. Besides providing work for loggers, truck drivers, and millworkers, the rainforest sustained virtually every other part of the economy. Its cool shade protected some of the richest salmon spawning grounds in the world, allowing the region's fishing industry to thrive. A dairy industry grew up in the lush, low-lying coastal valleys that were nurtured by a climate of heavy rains and mountain streams, requiring forests to collect and hold the moist ocean air. And a plethora of small businesses serviced those working in the forests, at the fisheries, and on the farms.

But in the late 1970s and 1980s this economy went into a tailspin. Double-digit interest rates, the product of a global economic crisis, put a crimp on farmers and slowed the housing industry, thus plunging the timber industry into the worst depression since the 1930s. Meanwhile, overfishing and the destruction of the salmon spawning grounds by dams and clear-cutting wreaked havoc on the fishing industries: the salmon harvest in the lower Columbia River dropped by nearly 70 percent between 1981 and 1995. Many mills shut down, and employment in Oregon fell from 85,000 in 1961 to 60,000 in 1996. In some heavily logged areas, the problems were even worse. In Tillamook country on the North Coast of Oregon, the annual timber harvest fell from 262 trillion board feet in 1978 to 115 trillion in 1995, and the number of jobs in the sector declined by 23 percent between 1977 and 1996, producing a number of serious social problems. Between

1979 and 1989, median household income declined by nearly 10 percent to only $21,965, one of the lowest in Oregon; one child in four grew up in poverty. Meanwhile, crime rates soared by 40 percent between 1990 and 1994, the second largest rise in the state, and juvenile arrests jumped 82.2 percent, the fifth worst record in the state.[2]

By the late 1980s this crisis had laid the groundwork for one of the most vicious environmental battles in American history. U.S. laws allowed private landlords to cut any amount of timber on their own property, even if doing so destroyed valuable salmon spawning grounds, caused massive soil erosion, or prevented the regeneration of the forests that were the basis of the region's economy. But many people dismissed those problems because there were large federal and state-owned tracts of valuable timberland in Oregon and Washington which, in contrast to private lands, were supposed to be managed on wiser, more ecologically sound principles. Unfortunately, the Forest Service, the Environmental Protection Agency, and the Justice Department made little attempt to enforce existing environmental laws; for much of the twentieth century they even encouraged the environmental carnage by passing out multibillion-dollar subsidies to major timber companies. As millions of acres of old-growth timber disappeared, environmentalists complained that the federal government should enforce the Endangered Species Act. When those complaints were ignored, they finally filed suit against the federal government, charging that logging on federal land systematically violated existing environmental laws. In 1992, a federal judge, who had been appointed by the Reagan administration, agreed: he issued an injunction halting all logging on federal lands until the government came up with an environmentally sound way of protecting the spotted owl.

This sparked a familiar political dynamic. Public officials accustomed to ignoring federal laws protecting the habitat were forced to make painful political and economic decisions, apparently to protect just one small inhabitant: the spotted owl. The unelected judges who made the ruling were an easy target for populist anger. That allowed opponents of environmental regulations to seize the high ground. Unlike reluctant federal regulators, who made the case for the spotted owl in long-delayed, mind-numbing environmental reports filled with obscure technical jargon, the timber companies raised potent political issues—such as jobs and community survival. Not surprisingly, the majority of millworkers and loggers, who had endured the economic crisis of the 1980s in which one-fifth of Oregon's timber jobs disappeared, responded to the spotted owl debate with anger and contempt. "I Hunt Spotted Owl" T-shirts became fashionable along with bumper stickers reading "Kill a Spotted Owl—Save a Logger" and "I Like Spotted Owls—Fried."[3]

This kind of anger is both misguided and understandable. Like the spotted owl, two hundred species of salmon and many other plants and animals are in danger of becoming extinct because of rapacious logging practices. Similarly, many local timber communities rely on the bounty of the Pacific coast rainforests for their livelihood. The basic problem they all face is very simple. For more than a century, major corporations have engaged in unrestricted, environmentally disastrous, and economically wasteful logging that have decimated the rainforest of the Pacific Northwest. This devastation cannot be blamed on a wacky band of bird lovers. The Sierra Club did not found the major corporations that denuded whole mountain ranges. Greenpeace activists did not cut so much timber in a thirty-year period that sawmills on the Oregon coast had to go out of business because the basis of their livelihood had disappeared. The Natural Resources Defense Council did not design the dangerous mills that maimed thousands of workers. The Rainforest Action Network was not responsible for the kind of logging that ignited forest fires that incinerated the livelihood of whole towns. Timber barons, not environmentalists, destroyed the fragile ecological balance of the Pacific Northwest, leaving many communities to rot in a nasty stew of unemployment and poverty.

Yet the corporations have been remarkably successful in blaming environmentalists for the region's economic woes. Much of that success can be traced to the millions of dollars they have paid to lobbyists, public relations firms, and anti-environment groups. But mainstream environmental groups paid little serious attention to the economic needs of local communities. That is particularly unfortunate because these groups have managed to preserve tens of millions of acres of wilderness as federal and state parks. They showed how the destruction of rainforests changes the world's climate and explained why this destruction endangers other industries such as fishing and tourism. Their propensity to view the rainforests in purely ecological or aesthetic terms, however, made it difficult for them to propose political solutions that took into account the people who lived and worked there.

Why should these economically marginal communities—which lack the cash even to fund studies on how the damage to the forest might be repaired—bear the brunt of much-needed policies to save a spectacular natural resource? After all, the best-paid lumberjacks, sawmill workers, and log-truckdrivers rarely earn more than $40,000 a year, and most are paid far less. Their communities barely have enough money for decent schools, let alone the billions needed to restore the rainforest. It is unrealistic—and elitist—to expect them to bear all the costs of saving the nation's forests, particularly when one remembers that little of the wealth produced by this magnificent resource has remained in their communities. The cheap timber that fueled the postwar construction boom produced hundreds of billions of dollars in profits for S&Ls, banks, and real estate interests, as well as the timber companies. Simply enacting regulations to restrict logging is like passing an urban renewal program that requires the struggling residents of inner cities to tear down their own homes and then rebuild the city with their own money and labor. Not only is this idea grossly inhumane; it is completely unworkable.

Yet that was the position some environmentalists adopted. In the 1970s and early 1980s, when timber on private lands was becoming scarce, no major environmental groups called for a public works program or other government-sponsored measure to protect the communities that would bear the social costs of reduced logging. They advocated federal regulations that would impose huge costs on local businesses and communities but failed to champion policies that would force those sectors of the economy that disproportionately benefit from the region's natural resources to fund programs to protect the forests. Worse, some groups adopted a Malthusian, dog-eat-dog attitude toward these communities that would simply let them eat lectures on free-market economics once the logging stopped. "A market economy does not maintain an industry simply for the sake of employing workers," explained a 1990 article in *Forest Voice,* a publication of the National Forest Council, which has long fought to protect rainforests in the region. "When a product becomes obsolete or a resource runs dry, the economy adapts. Companies and industries have been changing or shutting down for 200 years and workers always find new jobs—the nation is not lacking jobs; it's a natural necessary component of capitalism. Chopping down forests for the sake of jobs is nothing more than social welfare—not something our nation prides itself on."[4]

Since 1990, fortunately, such attitudes have changed. Many activists have worked to forge links with local workers, arguing that the destruction of the forests by major corporations harms them as much as the local flora and fauna. But the movement's longstanding failure to treat area residents with the same reverence as the spotted owl has made environmentalism a dirty word throughout the region. Given a choice between jobs and the spotted owl, locals frequently chose the survival of their communities, even if this meant siding with timber companies that have never shown any interest in the region's long-term economic or ecological survival.

Similar struggles between short-term economic interests and long-term ecological catastrophe occur all over the world. In Brazil, where more than fifteen hundred people were assassinated between 1980 and 1989 in a vicious battle over the Amazonian rainforest, more than thirty-three million acres of rainforest disappeared between 1975 and 1988; compare the seven million acres lost in three previous centuries of European settlement. Official Brazilian government statistics indicate that the destruction grew from 14,896 square kilometers in 1994 to 29,059 square kilometers in 1995 before falling to about 18,161 square kilometers in 1996 and 13,037 (5,034 square miles) in 1997. Others place the figures even higher: in 1997 a Brazilian congressional committee estimated the loss at 58,000 square kilometers (about 22,393 square miles) each year. By the spring of 1998, rampant logging (which makes forests more vulnerable to fires) and the El Niño drought had ignited a 250-mile line of fire that destroyed more than sixty-five hundred acres of forest.[5]

In Chile the same military dictatorship that killed or tortured thousands of people provided massive financial incentives to the timber companies that cut down about 30 percent of the country's native coastal forests between 1978 and 1987, and a study by the Central Bank of Chile estimated the loss at more than 700,000 hectares (almost 1.75 million acres) between 1984 and 1994. Exports of forest products hit $2.2 billion in 1995, and at present rates of logging the country could lose all its forests by 2025. Likewise, in Guyana the government has sold off virtually all the forests to foreign timber companies as part of its plan to increase logging by 400 percent by 2002, a policy that will destroy 4.5 million hectares of one of the world's last largely intact rainforests. And Surinam is considering the sale of millions of acres of timberland to solve its mounting fiscal problems.[6]

In Africa and Asia there is even worse news. Rainforests are disappearing in West Africa at a rate of 5 percent per year. European timber companies have virtually destroyed all of the thirty million hectares of rainforest in Nigeria and the Ivory Coast, and foreign companies are doing their best to achieve similar results in Congo and Cameroon, where logging increased by 400 percent between 1993 and 1995. The World Wildlife Federation estimates that about 88 percent of Asian forests have already vanished and that the cutting continues at a rapid pace in many countries. Some 4 to 5 percent of all forests disappear each year in Pakistan and Thailand, rates that will denude these two countries by 2012. In less than twenty-five years, the forest cover in Cambodia has been reduced from 74 percent to around 30 percent, and all the remaining timberland has been sold off to private companies—many tied to corrupt Thai leaders—that are logging so fast that the forests there could disappear by 2002. In the Solomon Islands, where seven public ministers were accused of taking bribes from Malaysian timber companies, logging rates are so high that the country will be deforested by 2007. In New Guinea, where impoverished indigenous peoples get about $24 for a tree that logging companies sell for $600, timber exports jumped from 642,000 cubic meters in 1980 to 2.7 million cubic meters in 1993, or about three million trees. Critics claim that at current rates all the country's forests will be gone within a generation. In Vietnam, where forests have still not recovered from the toxic chemicals that U.S. forces sprayed on 20 percent of South Vietnam's jungles and 36 percent of its mangrove forests, more than 7,900 hectares were destroyed by fires in the first three months of 1998. In the Philippines, heavy logging has made forests more vulnerable to fire; twenty thousand hectares were ravaged in early 1998. In Malaysia only a severe financial crisis halted plans for a dam that would allow loggers to harvest $500 million worth of timber on the 80,000 hectares of forest that would be flooded, displacing large numbers of indigenous people (some of whom have been killed in clashes with the government), and construction of the $5.5 billion dam is still scheduled to begin as soon as the economy recovers. Finally, rampant logging and forest fires continue to plague Indonesia, where the world's second largest tropical rainforest is home to some ten thousand species of trees, fifteen hundred of birds, and five hundred of mammals. In late 1997 and early 1998, fires set by major timber companies and palm oil plantations started fires that got out of control, touching off a conflation that torched more than 1.7 million acres of the country's forests, threatened many species, and produced such serious pollution that more than a thousand people died.[7]

Although the press pays more attention to the developing world, severe problems of deforestation continue in Europe and North America as well. More than 62 percent of Europe's forests have disappeared, and local governments are protecting only 2 percent of what remains. In Sweden, logging continues even in the remaining 1 to 2 percent of old growth forests. Rampant logging in Latvia, which increased by 700 percent between 1992 and 1995, threatens Europe's finest swamp forest. In Russia, which has 25 percent of the world's remaining temperate forests, the United States and the World Bank are helping companies expand their logging.[8]

Adding up the cutting isn't easy, but some researchers have estimated that since 1680 the world has lost nearly six million square kilometers of forest, and two-thirds of that—an area about half the size of the United States—was lost between 1950 and 1990. During the last two hundred years the United States has lost 95 to 99 percent of its old-growth forests. In the Pacific Northwest alone, where 90 percent of the old-growth forests have been destroyed in the last 150 years, more than two square miles are cut each week. About 75,000 acres of tropical rainforest vanish each day, for an annual loss of about twenty-seven million acres—an area about the size of Austria or Pennsylvania. Likewise, the developing world lost 33.8 million acres of forests a year between 1990 and 1995, or an area the size of Italy every 2.5 years. Overall, in 1997 the World Resources Institute estimated that only 20 percent of the world's virgin forests remained.[9]

Some of the forest destruction must be placed in the context of a global economy that has allowed dictators, organized crime groups, and multinational corporations to thrive. In Indonesia the family of President Suharto, who came to power in a U.S.-supported military coup that led to the massacre of half a million leftists, owned huge timber companies, palm oil plantations, and pulp and paper factories that were directly involved in massive deforestation. Worse, the Suharto firms were among those that started fires to clear land for plantations in the fall of 1997, thus touching off the massive forest fires that raged throughout the country.[10]

Likewise, in the Golden Triangle, the same military and political leaders who were heavily involved in the heroin trade also founded and ran timber companies that were given lucrative government concessions to cut spectacular rainforests in Thailand and Burma. Leaders of the Nationalist Chinese army, there ostensibly to fight the Cold War, profited from logs as well as drugs. They levied a tax on local peasants, forcing them to clear forests to grow opium, and set up timber companies or sold logging rights to Thai companies. Similarly, opium warlords such as Khun Sa sold timber rights to Thai politicians and top military leaders for huge fees. In the late 1980s the military junta in Burma, which had close ties to major opium warlords, also sold off rights in Burma's rich forests, mines, and natural gas fields to major corporations in the United States, Europe, and Asia, using the money to buy $1.4 billion worth of arms to fight political dissidents.[11]

Over time, some of Thailand's most powerful politicians have owned logging companies operating in Burma and profited from this nasty mix of drugs, deforestation, and dangerous dictators. Multinational investors are financing the construction of a 260-kilometer pipeline from Burma to Thailand, which will carry natural gas from fields owned by the French oil giant Total, Unocal, Burma's Myanmar Oil and Gas Enterprise (MOGE), and Thailand's Petroleum Authority. This project is destroying a spectacular ecosystem that is home to 120 species of land mammals. Thai environmentalists set up camps in December 1997 to block construction—despite death threats. Villagers on the Burmese end of the line have filed a lawsuit against Unocal, seeking compensation for the human rights abuses, rape, torture, extrajudicial killings, forced labor, and other "crimes against humanity" and MOGE has long been accused of being a principal means by which Burmese drug dealers launder their profits. Yet a number of major corporations (among them Mitsubishi, which is also involved in logging teak, constructing dams, and selling automobiles in Burma) are supplying materials for the pipeline, which will cost about $6.5 billion.[12]

As a result of such practices, some of Asia's finest forests have vanished. In 1962, 53 percent of Thailand was forested, but today trees cover as little as 20 percent, and they could disappear early in the twenty-first century. In 1988, when it became apparent that much of the logging had been done illegally by companies owned by top Thai military leaders and politicians, the government responded to mounting political pressure and banned all logging. But that simply shifted the environmental carnage to Burma, where the junta granted concessions covering half a million acres in Asia's last virgin teak forests to dozens of Thai firms in exchange for $112 million, which was used to make down-payments on arms to fight pro-democracy guerrillas. "Teak sales facilitated arms purchases from China to the value of over $1 billion in 1991 alone," environmentalist Kate Geary contends. And since many of the concessions were granted in areas that the government didn't control, companies were free to cut trees indiscriminately, failed to replant the clear-cut areas, and logged in areas outside their contracts. To make matters worse, SLORC units drove some villagers off their land so that logging could continue or sold tracts of land in areas controlled by a variety of guerrilla groups. Desperate for money to buy arms, some rebel groups allowed the cutting in exchange for a small "logging tax," thus mortgaging their future for the exigencies of today's armed struggle. "The Thai loggers are cutting indiscriminately because they don't care for the future," one Karen leader complains. "One year of their cutting is equal to ten of ours and they don't replant teak as we did." By 1993, the Rainforest Action Network estimated that about 800,000 to 1,000,000 hectares of forest were being lost each year, the fifth highest rate in the world and in the first nine months of 1997, Burma earned more than $71.4 million by exporting teak and hardwood products. Not surprisingly, forests now only cover about 20 percent of Burma, down from 80 percent in 1900.[13]

The story of old-growth forests in the Pacific Northwest is at first glance less horrifying than the rarely published history of drugs and logs in the Golden Triangle. But substance abuse, corruption, and government policies designed to boost the profitability of multinational corporations at the expense of local communities also played a key role in destruction of the Pacific rainforests. Whites used cheap rum and whiskey to steal rich timberlands from the Indians in the early nineteenth century and timber companies of the early twentieth century relied on alcoholism and the creation of crime-ridden red-light districts in major cities to preserve a captive, impoverished work force. Many of the large timber companies that seized control of rich forestlands—often through graft and corruption— ruled their fiefdoms with goons and blacklists, forcing thousands of men to work in brutally dangerous jobs. Throughout much of the nineteenth and twentieth centuries, they treated the land no better than they did their workers, clear-cutting millions of acres without bothering to replant a single tree and engaging in dangerous logging practices that allowed man-made fires to destroy millions more.

The indigenous peoples of the Pacific Northwest had established a variety of cultures between Alaska and northern California, but they were all based on a successful understanding and use of the region's natural resources. In British Columbia, for example, four-hundred-year-old coni-fers were selectively harvested and laboriously dragged to the coastal villages by Native Americans, where they were carved into oceangoing vessels used for war, whaling, and fishing. Large boards were assembled into huge lodges that could house a hundred people or more. Bark was woven into rope for fishing nets and clothes and blankets for warmth and fashion. Young saplings became bows and arrows that were used to hunt the deer, mountain antelope, and other animals that made their homes in the forests. And the diverse ecology of the old-growth forests allowed a variety of trees and other plants to grow in areas that had been cleared by fire, storms or native peoples. From these woods, the tribes harvested edible roots, nuts, grasses, and berries, as well as grasses, cedar, and roots for weaving baskets, nets, and blankets.[14]

The forests also protected the salmon spawning grounds. The deep, sturdy roots of conifers and the duff and humus on the ground regulated the flow of water out of the mountains when the snow was melting, thus preventing massive soil erosion, landslides that could block the clean gravel streams, or raging torrents that could damage the salmon eggs. As the eggs grew into young fish, the shade of the huge conifers kept the streams cool and provided an ideal habitat for the insects that the salmon ate. Fallen logs also held vegetable matter and created deep pools that nurtured the young salmon until they could make their way to the sea. At the age of four or five, when the salmon migrated back to the same stream where they were born and traveled upriver to its headwaters, they spawned in the same spot as their parents. This ecological system produced salmon runs so bountiful that the early white settlers were only slightly exaggerating when they claimed it was possible to walk across rivers on the backs of the fish.[15]

Before the arrival of the whites, although choice streams had to be bitterly defended from rivals, the bounty of the salmon and the forests allowed the coastal tribes of northern Washington, British Columbia, and Alaska to develop relatively dense settlements and sophisticated cultures.[16] But their way of life changed forever with the arrival of European and American traders in the late eighteenth century. Russian, British, and American ships quickly established a booming trade in rum, guns, trinkets, and steel tools for pelts. By 1795 American traders were crowding out the British and the Russians, and by 1809 John Jacob Astor had founded at the mouth of the Columbia River a trading post that Thomas Jefferson called the "germ of an Empire." Americans who made huge fortunes trading firewater for furs also dominated the North American fur trade with China and profited from the Chinese opium trade.[17]

Initially, many of the coastal tribes profited as well, proving to be sharp traders and middlemen for the interior groups who trapped and skinned the animals. But as time wore on, arms supplied by maritime traders fueled the fierce warfare between tribes seeking to control certain rich salmon spawning grounds. As early as the 1780s one Indian village had acquired two hundred muskets, and in later years villages even purchased swivel guns and cannons to be mounted on their forts. The tribes and the traders frequently sold prisoners of war to other villages, and the white traders' practice of selling quantities of cheap booze created social problems that exacerbated the spread of European diseases, which wiped out whole villages. Between 1770 and 1900 the number of Indians on the British Columbian coast is believed to have declined from about eighty thousand to less than twenty-five thousand.[18]

Meanwhile, overhunting reduced the available pelts, and many of the tribes lost their valuable fishing, timber, and hunting lands to white settlers. The British Navy regularly bombed villages that attacked settlers who were stealing Indian land and white officials forced the tribes to sign treaties that gave away valuable land and timber resources. Some tribes attempted to compete by establishing their own sawmills, but government authorities in both Canada and the United States, wrecked these enterprises by placing severe restrictions on the Indians' legal rights (making it harder for them to do business in the white economy) and by giving away vast tracts of valuable timberlands to rich speculators and politically well-connected entrepreneurs. "By 1910 much of the then commercially retrievable timber along the coast [of British Columbia] had been alienated by some form of lease to large private lumber holdings," writes historian Rolf Knight.[19]

In the United States some of the biggest subsidies were handed out to major railroads. In 1869 when Jay Cooke, America's most powerful financier, was awarded a franchise to build the Northern Pacific, Congress also gave him forty-seven million acres of valuable timber, mineral, and farmland along the Canadian border. The Central Pacific, awarded a franchise to build the western half of the first transcontinental railroad, got nine million acres of free government land and $24 million in government bonds; the Union Pacific, which built the eastern half of the road, got twelve million acres and $27 million in government bonds to finance construction. Frequently, these enormous land grants were obtained by bribing government officials. In 1873 a congressional investigation into Credit Mobilier, a railroad holding company, found that it had given bribes or stock to James Garfield (a future president), the Democratic congressional floor leaders, a former vice president, the incoming vice president, and numerous senators and representatives.[20]

Grants to the railroads were part of the much larger U.S. government policy of subsidizing big business by handing out public lands and underwriting construction of major capital projects. Corporate interests took advantage of the Homestead Act of 1862, which opened public lands to individual ownership; by 1870 the railroads held about 131 million acres. Similarly, huge public assets were handed over to private business for almost nothing as a result of the Desert Land Act, the Timber Culture Act, and the Timber and Stone Act, which allowed private parties to purchase 160 acres of forestland for only $2.50 an acre. As late as the 1970s the Burlington Northern, Southern Pacific, Santa Fe, and Union Pacific railroads still owned 13.9 million acres of land, much of which had been acquired during the mid-nineteenth century period of permissive federal corporate welfare policies. It included large western forestlands and areas rich in coal, oil, and natural gas, and mineral rights on another 7.3 million acres.[21]

As the nineteenth-century railroads advanced west, so did the timber barons, using corporate giveaways (eventually worth billions of dollars) to denude the woodlands of New York, Pennsylvania, Michigan, Wisconsin, and Minnesota. Nationwide, about 190 million acres of forest were chopped down between 1850 and 1910—more than all the timber that had been leveled in the first two hundred and fifty years of European settlement. Federal and state governments encouraged the cutting by virtually giving away hundreds of millions of forested acres under the theory that settlers would clear the land and establish small farms. In practice, however, a great deal of land fell to large landowners and corporations. Of the 5.6 million acres that Michigan sold under the Swamp Land Act of 1850, one million acres went to one iron company; Florida sold four million acres to a single wealthy buyer. In many cases the increasingly powerful lumber barons sent out employees to claim the land or quickly repurchased the holdings of impoverished immigrants, which they then clear-cut "as bare as the scalp of a Marine recruit at boot camp," one researcher notes.[22] These massive acquisitions created many of the major corporations that continue to wreak havoc on the nation's forests.[23]

But no timber baron was more successful in turning corporate welfare and environmental degradation into a huge business empire than Frederick Weyerhaeuser, the founder of a company that owned 7.1 million acres of forestland in the late 1970s, most of it in the Pacific Northwest. He got his start in the Wisconsin timber boom, bought cheap land from railroad interests (which financed the construction of their lines by selling the public land Congress had given them), and by the end of the nineteenth century controlled twenty lumber and railroad companies. Even bigger power would come his way following a lucrative deal James Hill cut with Congress in the 1890s. Hill had already been granted twenty square miles for every mile his Northern Pacific railroad advanced across the continent. Unsatisfied with this lucrative bit of corporate welfare, Hill and other major campaign contributors got Congress to pass the Organic Administration Act of 1897. This law allowed Hill to trade mountain cliffs and glaciers in the Rockies for public lands in the Pacific Northwest that contained rich old-growth forests. Then Hill sold 900,000 acres of valuable timberland for $5.4 million to Weyerhaeuser—a government-sponsored windfall profit for Hill and his financial backers, including the not exactly needy tycoon J. P. Morgan. Meanwhile, Weyerhaeuser continued to buy land from the Northern Pacific and others. By the start of the Great Depression, he had made Washington state the largest timber-producing region in the United

States, and his company had accumulated more forest property than any other private landowner in the Pacific Northwest.[24]

In these ways a tiny elite of exceedingly powerful corporations acquired ownership of the large rainforests of the Pacific Northwest, which accounted for about half of all the privately owned timberland in the U.S. in 1914. At the start of the First World War three timber barons controlled about one-quarter of all the region's timber, and as late as 1996 the fifty largest owners held 77 percent of the private forestland in the Coast Range of Oregon (59 percent being held by just ten companies). In sharp contrast to this concentration of wealth, the other 23 percent of the land was held by 13,175 owners.[25]

Consider Tillamook County on the north Oregon coast, which had one of the world's largest temperate rainforests. Here the Oregon and California Railroad was legally given some 27,450 acres of land, while speculators acquired a great deal more through graft and fraud. Between 1888 and 1891 wealthy speculators, primarily backed by eastern financial and timber interests, had spent almost $500,000 to acquire timberland there. By 1892 the local newspaper noted that "wealthy men . . . have succeeded in gaining control of most all the timber land in the county that are now surveyed, some of the firms owning as much as 40,000 acres."[26]

Although here, too, the sale of public land was designed to encourage small settlers, timber barons used a variety of illegal techniques to gain control. Typically, they bribed poor settlers to act as front men, and these land transfers to politically well-connected speculators would be recognized immediately by bribed officials while local settlers who had put in honest claims had to wait months or years to obtain their titles. By 1904, corruption had reached such a level that the U.S. government handed down dozens of indictments against speculators and powerful public officials, including U.S. Senator John Mitchell, Congressman John N. Williamson, U.S. Attorney John Hall, former U.S. Attorney and State Senator Franklin Pierce Mays, and former Land Commissioner Binger Hermann. Stephen Puter, who was known as "the king of the Oregon land fraud ring," admitted that "thousands upon thousands of acres, which included the very cream of timber claims in Oregon and Washington, were secured by Eastern lumbermen and capitalists, the majority of whom came from Wisconsin, Michigan and Minnesota, and nearly all of the claims to my certain knowledge were fraudulently obtained." By 1933, "most of the land [in Tillamook] was owned primarily by Eastern timber syndicates," notes Paul Levesque in his unpublished two-volume history of the county's timber industry, and most of the purchases occurred "during a period clouded in ... scandal, for it was indeed a dark age in the administration of the public domain."[27]

While Weyerhaeuser, James Hill, and other wealthy businessmen benefited from the corporate welfare that virtually gave away public assets, timber workers were denied even the most basic government protection regarding wages and working conditions. The European immigrants and Native Americans who did most of the work soon became known as bindle stiffs because they migrated from area to area in search of employment with their clothes and bedding—in bindles—on their backs; wealthy timber barons were too cheap even to provide blankets. Worse, anyone seeking a job had to pay fees to labor contractors, who kept a blacklist of rebellious or pro-union workers.[28] And anyone who survived the blacklist then faced some of the most murderous working conditions in America. Many men were struck down by falling timber or fell hundreds of feet to their death in the process of topping the mighty conifers. Others had their arms or legs ripped off by the steel chains used to pull the logs out of the forest, or were crushed by the logs they transported down rivers, or killed in sawmill accidents as the huge trunks were processed into finished lumber. Very few statistics were kept on the extent of this carnage, but death counts could reach appallingly high levels; for example, one hundred men died in the Grey Harbor region of Washington in just one three month period in 1925.

As for life in the logging camp after a day of dangerous work, one union organizer told Congress that the forest workers were known as "timber beasts" because "the logger ... works hard. ... And what does he get? He gets wages that are below ... the line necessary to keep him alive. ... They are murdered on the installment plan. ... They breathe bad air in the camps. That ruins their lungs. They eat bad food. That ruins their stomachs. The foul conditions shorten their lives and make their short lives miserable. ... It rains a great deal and they work in the rain. ... They get into a dark barn, not as good as where the horses are, and the only place to dry their clothes is around the hot stove. ... Business is business. ... The logger, he finds that he is nothing but a living machine."[29]

In periods of peak production these living machines worked ten to sixteen hours a day, six or seven days a week, without being allowed to leave the lumber camp for three to six months at a stretch. Many loggers left the woods only twice a year, for the Fourth of July and Christmas. And since the work schedule was not conducive to stable family life or community development, the leisure activities available during these rare escapes were frequently limited to the red-light districts, gambling dens, and saloons that were prominent features of the larger Pacific Northwest towns. A few days of drinking, whoring, and gambling often stripped forest workers of six months' hard-earned wages, forcing them to return to the lumber camps in order to eat.

Although many reformers and local residents railed against the saloons and the red-light districts, the local political machines in Seattle, Portland, Tacoma, and Vancouver displayed little interest in cleaning them up, primarily because vice was such a profitable business. In Portland, Oregon, an 1892 study found that many gambling dens and houses of prostitution were located on properties owned by leading members of the city's establishment, including Cyrus Dolph (brother of a U.S. senator), a law partner of County Judge Julius Moreland, brewer Henry Weinhard, Ainsworth Bank vice-president William K. Smith, former mayor and banker Van DeLashmutt, Northern Pacific Lumber president Lauritz Therkelsen. Overall, more than fifty prominent citizens were named as profiting from the vice trade.[30]

Seattle Mayor Hiram Gill, elected in 1910, promised his business friends that he would restore the city's prosperity by luring loggers from all over the Puget Sound region to the gambling and prostitution houses of the city's vice district, prompting one newspaper to label him "a businessman in politics who believes that gambling, drinking, prostitution and free-and-easy public conscience spell industrial prosperity." Under Gill's administration Police Chief Charles Wappenstein also cut a deal with leading gangsters whereby the police would be paid $10 a month for each working prostitute—a practice that encouraged the badly paid police to spend more time counting hookers than enforcing the law. Wappenstein even became a partner in a five-hundred-room brothel before losing his job.[31]

In Everett, Washington, a 1902 crackdown on vice angered a number of prominent local merchants and sawmill owners. The owner of a major logging company, Joe Irving, was "outraged because he wanted his men to be able to come into town on Saturday nights, find a girl and get drunk," explains historian Norman Clark. "It was easy enough for him to pick his men out of the saloons or the city jail each Monday morning, but if they went to Seattle [brothels and saloons] he had real trouble filling his crews. The mill owners stood with Irving.... They may have seen some advantage in keeping around the town the kind of casual and cheap labor—always a useful threat to the unions—that drifted in and out of the dives."[32] In short, alcoholism, rape, gambling, and violent crime helped perpetuate a class of desperate, underpaid workers who produced windfall profits for the timber barons and petty cash for local political leaders, tavern owners, and corrupt police officials. Not surprisingly, the Pacific Northwest in the early twentieth century had astonishingly high levels of violence and alcoholism, problems that persist to this day.

Such conditions quickly fueled the rise of radical political movements. During the 1894 depression, thousands of unemployed workers decided to march on Washington, D.C. Some protesters even stole trains and drove them east. "There seems to be absolutely no way of enforcing municipal or state authority," railroad baron James Hill complained in a letter to the president. This army of the unemployed, with its modest demand that Congress finance public works programs to put destitute people back to work, was quickly dispersed. But massive wage cuts, abusive corporate power, and dismal working conditions set the stage for even more violent struggles. The Knights of Labor had made some unsuccessful attempts to organize timber workers and longshoremen in the early 1890s, and the AFL maintained a few locals throughout this period. The radical Industrial Workers of the World (IWW) was more successful. The IWW actively recruited all races and sought to organize all workers, skilled and unskilled, into "one big union"—unlike the AFL, which targeted only skilled workers and organized different crafts within an industry into separate unions. By 1907 the IWW had established locals in Portland, Tacoma, Aberdeen, Hoquiam, Ballard, North Bend, Astoria, Vancouver, and Seattle. Native American workers who handled timber on the docks in British Columbia also formed an IWW local in 1906, and many Indians were active in labor struggles.[33] In 1907 the IWW assumed new prominence when it took control of a spontaneous walkout at a Portland, Oregon, sawmill:

organizers quickly shut down every sawmill in the city and pressed for employers to grant wage hikes and a nine-hour day.

The strike was broken, in part because the conservative AFL locals refused to help, but the incident sent shock waves throughout the region. Some employers instituted cosmetic improvements in working conditions to head off future labor agitation, but most responded brutally. In 1912 hundreds of timber workers were beaten up and jailed during a strike in Aberdeen that eventually forced sawmill employers to raise wages to $2.50 a day. Government officials aided the crackdown by arresting labor leaders and by assigning sheriff's deputies to guard company property. Private investigators employed by the timber barons also compiled huge files on union members; labor activists were blacklisted; and armies of labor spies were employed to weed out potential agitators. Attacks from state and local law enforcement—more concerned with fighting demands for a nine-hour day than they were with cleaning up local graft and high-crime red-light districts—eventually caused union membership to drop, and labor strife declined dramatically between 1913 and 1915.[34]

The onset of war in Europe boosted the industry's fortunes. The timber barons, displaying their usual patriotic fervor, profited heavily from the U.S. entry into the First World War by hiking timber prices. Seeking to capture some of these windfall profits and to improve conditions in the industry, the IWW embarked on a wave of labor agitation in 1916 and 1917, which was met with renewed repression. In October 1916, sheriff's deputies in Everett, Washington, rounded up forty union organizers and took them to a local forest preserve, where they were stripped naked and brutally beaten by hundreds of local vigilantes armed with guns, clubs, and whips. Hearing of this officially sponsored crime wave, 250 IWW activists traveled to Everett by boat, but when they arrived on November 5 they were greeted by drunken local vigilantes and law enforcement officials who had hidden in buildings around the docks. Someone fired a shot—no one knows which side—and a gun battle broke out. By the time it was over at least five people were dead (more bodies were probably washed away by the water) and more than fifty people wounded.[35]

The massacre attracted many new members, however, and led to several successful strikes. By the summer of 1917 an estimated twenty thousand men were on strike, and the IWW had shut down about 75 percent of the timber business west of the Cascades in Oregon and Washington. Responding to the labor unrest, many western states passed criminal syndication laws that made it illegal to strike or organize unions, and government authorities began rounding up union organizers and interning them in camps, where a number of people simply starved to death. "Thousands of strikers clapped into jail and when jails were filled up 'bull pens' were erected," writes Louis Adamic. "Men were slugged in the streets, killed in open daylight . . . [and] union halls were raided. Thousands were herded into box-cars and 'deported'—that is taken into lonely country, hundreds of miles from habitation. . . . Scores of men were tarred and feathered. Several were taken to lonely railroad bridges at night and hanged." Federal officials, who displayed no interest in the industry's antitrust violations or its abominable record on workplace safety, ignored these vigilantes. Instead, they arrested IWW organizers, sent in troops to break strikes, interned striking workers, used military police to keep union organizers out of lumber camps, and put military units to work in the woods. Then the U.S. military officials who had played a key role in quashing the strike convinced the timber barons to set up company-run unions and limit the workday to eight hours. These company unions were not allowed to strike, and for many years they blacklisted known radicals, but they did increase wages, shorten the working day, and improve workplace safety. These changes, coupled with massive repression, annihilated the radical labor movement and kept the AFL and other independent unions out of the region for many years.

During the same period, however, the timber barons were also coming under attack for massive environmental degradation. In the late nineteenth century the young environmental movement and some politicians began worrying about the future of the nation's forests. Fearing that rapacious logging practices would send the nation's supply of lumber the way of the dodo bird, Congress passed the Forest Reserve Act of 1891. The government began establishing National Forests—eventually comprising some 192 million acres—and the railroads reduced their use of lumber. By the late 1950s major corporations began to see the forestlands as a kind of agricultural asset that could be replanted and harvested over and over.[36]

By that time, however, the industry's dismal environmental record and its practice of pushing loggers to work overtime in unsafe conditions had already produced ecological disasters, including one of the worst forest fires in recent history: the Tillamook burn. In the early twentieth century the forests near Tillamook on the north coast of Oregon contained some of the world's most spectacular old-growth trees. "From the summit of the Coast Range to the tidewater lines, it is simply one vast and dense forest," one journalist wrote in 1902. "It is a forest area of the giant breed, with trees ranging from eight to thirty feet in circumference and reaching upward of 150 to 300 feet."[37] Most of this, however, disappeared in August 1933. Earlier that summer a major drought hit the Tillamook forests, and by August the woods were so dry that dragging a log out of the woods could easily ignite a spark. Under today's regulations, the government agencies would have halted all logging—the risk of fire was simply too great—but in the unregulated timber industry of the 1930s, work continued. Reportedly, one logging company ordered its crews to "drag out one more log" before stopping work, and that log ignited the spark that started the fire.

The veracity of this widely repeated story has never been proved, but there is little doubt that the fire was man-made. The results were disastrous. As the flames spread, an extremely dry east wind caused the forest to explode with the force that some later observers have compared to the ferocity of an H-bomb or the volcanic eruption of Mount St. Helens. Many older residents of Tillamook still remember using garden hoses to protect their homes from sparks that fell from the sky. Ashes rained down on ships five hundred miles out at sea and as far east as Boise, Idaho. Smoke clouds billowed forty thousand feet into the sky and so darkened the midday sun that chickens went to roost. By the time it was over, the fire had burned 285,733 acres in Tillamook, Washington, and Yamhill Counties in Oregon, destroying more than eleven billion board feet of timber.[38]

Unfortunately, the Tillamook burn was not the last ecological disaster engineered by the serial corporate criminals of the timber industry. In the late 1940s, the multibillion dollar subsidies secured by industry lobbyists for the timber, real estate, and home construction sectors boosted the demand for lumber. In 1952 the *Oregonian* noted that enough timber was removed from private lands "to house the state's entire 2 million population together with San Francisco's 700,000 residents."[39] But seventy years of unrestricted logging had reduced the supply of privately owned timber, and the industry realized it needed access to new forests in order to profit fully from the suburban housing boom. Having successfully lobbied against public housing for poor people by labeling it a Communist plot that would destroy the nation's entrepreneurial spirit, industry spokesmen went begging to Washington for a new round of corporate welfare. Beginning in the early 1950s, thanks to contributions from the timber barons, Congress's annual appropriations for the Forest Service included provisions that the government must sell enormous quantities of timber each year. That shifted the real power over federal lands from the biologists at the Forest Service to lobbyists in the timber industry and their allies in Congress.[40]

Armed with this power, the industry inked billions of dollars worth of below-market contracts with the Forest Service to log timber on public lands. In 1954, for example, the U.S. government signed a fifty-year deal with Ketchikan Pulp Company (KPC, now owned by Louisiana Pacific, one of the largest timber companies in the world) to log vast tracts of the Tongass National Forest in Alaska, an area that includes spectacular eight-hundred-year-old trees and some of the world's most important salmon spawning grounds. In the 1980s, researcher Keith Erwin estimated, the Tongass sales produced only one dollar for the U.S. Treasury for every ten dollars the government spent on roads and other services that allowed the loggers to clear-cut the trees. A Congressional report stated that between 1982 and 1988 alone, the Forest Service spent $386 million to help loggers in the Tongass forest but received only $7.6 million in payments from lumber companies. That is, the timber barons received a subsidy that covered 98 percent of the real cost of harvesting the timber in those years, while the government lost an average of $55 million a year.[41]

Since 1950, in fact, government officials have allowed the timber barons to clear-cut more than twenty million acres of federal land, often charging them less than what government agencies had to spend on the roads and other services that made the harvest possible. Between 1970 and 1998, various researchers estimate, the federal government has lost more than $10 billion in below-cost timber sales on the 192 million acres of national forests. As late as 1996—while slashing benefits for the poor—Washington still handed out about $153.9 million in corporate welfare by selling tax-payer-owned timber to hugely profitable corporations at below-market prices; in the Northwest alone, the government lost $115.9 million in sales on federal lands.[42]

Not surprisingly, this policy has been an ecological disaster for both the environment and local communities. A study by the National Biological Service in 1994 concluded that the massive ecological damage done to the nation's forests had endangered or threatened 126 of 261 major forest ecosystems. Jeffrey St. Clair adds, "With less than 5 percent of the native forest left in the West (and a fraction of 1 percent East of the Mississippi), many of the ecosystems across the continent are in a state of functional collapse. In the Northern Rockies, the wildest region in the lower 48 states, the grizzly bear, timber wolf and bull trout are all imperiled by Forest Service logging and road building. In the Southwest, where less than 2 percent of the original forest remains, the Mexican spotted owl and northern goshawk are threatened by the timber-first management of the national forests. In southeast Alaska, the 16 million-acre Tongass National Forest is being eviscerated by an economically irrational timber-sales program that essentially gives away 800-year-old Sitka spruce tress to multinational pulp companies."[43]

Industry apologists have long contended that these sales more than pay for themselves in new jobs and economic activity, but this argument falls apart when the industry's record of dealing with small businesses and local communities is closely examined. More often than not, government sales of taxpayer-owned timber give large timber companies an enormous competitive advantage over smaller, independent loggers and mills, forcing many out of business and leaving many timber communities dangerously dependent on one or two large employers.

Even though Congress mandated that a certain amount of public timber be set aside for smaller companies, lax enforcement of antitrust rules and secret deals allowed the timber barons to log those lands as well. In the Tongass, dozens of independent logging companies have gone out of business or have been acquired by larger companies since KPC and the Alaska Lumber and Pulp Company (ALP) signed a fifty-year deal with the Forest Service in the 1950s. In 1973, one of these companies, Reid Brothers, sued ALP and KPC, alleging a variety of antitrust violations, and eventually won a $1.5 million settlement; the two large companies were forced to pay other independent loggers, as well. Federal investigators also uncovered evidence that in the 1970s Louisiana Pacific executive John Crowell (who was put in charge of forest management during the Reagan administration) recommended to Henry Merlo (subsequently in charge of Louisiana

Pacific) that KPC use its subsidiary, Anette Timber, to gain access to the timber reserves of small loggers. This allowed Louisiana Pacific to earn windfall profits from timber that should have been sold to financially strapped small loggers and sawmills. A Forest Service investigation also determined that ALP and KPC had cheated the U.S. treasury out of $63 to $81 million by rigging bids. Yet the supposedly tough law-and-order Reagan administration ignored these rapacious attacks on small business and granted the two companies a rate reduction on the price of timber that allowed KPC to pay only $2.12 to $3.09 a board foot between 1982 and 1988, far below the market rate of about $55 a board foot which independent operators were forced to pay. Thus two hugely profitable companies prospered while many smaller operators went broke, legions of local workers were fired, and small towns dependent on the timber economy went into a deep depression.[44]

Similar stories can be found all over the Pacific Northwest. In 1972 an antitrust lawsuit forced Georgia Pacific to spin off 20 percent of its operations, thus creating Louisiana Pacific—which went on to engage in more antitrust violations. In the 1970s the major paper companies (including Weyerhaeuser, Champion International, Boise Cascade, Diamond, and St. Regis) were forced to pay $535 million in fines and damages for illegally fixing prices on paper bags, plywood, and other products—one of the largest antitrust cases ever prosecuted up to that time—yet researchers Marshall Clinard and Peter Yeager found that criminal activity remained a persistent feature of the industry. In just two years, 1975 and 1976, companies in the paper, fiber, and wood industries racked up eighty-one (including twenty-eight serious and moderately serious) violations of federal regulations: fifty were for environmental infractions, fifteen for labor law violations, and ten for antitrust activities, price fixing, or restraint of trade.[45]

Since then, despite legal charges and fines, these recipients of massive government aid have continued to pollute the environment and to endanger the lives of their workers. In 1989, as the spotted owl debate heated up, two major paper companies, Louisiana Pacific and Weyerhaeuser, were responsible for nearly one-tenth (9.4 percent) of the 188 million pounds of toxic chemicals that corporate America dumped into U.S. waterways. Pollution from Weyerhaeuser's operations has been linked to thirteen Superfund sites; it is a defendant in a $100 billion class action suit alleging widespread poisoning of U.S. streams with dioxin; and the Washington Department of Ecology took 137 enforcement actions against the company between 1985 and 1991. Similarly, the EPA fined Georgia Pacific seven times between 1977 and 1990 for a total of $1.16 million. Only chemical maker Du Pont and steel producer USX had a worse record.[46]

Once again it needs to be stressed that wild animals and plants are not the only species endangered by the timber barons' corporate crime. One study by the research group Essential Information notes that between 1977 and 1990 Weyerhaeuser had the third worst record in corporate America for violations of workplace safety rules. Logging kills five times more workers in Washington state than heavy construction, the second most deadly occupation. In 1991 about 42,200 cases of occupational injury and illness in the forest products, wood, and pulp industries kept workers off the job for more than 400,000 days, making accident rates in these sectors about twice the national average for private companies.[47]

This cavalier attitude toward the law and the environment also put local communities in an increasingly precarious position. Because most major timber companies did not replant clear-cut lands until the 1960s, they had to expand overseas or into the American South to find new sources of lumber. By the early 1980s the paper and sawmill plants of the Pacific Northwest faced stiff competition from more modern plants in the South and from regions that still had huge harvestable forests. In effect, the environmentally disastrous practice of clear-cutting Pacific Northwest forests allowed the timber barons to export billions of dollars worth of profits out of the region, using that money to invest in other regions. This flow of capital left sawmills in Oregon and Washington, which faced a timber shortage, increasingly vulnerable to outside competition.

Congress attempted to bail out the industry by passing the Federal Timber Contract Payment Modification Act of 1984. In 1981 the Reagan administration named former Louisiana Pacific executive John Crowell assistant secretary of natural resources and the environment, despite his role in the antitrust scheme that had defrauded taxpayers and wrecked local businesses in Alaska. Given his record, it isn't surprising that soon after taking office Crowell rejected the longstanding forest service policy of sustained yields and maintained that the potential annual yield of the national forests was actually thirty-five billion board feet—far more than the thirteen billion board feet the forest service traditionally sold. A firm advocate of clear-cutting, he also fought plans to designate new forests as wilderness areas and proposed that cutting in the Oregon and Washington national forests could be doubled from five billion board feet to ten billion by the 1990s. That proposal was not enacted, but in 1980 Congress had passed the law that required the federal government to spend millions per year helping the timber industry cut a whopping 4.5 billion board feet during the 1980s in the Tongass National Forest.[48]

While the industry and its political allies justified such measures as a way of preserving jobs, government subsidies were actually destroying the long-term ability of the region to create new jobs. As supplies of timber dwindled, an industry-wide restructuring shut down about 160 mills in Oregon and Washington. Between 1978 and 1990 the destruction of many forests, increasingly automated sawmills, and the movement of factories to new regions reduced employment in Oregon's timber and wood products industries by 21.9 percent. And it is important to remember that most of these losses, about 71 percent, occurred before the spotted owl became an issue in 1988.[49]

The problems were compounded by an economic crisis that cut a deep swath through the American economy. In the 1970s rising oil prices fueled inflation, making it harder for consumers to open their wallets, and manufacturers who were losing market share to foreign competitors laid off workers, thus creating a recessionary cycle at a time when prices continued to rise. To curb inflationary pressures, which threatened to wreck many banks and financial institutions, the Federal Reserve instituted a policy of tight money that ratcheted up interest rates to nearly 20 percent by 1980. This wrecked the housing market and further reduced demand for many natural resources, including timber. As the economy's downward spiral continued in the early 1980s, slumping profits hurt the stock prices for old-line U.S. corporations in the manufacturing, mining, timber, and natural resources sectors. Depressed stock prices, however, allowed speculators to buy companies' stock for less than the price of the underlying assets. Once in control, these corporate raiders spun off assets, laid off workers, and restructured operations to produce better short-term profits. Over time, this wave of mergers and corporate takeovers dramatically restructured the U.S. economy, making American corporations more profitable.

In the timber industry financial fraud and insider trading made it easier for corporate raiders and large financial institutions to carry out a wave of mergers that cost workers thousands of jobs. In 1978, for example, Sir James Goldsmith used his offshore empire to accumulate stock in Diamond International, a rather sleepy conglomerate with interests in matches and greeting cards. Its chief attraction for Goldsmith, however, was its 1.6 million acres of timberland in the Northwest and Northeast. During the recession of 1981 and 1982 he acquired the company for about $660 million; financing for the deal was arranged by Michael Milken and Drexel Burnham Lambert. Within seven months Goldsmith sold six of the company's divisions to pay off bank loans totaling $435 million. That left him with only $162 million in debt and the valuable forestlands, which were still worth more than $700 million. Next, Goldsmith launched a raid on St. Regis, which owned some 3.2 million acres of timberland. To avoid losing control of the company, the management bought out for $159.6 million the shares he'd acquired for $109 million, producing a quick profit of almost $51 million. With this cash in hand, he set his sights on the Continental Group, another forest products company, which owned 1.4 million acres of timberland. Again, his intentions were thwarted, but Goldsmith took away a profit of about $35 million. As his takeover machine picked up steam, in 1985 he acquired Crown Zellerbach, with more than two million acres of timber. By 1987, after selling off pieces of Diamond (for a profit of about $500 million) and Crown Zellerbach (for even larger profits), Goldsmith's personal fortune had ballooned to more than $2 billion, including 3.5 million acres of timberland in the United States.[50]

Lured by such riches others jumped into the game. As thousands of millworkers were losing their jobs in the Pacific Northwest, Champion International bought St. Regis for $1.8 billion and the James River Corporation bought Diamond's sawmills and Crown Zellerbach's paper products division from Goldsmith. Georgia Pacific, which had become the largest timber and paper company by borrowing heavily to buy timber and mills in the 1950s and 1960s, launched a new shopping spree in the 1980s, spending $216 million for U.S. Plywood in 1987, $228 million for timberland and mills from American Forest Products in 1988, $665 million for Brunswick Pulp & Paper in 1988, and $3.8 billion in a hostile bid for Great Northern Nekoosa in 1990. That gave the company, which had been convicted of antitrust violations in the 1970s, more than ten million acres of forest land.[51]

As the 1980s wore on, nearly 35,000 mergers, acquisitions, and divestments, valued at some $1.5 trillion, were consummated, including many in the paper and forest products sector. These takeovers obviously produced huge fees for investment banks—such as Goldsmith's Drexel Burnham Lambert—and the profits from these deals created a pool of capital for acquiring assets like timber that could be spun off and used to realize quick profits. During this period Milken's junk bonds financed a who's who of corporate raiders, arbitragers and speculators: T. Boone Pickens, James Goldsmith, Ivan Boesky, Ronald Perelman, Carl Icahn, Saul Steinberg, Victor Posner, S&L mogul Charles Keating, and insurance executive Fred Carr.

Less immediately apparent was the role played by financial crime in the takeover boom, and the corporate restructuring that put unions and workers on the defensive. When close associates of Drexel obtained advance information about pending takeovers, these leaks allowed investors with close ties to Milken and his band to accumulate large blocks of stock, making it easier for Drexel's clients to consummate the merger. For example, in the Crown Zellerbach case, Drexel investment banker Dennis Levine leaked information about the pending takeover to Ivan Boesky, who purchased large blocks of stock that were later sold to Goldsmith. That produced huge insider-trading profits for Boesky and Levine, and the sale of Boesky's stock to Goldsmith (who seems to have been unaware of these illegal activities) made it easier for the raider to acquire Crown Zellerbach.

Investors closely tied to Drexel, such as Boyd Jeffries and Ivan Boesky, also agreed to park large blocks of stock for Milken and his raiders. Stock parking basically means that one investor agrees to act as a front man for the real investor who later buys back the stock at a prearranged price. Having other investors hold or "park" the stock allows raiders to avoid Securities and Exchange Commission [SEC] rules that they disclose any investment that reaches 5 percent of a company's stock. As a result, a raider can continue purchasing stock at relatively low prices from unsuspecting investors who have no way of knowing that its price will go through the roof when the takeover is announced. This practice hurts long-term investors to the benefit of takeover speculators. Similarly, having stock parked or held in friendly hands strengthens the raider's bargaining position with his prey.

Finally, Milken created a network of investors, companies, corporate raiders, and financial institutions that had launched corporate raids or raised capital with Drexel's junk bonds. Companies that were financially dependent on Drexel for their expansion frequently purchased new junk bonds, making it still easier for Milken's corporate raiders to consummate a takeover and finance their acquisitions.

The impact of this system on the environment and local communities is particularly apparent in Charles Hurwitz's takeover of Pacific Lumber Company (PL), which owned 190,000 acres of the redwood forests. In the 1930s, when other timber companies paid no attention to the future, Pacific Lumber had adopted a policy of sustained cutting, meaning that it would log no more timber than what was naturally regenerated. By the late 1970s, when other companies had already cut their old-growth redwoods, PL's long-term thinking gave it a virtual lock on the market for premium redwood lumber, which could be sold for high prices at hefty profit margins.[52]

Unfortunately, as corporate takeovers swept the timber industry in the mid-1980s, the company's steady but less than spectacular profits failed to impress investors, and its stock began trading far below the value of its underlying assets—land, timber, and a pension fund with a $50 million cash surplus. To boost its profits and stock price, PL's management considered increasing production by abandoning its policy of not clear-cutting timber. But before it could implement this scheme, corporate raider Charles Hurwitz appeared on the scene. Like a number of Milken's other associates, Hurwitz already had a history of doggy financial dealings. In 1971 he was sued for stock manipulation by the SEC (a case he settled without admitting or denying any guilt), and in 1977 he was accused by New York State regulators of looting an insurance company (a case he settled for $400,000, again admitting no wrongdoing).[53]

Soon after Hurwitz publicly stated his plans to buy PL, the New York Stock Exchange (NYSE) launched an investigation into the fact that large amounts of stock had been traded shortly before the takeover announcement, a pattern that usually indicates insider trading. No charges were ever brought by the NYSE or the SEC, but a House Energy and Commerce Subcommittee on Oversight and Investigation found evidence of insider trading and stock parking: Boyd Jeffries had purchased 539,000 shares of PL stock and sold them for $29.10 to Hurwitz—well below the market price of $34—in a sweetheart deal with all the markings of a classic stock-parking scheme. Jeffries's only explanation was that he was in a "good mood" (though in a later case he pled guilty to charges that he parked stock for Ivan Boesky). The deal with Jeffries gave Hurwitz enough shares to force PL's board to negotiate a takeover deal with him and allowed him to buy the company's shares at an artificially low price. Angered by the appearance of stock parking, insider trading, and other securities violations, many shareholders sued. By the end of 1995 they had won more than $150 million in damages from Ivan Boesky, Michael Milken, Maxxam (Hurwitz's parent firm), and various insurance companies.[54]

Having cut a deal with PL's board of directors, Hurwitz needed more help from Milken's junk-bond network to consummate the purchase. Milken structured the junk bonds so that Hurwitz would not have to pay any interest until 1990, and Drexel sold $795 million worth of bonds to its junk-bond network. Like Hurwitz, who obtained more than $1.8 billion in financing from Drexel for corporate takeovers in the 1980s, many buyers of PL bonds were financially beholden to Drexel. For example, the United Financial Group, an S&L that was 23 percent owned by Hurwitz, purchased $1.4 billion worth of Milken's junk bonds in that period. Likewise, Executive Life Insurance (which purchased billions of dollars' worth of bonds from Drexel in the 1980s) bought $300 million worth of PL's bonds over the next two years, making the insurance company the largest owner of PL's debt. Not surprisingly, when Hurwitz decided to restructure the company's pension plan, he set up a new plan managed by Executive Life, a deal that allowed him to take out $50 million from the old overfunded plan, to shore up his cash-strapped empire. And it gave Executive Life, which had played a major role in financing the takeover, a lucrative new client.

The cozy deal between two speculators was very bad for retired forest workers in northern California. In 1991 Executive Life went broke, in the largest insurance failure in U.S. history, and the pension fund for PL's retirees lost 30 percent of its value. So far, Hurwitz has covered the deficit, but the Department of Labor eventually sued the speculator, claiming that giving Executive Life control of the pension fund violated federal rules requiring such decisions to be made objectively, on "an arm's length" basis.

The federal lawsuit argues that the crumbling insurance empire was already in trouble when the pension deal was announced and that Executive Life was given the contract to manage pension funds simply because its owner had purchased so many PL junk bonds.[55] Eventually, the company settled for $7 million, a tiny fraction of the $50 million Hurwitz took from the pension fund.

Meanwhile, even with all the aid, legal and illegal, that he received from Milken's gang of speculators, Hurwitz still faced the difficult task of paying off his heavy indebtedness. To boost revenues and profits, he announced that he would abandon the company's longstanding opposition to clear cutting and double the amount of timber cut each year. Unlike the old management practice of never harvesting more than 2 percent of its assets, thus ensuring a long-term supply of high profit redwood timber for its mills, the new plan meant that this largest privately owned old-growth redwood stand in the world would disappear in fourteen to twenty-five years. "Pacific Lumber existed for 120 years before Hurwitz took it over, cutting at a more or less sustainable rate," explained Earth First! organizer Judi Bari. "Yet, Hurwitz could wipe it all out in the next generation."[56]

Environmentalists filed legal suits that slowed some of the cutting, but while these cases wound through the courts, taxpayers all over the country were facing huge bills as many of the savings and loans that were big speculators in Milken's junk-bond network began going broke. In 1988 the United Savings Association of Texas (USAT), partially owned by Drexel and Hurwitz, was declared involved and seized by government regulators, prompting a bailout that cost taxpayers $1.6 billion—the sixth largest thrift failure in U.S. history. At that time Hurwitz owned 22 percent of USAT and 28 percent of United Financial Group (UFG), the thrift's holding company, of which he was the chairman. Drexel owned 9.7 percent of UFG, making the investment bank and Hurwitz its two largest shareholders. In 1991 the Federal Deposit Insurance Corporation (FDIC) filed a massive 202-page $6 billion suit on behalf of forty-four failed S&Ls, accusing Milken, Drexel, and other defendants of setting up a network of junk-bond buyers at USAT and other thrifts which "wilfully, deliberately and systematically plundered certain S&Ls." The complaint alleged that "by a wide range of unlawful means, the Milken group induced certain S&L's to use federally insured deposits to purchase many billions of dollars of junk bonds—many of these improperly issued without registration. The Milken group's wide range of illegal conduct included market manipulation, threats, bribes, coercion, extortion, agreements to control prices and numerous fraudulent misrepresentations about the value and liquidity of junk bonds."[57]

The forty-four S&Ls that failed had purchased at least $28 billion worth of junk bonds, thus creating huge profits for Drexel and Milken. Between 1983 and 1987 Milken alone earned more than $1.1 billion in salary and bonuses, and a group of some five hundred partnerships allied with the junk-bond trading scheme paid out more than $2 billion in profits. Drexel earned about $49.2 million in fees from its work on the Pacific Lumber takeover alone and received warrants to buy 250,000 shares of Hurwitz's parent company, Maxxam. And although federal regulators alleged that Drexel tricked many S&Ls into buying the bonds by not warning them of the risks, the owners of several S&Ls also profited, at least in the short term. In a network of financial deadbeats who could not raise money through normal channels, when one thrift needed capital, the other junk-bond buyers would buy its bonds. Outside investors, seeing that large and seemingly profitable financial institutions were buying the bonds, were tricked into believing they were good investments. To maintain this illusion, Milken and other members of the network traded the bonds back and forth, creating the impression that they were valuable and easy to sell. For much of the 1980s, for as long as the bonds traded at respectable prices, the S&Ls could maintain that they were solvent financial institutions because they owned billions in valuable bonds. This also allowed thrift owners to collect huge bonuses and salaries, and to pay large dividends to their shareholders—thus siphoning money out of institutions that were, for all practical purposes, bankrupt.

In Hurwitz's case, the FDIC alleged that "at the direction of the Milken group, USAT purchased approximately $1.4 billion of Drexel-underwritten junk. In exchange Milken financed a number of business schemes for Charles Hurwitz," totaling $1.8 billion between 1985 and 1988. Even though most of USAT's troubles could be traced to massive fraud and financial woes in the Texas real estate market—a problem ignored by the state's law-and-order politicians—the junk-bond scene certainly added to thrift's woes. By 1991 it had lost $8.3 million on its bonds, and it owned another $45 million worth of bonds that regulators doubted could be sold at face value. As part of the government's attempt to recover assets looted from S&Ls during the 1980s, the FDIC was seeking $548 million from UFG.[58]

Given the steep price that taxpayers, logging communities, and the forests have paid for this corporate crime wave, one might expect the perpetrators of the scheme to face severe legal sanctions. In fact, however, Charles Hurwitz continues to profit from the PL takeover. Besides the $50 million he took from the pension fund, he sold the welding unit for $350 million, an office building in San Francisco for $31 million, and some company land—for a total of $500 million. Hurwitz also had his parent company, Maxxam, bail him out of a bad real estate deal, and gave himself the right to buy one million shares of Maxxam stock for only $10.40 a share—far less than the market price of $35—thus increasing his holdings by a third.[59]

Unfortunately, the Hurwitz case provides only one example of how the corporate restructuring of the 1980s has affected the Northwest's environmental and social problems. Many companies that were acquired during the 1980s and 1990s suffered job losses, and those that remained independent frequently attacked labor unions to boost their profits and avoid a Hurwitz-style raid. After Georgia Pacific acquired American Forest Products, it cut the work force by one-quarter and slashed wages by up to $2.25 an hour. Likewise, the ALP—which is blessed with federal subsidies to log the Tongass old-growth forest—forced its workers to accept reduced benefits and wage cuts of $2.40 an hour in 1984, thus saving itself $100 million a year. When profits improved, ALP refused to restore wages, and it broke a strike to improve pay and work conditions by hiring three hundred replacement workers. (The National Labor Relations Board eventually ruled that the company had acted illegally when it broke the strike.) About the same time, during a bitter 1986 strike, Weyerhaeuser won concessions equal to four dollars an hour for six thousand unionized employees. As part of a corporate restructuring, more than eight thousand workers lost their jobs between 1988 and 1992. During the 1980s alone, as the major companies worked to break the unions, more than three thousand members of the striking United Paper Workers International were replaced by nonunion workers.[60]

As union workers stood on unemployment lines, the timber companies' rapacious cutting practices continued to produce massive environmental problems and cost the region thousands of jobs. In the 1970s and 1980s major U.S. lumber companies dramatically increased their sales of un-milled logs to Japan, China, and Taiwan. By 1989 about 4.3 billion board feet of unmilled logs were being shipped to the Far East each year. This practice of selling whole logs to Asia severely reduced the jobs available for millworkers and inflated log prices for smaller sawmill owners. Many such mills, forced to compete with foreign buyers willing to pay 40 percent higher prices, simply went out of business.[61]

Major timber companies, however, profited heavily. In 1979, one secu-rities analyst estimated that Weyerhaeuser made a 62 percent profit on the logs it exported but only 10 percent on the ones it milled into lumber. In 1987 Weyerhaeuser alone exported more than $1.5 billion worth of logs, and 37 percent of Washington's timber harvest was sold overseas that year. Some economists have estimated that milling these logs into lumber would have created about 17,200 U.S. jobs—more than the 14,000 jobs the Forest Service estimated would be lost by the impact of regulations to protect the spotted owl. "You could fully protect the owl and the ancient forests and offset the entire job losses by a total ban on exports," argues an economist at the Wilderness Society.[62]

All this puts the spotted owl debate in a new light. For more than a century the timber barons have displayed no discernible interest in the ecosystems or the communities and workers they exploit. Early in the twentieth century they beat, assassinated, deported, and imprisoned labor leaders. Today, as these same companies move toward the twenty-first century, they are cutting jobs, wages, and benefits in order to export cheap logs—harvested with billions of dollars of government subsidies—to Asian countries that have foolishly cut down most of their own forests. In between, the timber barons carried on a corporate crime wave of labor, environmental, antitrust, securities, and banking law violations that in-flicted billions of dollars' worth of damage on investors, taxpayers, workers, small businesses, local communities, and, of course, the natural environ-ment. No one familiar with the history of the region—the huge fires resulting from by unregulated logging, the lives that were lost in dangerous mills, the bloody labor struggles and wasteful logging practices that turned whole communities into ghost towns—would ever accuse these multina-tional conglomerates of putting lives before profits. Any rational war on crime would begin by imposing heavy penalties on the executives who masterminded this carnage. Yet in the early 1990s, these same timber barons were able to convince many local residents that they should be allowed to log millions of acres of the last old-growth timber in the region.

One reason was the media's poor coverage of the affair. Newspapers and magazines published by major media companies, who themselves often own forest land or paper mills, rarely mentioned the region's history. There was little discussion of the rapacious logging practices that had already destroyed millions of acres of timber or the industry's bloody labor history. In the absence of information about these two fundamental subjects, the entire debate turned into a battle between a cute owl and a lot of angry loggers. Forest workers sporting "I like Spotted Owl—Fried" T-shirts could easily be characterized as anti-environmental troglodytes—despite the fact that some of them knew more about the woods than the top leadership of the Sierra Club and the environmental movement, in turn, could easily be dismissed as a bunch of tree-hugging fanatics, a stereotype that ignores the many environmental activists who live and work in timber communities.

The generally superficial coverage of the issue also left local residents vulnerable to the deceptive tactics of the timber barons' ridiculously well paid public relations agents. For example, timber companies in British Columbia hired Burson-Marstellar, the multinational PR company that had previously attempted to burnish the image of Exxon after the *Valdez* oil spill, Union Carbide after the Bhopal, India, disaster, and an Argentinean military dictatorship that assassinated thousands of political opponents. Armed with $1 million from the Canadian timber industry, Burson set up the B.C. Forest Alliance, which masqueraded as a grassroots organization opposed to radical environmentalists who wanted to curb logging. Similarly, the timber industry provides large sums for the Center for the Defense of Free Enterprise, a Washington state organization with a $5 million annual budget which helped create the so-called Wise Use movement, the Oregon Lands Coalition (another pro-industry group with about 80,000 members), and dozens of other organizations that issue pro-industry propaganda. In many cases, lumber workers have been given a day off work and bused to large cities to lobby legislators, or companies have hired anti-environmental specialists to come and explain to timber workers how they can fight the environmentalists who want to take their jobs. Just how much money has been spent on these efforts isn't known, but the total surely adds up to tens of millions of dollars.[63]

Equally large sums pour out of the industry into federal, state, and local politicians. Between 1991 and the end of 1996, timber companies gave more than $8 million to federal candidates or the two major political parties, and it spent another $3 million lobbying Congress in 1997. Over time, this kind of investment also seems to have paid off. In the 1980s, when the industry was also a major political contributor, Reagan and Bush attacked environmental regulations and made little effort to enforce labor laws and antitrust laws that might have saved thousands of union jobs. Their administrations also fought a ban on exporting unmilled logs, another measure that would have created tens of thousands of jobs, and staunchly opposed any federal public works programs that might have aided displaced workers. In 1990, for example, the Bush administration repressed a Forest Service report that recommended an $86 million public works program for displaced workers, a ban on exports, and a proposal to return a share of federal timber sales to local communities.[64]

By 1992, however, environmentalists hoped that change was in the air. That year, a federal court ruling made by a Reagan administration-appointed judge forced the Bush administration to halt all new timber sales on old-growth forests because Forest Service policies violated numerous federal environmental laws. Environmentalists also hoped that the election of Bill Clinton and Al Gore would force Washington bureaucrats to enforce the law. Clinton initially encouraged those hopes by promising that any solution to the spotted owl debate would be ecologically sound and abide by the laws, and soon after taking office he convened a team of experts in Portland to formulate various options.

Yet even as its policies put hundreds of thousands of poor Americans in jail for minor drug offenses, the Clinton administration was engineering yet another massive bailout for the timber barons. Using the stated criterion that any plan had to be environmentally sound, the experts came up with eight options. But the most generous option would have allowed less than a billion board feet to be logged, whereas administration officials had promised the industry two billion. So the White House rejected those options and brought in more experts, who came up with Option 9, which would allow upward of two billion board feet a year. Environmentalists denounced the plan, even though it would reduce the average harvests of the 1980s by about half, because it would also destroy about 40 percent of the remaining old-growth timber on federal lands west of the Cascades and permit a billion board feet to be cut each year in forests inhabited by spotted owls.[65]

As usual, however, the industry wasn't satisfied with large government subsidies to destroy some of the best remaining old-growth forest. In the summer of 1995 the timber barons persuaded the Republican-controlled Congress to add the so-called "timber rider" to an appropriations bill. The rider exempted all federal sales of timber from existing environmental laws and regulations, thus making it impossible for opponents to challenge new logging contracts in the courts, and it dramatically increased federal sales of timberland that was supposedly damaged by fire, insects, or storms. These two measures once again allowed the timber companies to engage in the kind of rapacious clear-cutting that had been discouraged on public lands since the 1980s. Yet Clinton signed the bill.[66]

Since then the industry has engaged in another land grab, once again at the expense of taxpayers and the environment. The salvage sales have allowed the cutting even of areas that would have been protected under Clinton's massive giveaway of 2.3 million acres of old-growth forests. In 1997 alone more than 7,800 acres of old-growth trees—some five feet thick and two hundred feet tall—were chopped down on federal forest reserves in Oregon, Washington, and northern California, and another five thousand acres cut along streams—producing landslides and soil erosion that threaten the future of many salmon and trout species. "In a word, it's a disaster," explains the head of the Western Ancient Forest Campaign. "Everything we've learned about how not to log in the west has been thrown out the window. This is the old style, ugly clear-cuts the Forest Service said they'd never do again. It's the destruction of fish, pollution of waterways, the imperilment of wildlife, the liquidation of the last and the best of our forests."[67]

Chapter 12:
White-Collar Muggers

Why is it that despite the high numbers of victims, when people think of crime, they think of burglary before they think of monopoly (if they think of monopoly at all), of assault before they think of the marketing of harmful pharmaceuticals, of street crime before they think of corporate crime?

—Russell Mokhiber, *Corporate Crime and Violence*

THE IMPENDING LIQUIDATION OF SOME OF THE LAST AND BEST old-growth timber in the Pacific Northwest has made endangered species of both the spotted owl and high-paying unionized forest work. Here is found a fundamental and very peculiar aspect of the debate over crime in America. Crime is a major issue in the United States because of the destruction and violence it levels on local communities. Yet the politicians who have cried loudest for a massive crackdown on street crime have been silent on the issue of corporate crime. Meanwhile, they have frequently been the most vocal advocates of policies that encourage corporations to despoil the environment, maim workers, and defraud investors. They commonly throw the book at street criminals while they shower government subsidies on corporate criminals, imposing massive costs on the economy, most of which must be borne by the nation's least affluent.

Precisely measuring those costs in dollars and cents is simply impossible. In the Pacific Northwest dangerous forest jobs killed thousands of workers; antitrust violations pushed many small enterprises out of business; shady financial deals associated with corporate takeovers cheated investors out of hundreds of millions, maybe billions, of dollars and touched off an industry-wide restructuring, costing local communities many jobs. Environmental damage dealt a severe blow to the region's multibillion-dollar fishing industry, and long-term environmental destruction threatens the $6 billion Oregon and Washington tourism trade. Yet the destruction of these forests has also boosted the local economy in some ways and provided the rest of the economy with cheap building materials, paper, and other forest products.[1]

Beyond the difficulty of balancing these complex economic equations, how does anyone calculate the value of a sawmill worker's life? What is the real economic value of a salmon spawning ground destroyed by soil erosion? Is it possible to estimate the cost in dollars to local communities when a major corporation breaks labor laws to destroy a union? Can a dollar figure be attached to losses suffered by a family whose breadwinner, seeking relief from a dangerous and stressful job, turns to alcoholism? Who can quantify, in strict economic terms, the beauty of a rainforest or its value for the future of the planet?

Even though there are no easy answers, various studies have attempted to quantify the costs and extent of corporate crime. Investigators Marshall Clinard and Peter Yeager found that 1,553 federal cases were brought in 1975 and 1976 against the 582 largest manufacturing and service corporations in the United States for violating criminal statues, regulations, or civil laws. At that rate, the average major corporation was charged with breaking the law 2.7 times over a two-year period. Of the 582 corporations, 60 percent had at least one violation during this period, and the average among those firms facing federal charges was 4.4 cases. Moreover, many of these corporations were repeat offenders, charged with the same violations year after year.[2]

Other data confirm the conclusion that corporate crime is a widespread, serial phenomenon, not an isolated problem created by a few delinquent rich white men. Amitai Etzioni, a sociology professor, reported that 62 percent of all *Fortune* 500 companies were involved in one or more illegal acts between 1975 and 1985 and that 15 percent committed five or more violations. Similarly, a *Fortune* study in 1980 found that 11 percent of 1,043 companies had been involved in a major crime during the preceding decade, and a 1982 survey by *U.S. News & World Reports* determined that "of America's 500 largest corporations, 115 have been convicted in the last decade of at least one major crime or have paid civil penalties for serious misbehavior." This survey found that of the twenty-five largest U.S. corporations seven had been convicted of a crime and several more were forced to settle major civil charges. Between 1971 and 1980, 2,690 corporations had been convicted of violating federal criminal laws.[3]

Attempts to add up the costs that these crimes imposed on society have produced some mind-boggling numbers. The U.S. Chamber of Commerce—not noted for its anti-corporate stance—suggested in a 1974 study that white-collar crime was costing the economy more than $40 billion a year. Adjusting that figure for inflation and increases in population, Jeffrey Reiman estimates a total of $197.8 billion in 1991. More recently, such experts in corporate crime as Marshall Clinard and Russel Mokhiber have estimated that corporate crime and white-collar fraud total at least $200 billion a year.[4] Combining the estimates of researchers into various kinds of corporate crimes results in even larger totals.

Price fixing and monopolistic practices. In recent decades corporate power has become centralized in fewer and fewer hands, a trend accelerated by trillions of dollars worth of mergers in the 1980s and 1990s. This industrial concentration, which allows a few major corporations to supply our food, finance our credit card purchases, and even orchestrate our entertainment, obviously provides ample opportunity for abuse of power. By controlling key natural resources, wholesale markets, and retail sales, major corporations can set prices, use their market clout to drive out smaller competitors, and force consumers to accept shoddy goods and poor service. In the forests of the Pacific Northwest a long history of antitrust violations ruined many local businesses, forced consumers to pay excessive prices, and bilked taxpayers by rigging bids for timberland. Other examples can be found in the cable, electricity, and telephone industries (where consumers have long complained of rate gouging and poor service by local monopolies); oil and natural gas (where a few large companies have frequently been accused of reaping excessive profits); securities (where the larger firms used their quasi-monopoly status in the 1960s and 1970s to charge excessive commissions that unnecessarily raised the cost of buying stock); and pharmaceuticals (where the largest drugmakers have frequently been attacked for charging excessive prices). Just how much these abuses cost the economy is open to debate. Clinard and Yeager cite earlier studies from the 1970s estimating that faulty goods, monopolistic practices, and other violations cost consumers between $174 and $231 billion a year. More recently, Ralph

Estes pegged the cost of antitrust violations, price fixing, and deceptive advertising at $1.16 trillion dollars.[5]

Environmental crime. Whereas the concentration and abuse of corporate power by big business impose huge economic costs on consumers, environmental crime attacks their health and well-being, producing hundreds of thousands of deaths and injuries each year. Like antitrust violations, which are an intrinsic part of an economic system based on highly concentrated corporate power, most environmental problems are directly related to the workings of the American economy. In the Pacific Northwest, for example, the timber barons' logging was based on market forces. If the housing market was strong and the price of logs was high, they hired workers and cut down everything in sight. When the economy was weak and lumber prices were below their costs, they laid off workers and shut down mills. Nowhere in these equations did they consider the long-term ecological impact or the long-term health of the forests. This would have meant reduced logging, which would cut their short-term profits and, in turn, depress the price of their stock, making the company vulnerable to a corporate takeover such as Hurwitz's acquisition of Pacific Lumber.

This basic economic problem of short-term profits versus long-term economic viability runs through all environmental crime like the river of oil pouring out of Exxon's *Valdez* tanker. Until the late 1960s government failure to force corporations to recognize the costs their activities impose on the environment encouraged a tradition of doing business without considering its impact on animals, plants, local communities, and workers. Marketing campaigns dictated that food processors package their goods in disposable plastic containers, despite the environmental problem of disposing of millions of tons of unnecessary packaging. Cost considerations led companies to switch over to the use of synthetic materials in building cars and homes, even though the burgeoning petrochemical industry used thousands of tons of toxic chemicals to produce those materials. Coal, hydroelectric, and nuclear plants were built to satisfy the energy demands of industry and consumers with little regard for such problems as acid rain and nuclear waste. Public transportation systems were gutted and consumers were encouraged by tax and economic incentives to buy gas-guzzling cars for long suburban commutes, even though these autos filled the air with smog and increased health problems in heavily populated areas.

The United States moved to curb the worst of these abuses in the early 1970s, but the tradition of producing goods and services based on short-term profit-and-loss considerations continued to result in environmental degradation. In the early 1990s U.S. companies released more than 3.1 billion pounds of toxic chemicals into the environment, of which 272.9 million pounds were pumped into the nation's waterways. Between 1973 and 1992, oil and natural gas companies reported 175,194 accidents that released 210.8 million gallons of oil into U.S. waters. Each year, local governments must dispose of 196.7 million tons of solid waste, about 4.3 pounds per day from every American, much of which can be traced to the corporate practice of wrapping goods in environmentally dubious packaging. More than five billion metric tons of gases that contribute to the greenhouse effect are pumped into the atmosphere, and more than 150 million Americans live in areas that do not meet federal clean-air standards. The American Lung Association estimated in 1993 that thirty million preadolescent children and eighteen million elderly Americans were "at risk" of developing health problems created by ozone; another 8.5 million young children and 4.6 million elderly citizens faced potential health problems from particulate matter in the air; and 1.5 million pregnant women and 3.5 million people with heart trouble were "at risk" from excessive carbon monoxide. In the late 1980s the EPA estimated that the groundwater in twenty-four states was tainted by one or more of twenty-two different pesticides—many known to cause cancer. In 1993 a National Resources Defense Council report noted that seventy-one known carcinogens were included in the more than 2.2 billion pounds of pesticides used in the United States. As a result, 38 percent of all food samples analyzed by the FDA contain pesticide residues, and one in ten public water supplies contains at least one pesticide. Overall, in 1993 and 1994 about fifty-three million Americans drank water that violated EPA standards, which many scientists contend are far too lax to begin with. Water pollution was so bad in 26 percent of the nation's waterways that fishermen could not harvest shellfish, and about 18 percent of the nation's rivers and lakes are so polluted the EPA deems them unsafe for recreation.[6]

Putting a price tag on pollution isn't easy. Toxic chemicals and environmental degradation produce obvious short-term costs, such as the 3,500 people killed and 200,000 injured by the release of toxic chemicals in 1984 at a Bhopal, India, Union Carbide plant. Less obvious are the long-term costs, such as cancer caused by the cumulative effect of exposure to carcinogens. Nevertheless, it will cost from $300 billion to $1 trillion to clean up the 32,000 toxic waste dumps in the United States. The U.S. Energy Department estimates a cost of $500 billion over the next seventy-five years to clean up toxic and radioactive chemicals dumped at its nuclear weapons plants. Outsiders claim that this figure is unrealistically conservative.[7]

In one recent attempt to add up all these costs, accountancy professor Ralph Estes surveyed dozens of studies and updated them for inflation and population changes. Estes begins by estimating that carcinogens and other dangerous chemicals in the workplace produce deaths and injuries costing the economy $274.7 billion a year. Then he estimates that air pollution, water pollution, and hazardous wastes cost the economy another $307.8 billion a year. These estimates—which include only costs attributable to business and exclude environmental problems created by government agencies—ring up a whopping $582.5 billion worth of damage. Finally, it should be stressed that Estes's estimate, big as it is, excludes any attempt to examine long-term environmental catastrophes such as global warming or the destruction of rainforests around the world.[8]

Occupational injuries. While corporate crime is often viewed as either victimless or harmful primarily to rich people, labor-law violations illustrate the violence that annually maims and murders many less affluent Americans. Between 1984 and 1992 more than 95,000 American workers died on the job, and 21.8 million suffered injuries that forced them to lose at least one day's work. While some occupational injuries are of course unavoidable, researchers have estimated that about 30 percent of all industrial accidents resulted from violations of workplace safety rules. If so, then about 28,500 people were killed and 6.5 million injured between 1984 and 1992 by corporate criminals.[9]

No one can easily quantify the economic cost of industrial accidents, but in 1994 the National Safety Council estimated that occupational deaths and injuries cost the economy about $110 billion. Equally monumental is the long-term cost of injuries that won't be apparent for years or even decades. Estimates of cancer deaths caused by polluted factories and workplace environments range as high as $274.7 billion.[10]

Discrimination against women and minorities. Like labor and environmental crimes, discrimination imposes huge costs on society in both obvious and not-so-obvious ways. Obvious examples, disproportionally victimizing working and poor Americans, are violations of federal and local laws requiring employers not to discriminate on the basis of race or gender. No one knows just how frequently these laws are broken, but a 1978 study by Congressional Research Service found that discrimination cost nonwhites $37.6 billion a year in lost jobs or inequitable salaries. (Adjusted for inflation these bias crimes would impose social costs of about $75 billion a year.) Likewise, one researcher estimated that gender discrimination in 1985 cost women about $81 billion a year in lower salaries ($106 billion in 1992 dollars). Other researchers' estimates range from $165 billion to $215 billion.[11]

Even a bill of $180 billion for lost salaries and jobs, however, only begins to measure the impact of discrimination. Many of the worst problems date from periods when racial and gender violence were rarely prosecuted, or were quite legal. And although some of the worst features of this system were dismantled during the civil rights period of the 1960s, corporate crime continues to perpetuate the legacy of racism and gender bias in the United States. Bias and illegal lending practices by major financial institutions still make it difficult for people of color and women to obtain reasonably priced credit, insurance, and mortgages for homes and small businesses. Many real estate agents continue to make it difficult for members of marginalized racial groups to move to areas that offer good housing, safe streets, and high-quality public schools. Meanwhile, tax fraud by multinational corporations and wealthy business elites makes it harder for government officials to finance urban development programs. Lax enforcement of environmental laws discourages new businesses, and poorer communities—which are frequently located in polluted cities or old manufacturing areas—are subject to serious health problems.

Tax fraud. One of the side-effects of the restructuring of the global economy has been the remarkable increase in the U.S. *underground economy*—a term that refers to untaxed income from legal and illegal enterprises. The U.S. Trust Company has estimated that the average amount of untaxed income grew from $52.5 billion a year in 1971-1975, to $370.7 billion a year in the 1981—and by 1985 totalled about $431.7 billion. Other researchers have pegged the underground economy in the mid-1980s at 5 to 15 percent of GDP—with criminal activity accounting for 25 to 50 percent of total untaxed economic activity.[12]

The growth of underground economies has put a huge dent in the U.S. federal budget. In 1995, the IRS estimates that it was losing about $150 billion a year in taxes (up from $100 billion in 1990, $75 billion in 1981, and $15.5 billion in 1965). At least $100 billion, or two-thirds, of this federal bill can be attributed to business and wealthy individuals. Even higher figures may apply to state and local governments, simply because they lack the investigators and political will to crack down on the problem. But making the conservative assumption that they face the same rate of tax fraud as Washington, the state and local government loss came to about $87 billion in 1992, with about $58 billion (two-thirds) attributable to business and wealthy individuals.[13]

Financial crime. Few systematic studies have been attempted to quantify the costs of financial fraud and most information on the subject is anecdotal—pertaining only to the cost of a particular bank fraud or a specific case of insider trading. Two notable exceptions are securities fraud and the S&L crisis. In 1987, the North American Securities Administrators Association, a group of state security regulators, estimated that securities fraud costs investors about $40 billion a year and in the early 1990s federal regulators concluded the S&L bailout would cost taxpayers about $145 billion, a figure that does not include interest charges.[14]

The scarcity of good studies on the cost of financial crime since then may reflect the mainstream view that the era of financial excess and greed ended in 1990. Unfortunately, in the following years financial fraud has played a key role in banking crises around the world, ranging from the collapse of the Bank of Credit and Commerce International in 1991 and the Barings Bank in 1995 to the Mexican currency crisis of 1994, fraud in the derivatives market that bankrupted Orange Count California and the recent Asian economic woes, which were triggered by nearly $1.5 trillion worth of bad loans.

Although most of those losses can be traced to larger economic problems and lax government regulation, it is important to remember that many banks facing financial woe had been involved in shady practices such as laundering money. At least some of the problems in the Asian banking sector could be traced to banks that had loaned large sums of money to politically well-connected businessmen who were accused of paying millions of dollars in bribes to local politicians. Likewise, banks around the world that were heavily involved in laundering money for crime groups have suffered some of the largest losses—a problem that contributed to the collapse of the Venezuelan, Mexican, and Thai banking systems in the 1990s. In addition, some of the banks that suffered the worst losses in Japan's banking crisis had lent money to Yakusa crime groups that was used in shady real estate and stock market schemes.

Medical and health care fraud. Almost everyone agrees that the trillion-dollar medical-industrial complex is riddled with fraud, waste, and mismanagement. The Clinton administration has argued that fraud—payments for treatment not given, excessive prices for drugs and medical services, quackery, the sale of unneeded medical devices, and so on—accounts for about 15 percent of all health spending, or about $150 billion. Slightly lower figures come from a 1993 study by the General Accounting Office (GAO), which placed the cost of fraud at 10 percent of all expenditures, and other groups estimate 3 to 10 percent, or $30 billion to $100 billion.[15]

Consumer fraud and dangerous products. You don't have to visit a heroin shooting gallery in New York City to find products that are bad for your health. Notorious examples include asbestos (which will cost more than 240,000 lives by 2010), the Dalkon Shield (a birth-control device which produced such infections and birth defects that the manufacturer filed for bankruptcy protection in a desperate effort to avoid paying $2.5 billion in court costs), DES (prescribed to as many as two million pregnant women between 1940 and 1971 despite evidence dating from 1938 that it caused cancer), silicone breast implants (Dow Corning filed for bankruptcy in 1995 rather than pay billions of dollars in damages).[16]

Just how much such cases cost the economy each year is open to question. The Consumer Product Safety Commission has estimated that injuries related to products under its jurisdiction—a regulatory homestead that does not include autos, pharmaceuticals, or tobacco—would total $10 billion a year. A more complete bill would have to include other costs: auto accidents caused by defective designs or parts (about $9 billion a year); fraud in the $70 billion-a-year auto and products repair industry (one

Reader's Digest investigation found that 56 percent of auto repair shops did unnecessary work on cars that were working perfectly); telemarketing scams (said to cost consumers $1 billion to $10 billion a year); retail overcharges (electronic scanners frequently register full price for items that are on sale, studies have found); misleading advertising (Beech-Nut paid a $2 million fine for selling a concoction of sugar, water, flavorings, and coloring as "apple juice" for babies); shady trade schools (whose poorly educated graduates, frequently lied to about the courses they receive and their job prospects, account for about 40 percent of all student loan defaults); bait-and-switch tactics by long distance phone companies (not to mention the many consumers switched to another higher-priced carrier without their knowledge); overbilling by lawyers, doctors, and accountants (in the S&L scandal federal regulators filed dozens of suits alleging that accountants and lawyers padded their bills by tens of millions of dollars), and customer service that companies promise but don't deliver.[17]

Government contracts. There is little doubt that corruption and fraud have allowed corporation doing business with government agencies to bilk taxpayers out of tens of billions of dollars each year, money desperately needed for education and other programs. Much of this fraud can be traced to cozy ties established between government officials and major corporations, a problem particularly apparent in the military-industrial complex. The delivery of overpriced, shoddy weapons to U.S. soldiers has been a scandal in every American war; despite two and half centuries of complaints about the merchants of death, weapons fraud remains one of the most lucrative corporate crimes. Between 1990 and 1995, twenty top Pentagon suppliers paid the government more than $500 million in penalties and settlements for corporate wrongdoing. One GAO study found that half of all Pentagon contracts during a two-year period ending in June 1988 were overpriced and that the government had been bilked out of $1.1 billion in just 774 contracts. Ernest Fitzgerald and others have argued that as much as 25 percent of the military's procurement budget is lost through waste and fraud; if so, it has cost taxpayers hundreds of billions over the last two decades.[18]

While Pentagon purchases of sundries at ridiculously exorbitant prices have been widely publicized, less attention has been paid to a variety of scams used to cheat the U.S. Treasury out of money on timber, mining, and oil contracts. In 1995 the Project on Government Oversight accused seven of the largest oil companies of cheating the federal government out of $1.5 billion in royalties they owed for oil taken from federal lands. But the largest attacks on the government treasury are quite legal. Besides billions in subsidized timber sales, the U.S. government continues to give away at least $1 billion a year in rich minerals, coal, and oil. The 1872 Mining Act, for example, gave corporations rights to mine valuable minerals from federal land without paying a cent in royalties, and the option of purchasing the land for a mere five dollars an acre. As a result of this act American Barrick Resources got mineral rights to the Goldstrike mine in Nevada, a windfall now worth some $7 billion. The Phelps Dodge Corporation mined $500 million worth of copper in 1989 from a mine it claimed for five dollars an acre under the same law. Overall, a GAO study estimates the total value of minerals extracted from federal lands at $1.2 billion. Yet these corporate giants paid not one cent of mineral royalties to taxpayers. Worse, this bit of corporate welfare has also produced massive environmental damage. One 1993 report by the Mineral Policy Center estimates that 557,650 abandoned mines have released heavy metals, acid, and other toxics, polluting 12,000 miles of waterway and 180,000 acres of lakes and reservoirs. Ultimately, it will cost taxpayers more than $70 billion to clean up this mess.[19]

The total costs. Adding up all these costs isn't easy. Many major examples of corporate violence can't be quantified, and some very large costs that corporations impose on communities can't be called crime; it is quite legal for corporations to profit from lands and public assets obtained a century ago by bribery and corruption. But totaling the smallest estimates from these studies, corporate crime costs the U.S. economy at least $1.2 trillion a year, a figure that more than doubles to $2.5 trillion if you add up the larger estimates.

Although those numbers may include some double accounting, it must be stressed that this quick tour of corporate crime leaves out some very large enterprises—money laundering, redlining, political corruption, capital flight, insurance fraud, illegal attempts to destroy unions, accounting fraud, and so on—which would surely add hundreds of billions to either estimate. Ralph Estes, who has compiled the best available summary, arrives at an estimated cost of $2.4 trillion in costs in 1991 dollars—or $2.6 trillion in 1994 dollars—by adding up such costs as discrimination ($165 billion); workplace injuries and accidents ($141.6 billion); deaths from workplace cancer ($274.7 billion); price-fixing monopolies and deceptive advertising

($1,116.1 billion); cost of unsafe vehicles ($135.8 billion); health problems caused by cigarettes ($53.9 billion); other product injuries ($18.4 billion); environmental costs ($307.8 billion); defense contract overcharges ($25.8 billion); income tax fraud ($2.9 billion); violations of federal regulations ($39.1 billion); bribery, extortion, and kickbacks ($14.6 billion), and miscellaneous costs ($82.5 billion).[20]

Even the very conservative $1.2 trillion estimate, let alone Estes's $2.6 trillion, dwarfs the cost of street crime. In 1995 the Bureau of Justice Statistics estimated that the value of all goods stolen by street criminals totalled a mere $17.42 billion, and researchers at the National Institute of Justice estimate that violent crimes cost victims about $105 billion annually in property and productivity losses and outlays for medical expenses. Even the NIJ's larger estimate of $450 billion, which includes controversial calculations of the cost of pain, long-term emotional trauma, and disability, represents only about 37 percent of the $1.2 trillion cost of corporate crime and only 17 percent of the $2.6 trillion higher estimate.[21]

Given these costs, one might expect law enforcement to mobilize huge budgets and staff to fight corporate crime. Yet in 1991, after a decade of some of the worst corporate scandals in American history, the fifty-one U.S. regulatory agencies on the front line of the war against corporate crime employed 113,311 people—fewer than they did in 1980—and spent $12.2 billion, according to the Center for the Study of American Business. In contrast, federal, state, and local law enforcement officials spent some $30 billion to fight the war on drugs in 1993, and most of the $97.5 billion spent on law enforcement in that year was devoted to fighting street crime.[22]

Commentators have frequently justified this disparity by saying that corporate criminals do not terrorize their victims and that many of their crimes harm very few people. In fact, however, corporate crime is a very deadly business, as illustrated by the 95,000 American workers who died on the job and the 21.8 million that suffered injuries between 1984 and 1992. Moreover, most of these corporate crimes disproportionally harm less affluent Americans—which may help explain why such crimes are treated so laxly. Just as people who commit crimes against minorities face less severe penalties from the criminal justice system, the legal system is less harsh on corporate crime that harms poorer and working Americans. Although it is widely understood that everyone is affected by environmental crimes, there is very little research on the relationship between class and environmental crime. Working and poor Americans, who are much more likely to live in inner-city areas which have the highest levels of pollution, frequently find work in industrial and service jobs that involve working with toxic chemicals.

Estes concludes that exposure to carcinogens on the job causes about 150,000 deaths a year. (That would mean 1.5 million deaths in the last ten years, far more than all the battlefield deaths suffered in every American war since 1860: 566,000 U.S. soldiers during the Civil War, the First and Second World Wars, the Korean War, and the Vietnam War.) In sharp contrast, only 21,505 Americans were murdered in 1991, indicating that going to work in a toxic environment can be a lot more dangerous than walking through a high-crime neighborhood.[23]

On a local level, too, environmental crime provide a good example of how powerlessness makes poor communities particularly vulnerable to corporate misdeeds. In Puerto Rico, massive tax breaks to multinational corporations encouraged pharmaceutical companies, oil refineries, and petrochemical plants to turn the island into "one of the most heavily polluted places in the world." Likewise, in the American south, the white political establishment has systematically allowed—and frequently encouraged—the placement of toxic dumps and chemical factories close to minority communities. For example, the nation's largest hazardous waste landfill, which receives garbage from forty-five states and several foreign countries, is located in a predominantly African American section of Alabama known as the "black belt."[24]

The rest of the country hasn't produced a much better record. A 1987 study found that three of the five largest toxic waste sites, which handle more than 40 percent of the commercial landfill capacity in the United States, were in black neighborhoods. Nationwide, the survey found that, statistically, race was the most significant variable in the location of such facilities and that communities with the greatest number of hazardous waste facilities had the highest concentrations of people of color. Overall, three of every five African Americans and Hispanics and about half of all Asians, Pacific Islanders, and Native Americans lived in communities that have toxic waste dumps. In 1990 about 50 percent of all blacks and 60 percent of all Hispanics—versus only 33 percent of all whites—lived in counties where two or more air pollutants exceed permissible federal standards, a problem that many researchers claim contributes to the much higher levels of asthma and respiratory problems in poor minority communities. Moreover, 68 percent of all black children living in families earning less than $6,000 a year had lead poisoning. The main sources were peeling lead paint in substandard housing and pollution from cars using gasoline with lead additives.[25]

These situations maintain the subordinate status of poor and working-class Americans. They reflect the legal system's unwillingness to deal effectively with corporate violence, and are bolstered by a history of legal discrimination against working-class Americans, particularly minorities and women. Many of the worst problems faced by minorities and women date from periods when racial and gender violence was legal, or only rarely prosecuted. Wars against Native Americans to steal their land, which exterminated whole tribes, were heavily subsidized by the U.S. government. Slavery and then forms of indentured servitude left millions of blacks with few real legal rights or protections until the 1950s. Women, excluded from political power until recent decades, were all too often subjected to a wide range of sexual abuses. Between the 1620s and the 1960s, domestic violence, abuse, workplace harassment, and rape either were tolerated or were poorly prosecuted. Finally, unions that attempted to improve wages and working conditions faced enormous legal restrictions, imposed austerity, and violent repression. Minorities and women thus frequently ended up in dangerous or badly paid jobs and substandard services, housing, schools, and health care—resulting in many deaths, injuries, and shortened lives.

On the other side of the coin, white-collar crime has played a major role in bolstering the power of wealthy elites and big corporations. Political corruption shaped the giveaway of natural resources to railroads and timber companies. Bribes paid to corrupt dictators helped expand the economic power of multinational corporations.

A brief snapshot of the global business of exchanging bags of cash for contracts and investments came into public view in the mid-1970s. A post-Watergate Securities and Exchange Commission belatedly attempted to look into public corporations that were fraudulently claiming bribes as business expenses. That probe documented that 450 large U.S. corporations—including ITT, Northrop, Grumman, Textron, Exxon, Lockheed, United Brands, oil companies, arms traders, and pharmaceutical firms—paid more than $1 billion in bribes to foreign leaders. Of twenty major U.S.

drug companies, nineteen admitted substantial payments. Thus the pharmaceutical sector earned the dubious distinction of being the most corrupt American industry.[26]

The scandal led to the 1977 Foreign Corrupt Practices Act that made it illegal for U.S. companies to bribe foreign governments. But after years of lobbying by major businesses, the law was weakened in 1988, and companies have found a variety of mechanisms to avoid it. One common tactic is to pay middlemen or consultants who do the requisite dirty work. Even so, investigators continue to uncover major bribery scandals. In 1988 Ashland Oil paid $25 million in damages to two executives who had been fired after they questioned the $46 million Ashland paid in the early 1980s to obtain oil in Oman, Abu Dhabi, and other parts of the Middle East. In 1989 Goodyear Tire & Rubber pled guilty to offering bribes to an Iraqi trading company, and Napco International paid a $1 million fine for bribing officials in Niger to obtain a lucrative contract. Lockheed pled guilty in 1994 to paying $1 million worth of bribes to Egyptian officials to obtain a $79 million contract. In 1995 a top aide to the Brazilian president alleged, in a wiretapped conversation, that Raytheon may have paid bribes to obtain a $1.4 billion contract to set up a massive environmental surveillance system to monitor the Amazon, a charge the company denies. That same year IBM was accused by Argentine investigators of paying $21 million to obtain a $250 million contract to modernize the computer system at Argentina's central bank; the investigators alleged that the bribes inflated the contract from $125 million to $250 million. Although IBM has denied any wrongdoing, the scandal led to the resignation of the country's economy minister, a close aide to Argentina's president, the head of the central bank, and three top IBM executives.[27]

Meanwhile, major corporations continue to argue that heavy regulations on American industry have been imposed by a zealous band of environmentalists and left-wing Democrats. But a quick look at the history of government regulation and corporate crime reveals a very different story. Just as wealthy elites created a war on street crime that is more concerned with preserving property and wealth than creating safe, prosperous communities, government officials have created a regulatory system that is more concerned with preserving the profitability of American corporations than protecting the public's health, safety, and welfare from white-collar criminals.

Chapter 13:
Regulating for Profits

There are two things that are important in politics. The first is
money and I can't remember what the second one is.

—*U.S. Senator Mark Hanna, 1895*

I think I can say, and say with pride, that we have legislatures that
bring higher prices than any in the world.

—Mark Twain

ON AUGUST 15, 1971, PRESIDENT RICHARD NIXON APPEARED ON
national television to reveal his second surprise of the summer. Only one
month earlier America's most famous living Cold War politician had shocked
the world by declaring that he would visit mainland China. Now, in a startling
departure from the free-market economic policies he had defended all his
life, Nixon announced that he would impose government wage and price
controls to curb rising inflation. The idea obviously did not please him; he
looked even more nervous than usual—no easy accomplishment—and
beads of sweat formed on his upper lip.

But that plan, which received most of the press coverage, was in many
ways less notable than Nixon's speech announcing that the United States
would "close the gold window." This was a radical change from the entire
postwar financial system, which was based on the convertibility of the dollar
for a specified amount of gold. Currencies would no longer be tied to the
dollar and the dollar to gold at thirty-five dollars per ounce. All currencies
would now freely float on the international markets, rising and falling
according to the strength of their economies and the power of currency
speculators. Financial markets, not government policies, would play an

increasingly important role in the basic monetary policies, such as interest rates and the value of the dollar on foreign markets, that have an enormous impact on inflation, job creation, and economic growth. The era of speculative finance capital had come of age.

Nixon's decision to increase government regulation in one area—wages and prices—while deregulating another—the dollar—marked both a turning point in government regulation and a continuation of longstanding policies. The U.S. regulatory system has passed through several stages closely related to major economic and political changes, and the periods of major regulatory change occurred in periods of crisis. In the nineteenth century lax government regulation of the economy and financial system, coupled with severe legal restrictions on unions and on the political power of minorities and women, made it easy for wealthy businessmen to accumulate vast industrial empires. But this regulatory regime created a number of social, political, and economic problems that threatened future economic growth. To head off radical political movements, which wanted to impose severe restriction on major corporations, and to deal with the sources of economic instability, which created monopolistic abuses and vicious competition that hurt profits, the federal government passed significant antitrust, labor, transportation, telecommunications, food safety, and banking legislation in the late nineteenth and early twentieth centuries.

In many cases, major corporations actually played a dominant role in shaping such legislation. Railroads, for example, backed antitrust laws as a way of avoiding more onerous state rules. Meat packers lobbied for government regulation of the food industry, so they could export more goods to Europe—which already had tougher regulations—while reducing competition from smaller companies. Likewise, major banks, which had been buffeted by crises that were worsened by lax regulation, played a crucial role in passing the legislation that created the Federal Reserve.

The early agencies initiated one of the most enduring features of government regulation in America: major corporations working with government leaders to set up regulations, which were frequently designed to protect corporate interests and to head off more radical proposals. It is no accident that the significant periods of regulatory activity in the United States were also periods of political protest and economic crisis—the last turn of the century, the Great Depression of the 1930s, and the 1968 to 1984

period. The regulations often protected large corporations from competition, and corporate lobbyists were generally able to influence the policies
of regulatory agencies.

In the early twentieth century the new regulatory regime put corporations on a firmer legal basis for future growth but did not deal with issues
such as poverty, poor wages, poor educational opportunities, and income
inequality which limited the growth of a modern consumer economy.
When these problems exploded into the Great Depression, the Roosevelt
administration attempted to deal with them and with a new round of
radical political protest by instituting new forms of government regulation
and intervention designed to create a larger class of middle-class consumers
and to provide smoother economic growth in the private sector. Although
much of the business community was exceedingly hostile to programs that
increased government spending and made union organizing easier, corporate leaders once again played a crucial role in shaping regulatory policies.
They helped draft the National Industrial Recovery Act (NRA), which
created industry-wide cartels, and played a key role in the 1932 creation of
the Reconstruction Finance Corporation, which bailed out insolvent banks
and railroads. Federal officials worked directly with the Business Council,
a private trade group that represented forty to sixty of the nation's largest
corporations, to implement the NRA, even giving the group free offices in
the Commerce Department.[1]

Although the courts eventually ruled the NRA unconstitutional, the
notion that government should work closely with major corporations to
regulate the economy was enshrined in most New Deal regulatory reforms.
The Glass-Steagall Act divided the financial sector into securities (Wall
Street investment banks and brokerages), commercial banking (Citibank
and others), and housing finance (the savings and loan industry) and
created regulatory agencies to deal with each sector: the SEC for securities,
the FDIC and the Federal Reserve for commercial banking, and the Federal
Home Loan Bank Board (FHLBB) for the S&Ls. This system gave more
autonomy to the Federal Reserve and key regulatory responsibilities to
private industry. On Wall Street, for example, the SEC delegated the fron-
tline regulatory operations to the exchanges. The New York Stock Exchange,
the American Stock Exchange, the National Association of Security Dealers,

and so on—financial institutions owned by Wall Street companies—were given widespread powers to create rules and discipline brokers.

Many reforms had the effect, intended or unintended, of protecting established corporations from competition. Unlike reformers in the late nineteenth century, who sought to break up the power of big business, the New Deal saw large powerful corporations as an intrinsic feature of modern life. The issue was not to destroy their power but to work with them to create a long-term basis for economic prosperity. For example, the Motor Carrier Act of 1935 and the creation of the Civil Aeronautics Authority (CAA) in 1938 gave the federal government (which already regulated the railroads) regulatory control over the trucking and airlines industries. The resulting cozy, cartel-like environment for major companies and large unions in the transportation sector protected them from price competition. Similarly, the 1934 law which established the Federal Communications Commission (FCC), led to quasi-monopoliesthat were owned by major media companies in the radio and television sector.

In the long run, New Deal labor regulation also proved good for major corporations. The legalization of labor unions, and the establishment of the federal National Labor Relations Board to protect the right to organize, were bitterly opposed by many major corporations. From 1945 to 1965, however, in markets controlled by a few major producers, it was relatively easy to pass higher labor costs onto consumers. At the same time, improved wages and benefits gave consumers more disposable income and boosted economic growth. As a result, the consumer society, which had begun to emerge in the 1920s, bloomed in the postwar era. This was due in large part to massive government subsidies for the automobile industry (highways and lack of auto regulation); single-home construction (tax breaks and low-interest loans); cheap electricity (from federally built dams); education (college aid for veterans); oil (lucrative tax breaks); chemicals (lax environmental regulations before 1970), and the military (trillions of dollars worth of contracts for major arms manufacturers).

All this translated into more jobs in sectors closely tied to consumerism (service workers jumped from 6 to 10.2 million between 1940 and 1970, and white-collar employees from 16 to 37 million), higher wages (median family income jumped by 213 percent between 1947 and 1970), and more disposable income (up by 307 percent in those years). Also from 1947 to

1970, exponential growth occurred in advertising (which increased by 360 percent), the manufacture of consumer products (processed food production increased 100 percent, rubber and plastics 364 percent, chemicals 567 percent, paper products 189 percent), and retail outlets (sales of furniture and appliances skyrocketed 163 percent, autos 167 percent, gas sales 248 percent, clothing 208 percent). All these increases, it should be stressed, came in a period when population and prices grew by only 42 and 74 percent respectively.[2]

By the late 1960s, however it was clear that the economy was facing problems that the regulatory system was incapable of dealing with. Urban riots and the civil rights movement highlighted the system's lack of interest in racial justice, the economic difficulties of the cities, and the limited ability of the consumer society to deal with social problems. Environmental troubles—from smog and gridlock to polluted waterways and pesticide-soaked food—were reducing the quality of life, and the old wasteful methods of production were hurting such industries as fishing, mining, timber, and tourism. Increasingly affluent consumers wanted more protection from shoddy products that were engineered for short lives. A new generation of blue-collar workers demanded better working conditions. And government officials found that rising unemployment, inflation, trade deficits, and energy costs seemed to resist the old Keynesian solutions.

Once again, then, political protests and long-term economic problems produced an era of regulatory reform. Facing radical protests against racism, pollution, and corporate power, the Nixon and Ford administrations attempted to turn mounting political pressure for reform in less radical directions. On December 2, 1970, Richard Nixon signed an executive order creating the Environmental Protection Agency to enforce and administer the National Environmental Policy Act of 1969 (which required the development of a national environmental policy), the Water Quality Improvement Act of 1970 (which gave it power to regulate the dumping of wastes into water), and the Clean Air Act of 1970 (which set deadlines for reducing auto emissions and improving air quality). In upcoming years the EPA expanded its power into the regulation of hazardous pesticides (1972); the dumping of toxic wastes into oceans (1972); noise standards (1972); safe drinking water (1974); the control of toxic substances (1976), and the storage and handling of hazardous wastes (1976). By 1976, Nixon and Ford had also signed laws creating the Occupational Safety and Health Administration (OSHA, an agency in the Labor Department designed to protect worker safety); the National Highway Traffic and Safety Administration (a Transportation Department bureau to oversee auto safety and fuel efficiency); the National Credit Union Administration (to regulate credit unions), and the Consumer Product Safety Commission (to ensure the safety of consumer products). In 1973, they began the Federal Energy Administration (to manage short-term fuel shortages)and the Mining Enforcement and Safety Administration (an Interior Department agency to ensure mine safety), and in 1974, the Nuclear Regulatory Commission (to replace Atomic Energy Commission and oversee the use of nuclear power) and the Materials Transportation Board (to regulate the transport of hazardous materials).[3]

With this flurry of activity by two conservative Republicans the number of people employed in federal regulatory agencies grew by 43 percent, from 73,375 in 1970 to 105,052 in 1975 (the largest five-year increase in regulatory staffing since the New Deal), and total spending climbed from $1.4 to $3.5 billion—another record. Even in inflation-adjusted dollars, regulatory spending climbed 90 percent under Nixon and Ford. In sharp contrast, between 1975 and 1980 the supposedly tax-and-spend Carter administration increased staffing only 13 percent (105,052 (to 118,849) and total spending (adjusted for inflation) 27 percent (from $5.75 to $7.31 billion).[4]

A new alphabet stew of government regulatory agencies, employing thousands of new bureaucrats, was created by two conservative Republican presidents. This poses an interesting riddle. After all, both men owed much of their success and power to wealthy campaign contributors, and they had impeccably conservative credentials. Closer inspection, however, shows that their decision to increase government intervention in the economy was less radical than it might appear; it offered Nixon and Ford a way of diffusing pressure for more radical reforms and of paying back their political allies. Likewise, both men hoped that the new agencies, which had passed a liberal Democrat-controlled Congress, could be managed by a conservative White House to the benefit of wealthy elites. In creating the EPA, for example, Nixon hoped that consolidating all environmental regulation into one agency would enable him to set policy and to push it in conservative directions. Moreover, blue-collar voters had become increasingly important for the success of law-and-order politicians and Nixon's decision to create OSHA was payback to the conservative trade unionists that helped elect him.

In short, Nixon and Ford consistently attempted to mold government intervention in the economy to the benefit of their business allies. Despite Nixon's reliance on blue collar voters, his wage and price regulators consistently favored big business at the expense of organized labor, enabling corporations to raise prices while wages were frozen. Finally, Nixon and Ford's policy of using big government to solve the problems of their big business allies indicated just how much conservative views of the economy had shifted.

But by the late 1970s it was becoming clear that the country's economic problems were not responding to the old Keynsian nostrums. Inflation, touched off by heavy government expenditures for the Pentagon and for social programs in the 1960s, remained high in the 1970s as energy costs skyrocketed. Unlike earlier inflationary periods, however, these years saw the economy stagnate, posting dismal numbers for job creation, productivity, and trade deficits. Under pressure from the financial community, which was up in arms about rampant inflation, President Jimmy Carter appointed Paul Volcker to the Federal Reserve. To control the money supply, this former Wall Street investment banker, who championed the conservative monetarist policies of Milton Friedman, boosted interest rates to record levels. That pleased Wall Street and wealthy investors but sent the economy into a tailspin that wreaked havoc on the farming, manufacturing, and housing sectors.

This crisis quickly changed big business's attitude toward big government. Facing increased foreign competition and a stagnant domestic economy, major U.S. corporations found it increasingly difficult to pass on the costs of new consumer, environmental, and labor regulations to consumers. Further, as they struggled to cut costs and improve their position in the global economy, they became increasingly disenchanted with the cost of social programs. As a result, major business organizations and wealthy elites turned against government regulation, taxes, and social programs as unnecessary expenses that reduced their profits and made American business less competitive.

Carter responded to those criticisms by deregulating a few key economic sectors—notably trucking, airlines, and banking. He slowed the growth of regulatory agencies and issued an executive order asking them to weigh the costs of new regulations against their potential benefits. These trends—deregulation, budget cutbacks, and the emphasis on the costs of regulation—dramatically accelerated after the election of Ronald Reagan. He cut regulatory spending (in real 1982 dollars) from $7.8 billion in 1980 to $6.9 billion in 1983, and during his eight years in office spending rose in real terms by only 10 percent—a minor increase that did not keep pace with the total growth of the economy, which expanded by 25 percent in inflation-adjusted dollars. Equally important, Reagan significantly cut the number of employees at federal agencies. Full-time employees regulating the finance and banking sector dropped from 9,649 in 1980 to 9,370 in 1983 as financial fraud on Wall Street began to increase and the thrift crisis expanded. In consumer safety and health the number dropped 17 percent, from 66,016 in 1980 to 54,592 in 1988; employees regulating working conditions decreased 21 percent, from 18,201 to 14,409. Staffing at the Federal Trade Commission was slashed by 40 percent between 1980 and 1988, and the antitrust division of the Justice Department, in charge of curbing monopolistic abuses, was packed with Reagan loyalists who refused to enforce federal antitrust laws.[5]

Meanwhile, Reagan issued executive orders requiring that all new regulations had to be subjected to rigorous cost-benefit analysis and that agencies adopt the least costly alternatives. He further required that major rules had to be reviewed by the Office of Management and Budget (OMB), and he took pains to hire regulators who had long histories of being opposed to government regulation. Federal control over the prices and routes of truckers, buses, railroads, and airlines was significantly reduced. Thrifts were allowed to speculate in securities and commercial real estate; controls over the interest paid on savings accounts were phased out; and despite the Glass-Steagall Act, which separated commercial and investment banking, banks got limited powers to sell mutual funds, underwrite securities, and peddle insurance. The FCC loosened up federal control over the media, reducing the requirements for programming in the public interest, allowing media companies to own more television stations, making it easier for cable television operators to raise prices, and ending some restrictions on advertising in children's television programs.[6]

The most significant legacy of this period, however, might be called deregulation by mismanagement, corruption, and incompetence. Reagan's policy of hiring inexperienced political hacks, gutting staff, and adding red tape to the regulatory process made it virtually impossible for many agencies to do their jobs. Even as the nation faced a new health care crisis in the form of AIDS, the Food and Drug Administration reduced the number of its inspections from 32,778 in 1980 to 19,876 in 1988. By the end of the Reagan era the agency—which allowed AIDS-tainted blood to be given to thousands of patients and employed regulators who took bribes from drug manufacturers—had only 7,500 people to inspect the drugs, food, and other products that account for one-quarter of all consumer spending in the United States. And even though the FDA was supposed to test drugs within six months—a measure designed to allow patients to receive new medication quickly—the severely understaffed agency was taking an average of thirty-one months by the end of the Reagan administration and four of its nine testing laboratories were rated "unacceptable."[7]

Equally severe problems emerged in environmental and labor regulation. Reagan staffed the EPA with conservative ideologues who would eventually be removed from office for profiting from their ties to polluters, manipulating cleanup grants to influence elections, and shredding documents. Not surprisingly, these incompetent managers dragged their heels on the Superfund cleanup, thus endangering many Americans and boosting the ultimate costs of the program to as much as $1 trillion. Reagan's EPA also paid little attention to the ongoing destruction of old-growth forests and did little about acid rain. Moreover, as the Reagan administration reduced the number of OSHA inspectors (in charge of protecting workers from unsafe conditions) from 1,328 in 1980 to 1,044 in 1987, the seriously mismanaged agency failed to issue regulations on repetitive stress problems, even though these became the leading cause of occupational illness by the mid-1980s. Finally, having the OMB review all major regulations made the regulatory process so cumbersome and bureaucratic that it was harder for agencies to move quickly to solve new problems and protect consumers.[8]

The policy of deregulating the economy by mismanaging government agencies (and wasting billions of tax dollars) was cheered by corporations but imposed huge costs on consumers. Long-suffering taxpayers were promised relief by the Reagan administration, but quickly discovered that the gutting of federal regulatory programs to save a few million dollars would eventually cost them billions. In 1989 the General Accounting Office found that cutbacks in government agencies had exposed taxpayers to about $300 billion in potential losses from badly managed government-insured loans and deposits in the 1980s. About half of these were related to losses in the thrift industry, which had been exacerbated by cutbacks in bank examiners and deregulatory legislation. The GAO also noted that poor management of various programs and employee cutbacks had cost the taxpayers $38 billion in agricultural credits, $10 to $20 billion in arms sales, $5 billion in student loans, and at least $5 billion in mortgage loans. Such losses were often directly related to cuts in staff and systematic corruption. For example, the Department of Housing and Urban Development (HUD) was unable to monitor its loan methods adequately because some four thousand employees had been fired. By 1988 its bad debts had soared to $4.2 billion, and several people were eventually indicted and convicted for corruption because of federal housing grants given to private developers.[9]

Perhaps more important, neither the Republicans in the White House nor the Democrats who controlled Congress during this period attempted to revamp the regulatory system to reflect the workings of the global economy. A 1995 change in the regulation of the meat industry was the first major overhaul in almost three-quarters of a century. By 1997 OSHA had enacted rules pertaining to only twenty-five of the seventy thousand toxic substances used in the workplace. Rules regarding campaign finance and antitrust law had not been significantly revised in decades. As late as 1998 the financial system was ruled by a system of regulation enacted in the 1930s, an era when pension funds did not hold trillions of dollars in assets and computerized, twenty-four-hour trading didn't exist even in science fiction novels.

The thrift crisis revealed just how dangerous an outdated, corrupt regulatory system could be, but this lesson seems to have been quickly forgotten. By the time Clinton was elected president, both parties had enthusiastically embraced the neoliberal approach to regulation. Like Reagan and Bush, Clinton issued executive orders stipulating that regulations must be cost-effective and that federal agencies reduce the number of existing regulations by about 50 percent over three years. Regulatory agencies were gutted by staff and budget cuts. From 1989 to 1993 the Bush administration had increased total spending and staff for regulatory agencies by about one-fifth: from $11.8 billion (in constant 1992 dollars) to $14.3 billion, and from 103,649 employees to 126,264. Under the Clinton administration regulatory spending dropped to $13.6 billion in 1996 and staff to 124,915. Further, Clinton announced plans to lay off 250,000 federal employees to pay for his $30 billion crime bill, which will sentence tens of thousands of minorities and poor whites to long jail sentences for minor drug crimes. In effect, the administration decided to reduce enforcement of corporate crime while spending tens of billions to jail poor people.[10]

The popularity of these neoliberal ideas reflected the larger economic changes that reduced corporate support for government intervention in the economy. But the popularity of pro-business ideologies in Washington also reflected greed and corruption in all levels of government. Although corruption has long been a feature of American political life, there is mounting evidence that the economic changes of the last two decades have dramatically increased the power of big business over what is left of big government. The corrupting influence of that power became significant during the Reagan administration: two former White House aides were indicted for influence peddling, Attorney General Ed Meese was investigated for corruption, and officials at the EPA, the Pentagon, the FDA, and HUD were investigated or indicted for taking bribes. Congressional leaders, notably House Speaker Jim Wright and House Whip Tony Coelo, were also forced out of office for influence peddling during the S&L crisis.

But levels of corruption seemed to reach new heights in the Clinton administration. Soon after arriving in the White House Bill and Hillary Clinton faced a massive investigation into their involvement in the collapse of an Arkansas thrift that had made large contributions to his political career. By the end of 1996 that investigation had produced nine guilty pleas and three convictions. By early 1999, Clinton had been impeached but not convicted, and several cabinet officials either were indicted or were under investigation for taking bribes or collecting illegal campaign contribution.[11]

Far more important, however, are the institutionalization and legalization of corruption, leading to the power of money over all aspects of government. Lobbyists, most of whom represent the interests of the rich and powerful, spend $5 to $10 billion each year to influence federal, state, and local officials. About nine thousand lobbyists are registered in Washington, and another seventy thousand unregistered influence peddlers ply their trade there; tens of thousands more work on some local level.[12] In 1996 another $2.65 billion was spent on federal elections, triple the amount in 1976.

This tidal wave of cash has created a system in which a tiny elite of elected politicians, political consultants, fund raisers, think tanks, pundits, regulators, and affluent campaign contributors control the basic workings of the state. Wealthy contributors provide the money to elect political leaders who generally come from elite backgrounds and generally pursue policies that benefit the power brokers who bankroll their careers. More often than not they also appoint judges, cabinet officials, key staff members, and regulators from similarly privileged backgrounds. Many regulators have had cozy ties to major businesses prior to their government service, and many go to work for those industries after leaving the public sector. This revolving door reduces their willingness to pursue corporate criminals who might one day be their bosses. Finally, all of these officials, elected and unelected, are bombarded with advice and policy recommendations from lobbyists, consultants, and think tanks—many of which employ former regulators, congressional aides, and politicians—that are massively funded by major corporations.

Not surprisingly, a system that places more emphasis on collecting bags of cash from wealthy contributors than on the interests of the average citizen is open to enormous abuse, and it would be hard to find a branch of government that has not been tarred with scandal in recent years. Much press attention has correctly focused on the morally challenged exploits of the Clinton administration, but the Republicans in Congress have managed to produce an even worse record. During the 1996 presidential race Simon Fireman, the campaign finance vice-chairman for Bob Dole, was convicted on criminal charges that he laundered $125,000 in contributions for Dole and the Republican National Committee. Fireman's company, which laundered some of the money through Hong Kong banks, was fined $6 million, the largest penalty ever imposed for illegal contributions.[13]

Corporate lobbyists also played a key role in the drafting of the "Contract with America" in 1994, and the GOP leadership hosted weekly meetings with the U.S. Chamber of Commerce and the National Federation of Independent Business to receive advice on new legislation. Lobbyists actually wrote some of the bills introduced, and the Republican legislative agenda has consistently read like the wish list of a corporate lobbyist. After corporate campaign contributions allowed the Republicans to seize control of the House in 1994, they passed a law limiting the ability of shareholders to sue for securities fraud, and proposed legislation that forces the federal government to pay states for the cost of the new regulations (a move severely limiting the ability of regulators to propose new rules). In addition, House and Senate Republicans pushed through a number of bills offering regulatory relief to corporate polluters and white-collar criminals. Timber companies got the 1994 law that allowed them to clear-cut forests and ignore environmental laws. Both houses voted to prohibit the Interior Department from enforcing existing laws designed to protect endangered species, and the Senate voted to increase timber harvests in the old-growth Tongass National Forest. Both houses also agreed to open up the Arctic National Wildlife Refuge to oil drilling, and both Houses attempted to gut the Superfund cleanup and cut the already underfunded EPA budget.[14]

Not all of their proposals were signed into law, but public officials found it easier to raise money for expensive political campaigns by attaching themselves to corporate welfare schemes that had little chance of being enacted. In 1996, House Speaker Newt Gingrich attended 132 fund raisers and claimed to have helped Republicans raise $100 million, from which he paid $1.1 million in legal bills relating to his ethics charges and $6 million for his own campaign, the most expensive House race of 1996. More recently, as House Republicans were issuing subpoenas and denouncing Clinton's moral codes, they were accepting large checks from special interests in exchange for political access. In 1997, one hundred campaign donors and lobbyists forked over $5,000 apiece to play golf in Palm Springs with twenty Republican congressmen; some forty lobbyists each paid $3,000 to go skiing at a posh Vail, Colorado, resort with Republican Representative Michael Oxley (who plays a key role in securities, telecommunications, and utility legislation); and lobbyists paid $6,000 apiece to attend the Super Bowl with two powerful Republican congressmen. Likewise, in February 1997 Republican congressional leaders jetted to Florida to spend several days with Team 100—a group of more than two hundred donors who have given at least $100,000 in soft money contributions to the party during any calendar year since 1993. A week later Senate Majority Leader Trent Lott also met with Team 100 members to discuss the party's "upcoming legislative agenda." No wonder Republican literature boasts that Team 100 members "enjoy ... the greatest opportunity possible to meet and talk informally with party leaders, foreign dignitaries and special guests."[15] Corporate polluters who write large checks get private meetings with powerful politicians, while the communities that are directly harmed by their misdeeds are shut out of the corridors of power.

Many political leaders like to pretend that corporate cash has little overall effect on the political process. In fact, however, it played a key role in the congressional 1996 election. The Republicans faced a number of problems. Democratic Party efforts to court corporate contributors were paying off handsomely, while support for the Republican agenda dropped from 42 pecent in July 1995 to only 28 percent in January 1996, after a public backlash against Gingrich's crude attempts to gut social and environmental programs. By April, 49 percent of all voters said they were inclining toward a Democrat for Congress, and only 44 percent were ready to vote Republican. Yet as public support for the Republican agenda dropped, corporate campaign contributions skyrocketed, thanks in part to the strategy of introducing bills designed to protect powerful special interests. PAC contributions to Republicans rose from $20 million in 1993 to $42 million in 1995, while the cash flowing to Democrats dropped from $36.6 million to $25.6 million. And by June 1996 the Republicans had raised another $75.8 million in soft money (which enables a party to support its candidates indirectly), topping the $65.1 million collected by the well-oiled Democratic machines. Thanks to support from major corporations who stood to earn billions in profits from the right's political agenda, the Republican party was able to overcome early projections that the Democrats might regain control of Congress. With House and Senate incumbents eventually raising a total of $378 million (versus their challengers' $118 million), more than 95 percent were reelected—including many of the Republican freshmen in the House, who raised $69.5 million compared to only $31.5 million by their challengers. The freshmen "came to shake Washington up," the president of Common Cause quipped. "They stayed to shake it down."[16]

Unfortunately, the average taxpayer ends up paying for this system of legalized graft whereby major corporations collect huge amounts of corporate welfare each year. In a study of voting patterns of the 104th Congress, which finished its work in 1996, the Center for Responsive Politics found that the sixty-one senators who voted to preserve sugar subsidies, which will cost taxpayers an extra $1.4 billion a year in higher prices, had received an average of $13,500 in contributions from sugar industry PACs between 1991 and 1996; the thirty-five senators who opposed subsidies got only $1,500. The 213 House members who voted to spend an additional $493 million for B-2 bombers averaged $2,100 apiece from defense contractors in 1995 and 1996; the 210 who voted against this measure got only $100. Senators who voted to preserve laws that inflate drug prices for consumers by $2 billion to $5 billion a year, and add more than $350 million a year to government health care spending, were heavily funded by pharmaceutical companies that benefited from the loophole. Senators who supported subsidies to peanut growers, which cost consumers $314 million to $513 million a year, received an average of $2,720 in PAC contributions from the industry. Senators, who successfully defended a $15 billion government-funded program to help U.S. arms dealers peddle their deadly wares around the world received an average of $53,723 in PAC contributions from Defense Department contractors. Finally, the senators who supported laws that allow environmentally disastrous clear-cutting on federal lands received an average of $19,503 in timber PAC money between 1991 and 1996.[17]

Government by the rich for the rich not only disenfranchises less affluent Americans and costs them money but produces regulatory policies that have given the United States one of the worst occupational safety records in the developed world, at a cost to the economy of at least $110 billion annually. The fatality rate for U.S. workers is nearly six times that of Sweden, nine times that of the United Kingdom, more than double those of Italy and Japan. Overall, one of every eleven American workers is killed or seriously injured on the job—perhaps more, given the agencies' lack of resources to document the problem properly. One study of 1986 U.S. Labor Department data found that U.S. workers lost an astonishing 420 million workdays because of injuries and accidents—nine times the official Reagan administration's estimate of forty-seven million.[18]

Yet between 1980 and 1988 the Reagan administration cut the number of inspectors at the U.S. Labor Department from about 1,600 to 700, closed forty OSHA field offices, reduced inspections by about 5 percent, and slashed the number of cases citing companies for serious violations from 44,695 to 35,662. Reagan's policy of packing the National Labor Relations Board with conservative zealots—one of whom worked for a law firm that specialized in busting unions—also made it difficult for unions to protect their members: the number of cases on which the NLRB sided with employers over unions increased dramatically, and the understaffed agency developed a huge backlog of unresolved cases. Realizing that the government had little interest in enforcing the law, employers began using blatantly illegal tactics to defeat union organizing drives. In about one-third of the drives in the late 1980s, employers attempted to fire pro-union activists, and the number of workers who lost their jobs for attempting to organize a union increased by more than 500 percent over the late 1960s figures.[19]

Even after a Democrat returned to the White House, competent enforcement of labor laws did not return to Washington. Badly funded as it is, the EPA still gets twenty dollars for every dollar spent on OSHA, and there are six U.S. Fish and Game inspectors for every single OSHA inspector. The Clinton administration has heavily publicized its crackdown on sweatshops, but the number of labor inspectors at the end of 1996 was 20 percent lower than in 1990. Likewise, inspections of the meatpacking industry dropped 43 percent after 1994, even though 36 percent of all workers in this sector suffer illnesses and injuries every year.

Equally important to worker rights and workplace safety are official attitudes toward larger economic issues. For starters, Presidents Reagan and Bush made little attempt to enforce antitrust laws, a policy that has allowed trillions of dollars' worth of mergers to go unchallenged—many in heavily unionized sectors of the economy. Nearly 100,000 unionized jobs were eliminated as a result of mergers in the 1980s. Workers who survived those cutbacks faced an increasingly insecure future—a state of affairs that made it harder for unions to demand better wages and working conditions. At the same time, deregulation had an enormous impact on several heavily unionized industries. After deregulation of the phone and telecommunications sectors, which began with the breakup of the old AT&T monopoly in 1984, local phone companies eliminated more than 300,000 jobs—most of them unionized. Similarly, after President Carter and the Democratic Congress began deregulating the airlines and trucking industries in 1980 and government regulators ended their control over trucking rates and airfares, increased competition forced companies into bloody price wars and contentious battles with labor unions. In the trucking industry more than 140 carriers, employing 175,000 went out of business; real earnings dropped 27 percent between 1978 and 1990; and the number of truckers represented by a union dropped from 60 percent in 1975 to only 25 percent in 1995. Finally, increased competition convinced many companies to turn to outside suppliers (many of them not unionized) or to temporary employees for essential services. Today, 7,000 temp agencies provide employment for more than two million people a year, double the number in 1990, a trend that further reduces the power of unionized labor. As a result of the corporate restructuring, deregulation, and a tougher attitude toward labor, unionized workers dropped from 29 percent of the work force in 1975 to 18 percent in 1985 and less than 14 percent today.[20]

These changes also affected workplace safety. For example, following a wave of mergers in the oil industry (which produced the first huge profits for corporate raiders and a number of major cases of financial fraud), a large number of skilled workers were fired. Their absence or, in some cases, replacement with less experienced employees led to a sixfold increase in the fatality rate in the petrochemical industry and a notable rise in industrial accidents that released oil and other toxics into the environment. In less obvious cases, nonunion companies that grabbed market share from unionized operations apparently improved their competitive position by skimping on workplace safety. Between 1980 and 1990 aggressively antiunion Nucor Steel, which grew into the nation's seventh largest steel company during the 1980s, had the highest death rate for occupational injuries in the steel industry.

Finally, these broader attacks on labor produced enormous insecurity and stress. Millions of workers who lost jobs in the 1980s faced long periods of unemployment or were forced to accept lower wages. Of nearly 4.5 million Americans who lost permanent full-time jobs between 1991 and 1993, only two-thirds had found new jobs by February 1994, and nearly half of those (47 percent) were earning less than before. Moreover, the workers retained in downsized companies were often forced to do the same work that two or more people had once done. Not surprisingly, workers' compensation claims based on job stress doubled between 1980 and 1988 and accounted for about 15 percent of all claims by 1988. In the late 1980s the Office of Technology Assessment estimated that stress-related illnesses were costing business $50 to $75 billion a year. The drive for increased efficiency and production speedup offers a partial explanation for the dramatic increase in the growth of repetitive stress injuries from less than 50,000 a year in 1986 to more than 300,000 in 1993.[21]

This attack on labor also played a key role in the creation of underground economies, which can expose workers to dangerous, illegal working conditions. In the garment trade, for example, the United States lost an average of 3,451 garment industry jobs *every month* between 1979 and 1995, and the number of workers represented by a union dropped from 900,000 to only 350,000. Faced with increased global competition, U.S. garment factories began to rely on nonunion labor, children, and illegal immigrants. Between 1983 and 1989, Department of Labor statistics show, the number of children found working illegally increased from 9,200 to 22,500, and a 1994 Labor Department survey of California garment manufacturers found that 51 percent were not paying the minimum wage, 68 percent were cheating workers out of overtime, and 73 percent did not maintain proper payroll records—a practice that allowed fly-by-night companies to avoid paying workers back wages. By 1996 a U.S. Labor Department study found that about half of all the country's garment factories could be classified as "sweatshops," meaning that they routinely paid less than the minimum wage, refused to pay overtime, and violated other labor laws. In New York City there are believed to be some 4,500 sweatshops employing about 50,000 people, and in Los Angeles there are 75,000 garment workers in illegal sweatshops.[22]

Currently, two to three million workers are paid less than minimum wage, in part because federal and state governments make little attempt to enforce the law. Although the garment industry has received the most publicity, an estimated 50 percent of all long-distance nonunion truckers also get less than the minimum wage. And workplace conditions have deteriorated in other industries that were once heavily unionized. In the late 1970s and early 1980s, for example, most meat packers were unionized and decently paid; many earned more $30,000 a year, and wages and benefits topped $19 an hour. But in the 1980s employers cut wages and fired many union workers. Today, the rate of unionization is about half what it was in 1963, and the industry employs many illegal immigrants who make as little as $6.02 an hour to work in dangerous factories where the loss of limbs and repetitive stress injuries are common.[23]

In recent years, the government's lack of interest in protecting its own working citizens has been compounded by its policy of encouraging global expansion. Between 1980 and 1992 the U.S. government spent more than $1.3 billion helping American companies move jobs to low-wage zones around the world and financing the creation of tax-free havens abroad. By 1992, government aid had helped create more than two hundred export-processing zones in twenty countries in the Caribbean and Latin America, employing 735,000 workers who produced $14 billion worth of goods exported to the United States.[24] During this period, when the U.S. economy lost 2.6 million manufacturing jobs and nearly half a million apparel jobs, the federal government also provided more than $900 million in taxpayer-subsidized loans to help companies relocate, paid for ads promoting the fact that U.S. companies operating in El Salvador could pay workers as little as thirty-three cents an hour, and encouraged the creation of a computer-ized blacklist of Honduran union organizers. The Commerce Department even sent a letter to U.S. companies noting that "with labor rates that range from just $1.00 to $3.00 per hour, you can imagine the types of margins which these [offshore] firms are enjoying." In one case, the department encouraged Westinghouse to close a Connecticut plant and build five plants in the Dominican Republic, a move that cost six hundred American workers their jobs. In 1990 alone, more than one hundred U.S. apparel companies closed fifty-eight plants and fired twelve thousand workers in order to move to low-wage zones.[25]

Labor law provides an obvious illustration of how corporate power directly harms less affluent Americans. Less obvious are the financial crimes made possible by the burgeoning global economy for goods and services. New financial systems not only enable major multinational corporations to move capital and profits anywhere in the world and capitalize quickly on changing global markets but also make it easier to smuggle drugs, launder money, and avoid prosecution. This financial revolution, which has allowed organized crime groups to accumulate vast assets and impeded the work of law enforcement, has also made it harder for poorer communities stressed by job losses to sustain stable social structures and attract new investment.

Chapter 14:
Financial Fraud

President of the First Los Angeles Bank: "How much [cash] are you shipping today."
BCCI customer and head of a $1 billion drug money-laundering operation: "How much? I don't know. I have no idea."
"Ship me all you got."
"Okay, everything's yours anyway."

—*DEA surveillance tape*

I hope it doesn't shock you too much that we do have occasions of frauds in banks and if we closed down a bank every time we found an individual act or two of fraud we'd have rather fewer banks than we have at the moment.

—*Robin Leigh-Pemberton,*
Bank of England governor

IN THE EARLY 1980s AZIZ REHMAN WAS OVERJOYED TO FIND A JOB at the Miami offices one of the world's fastest-growing financial institutions, the Bank of Credit and Commerce International (BCCI). A recent immigrant from Pakistan, Aziz had arrived with dreams of success only to discover that the streets of Miami were not exactly paved with gold. With wages 40 percent below the national average, it was tough to make ends meet in an expensive city where the number of people on welfare had risen by more than one-third in 1978-1979. About the only thing that was booming in Liberty City and the other poorer sections of Miami was the murder rate—it was the highest in the nation.[1]

In 1980 the situation exploded into what the *New York Times* called "the worst race riot of this century" (an assessment rendered obsolete eleven years later in Los Angeles). Angered by the failure of prosecutors to convict four policemen who had killed a black insurance agent for no apparent reason, Liberty City seethed with violence. Passersby were beaten and in some cases doused with gasoline. Most of the area's businesses were destroyed and when President Jimmy Carter visited with promises of aid for rebuilding, blacks threw rocks and bottles at his motorcade. The federal aid never arrived.[2]

But if the people of Miami were hurting, its banks were booming. In the late 1970s well-dressed men had begun to appear with huge bags of cash, forcing bank managers to hire extra shifts of workers to count mountains of bills that were covered with strange white powder. Loan officers from Citibank, Bank of America, and Chase Manhattan battled for the privilege of lending billions to impoverished Latin American governments. And S&L executives, once happy to make modest profits lending money to middle-class homeowners, began investing hundreds of millions in office-building, certain that the real estate market would boom forever. New skyscrapers, housing some of the world's largest financial institutions, towered over Miami's skyline like stacks of silver dollars in a gigantic poker game. "There was so much money they couldn't keep it in the vaults," recalls Patrick M. Walsh, who worked on Operation Greenback, the federal investigation of money laundering.[3]

Aziz's new employer wasn't as big as many of the American banks, but BCCI was intent on catching up as quickly as possible. It had already established close ties to some of the country's most powerful people, and Aziz crossed paths with many of them. Some days he would drive out to the airport to pick up powerful foreign visitors, such as the governor of the Central Bank of Barbados. Or he would use his lavish BCCI expense account to entertain local politicians. "This was all part of the bank's trying to cultivate public official and powerful individuals," Aziz remembered years later. "Whatever the person wanted," BCCI pay for it—shopping, luxurious dinner, a nightclub visit, a Bahamas cruise. They would even provide women. It was "a full-service bank all the time."

But Aziz soon discovered that international finance had a less glamorous side. Two or three times a week, his supervisors would give him large postal bags filled with cash and order him to deposit the money at other Miami banks. Aziz was proud of his physical strength, but after a long day of lugging cash through the sweltering Miami heat, his muscles ached like a construction worker's. Once he badly injured his back carrying $700,000 cash. "I could not pull the bag," he remembers. "[But my boss said] ... this is part of your job. We do this same thing you know. . . . I had to so I did it. Seven hundred thousand dollars is a very heavy bag."

The bags of cash weighed on Aziz in other ways: each day he had to carry them through many of the city's poorest neighborhoods. While double-digit inflation and skyrocketing unemployment rates had devastated many parts of Miami in the 1970s, the drug trade boomed. Some analysts have estimated that Latin American drug money supplied about half of the $1.5 billion in foreign capital invested in Miami each year in the late 1970s and early 1980s. In 1981 alone foreigners accounted for 45 percent of all the real estate sold in Miami. Nicholas Aquiree, a founding member of the Florida Importers Exporters Association, admitted at the time that "the trafficking of drugs was developing at a very fast pace. . . . You can see that a great deal of construction and development [started] ... about that time. . . . Without drugs and the impact of [drug] monies ... I don't think that it would have been possible to see this rate of development."[4]

But there was a price for such progress. As drug gangs imported cocaine by the ton and battled for turf and market share, the violence escalated. In the late 1970s, nearly a quarter of a million guns were sold in Dade County, and the murder rate jumped more than 400 percent. Aziz, terrified by the thought that someone might find out what was in the bags he was dragging around Miami, finally complained to his supervisors. "That's why I open my mouth," he later told investigators. He was certain "somebody will shoot me. . . . [But] they say shut up. 'You don't know anything about banking. . . . You do your job. You deposit it and you come back.'"

When Aziz refused, he was fired. Angry at the bank, he took piles of computer printouts with him and began a three-year crusade to get someone to investigate BCCI. "I called the Federal Reserve," Aziz says. "They said no. . . . I called the FBI. They said it's not my case and you better talk to the IRS. Money laundering is their business. So, I called them at the IRS." In 1984, when Aziz sent the IRS computer printouts that detailed many of the bank's illegal activities, local investigators realized that they had stumbled upon a tremendously important case. But their superiors in Washington showed little interest, and a joint IRS and Customs Service investigation was slowed by lack of resources. By the time bank regulators shut down BCCI in July 1991, however, the financial scandal had prompted a global investigation into the bank's activities. But for Aziz the case provided little satisfaction. BCCI executives prevented him from finding new employment, saying he wasn't trustworthy. "I couldn't get another job because they wouldn't give me a good reference," Aziz remembers. Eventually he was forced to file for bankruptcy.[5]

Nor was he alone. As the global financial system has stumbled from boom to bust like a drunken sailor on the lookout for a better party, 132 of the 181 members of the IMF have suffered "significant" problems in their banking sectors, and fifty-two developing countries have lost most or all of their banking capital since 1980. In the developing countries alone more than $250 billion has been spent since 1980 to shore up insolvent banks, and Moody's Investors Service estimates that in 1997 fifty-eight banks around the world had an E or E+ rating—rank given only to banks in need of a financial bailout. And those estimates do not include the Asian, Eastern European, and Latin American financial crises that exploded in 1997 and 1998. By the fall of 1998 Asian banks had more than $1.5 trillion in bad debts, and most Russian banks were insolvent.[6]

This nasty mixture of crime, rampant speculation, and financial crisis has been a persistent feature of the global economy for three decades. Much of the reporting on these scandals has been limited to the business press, and even that has tended to minimize the importance of financial fraud to the average person. Yet financial fraud costing the U.S. economy tens of billions of dollars each year has a devastating impact on less affluent communities. Contrary to the popular perception that financial fraud consists primarily of rich people stealing from well-heeled dupes, these white-collar crimes have played a key role in the problem of violence in America. Financial crooks allow violent criminal gangs to thrive, steal billions of dollars from government agencies, and prevent less affluent people from obtaining the capital and jobs they need to sustain themselves and their communities.

A telling example of the way financial fraud affects the average American can be found in the workings of the offshore financial system and the Eurodollar markets. After the Second World War, U.S. corporations dreamed of becoming able to move their goods and services anywhere in the world. Initially, the job of constructing a global financial system that could service their needs fell to the U.S. government and U.S. banks, who followed their blue-chip clients into foreign lands. Eventually, however, multinational corporations, which had less and less allegiance to any one country, required a financial system that operated outside the control of any government. In the 1960s, such a system took shape in the Eurodollar market—based in London—and in offshore banking havens.

The Eurodollar market takes its name from the fact that central banks and foreign corporations began to accumulate dollars in their vaults as the United States increased its foreign trade and overseas military expenditures. In the 1950s these banks began lending out these dollars, and the Eurodollar market, operating completely outside any government control, grew by leaps and bounds—from $148 million worth of bonds or loans issued in 1963 to $721 billion in 1988, more than the total issued by Wall Street.[7]

Banks liked the Eurodollar market because it let them operate without strict government regulations and because most of the trading occurred in "offshore havens" that operate as a kind of capitalist utopia for transnational corporations. Strict bank secrecy laws protect depositors from the prying eyes of tax collectors or foreign investigators. Lax government regulations also allow foreign banks to carry on many activities, such as selling stocks and bonds, that may be illegal or tightly regulated in their home countries. Best of all, taxes are virtually nonexistent.

Some of these financial centers—Hong Kong, Switzerland, Luxembourg—have long histories, but the proliferation of unregulated havens really took off in the late 1960s and 1970s as the Eurodollar market boomed and the Western powers provided foreign aid to third world countries. U.S. aid money, for example, helped Panama set up an offshore financial center in the early 1970s, and international aid money allowed governments in the Bahamas, Aruba, the Caymans, and elsewhere to establish or expand their banking industry. The Cayman Islands, for example, didn't set up shop as an offshore center until the mid-1960s, but by 1990 it was home to more than five hundred banks—including forty-six of the fifty largest—holding more than $250 billion in assets. One of these was BCCI, which had established its headquarters in Luxembourg and subsidiaries in dozens of other havens. By 1990 its Cayman subsidiary held some $7.5 billion in assets.

Offshore financial zones assisted the growing global economy by providing multinational corporations with an unregulated, secretive system of moving capital all over the world. In addition, since many are located inside what economists call "duty-free zones" in the Caribbean, Central America, and Asia, they play a direct role in the global system of multinational production. For example, Panama allows multinational corporations to import parts from their manufacturing subsidiaries all over the world without paying duties. Then the parts are assembled into finished televisions, VCRs, and other goods by local workers—who are often paid as little as a one dollar a day—and reexported, again without the payment of duties.

Although this offshore system of finance and production was set up primarily to serve the interests of multinational corporations, it soon became apparent that it was also a boon for criminals of all stripes. The same features that attracted multinational corporations to offshore havens in Panama and Bermuda—bank secrecy, lax or nonexistent regulations, low taxes, and lucrative government subsidies—also allowed scofflaws to launder money or carry out major financial scams. BCCI capitalized on the lax regulation and secrecy of the system to embark on what investigators have called "the most complex deception in banking history." During the 1970s and 1980s its officials stole billions from depositors, helped various dictators loot their own countries, illegally purchased several large U.S. banks, laundered money for Khun Sa and the Colombian cartels, helped U.S.-financed Afghan rebels smuggle heroin, provided financial services for corrupt government officials who stole foreign aid from impoverished developing countries, participated in illegal arms deals that aided such dictators as Saddam Hussein, and helped corporations avoid taxes. Yet U.S. investigators virtually ignored the bank until the late 1970s. As Representative Charles Schumer (D-NY) once grumbled, "BCCI fell between the international [regulatory] cracks."

Congress has known about these cracks for some time. Long before the BCCI scandal hit the pages of *Time* in 1991, unregulated offshore financial havens played a key role in the Robert Vesco affair, the Vatican bank scandal, Watergate, the collapse of the Nugan Hand bank, the Ivan Boesky insider trading scandals, the S&L crisis, and the rise of global drug cartels. A key development in global organized crime has been its growing financial sophistication and its increased reliance on the international financial system. Whereas government regulators and police are constrained by borders, the crooks can move their profits and operations anywhere in the world. Press a key on a computer on Wall Street, and millions of dollars are transferred to offshore accounts in the Bahamas, Switzerland, or Hong Kong. Enter another command, and the money moves to a numbered account in the South Pacific, where organized crime groups do not have to worry about income taxes and inconvenient rules against money laundering. U.S. investigators estimated that in 1998, thanks to this system, about $57 billion in drug money has been laundered through American banking institutions and about $300 billion globally, an astronomical increase since 1970, when the U.S. heroin business was worth only $1.8 billion.

Despite this system's crucial role in the growth of organized crime groups, the leaders of the law-and-order crusade have been unwilling to act on money laundering, in part because many large multinational corporations and banks rely on the offshore financial centers to do business. Here again, BCCI provides a horrifying example. Allegations about its operations began cropping up in the press in the late 1970s, and in 1980 the Bank of America was so concerned that it sold its BCCI holdings. Aziz Rehman first approached the Miami office of the IRS in April 1984, and local agents recommended an undercover operation, but their superiors dragged their heels and terminated the investigation in 1986. In 1988, Tampa IRS agents brought evidence of BCCI wrongdoing to the Federal Reserve, which is in charge of regulating international banks, but the Fed failed to act on the information until 1991—after a massive money-laundering case had been filed. Similarly, the Customs Service learned in 1983 that one of BCCI's major customers, a Jordanian arms dealer, had been involved in a massive coffee-smuggling case, but the Justice Department waited so long to hand down an indictment that the statute of limitations expired. Meanwhile, DEA agents in many cities were reporting that BCCI was a well-known place to launder money. A congressional review of DEA files found 125 cases involving BCCI during the 1980s. For example, a BCCI official had been indicted in Chicago, a Los Angeles heroin dealer had bragged about his ability to launder money through BCCI, the Indian government had provided the IRS with evidence of BCCI's money laundering, the IRS had investigated a $60 million money-laundering scheme involving BCCI accounts in Panama and the Caymans, and an Oklahoma City heroin dealer was convicted of laundering more than $1 million through BCCI accounts.[8]

Unfortunately, the BCCI case is not an isolated example of the inadequate regulation of financial institutions that are major campaign contributors. As global drug cartels used the international financial system to build up multibillion-dollar empires, some of the nation's most prominent law-and-order politicians completely ignored money laundering. J. Edgar Hoover refused to let the FBI get involved in financial investigations until well into the 1960s. The IRS and some local law enforcement took a different tack; financial evidence was crucial in the convictions of Al Capone and Lucky Luciano in the 1930s. But generally, local officials lacked the expertise or resources to pursue such investigations throughout the 1960s and 1970s, when global narcotics groups were getting established.

As the battle against organized crime began to heat up in the 1960s, however, some law enforcement officials did push Congress for tough legislation to combat money laundering. The Nixon administration—which used the financial system to launder millions of dollars in illegal campaign contributions—and lobbyists for the banking industry attacked the legislation, but in 1970 Congress passed the inappropriately named Bank Secrecy Act (BSA), requiring banks to file currency transaction reports (CTRs) for all cash transactions greater than $10,000 and imposing sanctions for failure to do so. In theory, BSA gave Nixon a powerful tool in the war against organized crime—which he had promised to win during his term in office. Using the cash transaction reports, investigators could, for the first time, recreate a paper trail and follow illegal criminal income from its source through the banking system into legitimate assets. Yet while Nixon was urging draconian sentences for drug offenders and proposing law-and-order legislation that would severely restrict civil rights, his administration virtually ignored the issue of money laundering.

The counterproductive federal attitude toward financial investigations began to change in the late 1970s and early 1980s as the drug war assumed new political importance. The Carter administration was the first to attempt to enforce money-laundering laws. Chemical Bank was charged in 1977 and eventually pled guilty to more than two hundred misdemeanors in laundering about $8.5 million for drug dealers. In 1977 and 1978 reports of suspicious currency deposits prompted the IRS to begin investigating Deak Perera, a currency exchange dealer. Over the next eight years, investigators uncovered evidence that Deak and a number of banks were involved in a massive money-laundering scheme for the Colombian drug cartels. But initial efforts to enforce the 1970 law were badly funded, and had little influence in overall law enforcement strategies. According to Robert Powis, a consultant on money laundering for many banks, "The level of compliance by banks with strictures of the Bank Secrecy Act in the late 1970s and early 1980s was appalling. The level of scrutiny by federal bank regulatory agencies for compliance with those requirements was equally appalling. The result was that banks simply did not pay any attention to those regulations."[9]

On the surface, the Reagan and Bush administrations seemed to reverse the longstanding law-and-order policy of ignoring money laundering by major crime groups. As part of the crackdown on the Miami cocaine trade the IRS and U.S. Customs set up Operation Greenback to ensnare the cartel's financial allies. In 1981 Customs Service officials arrested Beno Ghitis-Miller, who was accused of laundering $242 million of Colombian drug money during an eight-month period; he was eventually fined $610,000 and sent to jail for six years. By 1984 Operation Greenback investigators had exposed $2.6 billion worth of money laundering by sixteen narcotics organizations; their work led to 164 arrests, 211 indictments, 63 convictions, $38.5 million in seized currency, $7.5 million in seized property, and $117 million in potential IRS assessments. Similar operations were set up nationwide, and 587 people were indicted in the first half of 1984. In 1985-1986 sixty banks admitted having failed to comply with anti-money-laundering regulations, and the U.S. Treasury—which was investigating 140 banks—slapped large fines on the Bank of America ($4.75 million), Crocker National Bank ($2.25 million), Chase Manhattan ($360,000), Manufacturers Hanover ($320,000), Irving Trust ($295,000), Chemical Bank ($210,000) and the Bank of Boston ($500,000).[10]

In the mid-1980s money laundering was made a criminal offense, a move that allowed law enforcement officials for the first time to press more serious charges. And in 1992 Congress passed the Anti-Money Laundering Act, which closed a number of loopholes and made it easier for law enforcement officials to both investigate and prosecute violations. By that time, money-laundering investigations had become a key law enforcement tool against narcotics and many other crimes. Using anti-money-laundering statutes and RICO, which allowed the seizure of assets obtained from organized criminal activities, law enforcement officials grabbed about half a billion dollars in criminal funds in 1988. In sixty-eight cases between 1970 and 1993 the U.S. government imposed $25 million in civil fines for violations of the Bank Secrecy Act. In 1990 BCCI was hit with the largest fine ever levied on a bank for money laundering—$15 million—and this case was quickly dwarfed by others. In 1992's Operation Green Ice, investigators from seven countries cracked a money-laundering operation by the Italian Mafia and the Colombian cartels that resulted in 167 arrests and the seizure of $54 million in cash and property. In 1993, ten Atlantic City casinos were hit with fines totaling $2.5 million, the first ever imposed on casinos. Then, in 1994, federal investigators set up their own Caribbean bank and in just seven months managed to ensnare eighty-eight alleged money launderers and seize $54 million in assets.[11]

Under mounting public pressure to deal with the international aspects of the drug problem, U.S. officials also pushed foreign countries and international organizations to crack down on money laundering. In 1988 the Kerry amendment to an anti-drug bill required the government to negotiate other countries' cooperation with U.S. investigators, and the law, though vigorously opposed by the Bush administration, gave U.S. officials the power impose sanctions on notorious money-laundering centers. In 1989 sixty-seven countries signed a United Nations convention promising to improve their enforcement; the European Commission issued a directive requiring all member states to pass anti-money-laundering laws and increasing their cooperation with U.S. authorities. Similar legislation was passed in 1989 in Hong Kong, which traced its origins as a financial center to its expertise in handling money from opium smugglers. Switzerland—which had signed a limited agreement of cooperation with U.S. narcotic investigations—made money laundering a crime. Between 1988 and 1992, thanks to this international campaign and the threat of U.S. sanctions, U.S. officials were able to ink bilateral agreements with some of the world's most notorious laundering centers—Colombia, Ecuador, Panama, Peru, Uruguay, and Venezuela. In 1992 Congress also revised the Kerry amendment to require the U.S. State Department to issue annual reports on the problem of money laundering, to negotiate with other countries for improved laws and cooperation, and to consider sanctions against countries that failed to cooperate.[12]

Unfortunately, these efforts came about forty years too late, for organized crime groups had by then grown into enormously powerful organizations. And when the Reagan and Bush administrations did change tack, they were unwilling to devote significant resources to the problem. Shortly after BCCI was indicted in 1988 for laundering drug money, Customs Commissioner William von Raab estimated that about $110 billion a year was being laundered through the U.S. banking system, with about $90 billion of that moving into the international financial system—an enormous increase over the $5 to $15 billion estimate offered by the President's Commission on Organized Crime in 1984. "Do you know what $110 billion looks like?" von Raab grumbled. "It weighs two million pounds. That has to be digested by the banking system, which means it has to be deposited somewhere. Then it has to be sent abroad. In the case of BCCI, we are serving search warrants on 40 different banks. . . . Because . . . if you are laundering $50 billion to $90 billion, this bank wasn't doing it all. I would be surprised if they could do a hundredth of it."[13]

Raab was not alone in this assessment. In 1989 U.S. prosecutors estimated that their investigations touched only about 2 percent of all drug money being laundered. That is, cartels were successfully moving 98 percent of their illegal profits out of the United States into foreign lands, thanks to larger conservative agendas that sabotaged the Reagan/Bush war on crime.[14] Consider a few examples of understaffing and lax investigation from the Reagan years.

• Between 1980 and 1984 the number of FDIC examiners dropped from 1,698 to 1,389, the Comptroller of the Currency axed 310 examiners, and thrift regulators reduced their ranks from 638 to 596—sharply limiting the government's ability to investigate violations and enforce the law. As a result, federal regulators failed to notice that sixty very large banks had been laundering money, and Treasury officials became aware of the problem only when the banks, not bank regulators, admitted violating the law.[15]

• In 1985 the Treasury Department processed about 700,000 CTRs but had only thirty to forty people handling this mountain of paper. Between 1970, when BSA was passed, and August 1984 the FDIC, the largest and most important bank regulator, filed only ten recommendations with the Treasury Department that banks be assessed civil penalties for failing to comply with money-laundering laws. Only four of these were acted upon by the Justice Department.[16]

• As late as 1984, fourteen years after the passage of BSA, the IRS had only eight full-time staff members in charge of making certain that 1,050 state banks, 4,700 national banks, 11,000 credit unions, 10,000 registered securities brokers and dealers, 3,500 S&Ls, and 8,900 state banks complied with the BSA.[17] It had identified only 3,014 of the 15,000 check-cashing businesses, rare coin dealers, jewelers, and secondary financial institutions that it should have been auditing for compliance—thus allowing drug dealers to launder money through these companies without fear of prosecution—and managed to inspect only 644, a two-thirds decline from 1981, when IRS enforcement was hardly energetic.[18]

The policy of jailing low-level drug dealers for long periods while gutting federal regulatory agencies and coddling corporate criminals wrecked several major money-laundering investigations. For example, investigators uncovered evidence that the Bank of Boston had laundered $1.2 billion from organized crime groups in the 1970s and 1980s, thus earning about $1 million in fees assisting the survival of the Boston mob. Under federal law the bank could have been fined up to $110 million for failing to report 1,163 cash transactions. Yet it was assessed a paltry $500,000—a punishment much like letting a mugger keep half the money he steals from an old lady's purse. Bank of Boston officials eventually admitted exempting the Angiulo family, customers for more than twenty years, from filing currency reports as early as 1976. A 1963 congressional investigation had determined that the Angiulo crime family was involved in organized crime, but federal officials and bank regulators had not bothered to pass on that information to the bank or to investigate the family's finances. In 1982, when Treasury officials told the Office of the Comptroller of Currency (OCC), which is in charge of regulating national banks, that the Bank of Boston was laundering money, the local examiners' claim that the bank was in full compliance with the law allowed the undetected mob-run money-laundering scheme to continue for another two years. Then, as a local U.S. attorney began closing in, the comptroller's office failed to cooperate and dragged its heels when asked to provide data to a grand jury investigation. "Organized crime, drug traffickers, tax evaders are delighted with a regulatory system that hears no evil, sees no evil, and speaks no evil—regulators such as the OCC," one congressman complained during hearings on the case.[19]

During the Bush years the Justice Department created an international office to coordinate its growing caseload of foreign investigations, and the federal government set up the Financial Crimes Enforcement Network (FINCEN) inside the Treasury Department—an agency that is now in charge of updating and administering the world's largest database on money laundering. Internationally, the United States signed the UN convention against money laundering and helped found the Financial Action Task Force, a Paris-based organization that has played an important role in analyzing the problem and in helping nations around the world beef up their anti-money-laundering efforts. The United States also imposed economic sanctions on Panama and in 1990 invaded Panama to removed a corrupt leadership that had allowed money laundering to thrive.[20]

Behind the scenes, however, despite its tough talk, the Bush administration continued to coddle major financial institutions that make large campaign contributions, gut regulatory agencies, and pursue Cold War foreign policies. As late as 1989, when the Group of Seven was estimating that global laundering of drug money had topped $300 billion, the entire U.S. federal government spent only $120 million attacking that problem—a tiny percentage of the $5.7 billion spent on the drug war. Bush's much-touted FINCEN program to centralize money-laundering data received funding of only $13.4 million in 1990, and by fiscal year 1996 its budget had grown to only $24.4 million, even though the agency's two hundred employees must process millions of CTRs each year. Worse, funding restraints have severely limited the use federal officials make of all that information and delayed regulators' response. For example, in 1992 the GAO reported that the Treasury Department took an average of 1.8 years to process cases and impose penalties—a record that one congressman called "pathetic"—and in 1993 that federal agencies rarely used the ninety-two million forms that had been filed under BSA since 1970. Moreover, many of those forms contained incomplete or inaccurate information, indicating that banks were not complying with or regulators enforcing the law.[21]

Worse, federal agencies failed to use the limited resources they were given, thanks to the administration's antipathy toward regulating wealthy corporate campaign contributors. For example, it had long been clear to law enforcement officials that drug dealers were using wire transfers to move vast amounts of money in and out of the United States. The Treasury promised to regulate the process in 1984 but met opposition from major trade groups. In 1989, with $615 billion in wire transfers moving in and out of the country every day, Treasury officials once again promised regulation, and opposition from trade groups once again derailed it. In 1992 an impatient Congress passed a law requiring the Treasury to issue regulations in 1994. By the time they were finally announced (significantly watered down by industry opposition) in late 1994, more than 277,000 wire transfers worth $834 billion a day were moving through Fedwire, a clearing system.[22]

Similarly, although organized crime groups had laundered money through casinos in Las Vegas since the 1940s, the Treasury Department waited until 1984 to propose that casinos be required to report currency transactions greater than $10,000. But even these modest attempts to plug a major financial conduit for criminal organizations drew the industry's ire and in 1985, intensive lobbying by Nevada casinos, which had close ties to the Reagan White House, persuaded the Treasury Department to exempt Nevada casinos from filing CTRs. Other casinos, which were required to file, widely ignored the rule, and the Treasury Department showed little interest in effectively regulating the industry, which is a major campaign contributor. In 1987 the IRS began uncovering hundreds of examples of money laundering by Atlantic City casinos and reported them to the Treasury Department—which failed to impose any fines in these cases until 1993. The department touted the $2.5 million in fines for some 11,000 BSA violations as a tough crackdown on money laundering. But that was less than 1 percent of the $275 million that could have been imposed by law. Worse, the casinos' highly paid lawyers and lobbyists managed to reduce even that slap on the wrist; the casinos eventually paid only $1.6 million.[23]

Likewise, in an exhaustive study of the thrift industry, which gave $11 million to federal candidates between 1980 and 1990, the authors of *Inside Job* concluded that "at nearly every thrift we researched for this book we found clear evidence of either mob, Teamster, or organized crime involvement." Organized crime figures had moved to the S&Ls "like German tank divisions in the early days of World War II" almost as soon as Congress deregulated the industry, yet a Senate investigation found that federal regulators "consistently dropped the ball regarding enforcement" of money-laundering legislation. Between 1970 and 1985 they cited only two thrifts for violations, a record that allowed mobsters to launder drug money and S&L executives to loot their own institutions. In 1990 Senator John Kerry claimed that shady thrift executives had used the international financial system and other sophisticated financial techniques to launder as much as $40 billion stolen from S&Ls.[24]

Similar complaints can be leveled against the SEC's investigations of money laundering on Wall Street. Even though the Treasury Department had issued a ruling in 1983 putting the SEC in charge of Wall Street compliance with the anti-money-laundering laws, as late as 1993 the SEC had undertaken action against only thirteen brokers; it had promulgated only one rule relating to money laundering; the Treasury Department had yet to impose a single fine against a brokerage firm for failure to comply; and an SEC official told a congressional investigating committee that the agency "did not have the statutory responsibility to enforce money laundering statutes directly."[25]

The SEC's lack of interest in money laundering allowed major crime groups to use financial markets to hide assets. In one particularly egregious example two Wall Street firms, Merrill Lynch and E. F. Hutton, helped Sicilian mobsters launder $1.65 billion in heroin receipts in the infamous Pizza Connection case. Neither firm was ever charged in the case, even though Hutton's decision to warn the Mafia of the investigation prevented U.S. prosecutors from indicting other mob financiers. Hutton was, however, fined $1 million in a separate case of money laundering that occurred at its Providence, Rhode Island, office.[26]

Ingo Walter, one of the world's best-known experts on offshore finance, has also pointed out that in 1985, at the height of the cocaine boom, Latin American and Caribbean investors increased their purchases of stocks and bonds issued by U.S. corporations by 250 percent, to $1.7 billion. In addition, purchases of U.S. Treasury bonds tripled between 1984 and 1985, to $4.3 billion—not all necessarily drug-related, "but it strains credulity to suggest that drug money is not at least a significant factor," Walter concludes. In February 1994, two Merrill Lynch executives were indicted for helping drug dealers in Panama launder millions of dollars. And between 1992 and 1997 executives at every major Japanese securities firms have been indicted for lending money to members of Yakusa crime families, paying them kickbacks, laundering money for them, or helping them bilk investors. One Japanese mobster managed to extort more than a quarter-billion dollars from just one Japanese bank, Dai-Ichi Kangyo.[27]

Corporate agendas and conservative foreign policy objectives continued to derail the war against money laundering. Because offshore finance (always a boon for crooks of all stripes) played a key role in the global economy, governments all around the world were unwilling to attack vigorously the features that made it so attractive: secrecy, market-driven efficiency, low taxes, and lack of government control. In the late 1980s very few countries had enacted effective anti-money-laundering statutes. When the European Union issued a directive requiring members to tighten their standards, only one member country had already passed legislation making money laundering a crime, and that law applied only to drug money. Hong Kong, which was cited by the President's Commission on Organized Crime as the world's largest money-laundering center for heroin in 1984, didn't pass anti-money-laundering laws until 1989 and as of October 1993 had managed to seize only $47 million in assets from drug dealers, even though billions of heroin dollars were flowing through its financial institutions each year. Switzerland waited to criminalize money laundering until 1990, and its rules do not apply to tax fraud—an exemption that makes it much harder to attack global crime groups. As late as 1995, U.S. authorities identified eight major money laundering countries (Brazil, Colombia, Pakistan, Russia, Thailand, Turkey, the United Arab Emirates, and Uruguay) that had not criminalized the practice and fourteen others (Argentina, Aruba, Costa Rica, Ecuador, Hong Kong, India, Liechtenstein, Mexico, Netherlands Antilles, Nigeria, Panama, Paraguay, Singapore, and Venezuela) that had not met the goals of the 1988 UN convention.[28]

Over the last quarter-century the reluctance of law-and-order politicians to push for a global crackdown on money laundering has seriously impeded the war on crime. In the drug trade, of course, lax financial regulation allowed multinational crime syndicates to launder billions in revenues, accumulate huge assets, and expand their operations. But lax financial regulation also allowed white-collar crooks to commit crimes whose impact is rarely obvious and rarely covered in the mainstream press. Yet the effects of tax fraud, bond fraud, and racial discrimination in the banking system are arguably more damaging to poor people all over the world than the drug trade, obstructing their ability to obtain the capital and government revenues they need to rebuild their communities.

Just as unregulated financial havens enabled wealthy third world elites to loot their own countries and drug gangs to launder large profits, multinational corporations use this financial system to hide their profits and avoid taxes. The Clinton administration estimates that tax fraud by major multinationals totals about $11 billion a year, and outside researchers put the total much higher. In 1993 Simon Pak and John Zdanovicz, professors at Florida International University in Miami, estimated that multinational corporations use the international financial system to carry out tax fraud schemes costing the U.S. federal treasury from $28.6 to $109.4 billion a year. Their lowest figure could pay for more than half the $56 billion spent on Aid to Families with Dependent Children in 1996; the larger figure would pay for the same welfare program for nearly two years or, in a ten-year period, provide more than $1 trillion that could be used to develop jobs and industry in less affluent neighborhoods all around the country.[29]

Thanks to tax fraud, many government agencies have seen their tax base erode in recent years, making it harder for them to finance programs that might actually do something about violence in America, and public bodies have increasingly turned to the bond markets to finance their operations. Unfortunately, lax regulation of the securities and bond market has allowed many major corporations to bilk government agencies out of badly needed cash. Obvious examples are the huge losses in the thrift sector during the 1980s.

The first major hint that white-collar crime had become a way of life in the thrift sector came in 1985, when a $400 million fraud by Florida bond dealer E.S.M. Government Securities brought down the Home State chain of thrifts owned by Marvin Warner and prompted a run on Ohio thrifts that bankrupted the entire state insurance fund; depositors, investors, and the state of Ohio sued Warner for $4.4 billion. This case should have set off alarm bells in Washington and statehouses around the country, but bond scams continued to proliferate. In the early 1980s, Salomon Bros. had used tax breaks and the regulatory changes that allowed thrifts to speculate in securities to create a booming market for mortgage-backed securities, which grew from virtually nothing in 1978 to a $1 trillion market in 1986. That year, Salomon Bros. was making as much as $100 million a year by buying and selling securities to S&Ls. Other Wall Street firms, primarily Drexel Burnham Lambert, began selling S&Ls junk bonds or charging thrifts huge fees to issue junk bonds. Some securities firms began helping thrifts issue Eurobonds in offshore havens to raise further capital. By 1988 S&Ls had accumulated about $135 billion in corporate paper—much of it in junk bonds—and more than $214 billion in federally guaranteed mortgage-backed securities. Frequently, the Wall Street firms failed to mention the risks these investments carried. Some of the country's largest thrift failures can be traced to bad investments in securities. For example, FCA, which expanded its speculative operations with Wall Street money and invested more than $6 billion in mortgage-backed securities, by 1987 had lost $1.8 billion. And in 1989 alone, at least four thrifts went broke by speculating on the futures market. Eventually, the FDIC sued Drexel and some of the other players in the junk-bond trade, alleging a fraudulent scheme that cost taxpayers billions.[30]

Less obvious but even more costly to taxpayers is the way major securities firms have used lax regulation of the issuance of government bonds to enrich themselves. Each year federal notes worth about $2 trillion are issued, and every day federal bonds worth about $120 billion are traded. The market in U.S. government bonds plays a crucial role not only in financing federal programs but also in the nation's economic stability, acting as a bellwether for interest rates and other key indicators. Yet in 1991 *The Economist* called the government bond market "a curious mixture of cozy cabal and loose regulation." Close ties between the Treasury Department (typically run by former Wall Street executives) and major financial institutions meant that the market was structured to be extremely profitable for a tiny group of brokers. Between 1987 and 1990 the Treasury Department designated only forty to forty-five firms as primary dealers—those allowed to bid on the issuance of new federal government notes—and these firms capitalized on the lack of competition to earn $1.7 billion in profits by trading these notes. Just five Wall Street firms—including Salomon, Goldman Sachs, and Morgan Stanley—got about half of the $800 million in pre-tax profits the industry made selling government bonds in 1990.[31]

The lack of competition also offered enormous potential for abuse, a problem that became apparent in the summer of 1991, when Salomon Bros. managed to corner the market on Treasury bonds. When investigators uncovered the illegal scheme, the Wall Street firm was forced to pay $54.5 million to the SEC and investors. The *Wall Street Journal* and other newspapers quickly uncovered evidence that the Salomon Bros. case was not unique; other major securities firms had carried out similar schemes that boosted their profits and allowed them to manipulate prices. Just what such fraud costs is open to question—in the Salomon Bros. case, outside investors lost money but not the Treasury Department. Still, economists have long warned that the system was open to abuse. In late 1950s Milton Friedman argued before a congressional committee that the power of a few Wall Street firms over the auction of Treasury bonds could easily lead to inflated borrowing costs, and in the 1970s an unpublished study by two Treasury economists found that the Dutch auction (a way of selling bonds that would reduce the power of major Wall Street firms) would have saved the government about $60 million for just ten issues of bonds, or about 0.75 percent of the money it raised from the sales. If similar savings were achieved from the $2 trillion in bonds the federal government sells each year, taxpayers would save about $15 billion annually on the cost of financing the federal deficit.[32]

Even worse problems can be found in municipal bonds, a huge and enormously important market subject to very lax government regulation. In the 1980s and early 1990s, as the federal government sought to curb spending for social programs, many state and city agencies turned to bonds to pick up the slack. By 1993 the municipal bond market was worth $1.2 trillion, and more than 50,000 government agencies had issued notes. That same year some $250 billion worth of new debt was sold, more than double the $110 billion dumped on the market in 1988. Yet *Business Week* found that "regulation of the market ranges from cursory to nonexistent," and the magazine's lengthy investigation also uncovered extensive evidence of political corruption, fraud, and mismanagement. As late as 1993 the industry's sole regulatory body was governed by industry volunteers and deferred to NASDAQ, which has a miserable regulatory record. "A kind of conspiracy of silence about malfeasance reigns in the muni market because so many powerful groups benefit from the market's current structure," *Business Week* alleged. "Politicians are happy with the lush flow of campaign contributions. Executives at Wall Street Firms, while fed up with local officials extending their palms, keep playing the game to get business. Muni dealers can reap handsome profits from the market's inefficiencies"—which is to say the market structure provides dealers with ample opportunities to bilk investors by charging them inflated prices.[33]

In many cases the lack of regulation and corrupt ties between bond companies and local politicians increased the cost that government agencies had to pay to borrow money. A typical example can be found at Lazard Frères, which became one of the largest investment advisers to government agencies issuing bonds in the late 1980s. To beef up its municipal bond department, Lazard hired Michael Del Giudice, a top aide to Mario Cuomo (then New York State governor), Grover McKean (an ex-aide to California Treasurer Jess Unruh), Norman Steisel (a former New York City sanitation commissioner), Mark Ferber (a former budget director and chief counsel of the Massachusetts Senate Ways and Means Committee who had close political ties to top Democratic Party politicians), and Richard Poirier (a former Prudential Securities muni-bond powerbroker with political ties to officials in New Jersey, Kentucky, and Florida). Thanks to this team of political heavyweights, Lazard went from the twentieth largest muni-bond underwriter in 1990 to tenth in 1992 and third largest for advisory work.[34]

Political clout got the Wall Street firm lots of new business but cost taxpayers a bundle. For example, after Lazard gave $53,000 in political contributions to the New Jersey Democratic State Committee and spent $15,000 for three inaugural balls for Governor James Florio, officials named the firm the lead underwriter in a $1.8 billion bond issue without putting the contract up for competitive bidding. Political ties to New Jersey officials, the lax regulation of the bond market, and the absence of competitive bidding allowed Lazard to sell the issue in a way that reduced its risks while increasing the state's costs. Ian MacKinnon of Vanguard Group has complained that pricing bonds too favorably for investors is a widespread practice that boosts profits for Wall Street firms but increases the costs for taxpayers: "They are earning an underwriting fee, but they're not taking an underwriting risk. The underwriting community is mispricing these securities. The issuers are costing the taxpayers money." *New York Times* reporter Allen Myerson noted that the bonds quickly rose in price after the sale, indicating that the pricing was too low: "The strong demand suggests the sale should have done better. A seemingly narrow savings of a tenth of a percentage point on such a huge issue could free $18 million a year—

enough to pay 300 more teachers. Over the life of the bonds, the total expense could reach hundreds of millions of dollars."[35]

Taxpayers in other states were also suffering from Lazard's cozy political ties, which protected it from effective government regulation. In 1992 Kentucky officials complained that Poirier made unauthorized trades during a $250 million bond issue and overcharged the state by more than $1 million. The *Wall Street Journal* alleged that "a group of well-connected lobbyists, lawyers, state bureaucrats and Legislators" helped Poirier get a lead managing role in the $861 million Florida State Board of Education bond package; later, Lazard was accused of selling the bonds too cheaply, prompting a scandal that forced the state to prohibit bond underwriters from making political contributions to state candidates. Poirier's involvement in a $2.9 billion New Jersey Turnpike Authority bond financing, which earned Lazard $2.3 million in fees in 1991 and 1992, subsequently became the focus of U.S. attorney and SEC investigation into corruption and fraud in the bond market. Finally, the SEC and the U.S. Attorney indicted Lazard partner Mark Ferber, who played a key role in arranging the $6 billion financing to clean up Boston Harbor, on sixty-three counts of fraud, accepting gratuities, and attempted extortion. Ferber, who was also investigated in Washington deals, was eventually convicted, and Lazard Frères and Merrill Lynch were each forced to pay $12 million in civil fines for their role in the illegal Boston scheme, which, Massachusetts officials contend, cost taxpayers millions of dollars.[36] The involvement of Merrill Lynch, one of the world's largest securities firms, in the Massachusetts deal indicates that Lazard's actions were not particularly unusual.[37]

In New Jersey, for example, Merrill Lynch was the lead manager in the same $2.9 billion highway bond deal that involved Lazard and Poirier. Merrill agreed to let Armacon Securities, of which Governor Florio's chief of staff owned half, help sell some of the bonds and thus earn huge fees—even though the *New York Times* later pointed out that the firm "had no sales staff to sell the bonds, no clientele of retail customers to buy them and little capital of its own to finance an inventory of bonds." No matter: in 1991, Armacon was given $727,800 in underwriting fees.[38]

Likewise, New York City Comptroller Elizabeth Holtzman gave Fleet Bank a lucrative contract for financing work with the city after Fleet gave her senate campaign an unsecured $450,000 loan.

In Chicago, bond underwriters such as Goldman Sachs contributed more than $400,000 to the campaign of County Board President Richard Phelan, who had a key say in bond contracts. ("If you want to be involved in a bond deal in Cook County, you have to give money to the politicians," says Cook County Commissioner Maria Pappas.) In Michigan, prominent bond lawyers contributed more than $200,000 to cover the office expenses of Governor John Elder.[39]

Investigators in New Orleans, Atlanta, Florida, Alabama, Washington, D.C., and Texas have found financial deals between bond underwriters and local politicians. And in Kentucky, Billy Colling, the husband of a former governor, was put on trial for extorting money from two bond firms—Donaldson, Lufkin, and Jenrette and Cranston Securities.[40]

Overall, the twelve largest bond underwriters gave $2.4 million to state and local politicians in the 1991-1992 election cycle, and only 19 percent of all bond contracts were put up for competitive bidding (41 percent were competitively bid in 1980). "The industry started this, the politicians did not," admits Kenneth Glover, an investment banker at W. R. Lazard. "In some cases it became a bidding war. If firm A had a relationship with the city and Firm B wanted the business, they would see what firm A had contributed and they would do better."[42] How much this cost government agencies is hard to say, but there is little doubt that graft, corruption, and fraud in the municipal bond market cost taxpayers billions in the 1980s and 1990s.

Another costly example of corporate crime involves bias in the financial system. This discrimination—sanctioned for much of the twentieth century by government, both directly (through urban policies) and indirectly (through lack of regulation)—played an important role in channeling capital out of cities with large minority populations into more affluent white suburbs. And it continued more or less unabated even after the passage of civil rights and consumer legislation in the 1960s and early 1970s, laws that theoretically prohibited racial bias in the workplace and in business dealings. As it became increasingly apparent that inner city communities were starving from lack of capital, Congress attempted to address the problem specifically by passing the Community Reinvestment Act (CRA) of 1977. This law required banks to invest a certain proportion of their deposits in the communities where they did business and gave federal banking regulators the power to impose sanctions on banks who failed to do so.

But "until June 1990 bankers largely ignored the vaguely drafted act, and regulators did little to make them pay more attention," *The Economist* has noted. As late as 1989, when HUD received 1,548 complaints about discrimination in mortgage-lending practices, the severely unstaffed agency acted on only ten complaints. A study by the Federal Reserve of 6.3 million mortgage applications at 9,300 lending institutions in 1989 found that only 14 percent of white but 34 percent of black applicants were rejected. This study, the first massive analysis ever attempted by long-uninterested federal regulators, was widely criticized by bank lobbyists because it made no attempt to analyze such factors as income level and credit history, which are important to lending decisions. A followup study found that criticism misguided, however. After reviewing 5.3 million mortgage applications at 9,300 banks, the Boston Federal Reserve found that among upper-income applicants 8.6 percent of whites were rejected but 20.8 percent of blacks and 14.2 percent of Hispanics. The same pattern of discrimination was found for upper-middle-income groups, lower-middle-income groups (24.8 percent of blacks, 17 percent of Hispanics, 10.6 percent of whites were rejected), and lower-income groups (29.4 percent of blacks, 22.4 of Hispanics and 14.7 percent of whites).[42]

These disparities persist even if one applies more sophisticated measures of financial racism. A Federal Reserve Bank of Chicago study screened mortgage applicants for thirty-eight factors that banks use to evaluate loans and found that nonwhites with the same income and credit history as whites were 60 percent more likely to be rejected. Likewise, in a study of nearly 700,000 applicants for mortgages to buy one- to four-family houses in twenty-one cities, Essential Information found that blacks were rejected at much higher rates than whites in *every* city—even if the data were broken down into three income levels. In short, thirteen years after the federal government had outlawed redlining and twenty-three years after it had outlawed discrimination in lending, racial discrimination was still standard banking practice.[43]

Other examples can be found in every stage of the search for decent housing. In 1989, federal researchers who paid 3,800 visits to real estate agents in twenty-five cities found widespread discrimination all over the country. In New York City and the surrounding suburbs, Hispanics experienced some form of discrimination 61 percent of the time when they tried to buy a home and 53 percent when they tried to rent. Blacks met with discrimination 44 percent of the time when trying to buy, and 40 percent when trying to rent. Nationwide, the study found that 8 percent of black and Hispanic applicants who responded to newspaper advertisements were told that a home had already been sold, although it was later shown to white applicants. Likewise, 12 percent of Hispanics and 15 percent of blacks were told that an apartment had been rented when in fact it was still on the market and would later be shown to whites. Overall, the study found that 23.9 percent of all blacks and 24.6 percent of Hispanics received less favorable treatment than whites in that brokers forced them to pay larger security deposits or an application fee.[44]

Those who were lucky enough to survive this process frequently faced more illegal discrimination once they convinced a landlord or homeowner to rent or sell a property. They were likely to have a harder time getting home insurance (without which it can be impossible to get a home loan) and typically paid much higher rates for it. For example, State Farm charges $630 for a $100,000 fire insurance policy in Harlem but only $309 in New York's wealthy suburbs. Similar tales can be told of other cities: St. Louis (where government investigators found maps in one company's files that labeled heavily black areas as "ineligible" for policies), Milwaukee (where American Family Mutual Insurance paid $14.5 million to settle discrimination charges), Toledo (where State Farm was forced to change its racially biased sales practices), Los Angeles (where many small businesses were unable to rebuild after the riots of 1965 and 1991, because they were unable to obtain insurance), and San Francisco (where California regulators have charged insurance companies with refusing to issue policies in areas that have large concentrations of blacks, gays, and people with low incomes). Nationwide, a *U.S. News & World Report* investigation found that "the number of poor and minority homeowners who cannot obtain full-coverage property insurance is nearly 50 percent greater than residents of mostly white, middle-class areas. Poor Americans also pay more than twice, on average, what residents of middle-class neighborhoods pay for property insurance" ($7.21 versus $3.53 per $1,000). In addition, a National Association of Insurance Commissioners study of thirty-three metropolitan areas in twenty states found that only 57.6 percent of the homes in poor minority areas were covered, versus 81.5 percent in wealthy white neighborhoods.[45]

The poor record of major financial institutions in lending to poor communities is compounded by minimal government regulation of the companies that *are* willing to do business with less-affluent Americans. Because brokerages on Wall Street and major commercial banks provided few services for working Americans in the nineteenth and early twentieth centuries, many people were forced to borrow from wildly exploitive sources. In the South, poor blacks and whites borrowed money from landowners to pay their poll taxes, to buy seed and tools, and to acquire basic necessities. Since the money they earned from their crops or labor rarely covered these debts, sharecroppers gradually slipped into a state of debt peonage that was passed down from generation to generation. Similar arrangements could be found in the company stores of mining towns or isolated manufacturing centers in the Appalachians, the Midwest and the West. Paid bare subsistence wages for grueling and dangerous labor, workers frequently had to obtain food, medicine, or supplies on credit from employers who had a monopoly on the sale of these goods, inflated the prices, and charged usurious interest. City dwellers, though able to avoid some of these problems, frequently turned to pawnshops, finance companies, gangsters, and local merchants for credit. Small loan companies for the urban poor appeared after the Civil War and by the early twentieth century were notorious for their high-pressure collection tactics and interest rates as high as 120 percent.[46] Immigrants, less affluent workers, and small businesses that were unable to obtain credit from legitimate financial institutions also turned to gangsters and loan sharks. Even after the Second World War, merchants in ghetto areas who sold furniture and appliances on time often used high-pressure sales tactics, charged exorbitant prices, imposed usurious interest rates and added hidden charges.

After the ghetto riots of the 1960s—which the Johnson administration's National Advisory Commissions on Civil Disorders blamed partially on exploitive financial arrangements—federal and state laws were passed to protect consumers from the worst abuses. But regulation remained lax, and many blacks, immigrants, Hispanics, Asians, and less affluent whites still relied on check-cashing places, credit cards, consumer finance companies, and high-interest mortgage lenders to meet their financial needs. Today, it's estimated that as many as sixty million turn to these sources because they can't obtain financial services and credit from mainstream banking and financial institutions. The number of check-cashing places, which typically charge 3 to 6 percent of the check's face amount, has tripled since the late 1980s, to more than 5,500. The difficulty of finding bank loans has created a $100 billion market for finance companies, who charge 30 to 300 percent annual interest rates. High-interest charges can also be found in the credit card business, the rent-to-own business, firms that make auto loans to consumers with bad credit histories, and pawnshops.[47]

Much of the booming business of charging poor people very high interest rates can be traced to the fact that banks have done their best to ignore less affluent communities—despite federal and state laws that require them to lend to low-income areas. Deregulation of the financial system in the 1980s allowed them to charge their customers higher fees, a trend that pushed many poor people out of the mainstream finance system. Even earlier, banks adopted a policy of paying less attention to poorer communities. In 1970 white and black areas in twelve major cities had about the same number of branches per 100,000 residents, but by 1993 there were three times as many branches in the white areas. Today there are only nineteen bank branches in South Central Los Angeles—who might charge customers five to fifteen dollars a month to maintain a bank account—but more than 130 check-cashing places, where a family earning $24,000 a year would pay from $720 to $1,440 to cash their checks. According to the Federal Reserve, at least 14 percent of all Americans no longer have a bank account, up from 8 percent in 1977. We have "two financial systems for two Americas. One for the rich and one for the poor," complained an activist at ACORN, a group involved in the fight against redlining. But the profits for this financial apartheid are very rich. The business of providing financial services to less affluent Americans, Michael Hudson notes in his book *Merchants of Misery*, was worth $200 to $300 billion a year.[48]

Over time, the role of major financial institutions in destroying poorer neighborhoods has directly contributed to inner-city violence, which most law-and-order politicians have attempted to blame on poor minorities. For a community to remain stable and wage an effective war on crime, it must provide jobs, services, and tax revenues. If the federal government had enforced the laws of the land and if major financial institutions had bothered to respect those laws, poorer Americans and minorities might have obtained loans to buy homes or start businesses, thus strengthening their communities. Instead, given blatant discrimination and government inattention, businesses and services disappeared, making communities less habitable, and the more affluent residents moved out. As poorer communities lost the upwardly mobile residents, businesses, and professional people they needed for economic and political survival, violent crime, not surprisingly, became a basic fact of life.

No one knows how many kids got involved in gangs because their parents couldn't get a mortgage for a home in a safer community, or how many young men dropped out of school and turned to crime because local governments couldn't afford decent schools and because there were no jobs in their redlined communities. But it's clear that discrimination by financial institutions was yet another spike in the heart of poor communities already struggling with the toxic effects of a global financial system that helped drive armies of impoverished peasants into the drug trade—thus ensuring a steady flow of narcotics into U.S. communities—allowed organized crime groups to launder hundreds of billions of dollars' worth of profits. Meanwhile, the U.S. government pursued policies that encouraged the movement of capital out of poorer communities and made little attempt to deal with their mounting social problems. Many communities, lacking equal access to credit and capital, found it virtually impossible to maintain stable and strong social institutions.

The role of financial activities—such as capital flight, bond fraud, transfer prices, and offshore banking—in creating these conditions illustrates four fundamental points. First, corporate crime helps create street crime, both by nurturing violent criminal gangs and by creating the social conditions that encourage violence. Second, both street and corporate crime develop according to changes in larger economic structures, adapting their operations to the opportunities offered by new institutions such as offshore banking. Third, the result of class relations and exploitation in the world of crime is that while poor people's lives are made much harder by corporate and street criminals, wealthier classes are allowed—often encouraged—to engage in activities that create violence and impose huge economic costs on the less affluent. Finally, the movement of capital plays a crucial role in the prevalence of violence: communities that are able to mobilize re-sources to sustain families, jobs, businesses, educational institutions, and other social structures over a long period of time are able to reduce crime, whereas those that face long-term disinvestment or capital flight generally see rising violence.

These seemingly abstract economic points may seem far removed from the deadly world of gang warfare and serial muggers. Yet they go a long way toward explaining the persistence of violence in America and the bizarre refusal of our elected officials to abandon policies that have obviously failed. The very same economic structures that have created so much violence—providing street and white-collar criminals with both the means and the opportunity to carry out a wide array of crimes—have also created powerful economic interests that would be objectively harmed by a real war on crime. An effective crackdown would hurt the legitimate business activities of multinational corporations as well as their dodgy deals to avoid taxes and capital flight rules. No wonder that economic powerhouses have spent billions to support political leaders who are committed to protecting their interests.

These politicians have paid back their corporate benefactors by pursuing a war against illegal activities committed by poor people while ignoring the even more vicious crimes carried out by major corporations. The ensuing violence proved a blessing in disguise for wealthy elites and their thoroughly compromised political allies. Violence in poor communities decimated by disinvestment, economic exploitation, racism, and corporate crime allowed right-wing politicians to build political support for a crackdown on street crime—one that ignored the actual sources of the problem but bolstered odious stereotypes of minorities and other poorer Americans—and for a larger conservative agenda of economic deregulation and cutbacks in social spending. By any objective measure, this policy was exactly the opposite of what was needed to interrupt the circle of violence.

Conclusion:
Ending the Violence

IN LATE 1998 NEW YORK CITY POLICE COMMISSIONER HOWARD Safir proudly announced that the homicide rate for 1998 would be the lowest since 1964. When he made the announcement on December 23, 1998, the year had seen only 606 New Yorkers murdered, a huge decline from the record 2,262 murders in 1990.

Criminologists remained divided on the exact causes of the drop. They pointed to such diverse factors as improved economic conditions, fewer young people, tougher prison sentences, and the decline of the crack plague. Some even noted that the declines had begun under the liberal administration of David Dinkins, which was voted out of office by Rudolph Giuliani's tough law-and-order campaign.

But Safir had no doubts about why the city was finally winning the war on mayhem. He claimed the numbers vindicated the NYPD's rejection of liberal community policing strategies, which had attempted to reduce crime by building better relationships between cops and local communities. "I'm not going to be bullied by community activists who say, 'we want feel-good cops,' " he declared. "The bottom line is crime reduction."

Several weeks later, Safir may have come to regret his bravado. In February 1999, four New York City police officers gunned down Amadou Diallo, a Guinean immigrant, in the vestibule of his own apartment. When community leaders heard that the unarmed man had no criminal record and that police officers had killed him with a fuselage of forty-one bullets, a long series of militant protests broke out around the city. Many New Yorkers wondered why police opened fire on an unarmed man, and why they continued firing until he was literally pinned to the doorway by the bullets. Safir had no answers to those questions in the days following the shooting.

The entire affair highlighted a number of major problems with the law-and-order crusade against crime. The recent declines in crime are welcome, saving the lives of thousands of Americans each year. Yet in New York City, those declines had merely reduced the carnage to the same level it was in 1964, a pivotal year in America's war on crime.

That year, as Barry Goldwater kicked off his law-and-order presidential campaign, a young woman was brutally and repeatedly stabbed to death on the streets of New York. As Kitty Genovese screamed for help, thirty-eight people watched the stabbing, but no one came to her aid. The case sparked a nationwide outcry against crime in America.

Many conservatives latched onto the Genovese case to justify a tough crackdown on crime. But many others saw a different message in the affair. They wondered why no one had come to her aid, and began championing programs that might rebuild the cities' frayed neighborhoods and community ties. In 1964, as part of an effort to improve relationships between the police force and minorities, Lloyd Sealy was named the NYPD's first black precinct commander; in 1966, Mayor John Lindsay created the Civilian Review Board to deal with widespread complaints about police brutality.

In the years that followed, these reformers lost the debate over crime in America. In New York City, police union opposition to the Civilian Review Board reduced its powers, and in 1969, newly elected President Richard Nixon launched a federal war on crime. New York Governor Nelson Rockefeller pushed through tough sentences for drug crimes in the 1970s and the state went on a prison-building spree during the 1980s. Yet the number of murders in New York City tripled from 630 in 1964 to 1,896 in 1988 and the police department was once again rocked by a series of corruption and brutality scandals in the 1990s.

The persistence of violence and police brutality, despite a trillion-dollar-plus war on crime, highlights one of the enduring problems with the law-and-order crusade. In the 1960s, politicians offered the nation a choice between building prisons and rebuilding communities. The decision to let poor urban neighborhoods "eat prison" created a cycle of economic decay, disinvestment, violence, heightened racism, and political opportunism that allowed crime rates to reach epidemic levels in the early 1990s.

Breaking out of this political cul-de-sac won't be easy. Footloose capital has already moved many low-skilled jobs overseas, making it harder for young people with little formal education to find jobs. Law-and-order politicians have cut social services that might help young people avoid a life of crime. Such problems raise serious worries that crime will once again begin to rise as the number of young people increases in the first decade of the twenty-first century. If the lack of jobs and decent social services once again boosts crime, conservatives will undoubtedly call for yet another war on crime.

Still, there are some encouraging signs. The recent drop in crime has removed some of the political risks faced by critics of the law-and-order crusade. The monumental costs of financing our penal system prompts debate over alternatives and a number of officials around the country are experimenting with programs that offer less expensive and more humane approaches to law enforcement.

Some may claim, with some justification, that this book indicts the behavior of an entire economic system without offering any useful alternatives. Still, there are several good reasons to emphasize the causes of crime over its solutions. The problem with our war on crime has not been so much the lack of workable alternatives. After all, many criminologists and organizations, such as the Sentencing Project, the Vera Institute of Justice, the National Center on Institutions and Alternatives, National Council on Crime and Delinquency, and the National Criminal Justice System have excellent and comprehensive programs to reform the current system. Reformers have been making useful proposals for years, and today there are thousands of books and articles on the subject.

The real problem has been the lack of political will to implement these reforms. During the last thirty years, conservatives won the debate over crime because they were able to offer a coherent and politically compelling solutions. It didn't really matter whether their policies worked—generally they were a dismal failure. What mattered was that they offered a coherent view of crime and spent a great deal of time, money, and effort to convey that message. Until reformers learn to offer an equally compelling message and place the same emphasis on the problem, there is little hope that the current system can be effectively challenged.

Conservatives, by definition concerned with the preservation of the status quo, have always understood that "Crime Matters." As long as they were in power, any violation of any law—even if that law was created by a corrupt official—was an attack on their power and privileges. In this way, the rule of law became an expression of their own self-interest, and the punishment of all transgressors was a reaffirmation of their own power.

For reformers and radicals, crime has always been a more complex matter. They were happy to expose political corruption and corporate misdeals, since such activities illustrated the problems in a system they wanted to change. Street crime, however, was a more difficult subject, in part because it was frequently committed by the lower classes they championed. Most responded by arguing that such violence was created by the society they wanted to change; thus, the best way of ending it was to address such social and economic problems as poverty and unemployment. But as the debates over crime heated up, reformers increasingly found themselves on the defensive. They argued, accurately, that crime rates were not rising as rapidly as conservatives claimed and that corporate crime, which conservatives ignored, was a much worse problem. But these are essentially defensive arguments. Judging by their actions, reformers behaved as if they hoped crime would simply disappear. Unlike conservatives, they did not make crime and violence an important part of their program. Anti-crime proposals were frequently put forward as "an alternative" to the existing law-and-order strategies, not as an integral part of a larger attack on social injustice.

The failure to confront seriously one of the most deadly problems facing less-affluent Americans allowed conservatives to monopolize the issue of crime. Today, many liberals and moderates have firmly embraced the law-and-order crusade, perhaps hoping that demonstrating their toughness on crime will enable them to pursue other liberal values. But this tactical retreat has also allowed conservatives to carry out a much larger right-wing agenda and severely weakened the power of the left. Until progressives make dealing with crime a central part of any program for social justice, there is little chance that the right's power over American politics will be really challenged.

A second approach emphasizes "The Big Picture." For far too long the war on crime has been extremely limited in its view of the world, its strategies for reducing violence, and its vision of the future. Just as policymakers used to obsess about body counts during the Vietnam War, the generals in our war on crime have measured their success or failure by a few simple numbers. As long as government officials spent more money for police (who arrested more people) and for prisons (filled with convicts serving increasingly long sentences), law-and-order politicians believed that the violence would end. The fundamental fallacy in this argument is that locking up a hundred thousand people or ten million people will have no effect on crime rates if there are millions of other potential criminals willing to take their place. Short of incarcerating everyone who belongs to a high-crime demographic—a notion that would surely bankrupt the entire country both morally and economically—punishment offers only a temporary solution.

The limits of law enforcement as a solution to the problem of violence indicate that policymakers must revisit the old debate about the sources of crime. Admittedly, this is a thorny subject. Debates over the causes of crime have consistently produced more confusion than enlightenment, and many of the most important issues relating to the problem have been virtually banished from mainstream political discourse. But progressives can make valuable contributions to this debate. The left has a long tradition of analyzing crime in terms of economic exploitation, class relations, and political powerlessness. During the 1960s and 1970s, for example, radical student groups and civil rights leaders illuminated the American criminal justice system by highlighting such problems as police brutality, inhumane prison conditions, the treatment of political prisoners, and the practice of using illegal break-ins, wiretaps, and agents provocateurs to harass political groups. During the same period civil rights leaders opened up a debate over the lack of equality under the law and the problem of institutionalized racism. Consumer and environmental groups documented that corporations commit some of the worst and most brutal crimes. And the growing power of organized labor among police departments gave the foot soldiers in the war on crime a way of fighting the political influence of corrupt political machines over the hiring, promotion, and work of police officers, a development that played a crucial role in the move to upgrade the educational and professional standards of American law enforcement.

Unfortunately, many of these groups failed to offer a larger critique of the criminal justice system and to build alliances with related groups. In the

1960s and 1970s many environmentalists paid little attention to the fact
that poor people, particularly minorities, were disproportionally victimized
by toxic chemicals and lax environmental rules. Mainstream civil rights
leaders, meanwhile, paid little attention to corporate crimes that did not
directly involve race, and they were reluctant to take up the issue of minority
violence, fearing—accurately—that conservatives would use a debate over
black-on-black violence to reinforce many racist stereotypes. Unions frequently failed to explain to their members how the global economic
changes that were costing them jobs were also destroying the cities and
increasing crime. Civil libertarians, who led a lonely fight to preserve the
constitution, all too often failed to explain why constitutional rights made
law enforcement more effective. And police unions, which have generally
been closely allied with the right, failed to recognize the extent to which
police brutality and corruption made it harder for most cops to do their
jobs.

Even though many of these attitudes changed over the two decades that
followed, the failure of these groups to forge alliances with one another
allowed the right to dominate every aspect of the issue. To change that,
progressives will need to make crime one of their core issues and come up
with a clear program for addressing violence. That isn't easy. It requires first
an understanding of the broad connections between different types of
crimes and the problems that face many working and poor Americans.
Financial crimes hurt not only investors but timber workers, residents of
inner-city ghettos, and suburban school districts. Environmental disasters
destroy the economic sustainabiility of communities in both Oregon and
Burma. Racism in the judicial system not only short-changes black victims
of crime; it also leaves blacks and other marginalized racial groups power-
less to head off the spread of environmental pollution. Disinvestment not
only costs union members jobs; it also destroys peasant communities in Asia
and minority neighborhoods in urban ghettos. The drug trade not only
destroys the lives of addicts; it also creates environmental damage in Asia and
Latin America and encourages bank fraud, which can wreck entire economic
systems. Organized crime groups not only make millions off the drug trade,
they also help destroy the economies of cities and corrupt the political
process. U.S.-backed dictators not only engage in massive human rights
abuses, they also protect organized crime groups and pursue economic

policies that exacerbate the problems of crime. In short, social injustice creates crime. Any movement that cares about creating a more just society needs to care about crime.

Then there is the importance of *economics*. By this time it should be clear that many of the country's most costly crimes—burglary, auto theft, robbery, pollution, money laundering, tax fraud, and securities fraud—can be traced to a simple economic motive: greed. Nonetheless, there is little evidence that any single economic factor by itself can explain the problem of violence. Simply analyzing the impact of poverty on crime ignores the fact that most poor people do *not* commit crimes and that variables such as poverty are very little help in explaining why many white-collar crimes are committed by affluent Americans. Nor can the economics of crime be reduced to the simple laws of supply and demand. Many criminals commit their acts of violence under the influence of addictive substances or in the heat of passion—a state not conducive to rational calculation of one's economic interests. Underground economies are secretive by their very nature, making it difficult for the various actors to construct a rational approach to their business. Unlike those of legal markets, the supply-and-demand curves in the business of crime are also radically distorted by the impact of government regulations, crime syndicates, insufficient public information, and other factors. In short, crime rates do not rise and fall year after year in parallel with changes in poverty, unemployment, income inequality, or wage levels. People who lose their jobs do not automatically become muggers. Contrary to the odious stereotypes governing the law-and-order crusade, most minorities and most poor Americans do not turn to crime as a way of life. The majority hold jobs, work hard, raise families, and do not beat their loved ones.

The case studies presented in this book suggest that the critical economic theories of the left—which emphasize the accumulation of capital, class relations, abusive corporate power, imperialism, long-term economic changes, and labor conditions—provide a way past this conundrum. Although short-term changes in unemployment and poverty do not translate directly into rising or falling crime rates, the basic structures of the economy and their evolution over long periods do have an enormous impact. If one uses that approach to analyze drug use, which the right has attempted to explain as a toxic byproduct of the permissive cultural values of the 1960s, it quickly becomes clear that the trade was created by economic forces and that the drug business evolved over time in response to economic changes. For example, though seriously disrupted by the Second World War, the drug trade expanded rapidly in the late 1940s and 1950s when the U.S. government backed pro-American third world elites and adopted economic policies designed to aid large corporations. Those policies boosted foreign investment, profits, global trade, and the power of multinational corporations, but they also allowed corrupt governments in Thailand, Taiwan, and Vietnam to profit from the drug trade. Overtime, these governments, massive political turmoil, and the global economic changes that destroyed peasant economies pushed hundreds of thousands of peasants into underground economies, which were then organized into vast agribusiness enterprises by organized crime groups with close ties to U.S.-backed dictators. Not surprisingly, opium production skyrocketed throughout the 1950s and 1960s, long before anyone had ever heard of Timothy Leary.

Just as postwar global economic developments destroyed peasant economies in the developing world, they also pushed millions of whites, blacks, and Hispanics off the land in the United States. Then, as these groups moved to large urban centers, major corporations reduced their investments in the older industrial cities (a trend that was encouraged by government policies), destroying the job base in many urban centers and leaving many communities increasingly vulnerable to the ravages of the drug trade. Heroin addiction began to rise dramatically in the 1950s and topped 750,000 by the end of the 1960s. Eventually, the flow of drugs out of Southeast Asia and Latin America created new economic and social problems—such as addiction, crime, and disinvestment—which in turn were affected by changes in the structure of the global economy. For example, as the economic crisis of the 1970s convinced corporations to shut down more factories, the number of unskilled jobs in urban centers dropped dramatically, and the communities most buffeted by these changes witnessed an epidemic of violence in the 1980s. Many young men who might once have moved from petty gang violence in their teens to unskilled manufacturing jobs and families in their twenties were unable to find work in the legitimate economy, turning to crime or the drug trade to make a living. By the late 1980s the law-and-order policy, as it reduced millions of people to poverty, had created a vicious circle of violence. Global drug gangs could recruit millions of poor peasants in the developing world to grow and smuggle drugs, with millions of poor people consuming and peddling those drugs inside the United States.

This abbreviated sketch indicates that the economic causes of crime can't be reduced to rising or falling incomes. What is important is the economic sustainability of communities, that is, their residents' ability to raise children in prosperity, with educational, occupational, social, and cultural opportunities. Policymakers who want to deal with the economic causes of crime need to see the problem of violence in these larger economic terms and conceive of programs that go far beyond writing welfare checks, building a few apartments, or providing some college scholarships. Even the extensive government programs to attack poverty in the 1960s and 1970s were dwarfed by other government and private policies that encouraged much larger sums of money to move out of the central cities.

If the past is any guide, there is little chance that the problems of the cities will be corrected without massive investments in the poorest neighborhoods. Making certain these neighborhoods get the capital they need will require more controls over the multinational corporations that dominate the global economy. Footloose capital is encouraged by government policies to move to any region that offers the lowest costs and the highest profits, while local governments are unable to raise the tax revenues they need to revive poor communities and effectively regulate abusive corporate power. Global problems demand international political alliances of progressives. Unions that complain about trade pacts such as NAFTA, which encourage capital to move into low-wage zones, need to understand that their long-term health rests on improving the prosperity and wages of workers all over the world. Their members have to realize that the enemy isn't impoverished factory workers in Mexico but a callous global economic system that exploits those workers while shutting U.S. factories. Likewise, blacks whose communities are plagued by the drug trade need to support programs that can improve the lives of peasants in drug-producing regions. All these groups need to work together, across borders, to bring multinational capital under control. Although local governments can do many things to improve the lives of their citizens, the problems created by a global economy dominated by multinational corporations will ultimately have to be solved by international political pressure.

Another social and economic issue that deserves closer attention is *class*. Although violence obviously cuts across class lines and the state has a duty to guarantee the safety and security of all citizens, rich and poor, there is little hope that America will be able to reduce its appallingly high levels of violence significantly until policymakers recognize that crime disproportionally harms less affluent Americans. Working-class Americans are far more likely to die on the job than professional and managerial workers. People who live in households with an annual income of less than $15,000 are three times more likely to be raped or sexually assaulted, two times more likely to be robbed, and one and a half times more likely to be victims of aggravated assault.[1]

Those who would have us believe that crime is simply a problem of moral decay have systematically refused to recognize these facts and have generally crafted anti-crime policies that are designed to protect wealthy elites. For many years poorer neighborhoods were underserved by the law enforcement community, a neglect that encouraged the economic decay of many urban neighborhoods and allowed open-air drug markets to thrive in the late 1970s and early 1980s, which in turn promoted the revival of gang violence and the spread of crack. Worse, law enforcement strategies primarily designed to protect wealthy elites do not adequately protect working-class and poor Americans from the violence inflicted on them by major corporations and businesses: dangerous workplaces, the environmental degradation of inner cities, the outflow of capital that makes their communities less attractive places to live, and other corporate crimes. Until this class violence—both the problem of poor people harming poor people and the problem of rich people committing acts of brutality against less affluent Americans—is understood and systematically faced, crime will continue to be a way of life in many American communities.

It is important to acknowledge that although most of these problems can be blamed on the right, progressives have done a poor job of addressing them. During much of the law-and-order crusade, progressives have attempted to downplay the entire problem of street crime, arguing that corporate crime was a much more severe problem and that official statistics on official crime are misleading. There is much to be said for this point of view: the hysteria surrounding street crime is rarely linked to the reality of the problem, and the failure to appreciate the costs of corporate crime has done enormous damage. Nonetheless, progressives need to recognize why street crime is such a crucial issue for their natural constituency—working and poorer Americans. Arguing that corporate crime is more important than street crime is much like telling someone dying of AIDS that far more people die of cancer or alcoholism. Street crime may not be the worst problem facing less affluent Americans, but it is a very serious issue that deserves to be part of any progressive agenda for social change. By failing to address the problem of violence in America, the left allowed conservatives, who have little or no concern for working Americans, to dominate and define the issue. Progressives need to own up to their past mistakes in this regard and take a hard look at the class-based biases that have prompted them to pay so little attention to the violence suffered by poorer Americans. It is possible, as this book has attempted to do, to examine the problem of poor people committing crimes against other poor people without surrendering to the assumption that most poor people are violent criminals.

Another crucial factor is *corporate crime*. The distinction between street crime and corporate misbehavior, a distinction that runs through much of our criminal justice system, must be discarded, both in the way our legal system approaches violence and in the way we think about crime. It is one of the key reasons why the law-and-order crusade has turned into a hugely expensive catastrophe. While spending hundreds of billions of dollars to put poor people behind bars, the right has ignored problems such as money laundering, which directly produces street crime, and has made little attempt to protect poor Americans from the corporate violence that destroys their communities.

Here again, however, the left has a great deal of work to do. During the 1980s there was virtually no original reporting from the left on the decade's major financial scandals—securities fraud on Wall Street and the S&L collapse—even though these stories had been front-page news in the business press since the late 1970s. The failure to investigate financial crime seriously—a tendency that has continued with its lack of serious coverage of derivatives scandals or the Asian financial crisis—is particularly unfortunate because these crimes cost the economy tens of billions of dollars each year and have a devastating impact on less affluent communities. Contrary to the popular perception that financial fraud primarily consists of rich people stealing from well-heeled dupes, major financial institutions allow criminal gangs to thrive by laundering money; they steal billions from government agencies; they make it much harder to protect less affluent neighborhoods from violence; and they prevent poor communities from obtaining the capital and jobs they need to sustain themselves. In fact, the whole subject of corporate crime, which has largely been cast as afflicting consumers of all backgrounds, needs to be reformulated as part of a much larger economic critique of modern capitalism.

The cycle of violence and cynicism *can* end. Other countries do not suffer such high levels of crime, and in the past some American politicians found ways to reduce it. But permanent victory won't come until some basic problems—economic exploitation, class violence, racism, human rights— are addressed. Making these subjects the center of any new debate on crime in America is a difficult assignment. Powerful economic forces continue to support the phantom war on crime, and can be expected to meet any challenge from the left with every resource at their disposal. Still, a progressive campaign against the real causes of crime can begin to ameliorate the climate of fear and desperation. In the process, the left, which has a long history of battling for social justice, has a chance to show that its views are more relevant now than they have ever been.

Acknowledgments
and Sources

THIS BOOK, WHICH TOOK FIVE YEARS TO WRITE, WAS MADE possible by the help of a number of people. I'm particularly indebted to Jim Winslow and David Mitchell, who worked as research assistants, providing background data and invaluable suggestions on the subject.

In the course of writing, I also received a great deal of help from my friends and fellow journalists—notably Joanne Koeller, John Cooney, Lee Cokorinos, Larry Jones, Ralph Rivera, Margaret Harris, Anna Carugati, Bill Hartung, Montana Katz, Suzanne Fletcher, Hanna Liebman, and Rana Dogar—who listened to my arguments, read the manuscript and offered intelligent critiques. I'd like to thank my employer Ricardo Guise, who gave me time off to work on the project, and my parents, who offered me continuous encouragement and a place to work while I was researching the timber industry in Oregon. Many of those who offered their help won't agree with my conclusions but their assistance greatly improved every aspect of this book.

At Monthly Review Press, I'm indebted to Susan Lowes who had the foresight to commission the project, and to editorial director Christopher Phelps and Ethan Young, who did a marvelous job of shepherding this project to completion. Patricia Sterling did a spectacular job of editing the book, improving my writing and streamlining the manuscript. All of them reminded me why good editors are so important in any writing project.

Parts of the book are based on original reporting and travel to various parts of the world—notably the sections on the Asian heroin trade, the timber industry, and BCCI. I am particularly indebted to a number of human rights workers in Thailand and Burma and Burmese dissidents who provided me with a wealth of data and information, often at considerable personal risk. I would also like to thank the Hong Kong Information Bureau for arranging interviews and various employees at the UN's office of crime control in Vienna, who allowed me to use their library and provided me with thousands of pages of documents on the problem of money laundering, drug trafficking and organized crime groups.

Most of the research for this book is based on printed sources. These include tens of thousands of newspaper articles and court documents, as well as hundreds of books and articles from libraries in New York City, Bangkok, Vienna, and Portland, Oregon. I'm particularly indebted to the libraries at Columbia University, where I conducted a number of major computer database searches.

Only the sources that are cited in the text are mentioned in the bibliography. Among those sources, several authors deserve particular mention. The research and writings of Bertil Lintner, who has written the best book available on the Burmese heroin trade, and those of Alfred McCoy were an indispensable guide to the Asian drug trade. Books by David Musto, Diana Gordon, and Dan Braun provide an essential introduction to the politics of the war on drugs. Works by such authors as Jonathan Kwitney and Alan Block offer many insights into organized crime.

In the area of street crime, I'm particularly indebted to research done by the Sentencing Project, The National Center on Institutions and Alternatives, the National Criminal Justice System, the National Council on Crime and Delinquency, Elliot Currie, and Jeffrey Reiman that have been particularly important in helping me understand this enormously complex issue. The sections on urban history and the politics of crime could not have been written without the help of books by John Mollenkopf, Thomas and Mary Edsall, Daniel Fusfeld, Timothy Bates, Douglas Massey, Nancy Denton, Thomas Cronin, Tania Cronin, Michael Milakovich, Thomas Ferguson, and Joel Rogers.

Finally, readers looking for addition information on the problem of corporate crime are encouraged to turn to works by Ralph Estes (whose work provides the single best summary of the costs of corporate crime), Ralph Monkhiber, Marshall Clinard, Peter Yeagar, and John Bellamy Foster. Such publications as *Money Laundering Alert, Multinational Monitor,* and the *Corporate Crime Reporter* were also particularly helpful.

Notes

Introduction: Crime Pays

1. Edward Jay Epstein, *Agency of Fear: Opiates and Political Power in America* (New York: Verso, 1990), 62.
2. Ibid., 60; Stephan Lesher, *George Wallace, An American Populist* (New York: Addison-Wesley, 1994), 414.
3. *The Economist*, 18 September 1993.
4. *New York Times*, 12 April 1993; *USA Today*, 23 February 1995, A3; "America The Violent," *Time*, 23 August 1993; *Portland Oregonian*, 15 March 1995, B8.
5. U.S. Department of Justice, Bureau of Justice Statistics, *Sourcebook of Criminal Justice Statistics* (Washington, D.C.: Government Printing Office, 1998).
6. Bureau of Justice Statistics, *National Crime Victimization Survey, 1973-1995* (Washington, D.C.: Government Printing Office, 1997).
7. Thomas Cronin, Tania Cronin, and Michael Milakovich, *U.S. v. Crime in the Streets* (Bloomington: Indiana University Press, 1981), 84-85.
8. Federal Bureau of Investigation, *Crime in the United States: 1991* (Washington, D.C.: Government Printing Office, 1993).
9. Alfred McCoy, *The Politics of Heroin: CIA Complicity in the Global Drug Trade* (New York: Lawrence Hill, 1991), 19; Epstein, *Agency of Fear*, 261; U.S. State Department, *International Narcotics Control Strategy Report (INSCR)*, 1995, 27; *NCADI: 1995 National Household Survey*; and *The National Drug Control Strategy: 1996*.
10. Cronin, Cronin, and Milakovich, *U.S. v. Crime in the Streets*, 84-85.
11. Marshal Clinard and Peter Yeager, *Corporate Crime* (New York: The Free Press, 1980), 54-55.
12. *The Nation*, 11 August 1997, 12.
13. *Public Citizen*, July-August 1990, 24; *Washington Post Weekly Edition*, 21-27 February 1994, 12; Vicente Navarro, "Class and Race: Life and Death Situations," *Monthly Review* 43, no. 4 (September 1991); *Business Week*, 27 March 1995, 28.
14. U.S. Department of Commerce, Economics and Statistical Administration, Bureau of the Census, *Statistical Abstract of the U.S., 1994* (Washington, D.C.: Government Printing Office, 1998).

Chapter 1: Supply and Demand

1. Two books were essential in shaping this chapter. Alfred McCoy, *The Politics of Heroin: CIA Complicity in the Global Drug Trade* (New York: Lawrence Hill, 1991), certainly the best single source on the trade; and Bertil Lintner, *Burma in Revolt: Opium and Insurgency since 1948* (Boulder: Westview, 1994), a compelling analysis of the forces that have created the Burmese heroin trade. The influence of these two writers goes far beyond the number of times they are cited.

2. *Far Eastern Economic Review,* 20 January 1994, 22.

3. James Brady, "The Social Economy of Arson: Vandals, Gangsters, Bakers, and Officials in the Making of an Urban Problem," in David Greenberg, ed., *Crime and Capitalism: Readings in Marxist Criminology* (Philadelphia: Temple University Press, 1993), 214; Christopher Mele, "The Process of Gentrification in Alphabet City," in Janet Abu-Lughod, ed., *From Urban Village to East Village: The Battle for New York's Lower East Side* (London: Blackwell, 1994), 171.

4. Robert Fitch's excellent account of the city's economic decline, *The Assassination of New York* (New York: Verso, 1993), viii.

5. White House Office of National Drug Control Policy; Drug Strategies, *Keeping Score* (Washington, D.C.: Drug Strategies, 1996); *New York Times,* 31 August 1994, A1.

6. Chao-Tzang Yawnghwe, "The Political Economy of the Opium Trade: Implications for the Shan State," *Journal of Contemporary Asia* 23, no. 3 (1993): 311.

7. *Sacramento Bee,* 23 July 1994, B7; cultivation from *INCSR,* 1997. Operating under Yawnghwe's estimate that a peasant family of four can produce five to twelve kilos a year, the U.S. State Department's estimated production of 2,900 tons of opium in the Golden Triangle would require from 966,000 to 2.3 million peasant cultivators. Most of these would be employed in Burma, which produces about 2,500 tons of opium per year.

8. *Far Eastern Economic Review,* 20 January 1994; *Boston Herald,* 13 June 1994. *Pac Rim Intelligence Report,* 2 June 1994, estimates 2,300 tons; however, the United States operates under the assumption that only about eleven kilos of opium can be produced a year from a hectare of poppy fields. The 42,000 hectares estimated in the same article could produce only about 460,000 kilos or 460 metric tons.

9. *Wall Street Journal,* 3 April 1987; McCoy, *Politics of Heroin,* 495; *Pac Rim Intelligence Report,* 2 June 1994; *Washington Post,* 16 March 1990, A37; *Inter Press Service,* 13 May 1994; *INCSR,* 1997; *New York Times,* 1 September 1994, B3.

10. *National Review,* 17 November 1994, 59-60; Abt Associates, *What Americans Spend on Illegal Drugs, 1988-1995,* November 1997. The data, commissioned by the federal government, available on the White House Office of National Drug Control Policy (ONDCP) web site.

11. Wholesale prices for cocaine, for example, have fallen from $45,000-$55,000 a kilogram in 1983 to $20,000-$35,000, according to DEA estimates compiled by the National Narcotics Intelligence Consumers Committee, which despite its strange

name, is a federal agency; *Christian Science Monitor,* 5 September 1989, 1; ONDCP data from its web site.

12. Drug Strategies, *What We Are Getting for Our Federal Drug Control Dollars* (Washington, D.C.: Drug Strategies, 1996); Braun, *Smoke and Mirrors,* 75, White House Office of National Drug Control Strategy, and Epstein, *Agency of Fear,* 11.

13. Interviews with UN officials in Vienna, who refer to data presented at a UN-sponsored conference on organized crime; author's interview with Kallstrom, August 1995.

14. See ANSA, *Crime Zoom, Colombia;* ANSA, *Crime Zoom, Venezuela;* ANSA, *Crime Zoom, Russia;* ANSA, *Crime Zoom, Mexico;* International Scientific and Professional Advisory Council of the United National Crime Prevention and Criminal Justice Program, *Preventing and Controlling Money Laundering and the Use of the Proceeds of Crime: A Global Approach* (Mont Blanc, Aosta Valley, Italy: Fondazione, Centro Internazionale su Diritto, Societa e Economia, 1994), 14, 16; President's Commission on Organized Crime, *The Impact: Organized Crime Today* (Washington, D.C.: General printing Office, April 1986).

15. *INSCR,* various years; McCoy, *Politics of Heroin,* 495.

16. *INSCR,* 1997.

Chapter 2: The Global Drug Trade

1. Scott Anderson and Jon Lee Anderson, *Inside the League* (New York: Dodd Mead, 1986), 145, 172, 174.

2. Immanuel Wallerstein, *The Modern World System: Capitalist Agriculture and the Origins of the European World-Economy in the Sixteenth Century* (New York: Academic Press, 1974), 39, 326, 328, 329; C. R. Boxer, *The Portuguese Seaborne Empire: 1415-1825* (New York: Knopf, 1969); D. R. SarDesai, *Southeast Asia: Past and Present* (Boulder: Westview Press, 1994), 60-62; J. R. Hale, *Renaissance Exploration* (New York: W.W. Norton, 1968), 11, 32 and 33.

3. SarDesai, *Southeast Asia,* 62-68, 130-31; Suehiro Akira, *Capital Accumulation in Thailand: 1855-1985* (Tokyo: Center for East Asian Cultural Studies, 1989); T. Wing Lo, *Corruption and Politics in Hong Kong and China* (Buckingham and Philadelphia: Open University Press, 1993), 77; and Economist Intelligence Unit, *EU Country Profile: India, Nepal, 1994-5,* 4-5.

4. SarDesai, *Southeast Asia,* 146. Justifying the carnage, one U.S. general said, "It may be necessary to kill half the Filipinos in order that the remaining half may be advanced to a higher plane of life than their present semi-barbarious state affords."

5. Jack Beeching, *The Chinese Opium Wars* (New York: Harcourt Brace Jovanovich, 1975), p. 104; Surachart Bamrungsuk, *United States Foreign Policy and Thai Military Rule, 1947-1977* (Bangkok: DK Editions, 1988), 17; John Curtis Perry, *Facing West: Americans and the Opening of the Pacific* (Westport, Conn.: Praeger, 1994), 80-87; U.S. Department of Commerce, *Historical Statistics of the United States: Colonial Times to 1970* (Washington, D.C.: Government Printing Office, 1975), 903-7.

6. Eric Hobsbawm, *The Age of Empire, 1875-1914* (New York: Vintage, 1989), 57-59.

7. U.S. Department of Commerce, *Historical Statistics of the United States: Colonial Times to 1970* (Washington, D.C.: Government Printing Office, 1975), 864, 869, 884-85; Harry Magdoff, *The Age of Imperialism: The Economics of U.S. Foreign Policy* (New York: Monthly Review Press, 1969), 55.

8. Alfred McCoy, *The Politics of Heroin: CIA Complicity in the Global Drug Trade* (New York: Lawrence Hill, 1991), 79-80. Much of this history is based on McCoy.

9. Ibid., 83-84; Bertil Lintner, *Burma in Revolt: Opium and Insurgency since 1948* (Boulder: Westview, 1994), 52.

10. Quoted in ibid., 51; Beeching, *Chinese Opium Wars*, 223; McCoy, *Politics of Heroin*, 82-83.

11. Ibid., 86, 88; Lintner, *Burma in Revolt*, 52.

12. McCoy, *Politics of Heroin*, 90, 92, 93, 107.

13. See Fenton Bresler, *The Chinese Mafia* (Briarcliff Manor, N.Y.: Stein and Day, 1980), 27-33; and Martin Booth, *The Triads: The Growing Global Threat from the Chinese Criminal Societies* (New York: St. Martin's Press, 1990), 1-16.

14. Quoted in William Appleton Williams, "The Large Corporations and American Foreign Policy," in David Horowitz ed., *Corporations and the Cold War* (New York: Monthly Review Press, 1969), 95. See also W. W. Rostow, *The World Economy* (Austin: University of Texas Press, 1978), app. A and B; U.S. Department of Commerce, *Historical Statistics of the United States: Colonial Times to 1970* (Washington, D.C.: Government Printing Office, 1975), 864, 869.

15. See Gabriel Kolko, *The Roots of American Foreign Policy* (Boston: Beacon, 1969); David Horowitz, *Empire and Revolution: A Radical Interpretation of Contemporary History* (New York: Vintage, 1969), 71-92; Richard Barnet, *Intervention and Revolution: America's Confrontation with Insurgent Movements Around the World* (New York: The World Publishing Co., 1968); William Appleman Williams, ed., *From Colony to Empire: Essays in the History of American Foreign Relations* (New York: John Wiley and Sons, 1972); Richard Freeland, *The Truman Doctrine and the Origins of McCarthyism: Foreign Policy, Domestic Politics and Internal Security, 1946-1948* (New York: Schocken Books, 1974); Magdoff, *Age of Imperialism* and *Imperialism: From the Colonial Age to the Present* (New York: Monthly Review Press, 1978); William Appleman Williams, *The Tragedy of American Diplomacy* (New York: Dell, 1972), 202-75; and Horowitz, *Corporations and the Cold War*.

16. Richard Barnet and Ronald Muller, *Global Reach* (New York: Simon and Schuster, 1974), 67-68; U.S. Department of Commerce, *Historical Statistics*, 872; Council on Economic Advisors, *Economic Report of the President* (Washington, D.C., Government Printing Office: 1991), 308, 402; *Survey of Current Business*, August 1992, 117.

17. SarDesai, *Southeast Asia*, 283.

18. See Bruce Cumings, *The Origins of the Korean War* (Princeton, N.J.: Princeton University Press, 1990), 2: 141-56, 234-35, 242-67, 704, 707, 720-21.

19. Description closely based on David Kaplan, *Fires of the Dragon: Politics Murder and the Kuomintang* (New York: Athenaeum, 1992), 46-47.

Chapter 3: The Narco-Dictators

1. Martin Smith, *Burma: Insurgency and the Politics of Ethnicity* (London: Zed Books, 1993), 101.
2. *Newsweek*, 3 October 1988; Smith, *Burma*, 16.
3. Author's interviews and U.S. State Department reports from 1989.
4. This paragraph is based on Bertil Lintner, *Burma in Revolt: Opium and Insurgency since 1948* (Boulder: Westview, 1994), 1-19; and Martin Smith's equally trenchant analysis of the country's history in *Burma*, 88-154.
5. Martin Booth, *The Triads: The Growing Global Threat from the Chinese Criminal Societies* (New York: St. Martin's Press, 1990), 45; Lintner, *Burma in Revolt*, 40, 61-62; Alfred McCoy, *The Politics of Heroin: CIA Complicity in the Global Drug Trade* (New York: Lawrence Hill, 1991), 266-69.
6. On the KMT opium trade, see ibid.; Lintner, *Burma in Revolt*; Booth, *The Triads*; David Kaplan, *Fires of the Dragon: Politics Murder and the Kuomintang* (New York: Athenaeum, 1992); Catharine Lamour and Michael R. Lamberti, *The International Connection* (New York: Pantheon, 1974), 93-113; Fenton Bresler, *The Chinese Mafia* (Briarcliff Manor, N.Y.: Stein and Day, 1980), 27-100; Gerald Posner, *Warlords of Crime: Chinese Secret Societies* (New York: McGraw-Hill, 1988); and Henrick Kruger, *The Great Heroin Coup* (Boston: South End Press, 1980), 129-40.
7. *Daily Telegraph Magazine*, 17 July 1993, 32; and McCoy, *Politics of Heroin*, 427; Lintner, *Burma in Revolt*, 187, 194, 249-53.
8. Ibid., 84, 172-73.
9. *Los Angeles Times*, 24 September 1990, 1; Bertil Lintner, "The Politics of the Drug Trade in Burma," unpublished paper, September 1993.
10. *Far Eastern Economic Review*, 20 January 1994 22; Andre and Louis Boucaud, *Burma's Golden Triangle* (Bangkok: Asia Books, 1992), 196-200.
11. *The Nation* (Bangkok), 10 July 1994; *BurmaNet*, October 1994; author's interviews.
12. Surachart Bamrungsuk, *United States Foreign Policy and Thai Military Rule, 1947-1977* (Bangkok: DK Editions, 1988), 150, 192, 194, and 196.
13. Ibid., 46.
14. Ibid., 56, 59-62.
15. All conversions were done at the 1995 currency rate of 25 baht to the U.S. dollar. Suehiro Akira, *Capital Accumulation in Thailand: 1855-1985* (Tokyo: Center for East Asian Cultural Studies, 1989), 187-89; Asian Development Bank, Economics and Development Resource Center, *Key Indicators of Developing Asian and Pacific Countries* (London: Oxford University Press, 1994), 38, 318-19; Bamrungsuk, *United States Foreign Policy*, 61-62, 109-111; and Robert Muscat, *The Fifth Tiger* (Armonk, N.Y.: United Nations University Press, 1994), 90-94.
16. Akira, *Capital Accumulation*, 138, 151, 152; Muscat, *Fifth Tiger*, 73.
17. Bamrungsuk, *United States Foreign Policy*, 63; Lintner, *Burma in Revolt*, 156, 184.
18. Bamrungsuk, *United Staes Foreign Policy*, 103-4.
19. Author's interview.
20. Chao-Tzang Yawnghwe, "The Political Economy of the Opium Trade: Implications

for Shan State," *Journal of Contemporary Asia* 23, no. 3 (1993): 325; Asian Development Bank, *Key Indicators*, (London: Oxford University Press, 1994), 316-17.

21. Lintner, *Burma in Revolt*, 114, 156; Akira, *Capital Accumulation*, 141, 142, 170, 191.
22. Ibid., 248; *INSCR*, 1994.
23. *Los Angeles Times*, 24 September 1994, 1; Lintner, *Burma in Revolt*, 243, 246, 259.
24. Ibid., 243, 246, 259.
25. Author's interview; *Bangkok Post*, 27 July 1994.

Chapter 4: Corporate Connections

1. *Periscope Daily Defense News Capsules*, 27 June 1994, citing Burmese television reports; *Asian Political News*, 4 July 1994; *Pacific Rim Intelligence Report*, 26 June 1994.
2. *Asian Political News*, 4 July 1994.
3. Ibid.; *New York Times*, 15 July 1994, A2-3.
4. Carolyn Skorneck, "U.S. Must Deal With Burma to Curb Heroin, Drug Policy Adviser Says," Associated Press, 16 June 1994; *Far Eastern Economic Review*, 20 January 1994, 26, and 18 November 1993, 23-24; Institute of Asian Democracy, "Towards Democracy in Burma," 1992.
5. Full text of Lawn's letter was reprinted in *BurmaNet*, 30 October 1994. See also John Dinges, *Our Man in Panama: How General Noriega Used the U.S. and Made Millions of Dollars in Drugs and Arms* (New York: Random House, 1990), 288-89.
6. The DEA's involvement in organizing these opium-burning ceremonies to rehabilitate SLORC's anti-drug image was first reported by *BurmaNet*, 17 October 1994 and Bertil Lintner, in *Far Eastern Economic Review*, 18 November 1993, 23-24; Agence France-Press, 18 July 1994.
7. Based on *BurmaNet*, 17 October 1994, and Lintner in *Far Eastern Economic Review*, 18 November 1993, 23-24.
8. Carolyn Skorneck, "U.S. Must Deal With Burma," Associated Press, 16 June 1994; *Bangkok Post*, 4 May 1994; *Wall Street Journal*, 29 November 1994; *Reuters North American Wire*, 2 December 1994.
9. *Daily Telegraph*, 10 August 1993.
10. *Los Angeles Times*, 22 February 1993.
11. *The Nation* (Bangkok), 8 April 1994; *Bangkok Post*, 8 June 1994.
12. Ministry of National Planning and Economic Development, "Myanmar: The Heart-Land of Asia," n.d.
13. Ibid.
14. *The Nation* (Bangkok), 27 May 1994; *Wall Street Journal*, 29 November 1994.
15. Asian Development Bank, *Asian Development Outlook 1994* (Oxford: Oxford University Press, 1994), 23; *The Nation* (Bangkok), 17 April 1994.
16. Martin Smith, *Paradise Lost: The Suppression of Environmental Rights and Freedom of Expression in Burma* (London: Article 19, 1994), 21.; Faith Doherty and Nyein Han, *Burma: Human Lives for Natural Resources Oil and Natural Gas* (Southeast Asian Information Network, 1994), May 1994, 5-8.
17. Author's interview with Kevin Heppner.

18. *The Nation* (Bangkok), 24 February 1994.

19. Author's interview with activist, November 1994. *Bangkok Post*, 20 March 1994; *The Nation* (Bangkok) 7 February 1994. Thai newspapers frequently refer to official involvement in the sex trade. For example, the *Nation*, 27 June 1994, reported a former Thai police officer's third arrest for bringing young Burmese girls to brothels in Thailand.

20. Asia Watch, Women's Rights Project, *A Modern Form of Slavery: Trafficking of Burmese Women and Girls Into Brothels in Thailand* (New York: Human Rights Watch, 1993), 3-4; *The Nation* (Bangkok), 21 and 25 March 1994.

21. *Washington Post*, 5 November 1990, A17; Lintner, *Burma in Revolt*, 187, 214, 225-27; Lintner, "Politics of the Drug Trade," 32.

22. Author's interviews with law wnforcement officials; Lintner, "Politics of the Drug Trade," 32-33.

23. Author's interviews with law enforcement officials; Lintner, "Politics of the Drug Trade," 34; *INCSR*, 1997.

24. Author's interviews, November 1994; *Far Eastern Economic Review*, 20 January 1994, 26; Reuters North American Wire, 10 April 1995.

25. Author's interviews, November 1994.

26. Reuters North American Wire, 27 April 1995; Reuters World Service, 2 May 1995.

27. Author's interview with Shan refugee worker.

28. *Ottawa Citizen*, 6 May 1995; *Inter Press Service*, 10 April 1995.

29. *Washington Post*, 5 November 1990, A17.

30. Author's interviews with researchers; the *Economist*, 6 April 1991, 31; quoted in Dennis Bernstein and Leslie Kean, "Singapore's Blood Money," *The Nation* (New York), 20 October 1997, 11-16.

31. Lintner, "Politics of the Drug Trade," 61-62; *Far Eastern Economic Review*, 20 January 1994, 26.

32. UN estimates; David Kaplan and Alec Dubro, *Yakusa* (New York: Collier, 1987), 38.

33. Gerald Posner, *Warlords of Crime: Chinese Secret Societies* (New York: McGraw-Hill, 1988), 70-71; Stanley Bachrack, *The Committee of One Million: "China Lobby" Politics, 1953-1971* (New York: Columbia University Press, 1976); and Sara Diamond, *The Road to Dominion: Right Wing Movements and Political Power in the United States* (New York: Guilford, 1995), 41-46.

34. Bachrack, *Committee of One Million*, 122-24; Alfred McCoy, *The Politics of Heroin: CIA Complicity in the Global Drug Trade* (New York: Lawrence Hill, 1991), 193-261.

35. Ibid., 124.

36. See Posner, *Warlords of Crime*, pp. 68-71; and McCoy, *Politics of Heroin*, 193-261.

Chapter 5: The Road to Violence

1. Author's interviews with law enforcement officials and BATF agents. See also *New York Times*, 8 November 1994, B3; 19 January 1995, B3; 7 November 1994, B5.

2. *New York Times*, 5 March 1994, A1.

3. *New York Times,* 19 January 1995, B3; 5 March 1994, 1; 22 November, 1994, B3.

4. Author's interviews with law enforcement agents; New York Times, 5 March 1994, A1; 14 March 1994, B1.

5. Author's interviews; Claire Sterling, *Thieves World: The Threat of the New Global Network of Organized Crime* (New York: Simon and Schuster, 1994), 37; *U.S. News and World Report,* 10 October 1994.

6. Author's interviews with DEA, August 1995; Sterling, *Thieves World,* 37.

7. Author's interview, August 1995.

8. U.S. Department of Justice, Office of Justice Programs, Bureau of Justice Statistics, *Drugs, Crime and the Justice System: A National Report from the Bureau of Justice Statistics,* (Washington, D.C.: Government Printing Office, 1992), 3-6; author's interviews; Bureau of Justice Statistics, *Survey of State Prison Inmates,* NCJ-136949, 1993 (Washington, D.C.: Government Printing Office, 1993).

9. Elliot Currie, *Reckoning: Drugs, the Cities, and the American Future* (New York: Hill and Wang, 1993), 170. Currie cites George Valliant "What Can Long-Term Follow-up Teach Us About Relapse and Prevention of Relapse in Addiction?" *British Journal of Addiction* 83, and Christopher A. Innes, *Drug Use and Crime* (Washington, D.C.: U.S. Bureau of Justice Statistics, 1988).

10. U.S. Department of Justice, Office of Justice Programs, Bureau of Justice Statistics, *Drugs, Crime and the Justice System: A National Report from the Bureau of Justice Statistics,* (Washington, D.C.:Government Printing Office, 1992), 4; Currie, *Reckoning,* 171-72.

11. These sentences are nearly verbatim from Edward Jay Epstein's excellent book, *Agency of Fear: Opiates and Political Power in America* (New York: Verso, 1990), 30-32.

12. Paul Goldstein, Henry Brownstein, Patrick Ruam, and Patricia Bellucci, "Most Drug-Related Murders Result from Crack Sales, Not Use," *Drug Policy Letter,* March/April 1990; Currie, *Reckoning,* 179.

13. Author's interviews with ATF agents, August 1995; Common Cause.

14. Bureau of Justice Statistics, July 1995, NCJ-148201; Violence Policy Center; *Village Voice,* 8 February 1994, 16; Peter Nye, "Violence: A Criminal Justice Issue Becomes a Public Health Issue," *Public Citizen,* March/April 1994.

15. *Economist,* 26 March 1994, 23-28; author's interviews with law enforcement officials.

16. Author's interviews with BATF agents; *New York Times,* 12 March 1994, B25; *Wall Street Journal,* 12 July 1994, 1.

17. *Business Week,* 25 October 1993, 120-21.

18. Ibid.

19. Violence Policy Center; Bureau of Justice Statistics, July 1995, NCJ-148201; *New York Times,* 16 October 1994.

20. David Burnham, *Above the Law: Secret Deals, Political Fixes, and Other Misadventures of the U.S. Department of Justice* (New York: Scribner, 1996), 130.

21. National Institute of Justice, *The Extent and Costs of Crime Victimization: A New Look* (Washington: Government Printing Office, 1996).

22. Downloaded from National Center on Institutions and Alternatives web site in July 1997; *Washington Post,* 18 August 1997, 34.

23. Bureau of Justice Statistics, *Sourcebook of Criminal Justice Statistics* (Washington, D.C.: Government Printing Office, 1994), 385; Ronet Bachman and Linda E. Saltzman, *Violence Against Women: Estimates from the Redesigned Survey, August 1995* NCJ-154348(Washington, D.C.: Bureau of Justice Statistics, 1995); Diane Craven, *Female Victims of Violent Crime* NCJ-162602 (Washington, D.C.: Bureau of Justice Statistics, 1996).

24. *New York Times,* 10 January 1994, B1.

25. This closely follows James Short's excellent survey of the literature in *Poverty, Ethnicity and Violent Crime* (Boulder: Westview Press, 1997), 6-25.

26. U.S. Department of Justice, Bureau of Justice Statistics, *Crime and the Nation's Households, 1992,* NCJ-143288 (Washington D.C.: Government Printing Office, 1993), 3; Bureau of Justice Statistics, *Sourcebook of Criminal Justice Statistics,* 624; Bureau of Justice Statistics, *Survey of State Prison Inmates* (Washington D.C.: Government Printing Office, 1995).

27. *Statistical Abstract, 1994,* 5, 18, 416, 479; *Washington Post,* 10-16 October 1994, 5.

28. Ibid.; *New York Times,* 12 December 1994, 1; Barbara Bloom and David Steinhart, *Why Punish the Children: A Reappraisal of the Children of Incarcerated Mothers in America* (San Francisco: National Council on Crime and Delinquency, 1993), 22.

29. Gary Becker, "Crime and Punishment: An Economic Approach," *Journal of Political Economy* 76, 1968: 169-217.

30. Bureau of Justice Statistics, *Sourcebook,* 267.

31. These figures and this description closely follow an article in *New York Times Magazine,* 12 June 1994.

32. Edna McConnell Clark Foundation, *Seeking Justice: The Cost of Incarceration* (New York: Edna McConnell Clark Foundation, 1995), 4; Bureau of Justice Statistics, January 1998, NCJ-167247; Michael Tonry, *Malign Neglect: Race, Crime, and Punishment in America* (New York: Oxford University Press, 1995), 17.

33. Sentencing Project, "Why 'Three Strikes and You're Out' Won't Reduce Crime," *Briefing Sheet; Village Voice,* 22 February 1994; *New York Times,* 2 June 1992, citing a 1992 Amnesty International report.

34. These studies are cited in Currie, *Confronting Crime,* 66-67.

35. Burnham, *Above the Law,* 364.

36. Ibid.; Manning Marable, *How Capitalism Underdeveloped Black America* (Boston: South End Press, 1983), 121-22; *New York Times,* 22 February 1995, 1; Federal Bureau of Investigation, *Crime in the United States: 1993* (Washington, D.C.: Government Printing Office, 1994), 60-66; *Economist,* 10 December 1994, citing Capital Punishment Research Project.

37. H. L. Mencken in *Liberty,* 28 July 1934.

38. *The Economist,* 10 December 1994.

39. *Newsday,* 10 November 1994, A26; Edna McConnel Clark Foundation, *Seeking*

Justice, 4, 29; Marc Mauer, *Americans Behind Bars: The International Use of Incarceration, 1992-1993* (Washington, D.C.: Sentencing Project, 1994), 10.

40. Edna McConnell Clark Foundation, *Seeking Justice,* 19; interview with Sister Marion Defies, who works with women in prison.

41. Bureau of Justice Statistics, *Women in Prison; Sourcebook,* 616; Bloom and Steinhart, *Why Punish the Children,* 13-15; Marc Mauer and Tracy Huling, *Young Black Americans and the Criminal Justice System: Five Years Later* (Washington, D.C.: Sentencing Project, 1995), 18; *Washington Post,* 10-16 October 1994, 5; *New York Times,* 12 December 1994, 1; interviews.

42. *Washington Post,* 10-16 October 1994, 5; *Statistical Abstract, 1994,* 18; Bureau of Justice Statistics, *Lifetime Likelihood of Going to State or Federal Prison,* NCJ-160092 (Washington, D.C.: Government Printing Office, 1997).

43. Rose Matsui Ochi, "Racial Discrimination in Criminal Sentencing," *Judges Journal,* Winter 1985.

44. *Dallas Times Herald,* 19 August 1990, 1.

45. Bureau of Justice Statistics, *Sourcebook of Criminal Justice Statistics, 1993,* 384-86.

46. *Statistical Abstract, 1991,* 281, 283, 287; *Emerge,* December 1992, 39; *New York Times,* 27 July 1994, 1.

47. *San Jose Mercury News,* 8 December 1991, 1; *Dallas Times-Herald,* 19 August 1990, 1 and 1 October 1989, 1; *Topeka Capital-Journal,* 9 October 1990, 1; *Times-Union,* 19 May 1991, 1; *Sacramento Bee,* 16 December 1990, 1; *Dayton Daily News,* 17 February 1991, 1.

48. See Stephen Klein, Joan Petersilia, and Susan Turner, "Race and Imprisonment Decisions in California," *Science* 247 (1990): 812-16.

49. Clarence Lusane quoted in Diane Gordon's excellent primer on the drug war, *The Return of the Dangerous Classes: Drug Prohibition and Policy Politics* (New York: W. W. Norton, 1994); Tonrey, *Malign Neglect,* 4-7, 59, 108-9, 146-47.

50. Ibid.

Chapter 6: Policing America

1. This account is based on Herbert Asbury, *The Gangs of New York* (Garden City, N.Y.: Garden City Publishing Company, 1927), 101-17.

2. Ibid., 103-4.

3. Jeremy Brecher, *Strike!* (Boston: South End Press, 1972), 4-21, 50-63, and 102-14.

4. W. E. B. Du Bois, *Black Reconstruction in America, 1860 to 1880* (New York: Atheneum, 1972), 698, 699; Lawrence M. Friedman, *Crime and Punishment in American History* (New York: Basic Books, 1993), 95.; Jacqueline Jones, *The Dispossessed: America's Underclasses from the Civil War to the Present* (New York: Basic Books, 1992), 90-93, 148-52.

5. Peter Kwong, *The New Chinatown* (New York: The Noonday Press, 1987), 12-13.

6. Fred Cook, *The Pinkertons* (Garden City, N.Y.: Doubleday, 1974), 116; Brecher, *Strike!,* 58-61; Du Bois, *Black Reconstruction,* 678-81; Kenneth O'Reilly, *Nixon's Piano: President and Racial Politics from Washington to Clinton* (New York: Free

Press, 1995), 123; John Hope Franklin, *From Slavery to Freedom: A History of Negro Americans,* 3rd ed., (New York: Alfred A. Knopf, 1967), 473-74.

7. Philip S. Foner, *History of the Labor Movement in the United States* (New York: International, 1964), 3: 15-17.

8. U.S. Department of Commerce, *Historical Statistics of the United States: Colonial Times to 1970* (Washington, D.C.: Government Printing Office, 1975), 607; John Commons, *History of Labor in the United States, 1896 to 1932* (New York: Macmillan, 1934), 3: 364.

9. Kenneth T. Jackson, ed., *Encyclopedia of New York City History* (New Haven: Yale University Press, 1995), 647; U.S. Bureau of Labor Statistics, *A Brief History of the American Labor Movement,* Bulletin 1000 (Washington, D.C.: Government Printing Office, 1976), 3 and 79.

10. Robert Heilbroner, *The Economic Transformation of America* (New York: Harcourt Brace Jovanovich, 1977), 71-72.

11. Ibid., 112-15.

12. Center for Responsive Politics, *A Brief History of Money in American Politics,* downloaded from CRP's web site in June 1997.

13. Quoted in ibid.

14. Quoted in John Higham, *Strangers in the Land: Patterns of American Nativism 1860 to 1925* (New York: Atheneum, 1972), 221.

15. Ibid., 227-31; Frank J. Donner, *The Age of Surveillance: The Aims and Methods of America's Political Intelligence System* (New York: Vintage, 1981), 37.

16. Samuel Walker, *Popular Justice,* (New York: Oxford University Press, 1998), 148; Louis Adamic, *Dynamite: The Story of Class Violence in America* (New York: Chelsea House/Vintage, 1958), 287-91; Murray, *Red Scare,* 269.

17. Ray Allen Billington, *The Protestant Crusade: 1800-1860* (Chicago: Quadrangle, 1964), 412; DAR president quoted in Higham, *Strangers in the Land,* 150, 227.

18. Quotes from Higham, *Strangers in the Land,* 150-51, 273, 314; Maldwyn Allen Jones, *American Immigration* (Chicago: University of Chicago Press, 1960), 276; David Bennett, *The Party of Fear: The American Far Right from Nativism to the Militia Movement* (New York: Vintage, 1995), 283.

20. Gary Walton and James Shepherd, *The Economic Rise of America* (London: Cambridge University Press, 1979), 2, 84-92; John Burnham, *Bad Habits: Drinking, Smoking, Taking Drugs, Gambling, Sexual Misbehavior, and Swearing in American History* (New York: New York University Press, 1993), 52-53, 57, 61; U.S. Department of Commerce, *Historical Statistics,* 690-91.

21. Dean Latimer and Jeff Goldberg, *Flowers in the Blood: The Story of Opium* (New York: Franklin Watts, 1981) 180; Alfred McCoy, *The Politics of Heroin: CIA Complicity in the Global Drug Trade* (New York: Lawrence Hill, 1991), 5-8; Musto, *American Disease* (New York: Oxford University Press, 1987), 2.

22. Morgan, *Drugs in America: A Social History* (Syracuse: Syracuse University Press, 1981), 5, 29.

23. Ibid., 93.

24. Musto, *American Disease*, 219-20; Dr. Alexander Lambert quoted in Morgan, *Drugs in America*, 96.

25. Ibid.; Musto, *American Disease*, 43-44.

26. Ibid., 65.

27. Ibid., 65-68; Higham, *Strangers in the Land*, 267-69.

28. Timothy Gilfoyle, *City of Eros: New York City, Prostitution and the Commercialization of Sex, 1790-1920* (New York: W. W. Norton, 1992), 87-88; Alan Block, *Space Time and Organized Crime* (New Brunswick, N.J.: Transaction, 1994).

Chapter 7: The Short Arm of the Law

1. U.S. Department of Commerce, *Historical Statistics of the United States: Colonial Times to 1970* (Washington, D.C.: Government Printing Office, 1975), 414; Federal Bureau of Investigation, *Crime in the United States: 1991* (Washington, D.C.: Government Printing Office, 1993), 14; *Newsweek*, 20 December 1949, 42; *U.S. News*, 8 May 1946, 30.

2. *Historical Statistics*, 135; Frances Fox Piven and Richard A. Cloward, *Regulating the Poor: The Functions of Public Relief* (New York: Pantheon, 1971), 117; Robert A. Beauregard's excellent survey, *Voice of Decline: The Postwar Fate of U.S. Cities* (Cambridge: Blackwell, 1993), 143.

3. Quoted in John Mollenkopf, *The Contested City* (Princeton, N.J.: Princeton University Press, 1983), 75.

4. Council on Economic Advisors, *Economic Report to the President* (Washington, D.C.: Government Printing Office: 1991), 308, 402; U.S. Department of Commerce, *U.S. Direct Investment Abroad* (Washington, D.C.: Government Printing Office, 1997).

5. Mollenkopf, *Contested City*, 103-9.

6. Ibid., 26, 27, 240.

7. Jacqueline Jones, *The Dispossessed: America's Underclasses from the Civil War to the Present* (New York: Basic Books, 1992), 224, 245, 251; Melvin Leiman, *The Political Economy of Racism* (Boulder: Pluto Press, 1993), 90-99; Christopher Mele, "Neighborhood 'Burnout': Puerto Ricans at the End of the Queue," in Janet L. Abu-Lughod, ed., *From Urban Village to East Village: The Battle for the Lower East Side* (London: Blackwell, 1994), 128-12.

8. Daniel Fusfeld and Timothy Bates, *The Political Economy of the Urban Ghetto* (Carbondale: Southern Illinois University Press, 1984), 93; Beauregard, *Voices of Decline*, 71; Douglas Massey and Nancy Denton, *American Apartheid: Segregation and the Making of the Underclass* (Cambridge, Mass.: Harvard University Press, 1993), 45.

9. *Historical Statistics*, 297.

10. Rachel Bratt, "Public Housing: The Controversy and Contribution," and Barry Checkoway, "Large Builders, Federal Programs and Postwar Suburbanization," both in Rachel Bratt, Chester Hartman, and Ann Meyerson, *Critical Perspective on Housing* (Philadelphia: Temple University Press, 1986); Sam Bass Warner, *The*

Urban Wilderness: A History of the American City (New York: Harper and Row, 1972), 240-41.

11. Mollenkopf, *Contested City*, 42, 90.

12. See Massey and Denton, *American Apartheid*, 96-109.

13. Ibid., 51-52.

14. Ibid., 52-54.

15. Studies cited in Fusfield and Bates, *Political Economy of the Urban Ghetto*, 144-48.

16. Don Wallace and Drew Humphries, "Urban Crime and Capitalist Accumulation, 1950-1971," in David Greenberg, ed, *Crime and Capitalism: Readings in Marxist Criminology* (Philadelphia: Temple University Press, 1993), 201-3.

17. FBI, *Crime in the United States* (Washington, D.C.: Government Printing Office, 1992), 186-87.

Chapter 8: The Politics of Retribution

1. Quoted in Thomas Cronin, Tania Cronin, and Michael Milakovich, *U.S. v. Crime in the Streets* (Bloomington: Indiana University Press, 1981), 18-24.

2. Ibid.

3. Thomas Edsall with Mary Edsall, *Chain Reaction: The Impact of Race, Rights, and Taxes on American Politics* (New York: W. W. Norton, 1992), 47-51.

4. Council on Economic Advisors, *Economic Report of the President*, various years.

5. John Mollenkopf, *The Contested City* (Princeton, N.J.: Princeton University Press, 1983), 112; Edsall, *Chain Reaction*, 41.

6. Ibid., 49, 61; Kenneth O'Reilly, *Nixon's Piano: President and Racial Politics from Washington to Clinton* (New York: Free Press, 1995), 285-86.

7. Sara Diamond, *The Road to Dominion: Right Wing Movements and Political Power in the United States* (New York: Guilford, 1995), 112-14; O'Reilly, *Nixon's Piano*, 284, 286; Cronin, Cronin, and Milakovich, *U.S. v Crime in the Streets*, 37.

8. Edsall, *Chain Reaction*, 61; Cronin, Cronin, and Milakovich, *U.S. v Crime in the Streets*, 60, 69.

9. Peter H. Irons, "American Business and the Origins of McCarthyism: The Cold War Crusade of the United States of Commerce," in Robert Griffith and Athan Theoharis, eds., *The Specter* (New York: New Viewpoints, 1974), 78-85; David Caute, *The Great Fear*, 349-50.

10. See Karl Schriftgiesser, *The Lobbyists* (Boston: Little, Brown, 1951), 95-97; Irons, "American Business," 74.

11. U.S. Department of Commerce, *Historical Statistics of the United States: Colonial Times to 1970* (Washington, D.C.: Government Printing Office, 1975), 178.

12. Frank J. Donner, *The Age of Surveillance: The Aims and Methods of America's Political Intelligence System* (New York: Vintage, 1981), 34-39; *Newsweek*, 2 September 1957, 22.

13. *The Nation*, 20 October 1963; author's interviews with FBI agents; O'Reilly, *Nixon's Piano*, 269-75; Morton Halperin, Jerry Berman, Robert Borosage, and Christine

Marwick, *The Lawless State: The Crimes of the U.S. Intelligence Agencies* (New York: Penguin, 1976), 3, 148-54.

14. Frank Donner, *The Protectors of Privilege* (Berkeley: University of California Press, 1990), 1, 51, 67.

15. See Jonathan Kwitney, *Vicious Circles: The Mafia and the Marketplace* (New York, W. W. Norton, 1979), one of the best books on organized crime and the best source for the mob's involvement in the legitimate economy. See also Stephen Fox, *Blood and Power: Organized Crime in the Twentieth Century* (New York: Penguin, 1990), 303; Virgil Peterson, *The Mob: 200 Years of Organized Crime in New York* (New York: Green Hill Publishers, 1983), 112, 216-20, 434; *Life,* 26 March 1951, 36; *Time,* 12 March 1951, 22-26.

16. Kwitney, *Vicious Circles,* 1-86, 231-47; author's interviews with former prosecutors who investigated the construction business in the late 1980s; *Newsday,* 11 May 1995, A3; *New York Times,* 23 April 1995, 33.

17. President's Commission on Organized Crime, *The Impact: Organized Crime Today* (Washington, D.C.: Government Printing Office, 1986), 423-25, 486-87.

18. Ibid., 463.

19. Putting that spending in perspective, Seymour Melman has written that between 1945 and 1973, the military "consumed sufficient resources to more than rebuild everything in the U.S. that is man made. That means the entire industrial infrastructure of the United States could have been rebuilt from the ground up. All the factories, roads, airports, ports, bridges, everything existing today could have been made anew. Imagine the effect this would have had on our nation's competitiveness."

20. Council on Economic Advisors, *Economic Report of the President, 1995* (Washington, D.C., Government Printing Office: 1996), 310, 326, 394; *Monthly Labor Review,* May 1990.

21. *Business Week,* 18 May 1992.

22. Figures computed from John Mollenkopf, *The Contested City* (Princeton, N.J.: Princeton University Press, 1983), 214, for 1970 and from *Strategic Abstract,* 44-47; Mark Alan Hughes with Julie E. Sternberg, *The New Metropolitan Reality* (Washington, D.C.: Urban Institute, 1992), 11.

23. Ibid., 10, 14, 22, 23.

24. William Junius Wilson, *When Work Disappears* (New York: Oxford University Press, 1997), 25.

25. Edsall, *Chain Reaction,* 240-42.

26. Wilson, *When Work Disappears,* 22.

27. Ibid.; see *Brooklyn Bridge,* March 1996.

28. Author's interviews at UN; *Business Times,* 20 July 1993, 27; Peter Andreas, *The Nation,* 16 April 1990, 515; *Latin American Newsletter; INCSR,* March 1995, 27; Bureau of Justice Statistics, *Drugs, Crime, and the Justice System* (Washington, D.C.: Government Printing Office, 1992), 36; National Institute of Justice, *Gang Crime Recordkeeping* (Washington, D.C.: Government Printing Office, 1994).

29. *North American Center on Latin America Report on the Americas,* March 1989, 35,

37; Chao-Tazang Yawnghwe, "The Political Economy of the Opium Trade: Implications for Shan State," *Journal of Contemporary Asia*, 23, no. 3 (1993): 311. Yanghwe cites production figures. I have recomputed his figures from current prices of opium supplied by *BurmaNet* and confirmed those figures with law enforcement sources. See Peter Reuter, R. MacCoun, and P. Murphy, *Money From Crime: A Study of the Economics of Drug Dealing in Washington, D.C.* (Santa Monica, Calif.: The Rand Corporation, 1990).

30. Author's interviews, December 1995; Agenzia ANSA, *Organized Crime* (Rome: ANSA Dossier, 1994).

31. "Does Free Market Reform Unintentionally Undermine Drug Market Prohibition? The U.S.-Mexico Experience," testimony of Peter Andreas, Research Fellow, the Brookings Institution before the House Subcommittee on Crime, *New York Times*, 24 May 1993.

32. Walter Wriston, writing in *Forbes ASAP*, 1993.

33. *Washington Post National Weekly Edition*, 11 May 1992; *New York Times*, 5 July 1992; *New York Times*, 2 February 1997, A1; *New York Times*, 27 July 1996, A1; 29 July 1996, A1; 30 July 1996, A1.

34. *Washington Post*, 18-24 March 1996, 13.

35. *New York Times*, 15 June 1992, B2; *Village Voice*, 14 February 1995, 17; 14 November 1995, 14.

36. Citizens for Tax Justice, *Tax Loopholes from A to Z: The Comprehensive Compendium* (Washington, D.C.: Citizens for Tax Justice, 1996); *Statistical Abstract, 1994*, 337.

Chapter 9: Addicted to Crime

1. Lou Cannon, *President Reagan: The Role of a Lifetime* (New York: Simon and Schuster, 1991), 792, 837.

2. *The Nation*, 26 August-2 September 1996, 18-19; Citizens for Tax Justice, *Tax Loopholes from A to Z: The Comprehensive Compendium* (Washington, D.C.: Citizens for Tax Justice, 1996).

3. *Dollars and Sense*, November-December 1996, 42; January-February 1997, 24-25; Urie Bronfenbrenner, Peter McClelland, Elaine Wethington, Phyllis Moen, and Stephen J. Ceci, *The State of Americans* (New York: The Free Press, 1996), 31, 56, 65, 71, 148, 149, 170.

4. Thomas Ferguson and Joel Rogers, *Right Turn*, (New York: Hill and Wang, 1986), 13-21, 24, 88; Thomas Edsall with Mary Edsall, *Chain Reaction: The Impact of Race, Rights, and Taxes on American Politics* (New York: W. W. Norton, 1992), 210.

5. Flo Conway and Jim Siegelman, *Holy Terror: The Fundamentalist War on America's Freedoms in Religion, Politics and Our Private Lives* (New York: Doubleday, 1982), 44-43; David Bollier, *Liberty and Justice For Some: Defending a free society from ten Radical Right's Holy War on Democracy* (Washington, D.C.: People for the American Way, 1982), 27-30, 113; Sara Diamond, *Spiritual Warfare: The Politics of the Christian Right* (Boston: South End Press, 1989), 10, 35-36, 53.

6. Sara Diamond, *Road to Dominion: Right-Wing Movements and Political Power in the United States* (New York: Guilford, 1995), 130, 233; Edsall, *Chain Reaction*, 132.

7. Ibid., 140; quotation in Dan Baum, *Smoke and Mirrors: The War on Drugs and the Politics of Failure* (Boston: Little, Brown, 1996), 233.

8. Diana Gordon, *The Return of the Dangerous Classes: Drug Prohibition and Policy Politics* (New York: W. W. Norton, 1994), 126.

9. Diana Gordon, *The Justice Juggernaut*, (New Brunswick, N.J.: Rutgers University Press), 188.

10. David Rasmussen and Bruce Benson, *The Economic Anatomy of a Drug War*, 122-27; *Washington Post*, 24-30 January 1994, 37.

11. On Carter's drug policy, see Baum, *Smoke and Mirrors*, 91-136.

12. Jimmie L. Reeves and Richard Campbell, *Cracked Coverage: Television News, the Anti-Cocaine Crusade and the Reagan Legacy* (Durham, N.C.: Duke University Press, 1994), 20, 26; parts of the paragraph paraphrased from ibid., 332, 334.

13. Gordon, *The Dangerous Classes*, 33; *The Justice Juggernaut*, 37; *Village Voice*, 22 February 1994; 12 April 1994; Reeves and Campbell, *Cracked Coverage*, 38.

14. Baum, *Smoke and Mirrors*, 260; ibid.; *In These Times*, 27 December 1993, 23.

15. "America the Violent," *Time*, 23 August 1993.

16. Ibid.; *Washington Post*, 28 October-3 November 1996, 32.

17. *New York Times*, 20 October 1996, A1; *Drug Policy Letter*, Fall 1996, 4; *Washington Post*, 28 October-3 November 1996, 9.

18. James Ridgeway, "Bill to Cities: Lock 'Em Up," *Village Voice*, 22 February 1994; The Sentencing Project, "Why 'Three Strikes and You're Out' Won't Reduce Crime," *Briefing Sheet;* White House Office on National Drug Control Policy data; Gordon, *Return of the Dangerous Classes*, 31-32; Bureau of Justice Statistics, *Felony Sentences in State Courts, 1994* (Washington, D.C.: Government Printing Office, 1997).

19. Peter Dale Scott and Jonathan Marshall, *Cocaine Politics: Drugs Armies and the CIA in Central America* (Berkeley: University of California Press, 1991), 23.

20. Ibid., 24.

21. Ibid., 104-5.

22. Arnold S. Treback, *The Great Drug War* (New York: Macmillan, 1987), 169-70; "National Security and the War on Drug in the Americas," Institute of Policy Studies briefing paper.

23. *NACLA Report*, April 1990, 9-10; *The Nation*, 1 January 1989, 8.

24. Reeves and Campbell, *Cracked Coverage*, 123-26.

25. Ibid.

26. *Village Voice*, 12 April 1994, 34; Marc Mauer and Tracy Huling, *Young Black Americans and the Criminal Justice System: Five Years Later* (Washington, D.C.: The Sentencing Project, 1995), 1-13.

27. Mauer and Huling, *Young Black Americans*, 18-20.

28. Baum, *Smoke and Mirrors*, 187.

29. *The Nation*, 14 November 1988, 492; Henrick Kruger, *The Great Heroin Coup* (Boston: South End Press, 1980), 16; *U.S. News and World Report*, 7 March 1988, 21.

30. After reviewing massive involvement in the drug trade by the Haitian military, Senator Kerry's Subcommittee on Terrorism, Narcotics, and International Operations concluded, "As long as the Haitian military continue to control virtually every government institution . . . the cartels will continue to operate unchallenged in that country." See U.S. Senate Subcommittee on Terrorism, Narcotics and International Operations of the Committee on Foreign Relations, *Drugs, Law Enforcement, and Foreign Policy* (Washington, D.C.: Government Printing Office, December 1988), 69-72. In addition, the *New York Times* reported (28 April 1993) that drug trafficking dramatically increased following a military coup in 1991: "International financial experts who are studying Haiti have said . . . that the country's economy appears to have been kept afloat in defiance of hemispheric embargo only by large scale laundering of profits from drugs and other contraband." See Henrick Kruger, *The Great Heroin Coup* (Boston: South End Press, 1980), for Strossner's involvement in the drug trade during the 1960s and 1970s. On Bolivia, see *New York Times*, 31 August 1981, 1. *The Nation* (25 April 1987) also reported that the 1980 coup led by General Luis Garcia Meza was financed by cocaine traffickers and "supported by an army of neofascist European mercenaries recruited by former Gestapo chief Klaus Barbie." See also Tim Bower, *Klaus Barbie* (New York: Pantheon, 1984), 210-16. Despite massive U.S. aid to fight the drug traffic in Bolivia, *The Nation* (11 February 1989) reported that "the local military command has shown no interest in the cocaine traffic flourishing under its nose. [And] . . . a congressional committee responsible for investigating the [failure of authorities to shut down one very large cocaine processing plant] alleged that high government authorities including a former Interior Minister and member of the national police were protecting the traffickers . . . [Moreover,] documentation obtained by the Catholic Church [shows] . . . the forcible use of street children by the Leopards, DEA trained anti-drug police, to tread coca leaves into paste. After two teenagers died at a police protected paste factory . . . in Central Bolivia . . . an exhaustive investigation . . . showed the youths had been illegally arrested, forced to tread the leaves in a vat with kerosene and sulfuric acid and then been killed . . . Despite the publicity generated by the two deaths, church sources say the practice continues."

31. Alexander Cockburn and Jeffrey St. Clair, *Whiteout: The CIA, Drugs, and the Press* (New York: Verso, 1998), 277-317; Gary Webb, *Dark Alliance: The CIA, the Contras, and the Crack Cocaine Explosion* (New York: Seven Stories Press, 1998).

32. See *In These Times*, 6-12 May 1992.

33. Scott and Marshal, *Cocaine Politics*, 42-50.

34. *Transnational Organized Crime*, Spring 1995.

35. U.S. Senate Subcommittee, *Drugs, Law Enforcement, and Foreign Policy*, 2, 32-61, 136; Scott and Marshall's excellent introduction in *Cocaine Politics; San Jose Mercury News*, 20 August 1996, 1; Webb, *Dark Alliance*.

36. Quoted in *Washington Post,* 25-31 May 1992.

37. *Statistical Abstract, 1994,* 472-76.

38. National Criminal Justice Commission, *The Real War on Crime* (New York: Harper Perennial, 1996), 156.

39. Ibid., 150.

40. Mauer and Huling, *Young Black Americans,* 21.

41. *Statistical Abstract,* 1994, 20; Office of Juvenile Justice and Delinquency Prevention, *Juvenile Offenders and Victims: A National Report* (Washington, D.C.: Government Printing Office, 1995); Bronfenbrenner, et al, *The State of Americans* (New York: Free Press, 1996), 48; *Time,* 15 January 1996.

42. Mike Males, *Scapegoat Generation* (Monroe, Me.: Common Courage Press, 1996), 108, 127.

43. National Criminal Justice Commission, *The Real War on Crime,* 157-58; Males, *Scapegoat Generation,* 119-20, 157-58.

44. *New York Times,* 5 July 1992; 27 July 1996, A1; Edsall, *Chain Reaction,* 245; Mauer and Huling, *Young Black Americans.*

Chapter 10: The Prison-Industrial Complex

1. This description is heavily based on William Booth, "Rattling Chains to make a point," *Washington Post,* 25-31 December 1995, 31-32, and Brent Staples, "The Chain Gang Show," *New York Times Magazine,* 17 September 1995, 62-63. In some places phrases and adjectives have been taken directly from those two very nicely written articles.

2. *New York Times,* 21 November 1995, A10.

3. *Washington Post,* 7-11 November 1994, 31; U.S. Department of Justice, Bureau of Justice Statistics, *Census of State and Federal Correctional Facilities* (Washington, D.C.: Government Printing Office, 1997), NCJ-164266.

4. Ibid.; from Stop Prison Rape's web site (http://www.spr.org) in December 1997. See also Stop Prisoner Rape, Inc., 333 North Ave 61 #4, Los Angeles, CA; Woman's Rights Project, Human Rights Watch, *All Too Familiar: Sexual Abuse of Women in U.S. State Prisons* (New York: Human Rights Watch, 1996), 18; David J. Rothman, "The Crime of Punishment," *New York Review of Books,* 17 February 1994; *Time,* 18 February 1994.

5. Quoted in Center for Research on Criminal Justice, *The Iron Fist and the Velvet Clove: An Analysis of the U.S. Police* (Berkeley: Center for Research on Criminal Justice, 1975), 35.

6. Samuel Walker, *Popular Justice: A History of American Criminal Justice* (New York: Oxford University Press, 1998), 197.

7. This sentence is nearly a direct quote from Rodney Stark, *Police Riots* (Belmont, Mass.: Focus Books, 1972), 70-78.

8. Tom McEwen, *National Data Collection on Police Use of Force,* NCJ-160113 (Washington D.C.: Bureau of Justice Statistics, 1996).

9. John DeSantis, *The New Untouchables* (Chicago: Noble Press, 1994), 25.; Paul

Chevigny, *Edge of the Knife: Police Violence in the Americas* (New York: The New Press, 1995), 40, 101; *New York Times,* October 1994; Walker, *Popular Justice,* 197; *In These Times,* 19 August 19 1992.

10. See Joseph Viteritti, "Police," in *The Encyclopedia of New York City;* Peter Maas, *Serpico* (New York: Bantam Books, 1974); *Village Voice,* 29 September 1992.

11. *Newsday,* 3 May 1995, A6; DeSantis, *The New Untouchables,* 153-56; Mike McAlary, *Good Cop, Bad Cop* (New York: Pocket Books, 1994); *New York,* 29-37.

12. *Washington Post,* 18-24 December 1995, 1-6; National Criminal Justice Commission, *The Real War on Crime* (New York: HarperPerennial, 1996), 166-67; *New York Times,* 28 August 1995, 1; *Newsday,* 6 July 1995, 33; *New York Times,* 23 December 1995, 1; and 14 December 1995, 1.

12. Walker, *Popular Justice,* 176-77, 208-9; Eric Cummins, *The Rise and Fall of California's Radical Prison Movement* (Stanford, Calif.: Stanford University Press, 1994).

14. Ibid.; Bureau of Justice Statistics, *State and Federal Prison Population (U.S.) 1960-1994;* Walker, *Popular Justice,* 217-18; William Selke, *Prisons in Crisis* (Bloomington: Indiana University Press, 1993), 42-44; David J. Rothman, "The Crime of Punishment," *New York Review of Books,* 17 February 1994; U.S. Department of Justice, Bureau of Justice Statistics, *Census of State and Federal Correctional Facilities,* NCJ-164266 (Washington, D.C.: Government Printing Office, 1997); Bureau of Justice Statistics, "Prisoners in 1996," Bulletin, June 1997, NCJ-164619.

15. *New York Times,* 2 July 1995, 1; Bureau of Justice Statistics, *Drug Enforcement in State and Federal Prisons,* NCJ-134724 (Washington, D.C.: Government Printing Office, 1992).

16. U.S. Department of Justice, Office of Justice Programs, Bureau of Justice Statistics, *Prison and Jail Inmates at Midyear 1997,* NCJ 167247(Washington, D.C.: Government Printing Office, 1998); David Anderson, "America's Best Buildings," *New York Times Magazine,* 20 February 1994, 39.

17. *Washington Post,* 18-24 June 1994, 31.; *Newsday,* 29 April 1995, 4-5; *Nation,* 20 February 1995, 22; Edna McConnell Clark Foundation, *Seeking Justice, Crime and Punishment in America,* (New York: Edna McConnell Clark Foundation, 1995), 8.

18. Lee Webb, "Repression—A New Growth Industry," in Anthony Platt and Lynn Cooper, *Policing America* (New York: Spectrum Books, 1974), 77; U.S. Department of Justice, Bureau of Justice Statistics, *Justice Expenditures and Employment Extracts: 1993,* NCH 163068 (Washington D.C.: Government Printing Office, forthcoming); Suzy Spencer, "Private Security," Phoenix Mosaic Group, 1997; U.S. Commerce Department.

Chapter 11: Clearcut Crimes

1. Keith Erwin, *Fragile Majesty: The Battle for North America's Last Great Forest* (Seattle: Mountaineers, 1989), p. 11.

2. *U.S. News and World Report,* 25 June 1990, 27.

3. *Forest Voice* 2, no. 2 (1990), quoted in John Bellamy Foster, "Capitalism and the Ancient Forest," *Monthly Review,* October 1991. 13.

4. *Multinational Monitor,* March 1989, 26; Susanna Hecht and Alexander Cockburn, *The Fate of the Forest: Developers, Destroyers and Defenders of the Amazon* (New York: Harper Perennial, 1990), 54; Rainforest Action Network, 26 January 1998; *Environmental News Service,* 28 January 1998; Associated Press, 15 December 1997; Environmental Defense Fund, 27 January 1998; InterPress Service, 16 March 1998; National Institute for Research in the Amazon, 5 January 1998; and Associated Press, "Fears of a Fiery Amazon Nightmare," 7 December 1997.

5. *Multinational Monitor,* November 1995, 13-18; Defensores del Bosque Chileno in Santiago Chile; Meso American Indian Rights Center; World Rainforest Movement, 28 November 1997 update on Guyana; and InterPress Service, 10/21/97.

6. *Multinational Monitor,* June 1987, 17; World Wide Fund for Nature, 7 December 1995; World Wildlife Fund; Cable News Network, 8 October 1997; Associated Press, "Asian Logging Giants Expand Reach," 18 August 1996; Global Witness 1997 estimates; Agence France-Press, 15 December 1997; and Reuters, 25 March 1998; Associated Press, 18 August 1996; *New York Times,* 5 June 1995, A1; Rainforest Information Center; Cable News Network, 30 March 1998; John Bellamy Foster, *The Vulnerable Planet: A Short Economic History of the Environment* (New York: Monthly Review Press, 1994), 101-5; Reuters, 3 April 1998; *The Economist,* 8 April 1995, 34; Earth Times News Service, 9 November 1997; Agence France-Presse, 9 November 97; Forest Networking, 16 December 1997 and 18 November 1997 reports.

7. World Wildlife Fund, 1997 data; World Wide Fund for Nature, *The Timber Trade and Global Forest Loss* (1996); World Wide Fund for Nature, 7 December 1995; *New York Times,* 30 January 1996; *Multinational Monitor,* January-February 1996, 19; Radio Free Europe, 14 November 1997; *Green Left Weekly,* 2 August 1997; *Worldwide Forest/Biodiversity Campaign News,* 14 November 1997 and 17 December 1997.

8. Foster, *Vulnerable Planet* (New York: Monthly Review Press, 1994), 24-30; Environmental News Network, "Habitat on the Edge," 13 March 1998; World Resources Institute, which estimates the 99 percent loss; Ellan Hosmer, "Paradise Lost: The Ravaged Rainforest," *Multinational Monitor,* June 1987, 6; UN Food and Agricultural Organization, cited by Reuters, 7 March 1997; World Resources Institute web page, 1997 data.

9. 1997 data from Rainforest Action Network, "Rates of Rainforest Loss," Rainforest Information Center, and "Indigenous People of the Rainforest," available at the group's very helpful website.

10. *Australian Financial Review,* 13 October 1997.

11. *Bangkok Post,* 29 March 1994; *The Economist,* 10 August 1994; Economist Intelligence Unit, *Country Profile: Thailand and Myanmar, 1994-95,* 45; *Far Eastern Economic Review,* 16 December 1993.

12. *Bangkok Post,* 4 January 1998. A number of the same politicians also have profited from illegal logging in Loas and Cambodia. Cable News Network, 25 February 1998; *Environmental News,* 10 March 1998; Rainforest Action Network.

13. Project Ecological Recovery, *The Future of People and Forests in Thailand after the Logging Ban* (Bangkok: Project for Ecological Recovery, 1992), x. Carl Parkes, *The Thailand Handbook* (Chico, Calif.: Moon Publications, 1992), 7, estimates that forest coverage has dropped from 70 percent in 1945 to 12 percent in the early 1990s; Martin Smith, *Paradise Lost: The Suppression of Environmental Rights and Freedom of Expression in Burma* (London: Article 19, 1994), 15; Kate Geary, "The Role of Thailand in Forest Destruction Along the Thai-Burma Border, 1988-1993," Earth Action Resource Center; author's interview with environmental activist Steve Thompson in Chaing Mai, November, 1994; S. Aung Lwin, "The Future of Burma's Environment," *Burma Buro Schriftenreihe* no. 2, 5; R. Harbinson, "Burma's Forests Fall Victim to War," *The Ecologist* 22, no. 2 (1992); Smith, *Paradise Lost,* 1; Cable News Network, 31 December 1997; Agence France-Presse, 25 June 1997.

14. Rolf Knight, *Indians at Work: An Informal History of Native Indian Labor in British Columbia, 1858-1930* (Vancouver: New Star Books, 1978), 216-17.

15. Based on Ervin, *Fragile Majesty,* 162-71.

16. Ibid., 32. Social stratification varied widely in the region, more egalitarian in Oregon and northern California and more stratified on the coast of Southern Alaska among the Tlingit. The further one moves from the bounty of the coast, the more egalitarian the tribes tended to be.

17. John Curtis Perry, *Facing West: Americans and the Opening of the Pacific* (Westport, Conn.: Praeger, 1994), 34; Dean Latimer and Jeff Goldberg, *Flowers in the Blood: The Story of Opium* (New York: Franklin Watts, 1981), 176-77.

18. Knight, *Indians at Work,* 29, 206, 222-3, 230.

19. Knight, ibid., 223, 234-235, 256-269.

20. Matthew Josephson, *The Robber Barons* (New York, Harcourt Brace Jovanovich, 1962), 78-79, 91-93, 163-65.

21. Robert Heilbroner, *The Economic Transformation of America* (New York: Harcourt Brace Jovanovich, 1977), 62; Milton Moskowitz, Michael Katz, and Robert Levring, *Everybody's Business* (New York: Harper and Row, 1980), 637-38, 642-43, 648-49.

22. *In These Times,* 24 August 1995, 17; Ervin, *Fragile Majesty,* 6, 63-64.

23. Moskowitz, Katz, and Levering, *Everybody's Business,* 567-90. St. Regis data from Geoffrey Wansell, *Tycoon: The Life of James Goldsmith* (New York: Athenaeum, 1987), 319.

24. Ervin, *Fragile Majesty,* 58-59.

25. Robert Tyler, *Rebels of the Woods: The I.W.W. in the Pacific Northwest* (Eugene: University of Oregon Books, 1967), 6; Landownership study by Coast Range Association, Newport, Oregon.

26. Paul Levesque, "A Chronicle of the Tillamook Country Forest Trust Lands," Vol. 1, "Background," unpublished, 64.

27. Ibid., 47-49, 58, 64, 65, 68; E. Kimbark MacColl, *Merchants, Money and Power: The Portland Establishment, 1843-1913* (Portland, Ore.: The Georgian Press, 1988), p. 369-372.

28. Melvyn Dubofsky, *We Shall Be All: A History of the IWW, the Industrial Workers of*

the World (New York: Quadrangle, 1969), 129; Louis Adamic, *Dynamite: The Story of Class Violence in America* (New York: Chelsea House/Vintage, 1958), 293; Ervin, *Fragile Majesty,* 60.

29. Quoted in Dubofsky, *We Shall Be All,* 128.

30. See MacColl, *Merchants, Money and Power,* 290-91.

31. Carlos Arnaldo Schwantes, *The Pacific Northwest: An Interpretive History* (Lincoln: University of Nebraska Press, 1996), 269-70; Gordon Newell and Don Sherwood, *Old Seattle* (New York: Ballantine Books, 1956), 162; Norman Clark, *Mill Town: A Social History of Everett Washington* (Seattle: University of Washington, 1990), 101; Richard Berner, *Seattle 1900-1920: From Boomtown, Urban Turbulence to Restoration* (Seattle: Charles Press, 1991), 118-21.

32. Clark, *Mill Town,* 103.

33. Matthew Josephson, *The Politicos* (New York: Harvest Books, 1966), 561; Knight, *Indians at Work,* 125-130; Dubofsky, *We Shall Be All,* 129.

34. Ibid., 131, 335-37; Adamic, *Dynamite,* 293.

35. Ibid., 294; Dubofsky, *We Shall Be All,* 339-41.

36. Ibid., 363-64, 378-98, 412, 414; Adamic, *Dynamite,* 295; Ervin, *Fragile Majesty,* 64.

37. Quoted in Ellis Lucia's excellent *Tillamook Burn Country: A Pictorial History* (Caldwell, Ida.: Caxton Printers, 1984), xxi.

38. This description is very closely based, both in language and facts, on ibid., xxi; Paul Levesque, "Chronicle," 203.

39. Barry Checkoway, "Large Builders, Federal Housing Programs, and Postwar Suburbanization," in Rachel Bratt and others, eds., *Critical Perspectives on Housing* (Philadelphia: Temple University Pree, 1986), 130, 131; *Oregonian,* 15 October 1990, quoted in Foster, "Capitalism and the Ancient Forest," 5.

40. See Jeffrey St. Clair, "Clinton and the Ancient Forests: Year One," *Lies of Our Times,* March 1994, 11.

41. Erwin, *Fragile Majesty,* 126-27; Jonathan Dushoff, "Razing Alaska: The Destruction of the Tongass National Forest," *Multinational Monitor,* July/August 1990, 18; Environmental News Network, 13 March 1998; Wilderness Society; Associated Press, 8 January 1998.

42. See St. Clair, "Clinton and the Ancient Forests," 11; Randall O'Toole, "Last Stand, Selling Out the National Forests," *Multinational Monitor,* January/February 1993, 25, estimates that the federal government has lost $1 to $2 billion a year since 1978. Associated Press, 8 January 1998.

43. Will Nixon, "The Forest for the Trees," *In These Times,* 24 July 1995, 18; St. Clair, "Clinton and the Ancient Forests," 11.

44. *Multinational Monitor,* May 1996, 5; Dushoff, "Razing Alaska"; Ronald Brownstein and Nina Easton, *Reagan's Ruling Class: Portraits of the President's Top One Hundred Officials* (Washington, D.C.: Presidential Accountability Group, 1982), 185-86.

45. Mitch Lansky, *Beyond the Beauty Strip: Savings What's Left of Our Forests* (Gardiner, Me.: Tilbury House, 1992), 29; *Multinational Monitor,* October

1994, 30; Marshall Clinard and Peter Yeager, *Corporate Crime* (New York: The Free Press, 1980), 340.

46. *New York Times,* 13 October 1991, F10; *Multinational Monitor,* October 1992, 32; *Multinational Monitor,* October 1990, 31.

47. *Multinational Monitor,* October 1992, 32; U.S. Department of Labor, Bureau of Labor Statistics, "Occupational Injuries and Illnesses in the United States by Industry, 1991," Bulletin 24, May 1993, table 1.

48. Ervin, *Fragile Majesty,* 104; Brownstein and Easton, *Reagan's Ruling Class,* 188-89; Foster, "Capitalism and the Ancient Forest," 7; *Multinational Monitor,* July/August 1990, 18.

49. *U.S. News and World Report,* 25 June 1990, 29; Bellamy, "Capitalism and the Ancient Forest," 12.

50. See Wansell, *Tycoon,* 268-69, 284-86, 301, 320-40, 359-60.

51. Ibid., 311, 321, 334; *Multinational Monitor,* October 1990, 30-31.

52. See *Mergers & Acquisitions,* various issues, for decade total; *Multinational Monitor,* September 1994, 11. For an overview, there are two excellent sources: David Harris, *The Last Stand: The War Between Wall Street and Main Street Over California's Ancient Redwoods* (New York: Times Books, 1996) and various essays by Earth First! activist Judi Bari in *The Timber Wars* (Monroe, Me.: Common Courage Press, 1994).

53. *Wall Street Journal,* 6 August 1993, 1.

54. For a useful summary of potential bank and securities law violations by Hurwitz, see Ned Daly, "Ravaging the Redwoods: Carl Hurwitz, Michael Milken and the Cost of Greed," *Multinational Monitor,* September 1994, 11-14. See also *Business Week,* 2 February 1987, 64; Harris, *Last Stand,* 345.

55. Ibid., 134-35, 344. See FDIC v. Milken, S.D.N.Y., 91 cv 0433, *Complaint-Class Action,* 82-84 and In Re: Drexel Burnham Lambert Group, U.S. Bankruptcy Court, S.D.N.Y., *Consolidated Proofs of Claim of the FDIC and the RTC,* 42-44; *New York Times,* 4 April 1993, B1.

56. Harris, Last Stand, 131; *Multinational Monitor,* September 1994, 11 gives a figure of fourteen. The higher number is based on doubling the 2 percent rate; Judi Bari, "The Redwood Curtain," *Lies of our Times,* November 1993, 7.

57. *The Economist,* 11 May 1996, 26; *Multinational Monitor,* September 1994, 14; FDIC v. Milken, etc. *Complaint-Class Action,* 34, 38-39, 82.

58. Ibid., 31, 40, 82, 97; In Re: Drexel Burnham Lambert, U.S. Bankruptcy Court, Chapter 11, 90-b-10421, 11, 44.

59. Bari, "Redwood Curtain," 7; *Wall Street Journal,* 6 August 1993; *San Francisco Examiner,* 10 October 1997.

60. *Multinational Monitor,* October 1990, 31; July/August 1990, 21; October 1992, 32.

61. *U.S. News and World Report,* 25 June 1990, 28.

62. Foster, "Capitalism and the Ancient Forest," 7; Ervin, *Fragile Majesty,* 11, 111; *U.S. News and World Report,* 25 June 1990, 28.

63. *The Greenpeace Guide to Anti-Environmental Organizations* (Berkeley, Calif.: Odonian Press, 1991), 16, 41, 42, 73.

64. "Timber Companies Donations to Political Parties Grow Lush," Associated Press, 17 December 1997; Foster, "Capitalism and the Ancient Forest," 15.

65. On the Clinton administration's capitulation to timber interests, see Alexander Cockburn, *The Nation,* 23 August 1993, 199-200; and St. Clair, "Clinton and the Ancient Forests."

66. *Washington Post,* 11-17 March 1996, 10.

67. "Logging Rules Fall in the Pacific Northwest," Associated Press, 4 February 1998.

Chapter 12: White-Collar Muggers

1. Keith Ervin, *Fragile Majesty: The Battle for North America's Last Great Forest* (Seattle: Mountaineers, 1989), 174.

2. Marshall Clinard and Peter Yeager, *Corporate Crime* (New York: The Free Press, 1980), 119.

3. Etzioni cited in *Multinational Monitor,* June 1990, 6; *Time,* 3 July 1989, 4; *Fortune,* 1 December 1980, 56-64; "Corporate Crime: The Untold Story," *U.S. News and World Report,* 6 September 1982.

4. See U.S. Chamber of Commerce, *Handbook on White Collar Crime* (Washington, D.C.: Chamber of Commerce, 1974); Jeffrey Reiman, *The Rich Get Richer and the Poor Get Prison* (Boston: Allyn and Bacon, 1995), 111-12; Marshal Clinard, *The Abuse of Corporate Power* (New York: Praeger, 1990), 15; Russell Mokhiber, "Soft on Crime," *Multinational Monitor,* June 1995, 25.

5. Clinard and Yeager, *Corporate Crime,* 8; Ralph Estes, *The Tyranny of the Bottom Line: Why Corporations Make Good People Do Bad Things* (San Francisco: Berrett-Koehler, 1996), 183.

6. Data for 1992: U.S. Environmental Protection Agency, *1992 Toxics Release Inventory Public Data Release,* and *Statistical Abstract,* 1992, 230, 233; *Newsday,* 1 March 1989; John Canham-Clyne, Patrick Woodall, Victoria Nugent, and James Wilson, *Saving Money, Saving Lives: The Documented Benefits of Federal Health and Safety Protection* (Washington, D.C.: Public Citizen's Congress Watch, 1995), 20; *Multinational Monitor,* March 1989, 32; *Corporate Crime Reporter,* 28 June 1993, 7, citing *After the Silent Spring: The Unsolved Problems of Pesticide Use in the U.S.;* National Resource Defence Council, *Multinational Monitor,* June 1995; *New York Times,* 24 September 1995, 26.

7. *New York Times,* 15 February 1989, 1; *Business Week,* 25 April 1994, 30; *The Economist,* "Survey of Waste and the Environment," 29 May 1993, 15; *Business Week,* 11 May 1992, 32.; *New York Times,* 16 June 1991, sec. 3, 1; *Bulletin of Atomic Scientists,* May/June 1995, 34; *Business Week,* 10 August 1992, 40.

8. See Estes, *Tyranny of the Bottom Line,* 181-89.

9. *Statistical Abstract 1994,* 436; *Multinational Monitor,* June 1990, 6.

10. Canham-Clyne et al., *Saving Money,* 11.

11. Mark Green and John F. Berry, "White-Collar Crime is Big Business," *The Nation,* 8 June 1985, 706; Estes, *Tyranny of the Bottom Line,* 179-80.

12. *New York Times*, 30 March 1995, B1; *Wall Street Journal*, 30 April 1990, A16; *American Demographics*, November 1985, 4.

13. *New York Times*, 30 March 1995, B1; *Wall Street Journal*, 30 April 1990, A16; *American Demographics*, November 1985, 4; *Wall Street Journal*, 25 August 1986, A1. State and local tax fraud is computed from the federal tax fraud rates. In 1995, when tax fraud was estimated at $150 billion, the federal government took in $1,346 billion, producing a tax fraud rate of 11 percent. In 1992, not counting $179 billion from the federal government, state and local governments took in revenues of $793 billion, 11 percent of which would be a tax loss of $87 billion.

14. *Forbes*, 27 June 1988, 270.

15. *Corporate Crime Reporter*, 8 February 1993, 10, and 22 February 1993, 15-19.

16. Russell Mokhiber, *Corporate Crime and Violence: Big Business Power and the Abuse of Public Trust* (San Francisco: Sierra Club Books, 1988), 174-75, 284; *New York Times*, 16 May 1995, A1.

17. *The Nation*, 8 June 1985, 707; *Forbes*, 14 July 1986; Mark Green, "Crime in the Suites: How Some Businesses Rip Us Off," *Washington Post Weekly Edition*, 7-13 December 1992, 25; *Time*, 3 April 1989, 38; *Newsday*, 2 May 1989, 51, citing Alliance Against Fraud in Telemarketing; *Business Week*, 16 January 1995, 32, which found overcharges on six of seventeen items in one New Jersey store (larger studies in California found overcharges on 2 percent of all items); *New York Times Magazine*, 24 July 1988, 18; *Wall Street Journal*, 28 March 1989, 1.

18. *Multinational Monitor*, May 1995, 27; *Corporate Crime Reporter*, 12 September 1988, 5-6; Estimate cited in Estes, *Tyranny of the Bottom Line*, 190. See also A. Ernest Fitzgerald, *High Priest of Waste* (New York: Norton, 1972), Fitzgerald, *The Pentagonists* (New York: Houghton Mifflin, 1989), and Richard Stubbing, *The Defense Game* (New York: Harper and Row, 1986).

19. *Multinational Monitor*, May 1995, 8, and January/February 1993, 16-20; *Corporate Crime Reporter*, 16 July 1993, 8.

20. Estes, *Tyranny of the Bottom Line*, 177-78.

21. Federal Bureau of Investigation, *Crime in the U.S., 1993*, 36; National Institute of Justice, *The Extent and Costs of Crime Victimization: A New Look* (Washington, D.C.: Government Printing Office, 1996).

22. Center for the Study of American Bussiness; White House Office on National Drug Control Policy.

23. Estes, *Tyranny of the Bottom Line*, 181; Center for the Study of American Business, *Statistical Abstract*, 362, 436; *Guardian* (New York), 25 April 1990, 5.

24. Ibid.

25. See United Church of Christ Commission on Racial Justice, *Toxic Wastes and Race in the United States: A National Reports on the Racial and Socio-Economic Characteristics of Communities with Hazardous Waste Sites* (New York: United Church of Christ, 1987); Robert D. Bullard, ed., *Confronting Environmental Racism: Voice from the Grassroots* (Boston: South End Press, 1993), 17-18, 20.

26. Clinard, *The Abuse of Corporate Power*, 121,124.

27. *Wall Street Journal*, 25 August 1988; *Wall Street Journal*, 29 September 1995, A, and 30 November 1995; *Business Week*, 11 December 1995, 39; *Wall Street Journal*, 11 November 1995, A1.

Chapter 13: Regulating for Profits

1. Ellis Hawley, *The New Deal and the Problem of Monopoly* (Princeton, N.J.: Princeton University Press, 1966), 41-43; Kim McQuaid, *Big Business and Presidential Power* (New York: William Morrow, 1982), 25, 31.
2. U.S. Department of Commerce, *Historical Statistics of the United States: Colonial Times to 1970* (Washington, D.C.: Government Printing Office, 1975), 10, 139, 210, 234, 303, 666, 848-49, 856.
3. Congressional Quarterly, *Federal Regulation Directory*, 5th ed. (Washington, D.C.: Congressional Quarterly, 1986), 18-19.
4. Melinda Warren and Kenneth Chilton, "Regulation's Rebound: Bush Budget Gives Regulation a Boost," *Occasional Paper* no. 81 (St. Louis: Center for the Study of American Business, 1990), 4-5.
5. Congressional Quarterly, *Federal Regulatory Directory* (Washington, D.C.: Congressional Quarterly, 1994), 28; Paul Tramontozzi and Kenneth Chilton, *U.S. Regulatory Agencies Under Reagan, 1980-1988* (St. Louis: Center for the Study of American Business, 1987), 4, 10.
6. Congressional Quarterly, *Federal Regulatory Directory*, 5th ed., 28; *Columbia Journalism Review*, May-June 1990, 46-47.
7. *Washington Post*, 21-27 August 1989, 31; *New York Times*, 4 December 1989, 1; *Washington Post*, 22-28 October 1990, 26.
8. Congressional Quarterly, *Federal Regulatory Directory*, 7th ed., 80-82; *New York Times*, 2 August 1987, sec. 3, 1; *Newsday*, 15 November 1990, 65.
9. *New York Times*, 19 December 1989, A1.
10. Christopher Douglass, Michael Orlando, and Melinda Warren, *Regulatory Changes and Trends: An Analysis of the 1998 Budget of the U.S. Government* (St. Louis: Center for the Study of American Business, 1997), 32-33.
11. Ibid.; *The Economist*, 18 January 1997, 21-23; *New York Times*, 29 June 1995, B6 and 8 June 1995, 1.
12. *Multinational Monitor*, May 1996, 28; *New York Times*,16 March 11995; *Washington Post*, 17 February 1997, 7; Center for Responsive Politics and *New York Times*, 18 October 1996, A27.
13. *New York Times Magazine*, 22 November 1996, 38-39.
14. *Wall Street Journal*, 20 April 1995, A14 and 11 August 1995, A6; *Washington Post*, 4-10 December 1995, 29.
15. *New York Times*, 23 February 1997, A1, and 26 January 1997, 1; "Private Party," *Common Cause*, 19 February 1997.
16. *Washington Post*, 31 July-6 August 1995, 13, and 15-21 April 1996, 38; *New York Times*, 18 February 1996, E4; Common Cause, "Soft Money Laundromat," and press release, 7 November 1996.

17. Nancy Watzman, James Youngclaus, and Jennifer Shecter, *Cashing In: A Guide to Money and Politics in the 104th Congress* (Washington, D.C.: Center for Responsive Politics, 1997).

18. *Multinational Monitor,* April 1990, 29; *New York Times,* 20 August 1995; *The Nation,* 3 February 1997, 12; *Multinational Monitor,* October 1989, 9; *New York Times,* 15 August 1993.

19. John Canham-Clyne, Patrick Woodall, Victoria Nugent, and James Wilson, *Saving Money, Saving Lives: The Documented Benefits of Federal Health and Safety Protection* (Washington, D.C.: Public Citizen's Congress Watch, 1995), 11; *Los Angeles Times,* 16 June 1996, A5; *New York Times,* 10 August 1986; *Multinational Monitor,* May 1987, 21.; *The Nation,* 14 December 1985, 647; *NewYork Times,* 30 October 1988, 4; *Business Week,* 23 May 1994, 76.

20. *Dollars and Sense,* July-August 1994, 14, and September-October 1995, 20-23; *Multinational Monitor,* November 1996, 14; *Wall Street Journal,* 4 June 1996, B2; *Fortune,* 24 November 1986, 64.

21. *Multinational Monitor,* April 1990, 31; *Wall Street Journal,* 10 May 1991; *Business Week,* 14 November 1994, 26; Washington Post, 25-31 January 1988, 6; *New York Times,* 16 April 1995, D1.

22. *Multinational Monitor,* June 1995, 14; May 1990, 5; October 1995, 6; *Los Angeles Times,* 16 June 1996, A5; *New York Times,* 13 September 1995, B1; *Minneapolis Star-Tribune,* 4 September 1995, 13A.

23. *Wall Street Journal,* 20 May 1996, 1; National Labor Committee Education Fund in Support of Worker and Human Rights in Central America, *Paying to Lose Our Jobs* (New York: NLCEF, 1992).

24. *The Nation,* 5 June 1997, 11-17.

25. Ibid.; National Labor Committee Education Fund in Support of Worker and Human Rights in Central America, *Free Trade's Hidden Secrets: Why We are Losing Our Shirts* (New York: NLCEF, 1993); *Sacramento Bee,* 8 June 1995.

Chapter 14: Financial Fraud

1. This chapter is based on "BCCI: The Big Picture," a two-part cover story originally published in *In These Times,* 23-29 October 1991 and 30 October-5 November 1991; tens of thousands of documents collected by government investigators; thousands of pages of documents filed in court cases in New York, London, Miami, Washington, D.C., and Atlanta; thousands of articles, information searches, and material from computer databases; and interviews with some government investigators. Unless otherwise noted, facts and details cited here are taken from that work.

2. *New York Times Magazine,* 19 July 1987, 22.

3. *American Banker,* 19 February 1985, 9.

4. *South Florida Business Journal,* 25 December 1989, sec. 1, 4; *New York Times Magazine,* 19 July 1987.

5. *Time,* 23 November 1991.

6. *Wall Street Journal,* 7 May 1997, 1.

7. Joel Kurtzman, *The Death of Money* (New York: Simon and Schuster, 1993), 87.

8. House Judiciary Committee, Subcommittee on Crime and Criminal Justice, *Subcommittee Staff Report Regarding Federal Law Enforcement's Handling of Allegations Involving the Bank of Credit and Commerce International*, 5 May 1991, 1-4.

9. President's Commission on Organized Crime, *The Cash Connection: Organized Crime, Financial Institutions and Money Laundering* (Washington, D.C.: Government Printing Office, 1984), 48-49; Robert Powis, *The Money Launderers: Lessons from the Drug Wars—How Billions of Illegal Dollars Are Washing Through Banks and Businesses* (Chicago: Probus Publishing, 1992), 9, 37-38.

10. *American Banker*, 28 September 1984; President's Commission on Organized Crime, *The Cash Connection*, 26-27; *American Banker*, 8 November 1985, 3; 19 June 1985, 1; 22 January 1986, 1; *Financial Times*, 12 October 1988.

11. *Money Laundering Alert*, 1 October 1992; *Financial Times*, 12 October 1988; *Money Laundering Alert*, April 1993; *U.S. News and World Report*, 10 April 1989, 14 and 21 July 1989, 22; *Money Laundering Alert*, February 1993 and January 1995.

12. *American Banker*, 30 April 1989, 17; *U.S. News and World Report*, 21 August 1989; *Money Laundering Alert*, December 1990, February 1991, June 1991, October 1992.

13. *American Banker*, 24 October 1988, 1; President's Commission on Organized Crime, *The Cash Connection*, 13.

14. *U.S. News and World Report*, 21 August 1989, 22; *Washington Post*, 5 November 1985, 17. One 1984 report that sampled currency reports in just two IRS districts found that ten people had deposited over $1.2 million, even though they failed to file tax returns.

15. Kathleen Day, *S&L Hell* (New York: W. W. Norton, 1993), 105.

16. *American Banker*, 17 April 1985, 2; President's Commission on Organized Crime, *The Cash Connection*, 24.

17. Ibid., 19.

18. *Washington Post*, 5 November 1985, 17.

19. Jeffrey Robinson, *The Laundry Men: Inside the World's Third Largest Business* (London: Pocket Books, 1995), 31-32; *American Banker*, 4 April 1985, 1; 22 February 1985, 1; 15 March 1985, 1.

20. *U.S. News and World Report*, 21 August 1989, 22; *Time*, 18 December 1989, 50; *Money Laundering Alert*, March 1995.

21. *Financial Times*, 17 July 1989, 2; The White House, *National Drug Control Strategy* (Washington, D.C.: Government Printing Office, 1989), 118; *Money Laundering Alert*, March 1995; July 1992; June 1993.

22. *American Banker*, 18 June 1984, 17; *U.S. News and World Report*, 21 August 1989, 22; *Money Laundering Alert*,1 October 1992; January 1995; February 1995.

23. *American Banker*, 27 August 1984; *Money Laundering Alert*, April 1992; February 1993; May 1995.

24. Stephen Pizzo, Mary Fricker, and Paul Muolo, *Inside Job: The Looting of America's*

Saving and Loans (New York: McGraw-Hill, 1989), 129, 299, 307; *American Banker,* 30 April 1990, 17.

25. *Money Laundering Alert,* January 1995, February 1995, March 1995.

26. Ralph Blumenthal, *Last Days of the Sicilians: At War with the Mafia* (New York: Times Books, 1988).

27. Ingo Walter, *The Secret Money Market* (New York: Harper and Row, 1990), 159; *Money Laundering Alert,* March 1994; *Bloomberg,* October 1997, 8-25.

28. *Money Laundering Alert,* March 1995; U.S. State Department, Bureau of International Narcotics Matters and Law Enforcement Affairs, *INSCR, 1995* (Washington, D.C.: Government Printing Office, 1995), 426-27, 494, and *INSCR, 1991* (Washington, D.C.: Government Printing Office, 1995), 380-81; *Financial Times,* 19 April 1989, 38.

29. *Wall Street Journal,* 6 July 1994.

30. James Ring Adams, *The Big Fix: Inside the S&L Scandal: How and Unholy Alliance of Politics and Money Destroyed America's Banking System* (New York: John Wiley and Sons, 1990), 143-91; Donald Maggin, *Bankers, Builders, Knaves and Thieves* (Chicago: Contemporary Books, 1989); Day, *S&L Hell,* 302-3; Michael Lewis, *Liar's Poker* (New York: Penguin, 1990); Martin Meyer, *Nightmare on Wall Street: Salomon Brothers and the Corruption of the Marketplace* (New York: Simon and Schuster, 1993), 74, 150-161; Meyer, *The Biggest Bank Robbery,* 112-13, 288-89; Paul Zane Pilzer with Robert Deitz, *Other People's Money: The Inside Story of the S&L Mess* (New York: Simon and Schuster, 1989), 131; Michael Waldman, *Who Robbed America?* (New York: Random House, 1990), 40-41.

31. Meyer, *Nightmare on Wall Street,* 235-43; *New York Times,* 3 September 1991; *The Economist,* 24 August 1991, 65.

32. *Washington Post,* 16-22 September 1991, 21. That number can be challenged— Dutch markets don't always reduce borrowing costs, and the market reforms since the 1991 Salomon scandal have made the market more competitive. Yet it is clear that the federal government wasted billions of dollars in recent decades by failing to police major Wall Street firms.

33. *Business Week,* 6 October 1993, 44-55.

34. *Business Week,* 20 November 1995, 142-43; *New York Times,* 15 May 1994, sec. 3, 1; *Wall Street Journal,* 21 May 1993, 1.

35. Quote from ibid.; and *New York Times,* 5 September 1993, F11.

36. *Wall Street Journal,* 21 May 1993, 1; *New York Times,* 15 May 1994, sec.3, 1.

37. *Business Week,* 20 November 1995, 142-43.

38. *New York Times,* 30 May 1993, 1.

39. *Business Week,* 6 October 1993, 44-55.

40. *Wall Street Journal,* 2 June 1993, 1; *Business Week,* 24 May 1993, 122-23.

41. *Business Week,* 6 October 1993, 44-55; 24 May 1993, 122-23; *Wall Street Journal,* 2 June 1993, 1.

42. *Economist,* 18 April 1992, 86; *Newsday,* 16 August 1994; *Wall Street Journal,* 31 March 1992, 1; *New York Times,* 22 October 1991, D1.

43. See *Multinational Monitor,* November 1992, 8-14, for a useful summary of many aspects of racial discrimination in the housing industry.

44. *New York Times,* 3 November 1991, sec. 10, 1.

45. *Wall Street Journal,* 31 March 1991, 1; *New York Times,* 30 October 1996, D1; *Business Week,* 19 July 1993; *U.S. News and World Report,* 17 April 1995.

46. Michael Hudson, *Merchants of Misery* (Monroe, Me.: Common Couage Press, 1996), 9.

47. Ibid., 5-6, 9, 55.

48. *U.S. News and World Report,* 17 April 1995; Hudson, *Merchants of Misery,* 2, 52-54.

Conclusion: Ending the Violence

1. Bureau of Justice Statistics, *Criminal Victimization in the United States, 1994,* NCJ-162126 (Washington, D.C.: Government Printing Office, 1997).

Index